KU-603-096

History of Universities

VOLUME XXX/1–2

2017

History of Universities

VOLUME XXX/1-2

2017

OXFORD

UNIVERSITY PRESS

Great Clarendon Street, Oxford, OX2 6DP,
United Kingdom

Oxford University Press is a department of the University of Oxford.
It furthers the University's objective of excellence in research, scholarship,
and education by publishing worldwide. Oxford is a registered trade mark of
Oxford University Press in the UK and in certain other countries

Published in the United States of America by Oxford University Press
198 Madison Avenue, New York, NY 10016, United States of America

British Library Cataloguing in Publication Data
Data available

Library of Congress Control Number: 82642421

ISBN 978–0–19–880702–5

Printed and bound by CPI Group (UK) Ltd,
Croydon, CR0 4YY

Contents

List of Figures and Tables

Benet Perera's Pious Humanism: Aristotelianism, Philology, and Education in Jesuit Colleges. An Edition of Perera's *Documenta quaedam perutilia*

Cristiano Casalini and Christoph Sander[*]

I. Introduction

Scholars commonly distinguish between different kinds of sixteenth-century Aristotelianism:[1] a secular, predominantly Italian Aristotelianism on one hand, and the so-called 'Christianized' Aristotelianism of the Catholic tradition, which was approved and fostered by the Church, and supposedly endorsed by the Jesuits more than by any other religious order, on

[*] The authors would like to thank Paul Richard Blum, Ulrich G. Leinsle, and Paul F. Grendler for their comments on an earlier version of this article, and Kasper Volk and Anke Timmermann for their linguistic revisions of the article. The authors also are very grateful to the Biblioteca Ambrosiana (Milan) and the Archivio Storico della Pontificia Università Gregoriana (Rome) for providing digital images of the manuscripts.

[1] See e.g. Charles H. Lohr, 'Jesuit Aristotelianism and Sixteenth-Century Metaphysics', in Harry George III Fletcher and Mary Beatrice Schulte (eds.), *Paradosis: Studies in Memory of Edwin A. Quain*, (New York, 1976), 203–20; Eckhard Kessler, 'The Transformation of Aristotelianism during the Renaissance', in John Henry and Sarah Hutton (eds.), *New Perspectives on Renaissance Thought: Essays in the History of Science, Education and Philosophy. In Memory of Charles B. Schmitt* (London, 1990), 137–47; Charles B. Schmitt, *Aristotle and the Renaissance* (Cambridge, Mass., 1983), 10–34; Antonino Poppi, *Ricerche sulla teologia e la scienza nella Scuola padovana del Cinque e Seicento* (Soveria Mannelli, 2001); Cornelis H. Leijenhorst, Christoph H. Lüthy, and J.M.M.H. Thijssen, 'The Tradition of Aristotelian Natural Philosophy. Two Theses and Seventeen Answers', in Cornelis H. Leijenhorst, Christoph H. Lüthy, and J.M.M.H. Thijssen (eds.), *The Dynamics of Aristotelian Natural Philosophy from Antiquity to the Seventeenth Century* (Leiden/Boston, 2002), 1–29, at 1; Sascha Salatowsky, *De Anima: Die Rezeption der aristotelischen Psychologie im 16. und 17. Jahrhundert* (Amsterdam/ Philadelphia, 2006), 21; Simone De Angelis, *Anthropologien: Genese und Konfiguration einer 'Wissenschaft vom Menschen' in der frühen Neuzeit* (Berlin/ New York, 2010), 64–5; Craig Martin, *Subverting Aristotle: Religion, History, and Philosophy in Early Modern Science* (Baltimore, 2014), 5–10.

the other.[2] This distinction is made both based on different methods of teaching and on the specific purposes for which Aristotle's works were studied: Catholic clerics are supposed to have adopted a medieval scholastic, mostly Thomistic reading of Aristotle in order to reinforce certain doctrines of faith, or at least to use Aristotelian philosophical doctrines that did not contradict the articles of faith that were at the basis of the study of theology. But from the fifteenth century onwards, another, more critical reading of Aristotle emerged. Philosophers at Italian universities, particularly at Padua, constructed a philological and historical approach towards the *Corpus Aristotelicum*. Those 'secular Aristotelians' are said to have read Aristotle's works for secular purposes, for example, as basis for the study of medicine or law, or by integrating the study of Aristotle's works in the humanities curriculum (*studia humanitatis*).[3] Their approach is, then, also related to the humanist movement of the period.[4]

Since such a distinction between two separate schools or distinct types of Aristotelianism seems rather too simple, several scholars have proposed a more nuanced picture to date.[5] The concept of Jesuit philosophy as a Thomistic reading of Aristotle, and as one to be contrasted with the approach of secular Italian humanists, however, remains firmly in place.[6] Admittedly, this concept has historical antecedents: when the Jesuits defined their order, at the point of its foundation, as a teaching order, they needed to decide which philosophical direction would serve their goals best.[7] The *Constitutions*, published in 1558, called for the following of Thomas Aquinas in theology, and of Aristotle in philosophy.[8] As a consequence, the Jesuits grew to be the early modern order most recognized for supporting Thomism, and for considering philosophy a handmaiden of theology.

In recent years, several studies have challenged, added to and refined this picture, particularly by highlighting the heterogeneous and complex

[2] This point has most recently been repeated in Martin, *Subverting Aristotle*, 6: 'In this [Jesuit] version, Aristotle was presented if not as pious himself, than [sic] as a handmaiden to true religion'.

[3] Schmitt, *Aristotle*, 14–15; Lohr, 'Aristotelianism', 204–5; and others.

[4] Paul F. Grendler, 'Humanism: Ancient Learning, Criticism, Schools and Universities', in Angelo Mazzocco (ed.) *Interpretations of Renaissance Humanism* (Leiden/Boston, 2006), 73–95 may provide first guidance on this topic. See also n. 91 below.

[5] The majority of scholars referred to in n. 1 similarly note and criticize a sharp distinction between two distinct schools of Aristotelianism.

[6] See e.g. Lohr, 'Aristotelianism', 215.

[7] Cp. John W. O'Malley, 'How the First Jesuits Became Involved in Education', in Vincent J. Duminuco (ed.), *The Jesuit Ratio Studiorum: 400th Anniversary Perspectives* (New York, 2000), 56–74.

[8] *The Constitutions of the Society of Jesus and Their Complementary Norms*, trans. George E. Ganss (St. Louis 1996), 182–3. However, the passage does not specify any manner in which Jesuit lecturers ought to follow these authorities.

nature of Jesuit philosophy.[9] Since sixteenth-century Jesuit scholars considered a wide range of sources, the definition of a 'secular', 'humanist' or
'Catholic Aristotelianism' would fail to grasp the complexities of actual
practice. Particularly interesting are the different and various intersections
between the Jesuits, their influences and other strands of early modern
philosophy. Moreover, the ambiguity of the *Constitutions* allowed for
much room for manoeuvre in and around the teachings of Aristotle (and
Aquinas), so that Jesuit philosophers inadvertently dissented, held conflicting views, and even disputed openly among themselves about various
topics. Accordingly, Jesuit philosophy was not a fixed concept, but rather
a complex and controversial one that resulted in significant differences
between Jesuits of different times and geographical origins. Finally, since
all Jesuit philosophers were also teachers, their scholarship and philosophy
were closely linked with teaching methods, and conflicting doctrines often
implied conflicting pedagogical ideals. Historians have shown a tendency
to underestimate this pedagogical basis of Jesuit philosophy. It is this
aspect that shall be addressed in the present study.[10]

This article aims to shed light on the philosophical pedagogy of the Jesuit
Benet Perera (1535–1610). Perera proposed a philosophical pedagogy that
would not be defined simply as either secular or Christian Aristotelianism.
He promoted a philological approach to Aristotle's works as a seed for a sound
and orthodox concept of philosophy. His approach was strongly criticized,
particularly in the Jesuits' own ranks. While Perera's students appreciated his
teachings, his critics accused him of 'Averroism' and identified his philosophical approach as potentially not serving the goals of Jesuit philosophy, or even
being at odds with central Council decrees of the Catholic Church.

In its analysis of Perera's philosophy, this article offers three contributions to scholarship: (1) It provides, for the first time, a complete study and
transcription of Perera's treatise on the useful, error-free study of Christian
philosophy,[11] the *Documenta quaedam perutilia iis qui in studiis philosophiae*

---

[9] See e.g. Alfredo Dinis, 'Censorship and Freedom of Research among the Jesuits
(XVIth–XVIIIth Centuries): The Paradigmatic Case of Giovanni Battista Riccioli (1598–
1671)', in Luís Miguel Carolino and Carlos Ziller Camenietzki (eds.) *Jesuítas, Ensino e
Ciência: Séc. XVI–XVIII* (Casal de Cambra, 2005), 27–57; Cristiano Casalini, *Aristotele a
Coimbra: Il Cursus Conimbricensis e l'educazione nel Collegium Artium* (Rome, 2012);
Michael John Gorman, 'The Scientific Counter-Revolution: Mathematics, Natural
Philosophy and Experimentalism in Jesuit Culture 1580–1670', Ph.D. thesis (Florence,
1998).

[10] Cristiano Casalini and Claud Pavur (eds.), *Jesuit Pedagogy (1540–1616). A Reader*
(Boston, 2016) provides a new overview of this field.

[11] A comprehensive study on Perera's work and further biographies are provided in
Marco Lamanna and Marco Forlivesi (eds.), *Benet Perera (Pererius, 1535–1610). A Renaissance
Jesuit at the Crossroads of Modernity*, special issue of *Quaestio. Journal for the History of
Metaphysics* 14 (2014).

cum fructu et sine ullo errore versari student. Its text is extant in a manuscript held at the Biblioteca Ambrosiana in Milan (MS D496 inf., ff. 25r–31v).[12] This treatise was previously mostly neglected in scholarship, or only used in part.[13]

(2) This article places Perera's treatise within its historical context—that of the Jesuit Roman college of the 1560s, the period during which Perera taught philosophy. Several themes developed the *Documenta* echo other pedagogical writings by Perera, as well as parts of his philosophical master-piece (*De communibus omnium rerum principiis*, 1576), which mostly derived from his lectures at the Roman college. A contextualization of Perera's treatise sheds new light on the question of how Perera's promotion of his own idea of a Christian philosophy for schools provoked criticism among his fellow Romans Diego de Ledesma, the prefect of studies at the college, and Achille Gagliardi.

(3) Finally, this article discusses Perera's conception of a humanistic approach to philosophy as a useful instrument for outlining a Christian philosophy curriculum for Jesuit colleges. It will become clear that Perera's concept of philosophy was strongly connected with contemporary Catholic and humanistic philosophical thought, and that his philosophical approach cannot be placed within the rigid dialectics of 'secular' vs. 'Catholic' Aristotelianism.

---

[12] This manuscript of 14 pages is written in one hand, with only few corrections or insertions. A codicological description of the manuscript may be retrieved from *Manus Online* (http://manus.iccu.sbn.it//opac_SchedaScheda.php?ID=35772, accessed on 18.05.2017). The present article will refer to specific passages in the manuscript by providing references to the specific *documentum* and paragraph. The title of the manuscript is derived from doc. 3: 'Quocirca convenit eos qui in Philosophia sine ullo errore versari cupiunt, si non se totos dederint ad perdiscendas & pertractandas res Theologicas, saltem ad eas cognoscendas et quasi degustandas aliquid opere studijque conferre'. The *explicit* ('Sed revertamur ad institutam tractationem') suggests that it was once part of a lecture—a strong possibility given that it is preserved together with some of Perera's philosophy lectures: *Institutio logica* (ff 1r–23v), *Metaphysicae disputationes* (ff 33r–82v), *Expositio operis Metaphysicae Aristotelis* (ff 84r–91v), *Principium librorum philosophiae* (ff 93r–117r).

[13] The following works all refer to the manuscript, primarily for the purpose of documenting Perera's alleged Averroism: Mario Scaduto, *L'epoca di Giacomo Lainez (1556–1565): L'azione* = Storia della Compagnia de Gesù in Italia 4 (Rome, 1974), 283–8; Paul Richard Blum, *Studies on Early Modern Aristotelianism* (Leiden/Boston, 2012), 141–7; Christoph Sander, 'The War of the Roses. The Debate between Diego de Ledesma and Benet Perera about the Philosophy Course at the Jesuit College in Rome', *Quaestio* 14 (2014), 31–50, 42–4; Cristiano Casalini, 'Pererio 'Cattivo Maestro': Su un cold case nella storia della pedagogia gesuitica', *Quaderni di Noctua* 2 (2014), 59–110, 103–8. The manuscript is also quoted in an editorial note in *Monumenta paedagogica Societatis Iesu*, ed. László Lukács, (7 vols, Rome, 1965–92), ii. 664 (quoted as MPSI, followed by volume and pages). Blum's book chapter of 2012 incorporates his own article, see Paul Richard Blum, 'Benedictus Pererius: Renaissance Culture at the Origins of Jesuit Science', *Science & Education* 15 (2006), 279–304.

II. Origin, Purpose, Content

A discussion of the dating of the manuscript, the purpose of Perera's treatise, and its intended readership, and a complete outline of its content shall provide an initial introduction to the subject of this article. Although some of this material will be repeated and discussed further in the next section, which introduces the broader context of Perera's treatise, this first overview will provide a more general if comprehensive introduction to the treatise.

Unfortunately, the manuscript does not survive with an explicit date of composition, so that we can only surmise that the *Documenta* are likely to have been composed at the Collegio Romano between 1565 and 1567. The *Documenta* were certainly written after 1565, as Perera refers to Carlo Sigonio's translation of Aristotle's *Rhetorica*, previously unpublished.[14] And since Perera started to lecture on scholastic theology in 1567, it is unlikely that the *Documenta* were drafted after this date.[15]

What might have been Perera's motivation or occasion to write the *Documenta*? It is known that Perera started to teach philosophy in 1558, and that he participated in a survey given to all philosophy teachers at the Collegio in 1561.[16] This survey was conducted by the later prefect of studies of the college, Diego de Ledesma, in order to understand the current practice of philosophy teaching. Perhaps thanks to this survey, lecturers spent time reflecting on topics including those incorporated in Perera's *Documenta*.[17] Perera also compiled a bibliography for philosophy teachers (completed after 1563); and two further of his educational documents survive, which date from 1564.[18] Together, these sources and the *Documenta*

---

[14] For the passage of the *Documenta* see below, n. 46. Aristotle, *Aristotelis de arte rhetorica libri tres*, transl. Carlo Sigonio (Bologna, 1565). Sigonio taught Aristotle's *Rhetoric* at Venice from 1553 onwards, and his lecture notes survived in manuscript; see William McCuaig, *Carlo Sigonio: The Changing World of the Late Renaissance* (Princeton, 1989), 18–19. If Perera did, in fact, refer to an unpublished translation by Sigonio, this would not have been written before 1561/2: the manuscript is preserved together with his Logic lectures, which Perera then delivered for the first time. On Perera's teaching activities, see Ugo Baldini, *Legem Impone Subactis: Studi su filosofia e scienza dei Gesuiti in Italia, 1540–1632* (Rome, 1992), 569–70; and Ricardo García Villoslada, *Storia del Collegio Romano dal suo Inizio (1551) alla soppressione della Compagnia di Gesù (1773)* (Rome, 1954), 327–31.

[15] García Villoslada, *Storia del Collegio Romano*, 52, assumes that Perera's shift towards theology resulted from the argument with Ledesma and Gagliardi.

[16] For Ledesma's survey of 1561/2, see MPSI ii. 457–9. Ledesma and his peers' comments on the survey can be found in MPSI ii. 464–81.

[17] Evidence from MPSI documents does not indicate that any prescriptive guidelines for philosophy teachers at Rome were in place prior to 1561. See also below n. 23.

[18] The bibliography was published in Charles H. Lohr, 'Some Early Aristotelian Bibliographies', *Nouvelles de la République des Lettres* 1 (1981), 87–116, 99–116. Lohr dates

form parts of Perera's comprehensive engagement with educational and pedagogical developments from 1563 to 1567.

The *Documenta* can be considered a propaedeutic manual: an introductory and preparatory work for an audience of students of Aristotelian philosophy at a Jesuit college. It is indeed very likely that Perera integrated his treatise into his philosophy lectures.[19] The scholastic context emerges, for example, from Perera's explicit advice on the structure of philosophy lessons (doc. 6) and on speaking in class (doc. 4). It seems likely that Perera here addresses teachers rather than students.[20] The propaedeutic goal then becomes clear in Perera's extensive reflections on the texts on which philosophy lessons are based, and on students' methods of studying those texts (doc. 7–8).

Structurally, the *Documenta* consist of eight individual *documenta*, each devoted to one specific topic; the first six provide the reader with rules for a pious and efficient course of philosophical study, while the last two engage with the textual basis of the course, and thus with Aristotle's writings and Aristotelian commentaries.[21]

At the beginning (doc. 1) Perera states that philosophy is subordinate to Christian faith. Hence, whenever faith conflicts with Aristotle's doctrines, it is faith (of divine origin) that is true, not philosophical doctrines generated by fallible human minds. Perera even warns his reader of arrogance and vanity by referring to Adam and Eve, and their fall in the Garden of Eden. The next three *documenta* analyse the relation between theology and philosophy further. Perera states (doc. 2) that it is impossible for a human being to understand by natural reason all Christian doctrines—the Creation of man and the resurrection are examples of ungraspable concepts. Therefore, Perera continues (doc. 3), all Christian philosophers ought to have a basic understanding of theological matters, be able to speak with confidence about them. Philosophers' statements in class are the subject of document no. 4, and Perera discourages pronouncements like, 'Since it is eternal, the world is true according to philosophy, but false according to

---

the bibliography to between 1563 and 1565 both due to the appearance of a publication of 1562 within it, and because it is preserved together with Perera's lectures of 1563 and 1565. Further educational documents by Perera were edited and published in: *Ordo classium rhetorices, humaniorem litterarum et grammatices* (1557, with potentially spurious attribution to Perera, cf. MPSI ii. 427–9); *Breve instruttione del modo di leggere il corso* (1564, cf. MPSI ii. 665–9); *Ratio studendi iis qui versantur in studiis bonarum artium apprime utilis* (1564, cf. MPSI ii. 670–85). The editor, L. Lukács, dates the documents by circumstantial evidence alone.

[19] Cf. above n. 12.

[20] It should also be noted that the Latin term 'legere' (used 23 times in the *Documenta*) may apply both to the reading act of a student, and to that of a lecturing teacher.

[21] The second part constitutes *c.* 87% of the text.

faith'. Since faith is always true, and philosophy is the science dealing with true and immutable things, it can by no means happen that the doctrines of faith contradict those of philosophy. However, faith may sometimes be at odds with Aristotle's doctrines, the product of a fallible human mind. Perera does not conclude that doctrines of faith that cannot be proven by natural reason are against reason, but that they are above reason. The subsequent document (doc. 5) addresses the moral condition of philosophers: it is disgraceful, Perera states, for philosophers not to strive for truth and wisdom but for their own glory and reputation. But it is even more disgraceful to corrupt philosophy with vices and immoralities, since the teachings of philosophy condemn vices, and advise to avoid them more than disease and death. And the most disgraceful way to philosophize is to pervert the truth intentionally. Perera then records his brief recommendations on the structure of an ideal lesson (doc. 6), starting with reading followed by reflection and disputation, and closing with the composition of a written record.

Document no. 7 discusses, in twelve paragraphs, principles for reading and studying Aristotle.[22] (1) First, Perera recommends a general *modus philosophandi*, which begins with what is known, such as sensory experience—the human intellect operates naturally in this way. (2) Since Aristotle's books are notorious for their clear general structure, but often more obscure in the individual chapters, those who analyse Aristotle may diverge from the rich Aristotelian text. (3) The richness and obscurity of Aristotle's writings may be cut through with a good knowledge of Greek, since Aristotle employs some expressions in a unique way, but others to denote different concepts in different contexts. (4) Perera then introduces a specific aspect of Aristotle's method: his use of different types of demonstration according to the tangibility of different subject matters. His demonstrations on the heavenly bodies, for example, can only be proposed as probabilities. This epistemic and methodological background is important for any evaluation of Aristotle's position. (5) Perera also points out that his own contemporaries often know pre-Socratic teachings (which are discussed and criticized by Aristotle) through the mediation of later authors alone, whereas the original philosophical intentions of any pre-Socratic author are elusive. Only the doxographical writings of ancient authors like Pliny, Plutarch, and Diogenes Laertius are extant. Furthermore, the manner of and motivation for Aristotle's discussion of another philosopher's opinion, refutation of a philosophical theory, or criticism of another's language need to be considered.

---

[22] We have not been able to determine a rationale behind the order of the individual paragraphs.

(6) Nonetheless, readers of Aristotle must focus on Aristotle's text without distraction, always in comparison with passages previously read, in order to identify correspondences or contradictions within Aristotle's writings. (7) Perera states that learning Aristotle's writing by rote is an almost futile exercise, and proposes that the reader recollect the most crucial passages from Aristotle's writings in order to record them in writing eventually. (8) The best way to explain a passage of Aristotle's text is by means of another passage from Aristotle, since a phrase obscure in one place may become clearer in the light of another, more comprehensible passage. (9) Perera further emphasizes the importance of knowledge of the principles of Aristotelian philosophy for the interpretation of Aristotle's writings, especially primary philosophical principles, e.g. the eternity of motion. These, however, should be evaluated according to their area of application. One should be aware if they contradict principles of faith (and if so, whether they can be refuted by natural reason), and they must also be compared to the principles of Platonic philosophy. (10) Perera encourages those who are able to read Aristotle in Greek to do so, because they might not only understand the text better, but also appreciate the beauty of Aristotle's expression. For those who read Aristotle exclusively in Latin, Perera provides a brief overview over Latin translations available, and recommends specific translation for specific pieces of Aristotle's writing. (11) He then briefly outlines a history of the transmission of Aristotle's works in the original Greek manuscripts, in order to explain the textual corruption and obscurity that occur in contemporary versions of the Greek text; and dispenses philological advice for dealing with these textual difficulties. (12) Finally, Perera invites students to reflect on their progress in Aristotelian philosophy and closes by reassuring students that they will understand the complexities of Aristotle's works as long as they continue to study them.

In his last and most extensive *documentum* (doc. 8), Perera weighs the value of commentaries on Aristotle's works, and distinguishes three types of authors: the ancient Greek commentators (Alexander of Aphrodisias, Themistius, Simplicius, and Philoponus); the Arabic commentators Avicenna and Averroes; and two Medieval Latin commentators, Albert the Great and Thomas Aquinas.

Of all these, Alexander is Perera's favourite, since Alexander increased Aristotle's popularity in the ancient period, but also because he was the first to truly clarify and elucidate Aristotle's writings. According to Perera, all of Alexander's commentaries (first published in the sixteenth century) are essential reading. Perera has no views on Themistius, except praise for his useful paraphrases of Aristotle's works. For Simplicius, Perera praises his commentaries on the *Physics* and on the *Categories*, but admits that the

Greek version of his commentary on *De caelo* is corrupt, and the Latin poorly translated. Further, Perera thinks Simplicius' commentary on *De anima* more Platonic than Aristotelian, and therefore questions the authorship of the text. Perera shows much less enthusiasm for Philoponus' work: his language might be elegant, but some of his arguments were rather sophistic; he was also criticized by Simplicius on this point.

With regard to Arabic authors, Perera first emphasizes Avicenna's renown as a medical authority. But while Avicenna's medical writings are a good read, Perera states, his philosophical works are less distinguished, and perhaps even only noteworthy because Averroes frequently criticized Avicenna, and some Latin authors acknowledged and referred to him frequently. Contrary to common praise for Avicenna's philosophical works, Perera regards them as obscure and not essentially Aristotelian.

The most extensive subsection is devoted to a highly favourable philosophical portrait of Averroes. Perera emphasizes the importance of Averroes for Aristotelian philosophy, especially his contribution to the interpretation of Aristotle's doctrines and to protecting them against incorrect interpretations. Consequently, Perera says, Averroes is admired by all scholars, except for those who have not read him at all or have not fully comprehended his writings. Perera recommends that not only Averroes' commentaries on and paraphrases of Aristotle be studied, but also certain of his extant original works (*De substantia orbis, Destructio destructionum*), and arguments made within his commentaries as digressions from the commentary proper. Perera explains Averroes' occasional failure to elucidate Aristotle with Averroes' corrupted sources. Averroists like Marcantonio Zimara have made a great effort to overcome the philological problems in Averroes' writings and to explain his doctrines, and thereby contributed to a better understanding of Aristotle.

Finally, Perera attends to the medieval Latin authors. Albert the Great's works can be divided into two groups: commentaries on Aristotle, and other works. Perera highlights Albert's erudition and his knowledge in natural history. Perera especially praises (Pseudo-)Albert's *Dialogus de apprehensione* (doubting, correctly, its authorship). But although Perera finds much to admire in some of Albert's philosophical doctrines (e.g. the conception of intelligences), he also admits to not understanding or subscribing to all of the concepts that Albert introduces. Perera also mentions existing criticism of Albert's writings in natural history, accusing him of using material from other authors rather writing from personal experience.

Perera then describes Thomas Aquinas as a promoter of Aristotle's writings both in his own commentaries and thanks to Aquinas' canonization, which popularized Aristotle's works to a Christian audience. According to Perera, this 'extrinsic' reason made Aquinas a model for the reading and public teaching of Aristotle, and he was acknowledged as conducive to the science of Christian theology. Perera praises Aquinas for his clarity of expression and his profound knowledge of divine things, as well as for his restraint in the criticism of other authors—Aquinas always defends his adversaries by identifying their mistakes as specific and limited; and even when a benevolent reading is not possible, Aquinas directs his criticism not against an individual, but always against the doctrine under discussion. With regard to philosophy, Aquinas' theological *Summae* (*Summa theologiae, Summa contra gentiles*) deserve students' attention even more than his succinct commentaries on the *Corpus Aristotelicum*. Of these, Perera especially recommends Aquinas' commentaries on *De interpretatione* and on *De caelo*, in which he follows the Greek commentators (Ammonius and Simplicius) comparatively closely. If Aquinas had followed this approach in all his commentaries—which was impossible, since the Greeks' commentaries were not available in the Latin West at the time, Perera admits—his commentaries would not just be supplements to those of the Greeks, but preferred to them. The section closes with a short defence of Aquinas against those who criticize his breaking up Aristotle's words into tiny divisions, which, as Perera agrees, makes Aquinas a demanding read (but these are not grounds for his general dismissal).

A final paragraph referring back to the first *documentum* reminds the reader to reject doctrines which are directed against philosophy and Christian faith, for example, Alexander's denial of God as an efficient cause and Averroes' doctrine of the unity of the intellect. Those errors are natural, Perera remarks, since their authors, human beings, were fallible by nature. Perera closes the *Documenta* with the request that the reader praise God for revealing knowledge concealed from pagan philosophers to his contemporaries (i.e. Christian philosophers).

III. Historical Context

When Perera started lecturing on philosophy at the Roman college in 1558, he did not find any explicit teaching guidelines in place for philosophy teachers.[23] The first known attempt to establish such guidelines was not made until 1561, when Diego de Ledesma conducted the abovementioned

---

[23] For the history of the Roman college and Ledesma's role within it, see Ernesto Rinaldi, *La Fondazione del Collegio Romano: Memorie storiche* (Arezzo, 1914); John M. Belmonte, 'To Give Ornament, Splendor and Perfection: Diego de Ledesma and Sixteenth Century Jesuit Educational Administration' (Ph.D. thesis, Chicago, 2006); Paul Gilbert, 'La preparazione della *Ratio studiorum* e l'insegnamento di filosofia di Benet Perera', *Quaestio*, 14 (2014), 1–30.

survey of philosophy teachers in order to find out which material they considered worth reading and discussing in class.[24] As soon as Ledesma was promoted to the position of the college's prefect of studies, and as soon as it was one of his duties to supervise studies at the college, in 1564, his own survey gathered his colleagues' insights into possible ways to improve the teaching of all disciplines; notably, his survey extended beyond the field of philosophy.[25] The results served Ledesma as a basis for a first 'plan of studies' or *Ratio studiorum* for the Roman college.[26] Perera himself had also reflected on pedagogy, especially with regard to philosophy teaching, and preserved his thoughts into two short pedagogical treatises (dating from around 1564)—with the *Documenta* a third significant supplement—and a bibliography of commentaries on the *Corpus Aristotelicum*.[27] In addition to Perera's pedagogical treatises, evidence of their actual implementation has survived in the form of his lecture notes for his philosophy lectures.[28] These were later incorporated to a significant extent into his philosophical manual *De communibus omnium rerum naturalium principiis*, which was published in 1576.[29]

As will be shown below, these well-known and well-analysed documents by Ledesma and Perera, once considered in addition to Perera's *Documenta*, appear in a new light. Indeed, the *Documenta* reveal connections to both Perera's own writings and the educational guidelines proposed

---

[24] See also above n. 16.

[25] See also above n. 16. While Perera contributed a paper to Ledesma's first survey of philosophy teachers, he was, surprisingly, not included in the later, more substantial survey, cf. MPSI ii. 466 n. 11: at the time, Perera was still teaching his philosophy course. Some have argued that this exclusion is indicative of early attacks on Perera's teachings. The scope of this present essay does not allow for a detailed account of the controversy around Perera's teaching methods; interested readers are referred to literature referenced above (n. 13).

[26] Plan of studies, 1564: MPSI ii. 481–90. This document is to be distinguished from the *Ratio Borgiana*, which was not authored by Ledesma according to László Lukács, 'De prima Societatis Ratione studiorum sancto Francisco Borgia praeposito generali constituta (1565–1569)', *Archivum Historicum Societatis Iesu*, 27 (1958), 209–32.

[27] For references for these works, see above n. 18.

[28] Blum, *Aristotelianism*, 140–1, provides an overview.

[29] Blum demonstrates this (see above, n. 28). On the publication of Perera's book, see MPSI iv. 664–5, and García Villoslada, *Storia del Collegio Romano*, 78–80. Benedictus Pererius, *De communibus omnium rerum naturalium principiis & affectionibus libri XV* (Rome, 1576) may be considered first edition of Perera's book: the alleged edition of 1562 appears to be spurious (according to Blum, *Aristotelianism*, 140 n. 3). The appearance of Ledesma's name as one of the committee of 1576, which was to discuss the potential print publication of Perera's work, poses an additional conundrum, since Ledesma died in 1575: an obituary provides evidence for his death, see *Monumenta paedagogica Societatis Jesu, quae primam Rationem studiorum anno 1586 editam praecessere*, ed. Cecilio Gómez Rodeles et al. (Madrid, 1901), 862. Martin, *Subverting Aristotle*, 90, appears to consider the Paris edition of 1579 the *editio princeps*, or at least reactive to the *censura* committee. The authors of this present article have not been able to detect any differences between the editions of 1576 and 1579.

by his critics.[30] We will address these connections by following the structure of the *Documenta*: first, 'rules concerning the relation between philosophy and faith', and second, 'rules relating to the textual basis for studying philosophy'. It will become clear that piety and philology are intertwined in Perera's concept of philosophical studies.

Piety

In the *Documenta*, Perera describes in certain terms how the doctrines of Christian faith and philosophy relate to each other.[31] While faith is above reason, the two domains cannot contradict each other in principle. However, some divinely revealed doctrines might not be completely understood by the human intellect or resist philosophical proof, since philosophy is necessarily guided by natural reason alone. Moreover, Perera is at pains to emphasize that each philosopher, whether Aristotle or another, is a mere fallible human being, and therefore not immune to errors.[32] In the preface of *De communibus*, which imports several passages from the *Documenta* verbatim, Perera refers to these errors as 'philosophers' errors', not 'errors of philosophy'.[33] This rather programmatic idea, however, poses a conundrum

---

[30] In contrast to Perera's other pedagogical treatises and a number of Ledesma's records, the *Documenta* do not seem to address strictly pedagogical questions—e.g. the ideal length of a teaching unit or the nature, time in the academic year and order of texts to be read—in any detail. Perera's audience for the *Documenta*, as stated in their title, may explain this: they are not written exclusively for teachers, but more generally for students of philosophy. Also, as we assume, the *Documenta* were integrated in a philosophy lecture. Some similarities with documents written primarily for teachers can, however, be detected: for example, in the *Documenta* Perera alludes to the sequential structure of lessons (*lectio, speculatio, disputatio, scriptio*), and in his *Il modo* he elaborates on this point in a more pedagogical manner: 'Perché alcuni sono più atti ad argumentare, altri a respondere, altri ad altre cose, procuri d'essercitare ciascuno principalmente secondo il talento suo; et in summa faccia che li suoi scolari si diano più tosto al speculare et disputare, che a leggere molte cose o scrivere'. Cf. MPSI ii. 669.

[31] Cf. doc. 1–5.   [32] Cf. doc. 1, 4 and 8. See also below n. 75.

[33] Pererius, *De communibus*, praef. reads: 'illi quidem errores Philosophorum, non Philosophia[e]; hoc est, hominum non scientiae'. On this passage, see also Blum, *Aristotelianism*, 149–50. Perera further remarks in his preface: 'Nec mirandum cuiquam accidat, Platonem et Aristotelem, caeterosqui sapientes viros, et philosophorum principes, nonnumquam graviter et turpiter errasse: videlicet, homines fuerunt, quorum erant fallaces sensus angusta ingenia, infirma iudicia, vita multis flagitiis inquinata, mens humanae inscitiae circumfusa tenebris et caelesti lumine destituta. Quin potius non immortales Deo gratias agamus qui ea nobis clarissime patefecit, quae acutissimos Philosophos latuerunt. Nec solum in iis quae tradit philosophia, quid nobis probandum sequendumque quid contra repudiandum et fugiendum esset, omnium errorum discussa caligine iudicavit: sed etiam earum rerum quae omnem humanae intelligentiae vim et facultatem superant cognitionem ad quam philosophia aspirare non potest, liberaliter impertuit'. These two passages may be compared with Perera's statement at the end of the *Documenta*: 'neque vero mirandum est hos viros caeterosque sapientes tam graviter & absurde lapsos & deceptos fusse, homines enim fuerunt, quorum errant fallaces, sensus, angusta ingenia, infirma iudicia, vitae multis

whenever a lesson results in a conflict between all three: faith, philosophy, and Aristotle. Perera offers a solution to this problem in the *Documenta*:

> Students are not to imitate the way of speaking of those philosophers who are used to explain philosophical controversies speaking like this: '"the world is eternal" has to be accepted as true according to philosophy, but as false according to faith'. This is so, since truth always is in accordance with truth and our faith is true. The same holds for philosophy, since this is the science which considers true and immutable things. Therefore it is impossible that the dogmas of faith contradict the doctrines of philosophy. Therefore, one should speak like this instead: 'something, namely that the world was created, needs to be accepted as true and certain according to faith. But Aristotle thought this false and impossible'. And this must not seem to be strange and absurd. For Aristotle, like all human beings, is capable of error, and from time to time he erred in one case or another, and one should not be surprised when the truth of faith clashes with the errors of Aristotle.[34]

If one compares Perera's ideal of a pious philosophy for schools with the results of Ledesma's survey and his plan of studies for the Roman college, the two seem to agree at a basic level on one essential point. Perera demands that philosophers always keep religious objects in mind and that they are equipped with a basic understanding of theological issues at minimum.[35]

---

flagitiis ingenerata, mens humanae inscitiae tenebris circumfusa, & celesti destituta lumine. Nos igitur immortales gratias Deo immortali agamus, eumque pie & caste semper colamus, atque veneremur, quod singulari beneficio suo: pro Christum senatorem, & doctorem humani generis: ea nobis clarissime patefecit, quae acutissimis doctissimisque philosophis obscura & occulta esse voluit, nec tamen in iis qui philosophiam tradit quod sequendum, aut fugiendum, quod ite probandum aut interpretandum nobis esset iudicavit. Sed etiam earum rerum: quae omnem intelligentiam vim atque facultatem, infinitis partibus superant, cognitionem liberaliter impertivit'. Cf. also doc. 5: 'tamen est repugnans doctrinae Aristotelis, neque hoc mirum et absurdum videri debet, nam cum Aristoteles more aliorum hominum, et potuerit errare et interdum erraverit, tum in hoc tum in alijs rebus, non est mirandum veritatem fidei pugnare cum erroribus Aristotelis'. A similar point is raised by Jacobus Pontanus, a Jesuit from Dillingen, in a speech which certainly alludes to Perera's *De communibus*, see Jacobus Pontanus, *Akademische Reden an der Universität Dillingen 1572–1582*, ed. Ulrich G. Leinsle (Münster, 2014), 137.

[34] Doc. 4: 'Caveant imitari consuetudinem loquendi eorum philosophorum, qui in explicandis controversijs philosophiae ita loqui consueverint. Hoc v.g. mundum esse aeternum, verum etiam et teneri debet secundum philosophiam, at secundum fidem Christianam falsum esse, nam cum verum semper vero consonet, fides autem nostra vera sit, et item philosophia si quidem est scientia quae in rebus veris et immutabilibus, necesse fieri non potest ut dogmata fidei adversentur decretis philosophiae. Quare sic potius loquendum est, hoc scilicet mundum esse de novo factum, pro vero et certo habendum est secundum fidem. Sed Aristoteles putavit esse falsum et impossibile. Itaque licet sit consentaneum fidei: tamen est repugnans doctrinae Aristotelis, neque hoc mirum et absurdum videri debet, nam cum Aristoteles more aliorum hominum, et potuerit errare et interdum erraverit, tum in hoc tum in alijs rebus, non est mirandum veritatem fidei pugnare cum erroribus Aristotelis'. The English translation is slightly adapted from Sander, 'The Debate', 43–4.

[35] See doc. 3.

Ledesma and his colleague Achille Gagliardi find that, among other things, 'nobody other than a theologian shall teach philosophy', and 'philosophy shall be taught in a manner appropriate to its serving theology'.[36] Therefore, these philosophers appear to have agreed on the point that philosophy was not a purely secular undertaking separate from all theological implications. Nevertheless, a controversy appears to have arisen regarding the role of Aristotle within this conception of pious philosophy, and the possibility of matters of faith to be proven by natural reason.

This alleged conflict took place on at least three different levels, the first epistemological. Ledesma had investigated Perera's teaching based on his students' lecture notes—an indirect piece of evidence.[37] Nevertheless, the points that seemed suspect in the eyes of Ledesma emerge clearly in the notes: Perera was recorded as denying that some doctrines of faith—especially those concerning the status of the immortal human soul—could be demonstrated by natural reason, and claiming that Aristotle held the opposite view.[38]

Secondly, the argument concerned doctrine. Ledesma and Gagliardi maintained that, within the Society of Jesus, doctrines like the immortality of the soul need to be considered true not only according to philosophy, but also according to Aristotle's authority.[39] Ledesma in particular was very eager to match doctrines of faith with Aristotle's doctrines: he wished to exert the power of natural reason also on religious doctrines.[40] The famous papal bull *Apostolici regiminis* (decreed in 1513 at the Fifth Lateran Council) was Ledesma's most potent justification for his measures.[41]

Thirdly, the argument revolved around pedagogy. Ledesma was pursuing practical pedagogical goals, for instance, in his juxtaposition of a sound way of teaching with the impious custom which was permitted at some Italian universities:

> It is an absurd and destructive way of disputing and of speaking, in which one thing is proven according to philosophy, and another according to the

[36] Cf. MPSI ii. 476 (signed by Gagliardi): 'Nullus doceat philosophiam aut philosophiae cursum, qui non sit theologus'; MPSI ii. 478 (signed by Gagliardi and Ledesma): 'sic doceatur philosophia, ut serviat theologiae'.

[37] Cf. MPSI ii. 502–3. This accusation is discussed in Casalini, 'Pererio'.

[38] See also Christoph Sander, 'In dubio pro fide. The Fifth Council of the Lateran Decree Apostolici Regiminis (1513) and Its Impact on Early Jesuit Education and Pedagogy', *Educazione. Giornale di pedagogia critica*, 3/1 (2014), 39–62; 49; Blum, *Aristotelianism*, 145.

[39] Cf. MPSI ii. 478: 'et ideo, notentur opiniones non tenendae in his quae fidem concernunt, ac eae quae sunt defendendae, ut omnes sic doceant, et totis viribus defendant, et ad id obligentur expresse, etiam secundum Aristotelem, ut de immortalitate animae etc.; ac per totam Societatem sic servetur'.

[40] On Ledesma's guideline, see Sander, 'In dubio pro fide'.

[41] This point is also analysed in detail in Sander, 'In dubio pro fide'.

truth [i.e. the Christian doctrine] or when the same thing is asserted to be true according to philosophy but false according to faith.

This would not be a love of wisdom [*philosophia*] but a love of error [*philopseudia*], which shuns the truth. And something that contradicts divine doctrine, i.e. faith, cannot be the truth. Truth always agrees with truth in such a way that truth cannot stand against truth. For this reason, the third [i.e. fifth] Council of the Lateran was right to repudiate this way of disputing and speaking in the strongest terms.

And it is not very different from this to say that this thing should be maintained in Aristotle but this in reality or in the faith. Although this might occasionally be necessary, it should still be done moderately, so that we do not give the impression that in matters pertaining to the faith and religion we are suppressing the faith itself, that is, the teaching received from God, by raising up Aristotle's authority against it.

This is actually done by those who strive with all their strength to show, in many cases, that Aristotle held opinions contrary to the faith, although it is clear that he disagreed with the faith in [only] a very few matters; and—even worse—they try to do the same in the many passages in which Aristotle certainly could quite reasonably be interpreted in favour of the faith, especially since men of great authority have openly testified that that opinion is Aristotle's.

They have done a disservice to Aristotle, whom they think they are supporting because this way they are turning him from a true to a false idea, and they are forcing him against his will to say what is false and to make disgraceful errors even in the most important matters. What about the fact that from this serious and frequent striving for Aristotle against faith and truth, certain serious disadvantages arise, both unworthy of a Christian man and entirely intolerable?

First, it does not contribute anything positive at all but rather presents a great obstacle to stir up recklessly so great an adversary against the faith, and to arm him with great zeal against it, and to help him fight it in all matters. Then, many people, when they hear that something is true according to Aristotle, understand that whatever it is, is so according to philosophy, indeed, according to the best philosophy of all (which they think to be Aristotle's), and what Aristotle thought, they believe to be in accord with natural reason and its light; and therefore disputing this way, as much as they can, they unwisely subvert the Council's decree, because they believe their faith stands opposed to reason and natural illumination. But it is quite damaging or a very serious matter that, when they are teaching that Aristotle thought something in contradiction to the faith, they strive to confirm it with arguments in such a manner that they themselves also seem to agree with Aristotle against the faith; especially when with all their zeal they strive to dissolve the reasons that could bring be brought forward to endorse faith and truth, just in order that they might protect Aristotle's opinion. It is clearly a serious obstacle to the faith and the truth when their arguments and reasons seem to be weakened and broken. [42]

These statements, although they were published a few years after the argument with Perera, openly contradict Perera's recommendations.[43] Ledesma conceded only few cases to the perceived conflict between faith and Aristotle, but these cases granted anyone the permission to consider Aristotle useless for true Christian philosophy. For Ledesma, the suspicion of Aristotle's doctrines as overall contrary to the doctrines of faith was an unfounded, overly strong conclusion. The few cases in which Aristotle and faith are at odds should not, he maintained, result in an overall mistrust of Aristotle's teachings. At first glance, Perera seems to agree with Ledesma on the metaphysical assumption that there is only one truth and that therefore, overall, faith and reason cannot contradict one another. However, Aristotle plays a different role in Perera's rationale. In the *Documenta*,

---

[42] Diego de Ledesma in Franciscus Toletus, *Commentaria una cum quaestionibus in octo libros Aristotelis de physica auscultatione* (Venice, 1573), praef.: 'Illud quoque absurdum et perniciosum est, vel disputandi, vel loquendi genus, quo, illud ex philosophia, hoc ex Veritate, asseritur: aut idem secundum philosophiam verum, secundum Fidem falsum esse affirmatur. Neque enim philosophia, sed [gr. philopseudia] erit, quae a veritate abhorret; neque, quae cum divina doctrina, id est, Fide pugnet, veritas esse poterit. Sic enim vero verum congruit, ut veritas veritati non possit esse contraria. Quocirca non immerito in Concilio Lateranensi tertio hoc disputandi, ac loquendi genus, verbis exterminatur gravissimis. Neque illud dissimile est, Hoc in Aristotele hoc vero in veritate, aut in Fide esse dicendum: ut enim id interdum necessarium sit, tamen ea fieri moderatione debet, ut ne in rebus, quae ad Fidem et religionem attinent, Fidem ipsam, hoc est a Deo acceptam disciplinam, obiecta Aristotelis authoritate praemere videamur: quod sane isti faciunt, qui summo conatur viribusque nituntur ostendere compluribus in rebus, Aristotelem contra fidem sensisse, cum tamen constet, paucissimis in rebus a Fide dissentire, et (quod peius est) idem conantur efficere multis locis, in quibus quidem Aristotelem possent non sine magna etiam probabilitate pro Fide interpretari, cum praesertim viri gravissimi Aristotelis sententiam eam esse aperte testentur. In quo sane de ipso Aristotele, cui favere se putant, male merentur, cum sic eum a vera ad falsam sententiam abstrahunt, et cogunt falsum dicere vel invitum, in rebus etiam gravissimis errare turpissime. Quid quod ex hac graviori, frequentique pro Aristotele contra Fidem et veritatem concertatione, gravia quaedam incommoda accidunt, et Christiano viro indigna, et omnino non ferenda? Primum enim, nihil prodest, obest autem plurimum temere excitare tantum contra Fidem adversarium, eumque summo studio contra illam amare, et ad eam oppugnandam omnibus rebus iuvare. Deinde plerique, cum audiunt verum quid esse secundum Aristotelem, id omnino intelligunt, quid est, secundum philosophiam, immo secundum omnium optimam (quam esse putant Aristotelis) philosophiam, et quod Aristoteles sensit, id credunt esse naturali rationi ac lumini consentaneum, atque ideo sic disputantes, quantum in ipsis est, idem illud Concilii decretum per imprudentiam evertunt, quod credant, rationi, et lumini naturali fidem adversari. Illud autem incommodum vel gravissimum est, cum enim contra Fidem docent aliquid sensisse Aristotelem, id sic confirmare nituntur argumentis, ut ipsi quoque contra Fidem cum Aristotele sentire videantur; praesertim cum quae pro Fide, et veritati adduci possunt, ea summo studio conentur dissolvere, ut Aristotelis sententiam tueantur; quod sane plurimum Fidei, et veritati obesse constat, cum eius argumenta et rationes infirmari, frangique videantur'. For the supposed attribution to Ledesma, see below n. 96.

[43] Cf. above n. 34.

Perera does not avoid a distinction between true philosophy and Christian faith on the one hand, and Aristotle's doctrines on the other. It is this historically accurate understanding of Perera's, of Aristotle as being a fallible human philosopher, that allows him to maintain this distinction.

Philology

While Ledesma's aims were primarily pedagogical, Perera's approach was largely philological, and hence essentially different. In Perera's view, the study of philosophy starts with reading Aristotle.[44] Firstly and notably, he recommends reading Aristotle in the original Greek, and ranks translations extant at the time in order of usefulness for those not versed in Greek.[45] Perera particularly recommends the *translatio vetus* of Aristotle's works on logic and physics, and for other works (including those that were not part of the Jesuit curriculum like the *Poetica* or the zoological works), he names reliable contemporary humanistic translators, including Carlo Sigonio (1524–84), Denis Lambin (1520–72), Juan Ginés de Sepúlveda (1490–1573), and Piero Vettori (1499–1585).[46] These recommendations indicate that Perera approved of the humanists' attempts to make Aristotle's texts more accessible.[47] Perera also frequently points out the advantages of

---

[44] Cf. doc. 6.

[45] Cf. doc. 7 §10: 'In scriptis logicis & physicis maxime omium probatur mihi translatio vetus quae nuper emendata fuit, & recens excussa parvis voluminibus circumfertur, nam etsi nonnunquam importuna quadam superstitione, singula verba Aristotelis eo quo greco sunt ordine, quasi numerata latine reddens, & formulas graece linguae proprias totidem verbis latinis satis barbare, & insulse exprimens faciat nobis Aristotelem obscurum & ferreum quendam scriptorem, tum contra vere et fideliter (quod imprimis requirendum est ab interprete) sensum eius – representat caeteris versionibus (quas adhuc vidi) praeferendam iudico – Demum in Metaphisicis probo versionem Bessarionis: in hisque de animalibus Theodori Gazae; in Ethicis Lambini, vel etiam Argiropuli; in politicis Johannis Sepulvedae, in Rhetoricis Caroli Sygonii, in poetica Petri Victorii'.

[46] According to Ferdinand Edward Cranz and Charles Bernard Schmitt (eds.), *A bibliography of Aristotle editions, 1501–1600* (Baden-Baden, 1984), the first few editions of the translations named by Perera are: *Metaphysica*, transl. Bessarion (Paris, 1515); *De animalibus*, transl. Gaza (Venice, 1504); *Ethica*, transl. Lambin (Paris, 1558); transl. Argyropylus (Leipzig, 1501); *Politica*, transl. Sepúlveda (Paris, 1548); *Rhetorica*, transl. Sigonio (Bologna, 1565); *Poetica*, transl./comm. Vettori (Florence, 1560); trans. Vettori (Venice, 1562). Jesuits using humanistic translations of Aristotle are also discussed in Christoph Sander, 'Medical Topics in the De Anima Commentary of Coimbra (1598) and the Jesuits' Attitude towards Medicine in Education and Natural Philosophy', *Early Science and Medicine* 19 (2014), 76–101, 82 n. 23. On texts called for by a Jesuit curriculum, see Paul Richard Blum, 'Der Standardkurs der katholischen Schulphilosophie im 17. Jahrhundert', in Eckhard Kessler, Charles H. Lohr and Walter Sparn (eds.), *Aristotelismus und Renaissance: In Memoriam Charles B. Schmitt* (Wiesbaden, 1988), 127–48.

[47] Cf. doc. 7, § 10: 'Esse legatiores autem versiones Aristotelis, quae multis additis et immutatis faciunt Aristotelem non modo suo, sed latine loquentem longe retroque ponendas censeo'. On the relatively recent popularity of translations of Aristotle's works, see also Katharine Park, 'Psychology: The Organic Soul', in Charles Schmitt et al. (eds.) *The Cambridge History*

being familiar with Aristotle's texts, to gain a good understanding of his teachings, and as a firm basis for the discussion of difficulties in the text.[48] Further, Perera points out that a lack of knowledge in the Greek language is at the root of some authors' misunderstanding of Aristotelian texts, not aided by the fact that many of them could not rely on the help of more recent ancient Greek commentators.[49]

It is, secondly, noteworthy that Perera rejects the common practice of teaching by rote, and, for students, of learning by rote.[50] He considers a systematic committing to memory of Aristotle's theories, by compiling lists or tables of his major tenets, much more useful. Perera refers to this method in his other pedagogical writings as well.[51] Like the reading of Aristotle in the original Greek, the creation of a structured excerption from Aristotle's works agrees with Perera's general hermeneutic strategy elucidating obscure Aristotelian passages with the aid of other, related and clearer passages.[52]

---

of Renaissance Philosophy (Cambridge, 1988), 464–84, 458; Brian Copenhaver, 'Translation, Terminology and Style in Philosophical Discourse', ibid., 75–110, 77.

[48] Some examples emerge from doc. 7, §3, §10 and §11. Perera's reference to the transmission of Aristotle's manuscript according to Strabo, *Geographicorum libri XVII* (Basel, 1539), 408, is also documented in its entirety in Pererius, *De communibus*, 128 (IV, 4). On Strabo's account see William K. Guthrie, *A History of Greek Philosophy*, vi: *Aristotle. An Encounter* (Cambridge, 1981), 59.

[49] The new Aristotle editions compiled by Greek commentators are discussed in Charles H. Lohr, 'Renaissance Latin Translations of the Greek Commentaries on Aristotle', in Jill Kraye and M. W. F. Stone (eds.), *Humanism and Early Modern Philosophy* (London/New York, 2000), 24–40. In his *Ratio*, Perera remarks: 'Scriptorum genera duo sunt: Unum eorum qui aliorum sententias suis vel scholiis vel commentariis explanant; alterum eorum qui nullius interpretationi adstricti non alienas, sed suas scriptis exponunt sententias. Priores, ut munere interpretandi probe fungantur, oportet primum quidem linguae, qua scripsit author quem interpretantur, scientes ac peritos esse. Huius enim ignoratio saepenumero interpretes, caeteroquin doctos viros, in multos ac faedos errores induxit. Cui rei fidem faciunt mille quaestiones frivolae, sescentaque figmenta in explicando Aristotele, ob inscitiam linguae graecae, a latinis philosophis excogitata. Deinde convenit eos in aliis scriptis eiusdem authoris probe versatos ac exercitatos esse, ut opus quod interpretandum susceperunt, vel ex aliis locis declarando vel cum aliis conferendo, ut quid vel simile vel diversum aut contrarium ab authore dictum fuerit, demonstrando accuratius et luculentius exponant'. Cf. MPSI ii., 678. References to Averroes and Aquinas appear in doc. 8. See also below n. 65 and 98.

[50] Cf. Ledesma's remark in MPSI ii. 477: 'Docendi modus sit, ut vel mediocria ingenia possint lectionem memoria concipere, et memoriter repetere'. Cf. Perera's doc. 7, §7. On this matter, see also Paul Nelles, '*Libros de Papel, Libri Bianchi, Libri Papyracei*. Note-Taking Techniques and the Role of Student Notebooks in the Early Jesuit Colleges', *Archivum Historicum Societatis Iesu* 76 (2007), 75–112.

[51] Cf. MPSI ii. 675–6, and 666–7, where Perera states: 'Deve ancora scrivere qualche cosa, almanco notare circa ogni materia alcuni belli concetti o resolutione, o sua o d'altri; alcuni testi et testimonii principali, o di Aristotele o d'altri antichi, acciò di queste cose possa aiutarsi un'altra volta'.

[52] Cf. doc. 7, §6 and §8. See also above n. 49.

Perera's two strategies for appropriating Aristotle's texts provide the basis for a critical and historical understanding of his philosophy. This basis becomes instrumental, for example, when Perera advises his readers to keep the following points in mind: (a) The certainty of a demonstration depends on the realm within which it is conducted;[53] (b) Aristotle's principles need to be gauged against those of Platonic philosophy and faith;[54] (c) Aristotle's criticism of his predecessors needs to be taken with a grain of salt, and his specific reasons for his criticism to be taken into account, especially given that his predecessors' original ideas are often only available in doxographical accounts.[55]

Many of these guidelines for the study of Aristotelian philosophy reappear later in Perera's *De communibus*; but there, they serve a different purpose. In the *Documenta*, Perera presents his ideas on a historical understanding of Aristotle's ideas as preparation for the study of his works; the doxographical accounts, the comparison of Aristotle's principles to those of other philosophers, and the transmission of Greek Aristotelian texts are all relevant in this context. By contrast, in the *De communibus*, book IV (*De antiquis philosophis, eorumque variis, circa rerum naturalium principia, opinionibus*), Perera's ideas emerge in the context of a history of philosophy, with particular focus on ancient philosophical schools and their chronology.[56] In this book, Perera proposes that some philosophers' theories are particularly useful:[57] in his discussion of the immortality of the soul, for example, Perera compares Aristotle's and Plato's approaches to the doctrine of faith directly with each other—a direct implementation of his guideline mentioned above. It should be noted that the chapters of *De communibus* which also survive in a separate manuscript copy are evidence of Perera's ambition to analyse the texts of ancient philosophers (other than Aristotle) in comparison with each other.[58]

---

[53] Cf. doc. 7, §4.   [54] Cf. doc. 7, §9.   [55] Cf. doc. 7, §5.

[56] Perera's history of ancient philosophy and the related refutation of Simplicius is examined in Constance Blackwell, 'Neo-Platonic Modes of Concordism versus Definitions of Difference: Simplicius, Augustinus Steuco and Ralph Cudworth versus Marco Antonio Zimara and Benedictus Pererius', in Stephen Clucas, Peter J. Forshaw and Valery Rees (eds.), *Laus Platonici Philosophi: Marsilio Ficino and His Influence* (Leiden/Boston, 2011), 317–42.

[57] Cf. Pererius, *De communibus*, 112–3 (IV, 1).

[58] Rome, Archivio Storico della Pontificia Università Gregoriana, APUG 1345, ff. 132r–146r, includes the following treatises: *Secundum Platonem Animam rationalem esse immortalem, Animum nostrum esse immortale etiam secundum Doctrinam Aristotelis, Probatur immortalitem animae rationalis rationibus Philosophicis, Anima rationalem esse veram, et naturalem formam hominis, De varijs sectis Philosophorum, Reprehenditur Simplicius, qui conatur ostendere omnes praedictas opiniones veras esse atque inter se contenientes.* This collection is erroneously ascribed to Ledesma in *Manus online* (http://manus.iccu.sbn.it//opac_SchedaScheda.php?ID=162831, accessed on 18.05.2017), and in Sander, 'The Debate', 40 n. 48. Rather, these short treatises are near-perfect copies of chapters published in Perera's

Perera understood that, in addition of his own efforts to achieve a proper critical reading of Aristotle's text, the project was also a collaborative undertaking. The longest part of the *Documenta* is therefore devoted to a critique of Aristotle's commentators.[59] Moreover, Perera wrote an extensive bibliography comprising the 131 commentaries he approved of the most, and he refers to it twice in his pedagogical treatises.[60] In three of his writings Perera divides the commentators (who are roughly the same across all three documents) into three major groups: Greek, Arabic, and Latin.[61] For the *Documenta*, two aspects of his 'literature review' are especially noteworthy. Firstly, Perera's appears to most approve of the commentaries by Alexander and Averroes. He acknowledges Alexander's importance for the peripatetic school, which led Averroes to pronounce that 'Nobody is an Aristotelian if not an Alexandrian'.[62] Perera clearly knew that this pronouncement was adopted by Giovanni Bernardino Longo, but in the variation of: 'nobody is an Aristotelian if not a perfect Averroist'.[63]

De communibus; and on f. 138r the scribe ascribed them to 'B.P'., i.e. 'Benedictus Pererius'. Yet the intriguing question of why only this particular selection is preserved in the manuscript—the treatises in the manuscript originate from two different sections in Perera's printed book and concern two unrelated topics—remains to be answered. One possibility is that these chapters were copied in order to be checked as part of the *censura* of Perera's work: they address the crucial questions of the immortality of the soul, and the accounts of ancient pagan philosophers, i.e. two issues that particularly concerned Ledesma.

[59] Perera's review of philosophical literature is the first to emerge from a Jesuit context. For later accounts, see Antonio Possevino, *Bibliotheca selecta* (2 vols, Rome, 1593), ii. 117–36; Andreas Schott, *Vitae Comparatae Aristotelis ac Demosthenis, Olympiadibus ac Praeturis Atheniensium Digestae* (Augsburg, 1603), 147–66.

[60] The number of titles is provided in Lohr, 'Some Early Aristotelian Bibliographies', 93. For references, cf. MPSI ii. 666: 'Habbi il catalogo delli migliori commentarii, che si trovano, sopra tutte le parti della philosophia, quale si è fatto in Roma'. Cf. MPSI ii. 677: 'Cathalogum autem eorum authorum, qui de omnibus philosophiae partibus (de aliis enim in praesentia mihi loquendum esse non duxi; quamvis haec omnibus accomodari queant) docte ac luculenter scripserunt, in fine huius tractationis ascribam'.

[61] Cf. MPSI ii. 666: 'Et benchè deve il maestro seguire li principali authori come sono tra li greci Alessandro, Simplicio, Themistio; fra gl'arabi Averroe, fra li latini Alberto e S. Thomaso; nondimeno non deve esser sectario, massime di authori latini, che discordano dalli antichi. Deve essere modesto in refutare le opinioni che riprende, principalmente se sono de gravi authori, benché deve essere resoluto nelle cose che insegna, et non dubbio né problematico'. Cf. Pererius, *De communibus*, praef.: 'Graecos Aristotelis interpretes Alexandrum Themistium, et Simplicium, in Aristotelicis sententiis et verbis explicandis praeter caeteros, secuti sumus'. This is followed by sections on the Latins (only Thomas Aquinas) and the Arabs (Avicenna and Averroes). See also ibid., 115 (IV, 2) and doc. 8.

[62] Cf. Pererius, *De communibus*, 115 (IV, 2). See also doc. 8: 'ut (quemadmodum refert Averroes) nemo Aristoteleus haberetur qui non esset Alexandreus'.

[63] This has been previously proposed in Sander, 'The Debate', 42. Cf. doc. 8: 'Is [quidam clarissimus philosophus] enim cum doceret publice philosophiam saepe numero dicere solebat, neminem unquam fore bonum Aristotelicum qui non esset perfectus Averroista'. Giovanni Bernardino Longo, *Expositio in Prologum Averrois in Posteriores Aristotelis* (Naples, 1551), praef., states: 'sententiis merito ab Alexandro mutatus est, ut NEMO ARISTOTELICUS NISI AVERROISTA'.

However, Perera does not credit Longo but another 'Averroist', Marcantionio Zimara, for rendering Averroes' ideas more comprehensible. In his guidelines for teachers of philosophy, Perera recommends Averroes' writings due to his good reputation in Italy, and mentions some of his followers, among them Zimara.[64] Perera discovers Averroes' contribution to Aristotelian philosophy in his efforts to defend Aristotle against others, and to explain his doctrines more clearly.

Secondly, Perera pays as much attention to philological issues in the commentators as he does in Aristotle's works. For example, he questions the authenticity of Simplicius' commentary on *De anima* and Albert's *De apprehensione*.[65] Perera emphasizes that all or most of Alexander's Greek commentaries were not available before his lifetime, and that even Thomas Aquinas was only aware of a few of them.[66] Further, the poor transmission of the Greek text of Simplicius' commentary on *De caelo* introduced errors into the Greek text itself, as well as into its later Latin version.[67] And even Averroes was only able to access Aristotle's texts via inadequate Arabic translations.[68] Finally, in his comparison of Aristotle's philosophy with the theories of others, Perera meticulously records several deviations from Aristotelian principles in the writings of philosophers like Simplicius, Avicenna, and Albert.[69]

---

[64] Cf. MPSI ii. 665: 'Leggere Averroe è molto utile, sì per la sua dottrina, come per la fama che ha in Italia; et per poterlo intendere, leggerà li suoi seguaci, come Janduno, Barleo, Paulo veneto, Zimarra, Nipho'.

[65] Cf. doc. 8: 'sed ego maxime omnium laudo & probo librum quod inscribitur de Apprehensione modo dialogi compositum, cuius libri doctrina quaedam & sententiae sine dubio sunt Alberti stili vero apertior, completior atque [30r] politior est: quasi ut credere possim auctorem eius fuisset Albertum'.

[66] Cf. doc. 8: 'Huius [Alexandris] igitur commentarii omnes qui nunc extant (utinam autem extarent omnes)'; '[Thomas] non potuit autem ut opinor quod graecorum scripta tum non dum reperta essent, aut Latinitatem donata'.

[67] Cf. doc. 8: 'Eandem plane laudem obtinerent, quos scripsit in libros de caelo nisi & graece multis locis corrupti essent, & in Latinum sermonem perversissime translati fuissent'.

[68] Cf. doc. 8: 'Constat tamen Averroim in explanatione verborum Aristotelis nonnumquam lapsum & hallucinatum esse propterea quod mendosam & corruptam versionem Aristotelis haberet, quod ipse non aut semel traduerit & conqueritur, sed quantum in eo fuit semper graecos interpretes sequutus & imitatus est, porro obscuritas et perplexitas orationis quam in commentariis eius apparet, tota provenit ex translatione Latina, nam cum lingua Arabica & Latina maximo intervallo disiunctae sint quod mirum est id quod Arabice scriptum fuit si verbum e verbo Latine reddatur, obscurum horridum, & insulsum existere'. Perera does not mention Averroes' lack of knowledge of Greek here explicitly.

[69] On Simplicius, see also above n. 56 and 67. Cf. esp. doc. 8: 'Opus autem eius in libros de anima valde dissimile est reliquorum scriptorum, continet enim doctrinam brevem ieiunam involutam & platonicam, potius quam peripateticam, cuius operis auctor quicunque fuit (nam multi putant non esse Simplicii) ita se gerit [28v] ut non tam Aristotelem explicare quam varias quasdam contemplationes Jamblici sequeri & declarare voluisse videatur'; on Avicenna: 'Opus eius philosophicum, Logicam, physicam, et metaphysicam complectens in laude est apud multos philosophos, sed in eo tametsi nonnunquam subtilis est tum

Overall, Perera considered philological analyses of commentaries on Aristotle an important part of their evaluation. They allow readers to determine how reliable and useful a commentary is by discovering (a) whether the author had access to the Greek text, (b) how faithfully the text they see has been transmitted to their own time, and (c) how great the discrepancies (philosophical and conceptual) are between the commentary and the Aristotelian teachings.

Thirdly, it is remarkable how much attention Perera pays to matters not strictly related to Aristotelian philosophy. For example, Perera recommends reading various of Averroes' digressions on cosmological questions as well as Averroes' *De substantia orbis*;[70] holds Avicenna's medical writings in high esteem;[71] and acknowledges (Pseudo-)Albert's epistemological dialogue *De apprehensione* as well as his writings on natural history.[72] He also considers reading Lucretius helpful for understanding Aristotle.[73] And finally, and perhaps unsurprisingly, Perera approves of consulting the theological works of Thomas Aquinas in philosophical matters.[74] Perera therefore clearly did not limit himself to a single concept of philosophy or to Aristotle's writings alone.

semper obscurus, perplexus, horridus, dissimilis peripateticorum et ab Aristotelica philosophandi ratione longissime remotus est'; on Albert: 'illud tamen vitiosum & dignum reprehensione videri potest quod in modo philosophandi nimis obscurus & horridus sit, et non tamen peripateticos quam Arabes, & Platonicos sequi & imitari studuerit, cum enim de rebus arduis & gravibus disputat'.

[70] Cf. doc. 8: 'Sunt etiam alia opera eius philosophica immortali laude digna ut libellus de substantia orbis'.

[71] Cf. doc. 8: 'Avicennam quanto in medicina aliis omnibus (Hippocratem et Galenum his non numero) superior fuit tanto in philosophia et se ipso & aliis quorum plurimis inferior extitit. Itaque quemadmodum scripta eius quae pertinent ad medicinam libenter legerem, ita quae spectant ad philosophiam, legere non magnopere curaverim, nisi ea de causa forte legenda sint quod is saepe reprehendatur ab Averroe, & a quibusdam Latinis philosophis in praetio habeatur, atque frequenter citetur'. Cf. Pererius, *De communibus*, praef.: 'Fuit is praestantissimus medicus, fuit etiam (quorundam iudicio) peracutus Metaphysicus, sed eum doctrinae Aristotelis (quam omnibus Philosophiae studiosis maxime probatam et cognitam esse oportet) nec valde studiosum, nec admodum intelligentem fuisse constat'. On Perera and the Jesuits' approaches to medicine, see Sander, 'Medical Topics', 91 n. 59.

[72] See above n. 65, and doc. 8: 'Deinde in his quae scripsit [Albertus] de metallis, animalibus & plantis valde accusatur a viris earum rerum doctissimis & peritissmis aiunt enim eum quaecunque ab aliis accepisset'.

[73] Cf. doc. 7, §5: 'Eius [Lucretii] lectio non parvam lucem afferet ad intelligenda multa loca Aristotelis'. Cf. also Pererius, *De communibus*, 277–8 (V, 1). This was repeated (certainly alluding to Perera) by Pontanus, *Reden*, 78. Yet some philosophers also referred to Aristotle in their interpretation of Lucretius, cf. e.g. Raffaele Franchi, *Raphaelis Fra[n]ci Florentini i[n] Lucretiu[m] paraphrasis, cu[m] appe[n]dice de animi immortalitate.* (Bologna, 1504), 18r–v.

[74] Cf. doc. 8: 'sed ea potissimum cognosci & iudicari debet ex scriptis theologicis [Thomae] maxime vero ex quadripartita summa theologiae'. Cf. also Pererius, *De communibus*, praef.: 'Sed D. Thomam eximium Philosophiae decus, et splendissimum Theologiae lumen, firmissimumque columen, prae caeteris miramur, et colimus'.

Finally, Perera is sensitive to any potential conflicts between Aristotle's commentators and the Christian faith. He names some doctrines by Alexander and Averroes as problematic, and reflects on these commentators' integrity and credibility on this basis, concluding that in spite of some difficult statements they are yet not to be dismissed altogether. As he had done for Aristotle, Perera attributes these errors to both the fallible human intellect and God's intention to withhold doctrines of faith—intended only for Christian believers—from these authors.[75]

Under consideration of these four aspects of Perera's approach to Aristotle's commentators, the conflict between Perera and Ledesma emerges clearly, in spite of the fact that both are Jesuits. Ledesma observes the same distinction between Greek, Arabic, and Latin commentators, and in 1573 compiles an even longer bibliography on commentators than Perera's;[76] from 1564 onwards, he emphasizes repeatedly that Greek or Arabic commentators are suitable for teaching purposes but may not be revered.[77] By contrast, the Latin commentators, above all Thomas Aquinas, must not be criticized but rather praised by Jesuit teachers, according to Lesdema. But, although Perera does not openly criticize Aquinas in the

---

[75] Cf. doc. 8: 'Si quod autem in libris eorum quos ante memoravimus erratum inest contra philosophiam & christianam veritatem, id nobis continua nulla vel dignitatis vel auctoritatis eorum habita ratione improbandum, reiiciendum & execrandum est, [...] cogitationes curam & providentiam habere [...] neque vero mirandum est hos viros caeterosque sapientes tam graviter & absurde lapsos & deceptos fusse, homines enim fuerunt, quorum errant fallaces, sensus, angusta ingenia, infirma iudicia, vitae multis flagitiis ingenerata, mens humanae inscitiae tenebris circumfusa, & celesti destituta luminem'. Cf. also above n. 32.

[76] Cf. Toletus, *Physica*, praef.: 'Dum de Aristotelis mente certabitur, optimis quibusque utemur Authoribus, Graecis, Latinis, Arabibus: ex Graecis Theophrastio, Alexandro, Ammonio, Philopono, Porphyrio, Simplicio, Themistio, Eustrathio, caeterisque, quorum nobis commentarios temporum iniuria non ademerit. Ex latinis autem D. Thoma, Boethio, Alberto magno, Aegidio, Scoto, Marsilio, ita tamen, ut et qui ex recentioribus praesant, suum quoque locum habeant. Scotus, Caietanus, Sonzinas, Iavellus, Iandunus, Burlaeus, Buridanus, Zimara, Nyphus, et caeterique, si qui alii in hoc genere excellere videbuntur. Unus sane D. Thomas instar erit omnium, in quo et diligentia interpretandi, et doctrinae gravitas cum pietate coniuncta, multa, varia ac solida eruditio, incredibilis praeterea methodus, integris etiam disciplinis pertractandis; nec commentariis solum quos scripsit in Aristotelem, sed multo etiam magis Summa Theologiae, Summa contra gentes, Quaestionibus disputatis, et caeteris eius scriptis, tantam (ut de Theologia taceamus) Philosophiae lucem attulit unus, quantam caeteri omnes (aliorum pace dixerim) possint explanatores afferre: in quo, ex nullius arbitror laude quippiam detrahi, si id dicitur de D. Thoma, quod ipsorum quisque, se et viveret, et adesset, de eodem videretur esse dicturus. Ex Arabibus autem (quamvis numero, doctrina, et eruditione, si vel cum Graecis inferiores) utemur Avempace, Alpharabio, Avenzoar, Averroe, et aliis: Avicenna potissimum, quod eius scripta omni memoria gravissimis hominibus probata sint, et quod unus inter omnes Arabes proxime ad verum Philosophiae Christianae decus et laudem videatur accesisse'.

[77] Cf. MPSI ii. 478: 'Item, ne laudent nimis, imo ne laudent quidem, Averroin vel alios impios interpretes; sed si qui laudandi sint, potius laudent D. Thomam, Albertum Magnum, vel alios christianos et pios. Quod si sit discedendum ab eorum sententia, id modeste faciant'. Cf. also MPSI ii. 487, 499, 502.

Documenta, he does not praise him very much, and mainly points out the brevity of his commentaries on Aristotle.[78] In his investigation of Perera's philosophical teachings, conducted through an analysis of his pupils' notes, Ledesma found that Perera dismissed Aquinas and the Latin commentators excessively.[79]

In a later treatise, Ledesma particularly condemned the doctrines of Alexander, Themistius, and Averroes, especially their philosophy of the soul, and found them 'impious'.[80] Averroes in particular seems to have troubled Ledesma and Gagliardi: they explicitly prohibited Jesuit teachers from confessing Averroist sympathies.[81] Gagliardi similarly recommended a prohibition of following Averroes' digressions; Averroes, however, was on the list of Perera's preferred authors.[82] Overall, Aristotle's commentators were one crucial aspect that caused the conflict between Perera on the one hand, and Ledesma and Gagliardi on the other.

This matter remained a sensitive issue among Jesuits for some time and was particularly discussed while the Jesuits drafted their *Ratio Studiorum* for all colleges.[83] Although the official versions of 1586, 1591,

---

[78] Cf. doc. 8: 'quae in eo fuit amplissima non tantum petenda est ex commentariis eius in Aristotelem quos ille breves & succintos esse voluit, ut ultimas sententias Aristotelis breviter & dilucide exponeret non ut ostentaret subtilitatem & copiam eruditionis'. Cf. also Casalini, 'Pererio', 106. Perera's *laudatio*, situated towards the beginning of the passage and addressing the topic of Aquinas, alludes to his historical role in relation to Aristotelian philosophy via his canonization, rather than by merit of his philosophical works.

[79] Cf. MPSI ii. 503: 'Item, parum reverenter [Perera] tractat D. Thomam, et contra illum ardenter disputat fere semper et contra latinos'.

[80] Cf. *Monumenta paedagogica*, 551–3: 'Nec quicquam obstat si, praeter aliquos impios interpretes, quales sunt Averroes Simplicius et olim Plato, qui non sunt sequendi. [...] Contraria stultitia est Averrois, qui unicam posuit assistentem in omnibus, et forte etiam Themistius sic posuit intellectum agentem [...] Imo vero et Themistius, et Theophrastus, et Averroes; nam, quamvis hic Averroes unam dicat intellectivam in omnibus, et fortasse alii de intellectu saltem agente idem dicant, tamen faciunt immortalem secundum Aristotelem. Nec obstat, ut quosdam recentiores omittamus, si Alexander impius et aliqui etiam ex antiquis christianis putent, secundum Aristotelem, mortalem'. This document is not edited in the MPSI. Cf. also Toletus, *Physica*, praef.: 'Hoc autem loco admonendus es, Lector pie, ne cum in hos, aut alios impios Aristotelis interpretes, sive Graecos, sive Arabes incideres, in iis praesertim, quae ad pietatem attinent, facile illis credas, atque committas. Nam, cum impii fere omnes fuerint, Ethnici, Idolatrae, nonnulli etiam Sarraceni, vel Mahumetani, de Deo, de divinis rebus, de ultimo fine, de divina providentia, de vita beata, de animis ipsis hominum non raro male scripserunt [...] ut [Averroes] non immerito apud aliquas celeberrimas provincias, impii cognomen invenerit'.

[81] Cf. MPSI ii. 478: 'Item, non se ostendant esse averroistas, aut graecorum fractionem sectare vel arabum contra latinos aut theologos'.

[82] Cf. MPSI ii. 478 (subscribed by Gagliardi): 'Item, prohibeatur ne magistri interpretentur digressiones Averrois vel Simplicii aut alterius; sed simpliciter proponantur opiniones eorum indiferenter'.

[83] On this project of the *Ratio Studiorum*, see e.g. Mario Zanardi, 'La "Ratio atque institutio studiorum Societatis Iesu": Tappe e vicende della sua progressiva formazione (1541–1616)', *Annali di storia dell'educazione e delle istituzioni scolastiche* 5 (1998), 135–64; John W. Padberg,

and 1599 echoed Ledesma's sceptical and critical tone in many respects, and especially his scepticism towards Averroes, Perera's approach was not ignored altogether.[84] Even before the first *Ratio* was established in 1586, Perera was a member of a committee whose aim was to reconsider the issue of philosophical censorship and to construct a syllabus of philosophical doctrine within the Society of Jesus. Naturally, Perera was not in favour of limiting philosophers' freedom of thought.[85] In spite of Perera's plea for this freedom, the *Ratio* of 1586 banned Averroes from the reading list and prescribed fifteen philosophical doctrines.[86] When this *Ratio* was reviewed by the Roman Jesuits later in the same year, all of them agreed on this prohibition, except for Perera, who emphasized once more that Averroes' doctrines, and those of other pagan authors, contain some true content which can be cited and taught.[87] The *Ratio* of 1586 also attempted to prescribe the doctrine of Aquinas to Jesuit theologians, and one of Perera's fellow Jesuits, Didacus Tapia (*d.*1591), reported that Aquinas was criticized by many. His review states that Tapia knows several men who praise Aquinas not as a philosopher, but as a theologian.[88] Aquinas, these critics say, did not know Greek and therefore he did not penetrate Aristotle's ideas to the extent that recent philosophers 'addicted to the Greek language' (*graecizantes*) are able to.[89] For Tapia, this critique is not valid, since Aquinas did, indeed, know translations and the works of the Greek commentators, and knew the works of Aristotle better than those moderns who oppose Aquinas. It seems very likely that Tapia knew about his colleague Perera's attitude towards Aquinas: Perera, too, had highlighted the problem of Aquinas' lack of knowledge in Greek.

'Development of the Ratio Studiorum', in Vincent J. Duminuco (ed.), *The Jesuit Ratio Studiorum: 400th Anniversary Perspectives* (New York, 2000), 80–100.

[84] Cf. MPSI v. 100–1, 283, 189–91; vii. 249.

[85] Sander, 'The Debate', 45–9.

[86] Cf. MPSI v. 95–109.

[87] Cf. MPSI vi. 261: 'De Averroe: Placet totus ut iacet; excepto P. Pererio, cui videntur quaecunque et in Averroe et in aliis gentilibus vere dicta sunt, simpliciter esse citanda atque docenda; praesertim cum in digressionibus Averrois uberior soleat esse philosophiae doctrina'.

[88] Cf. MPSI vi. 261: 'Scio nonnullos non ita celebrare S. Thomam in philosophia, ac in theologia celebrare illum videntur. Et hanc pro se adducunt rationem, quia S. Thomas graecam linguam non intellexit, et sic Aristotelis sensum non penetravit ita intense, ac alii antiqui et moderniores graecizantes. Horum rationem non esse tanti momenti, patet. Primo, quoniam S. Thomas, si graecam linguam non novit, vidit, legit, intellexit traductiones et commentaria graeco: tum, qui satius intellexerunt Aristotelem, quam illi moderni, qui S.ti Thomae philosophiae opponuntur'.

[89] The term *graecizantes* is often used by Jesuits in a pejorative sense, to refer to humanist philosophers of the time.

IV. Conclusions

A more thorough analysis might reveal more contradictions between Perera's and Ledesma's concepts of philosophical pedagogy, and further studies may also shed more light on the position of Perera's project within the multiple forms of Aristotelianism in the early modern period. However, the dossier at hand alone enables us to conclude that Perera's positive attitude towards some of Aristotle's commentators formed a core element of his conflict with Ledesma, since these commentators and their partial incompatibility with Christian faith were problematic at the time. Nonetheless, Perera was able to justify his own position as 'sufficiently pious' by relying on his critical, historical, and philological approach to philosophy.[90] It is this emphasis on philology that Perera shared with the sixteenth-century humanist movement in philosophy.[91]

It has been observed that Perera, perhaps in an attempt to make his theories less offensive, softened the tone of his praise for Averroes in the preface to his *De communibus* (1576). This appears to have been done in reaction to the investigation against him,[92] as is clear from a comparison of this preface with his admiration for Averroes expressed in the *Documenta*. This revision was motivated by an attempt to prevent the printing of Perera's book by Ledesma, Gagliardi, and other Jesuits. Eventually, the *imprimatur* had to be granted by Pope Gregory XIII himself.[93]

The very first philosophical *cursus* that was published by a Jesuit author was that of Franciscus Toletus, and the first tome was his commentary on Aristotle's *Physics*, printed in 1573.[94] Toletus was a colleague of Perera's and Ledesma's in Rome, and Ledesma was among the censors for the edition.[95]

---

[90] Initial insights into humanism, philology, education, and piety may be gathered from Charles G. Nauert, 'Rethinking "Christian Humanism"', in Angelo Mazzocco (ed.), *Interpretations of Renaissance Humanism* (Leiden/Boston, 2006), 155–80; Grendler, 'Humanism'.

[91] For a short overview on definitions and historiographical accounts of the term 'humanism', see Heikki Mikkeli, *An Aristotelian Response to Renaissance Humanism: Jacopo Zabarella on the Nature of Arts and Sciences* (Helsinki, 1992), 9–14. On the connection between philosophy and philology, see esp. Jill Kraye, 'Philologists and Philosophers', in Jill Kraye (ed.), *The Cambridge Companion to Renaissance Humanism* (Cambridge, 1996), 142–60.

[92] Blum, *Aristotelianism*, 140.   [93] See above n. 29.

[94] Cf. Toletus, *Physica*. It is further worth noting that Perera's *De communibus* (*omnium rerum naturalium principiis*) is primarily a work on Aristotle's Physics: see Ugo Baldini, 'The Development of Jesuit Physics in Italy, 1550–1700: A Structural Approach', in Constance Blackwell and Sachiko Kusukawa (eds.), *Philosophy in the Sixteenth and Seventeenth Centuries: Conversations with Aristotle* (Aldershot/Brookfield, 1999), 253.

[95] Ledesma was among the *censores* of Toletus' commentaries on the *Physica* (cf. Toletus, *Physica*, 77v, 192r, 249v) and the *De anima*. In *De anima* Ledesma seems to have included ten prescriptive propositions that were to be taught, cf. Franciscus Toletus, *Commentaria*

When Perera wrote the preface for his own book, he must have looked at the anonymous preface to Toletus' commentary, which was most likely written by Ledesma himself.[96] Accordingly, the prefaces share some common material on Averroes, and both of them mention the well-known yet disgraceful addiction to Averroist philosophy.[97] Further, both of them point out that Averroes did not have direct access to the Greek text of Aristotle.[98] Yet the more subtle differences between the two texts are even more noteworthy. Ledesma introduces the topic of an over-reliance on Averroes into a general attack against the habits of secular Italian universities. At first glance, Ledesma's critique of Averroes in itself is not so much a refutation of his philosophical tenets than an argument *ad hominem*. In Ledesma's opinion, the Muslim Averroes is harmful for Christianity.[99] However odd such an argument might sound today, it clearly echoes Ignatius of Loyola's advice in the *Constitutions* for the reading of suspect authors:

> Even though a book is without suspicion of evil doctrine, when its author is suspect it is not wise to read it. For through the book affection is stirred up for the author; and approval given to the author in what he says well may lead one later on to accept what he says poorly. Moreover, it rarely occurs that some poison is not mixed into that which comes forth from a heart full of it.[100]

---

vna cum quaestionibus in tres libros Aristotelis de anima (Venice, 1575), 6v–8r; Sander, 'In dubio pro fide', 57.

[96] As *censor* of Toletus' *Physica* Ledesma appears to have written or contributed to the anonymous preface himself: numerous coincidences with his thought can be observed. Yet this attribution remains an assumption at best, since it is only based on the circumstantial evidence: the resemblance of thought presented in the preface with Ledesma's ideology and Ledesma's role as one of the *censores* of the volume. This preface is discussed in Martin, *Subverting Aristotle*, 91–2; Luca Bianchi, *Pour une histoire de la double vérité* (Paris, 2008), 150; it is noteworthy, however, that neither scholar ascribes the piece to Ledesma. The preface also was known to Antonio Possevino, cf. Possevino, *Bibliotheca selecta*, ii. 106.

[97] Cf. Toletus, *Physica*, praef.: 'Nec vero satis mirari possum, sic quosdam in nonnullis Academiis esse Authoribus impiis addictos, ut tantum non apud illos, eorundem authorum causa, fides periclitetur, quo cum sermo devenerit, de uno Averroe pauca dicam'. Cf. Pererius, *De communibus*, praef.: 'hoc autem cuius Philosopho, turpe est, Christiano autem unius hominis, qui labi potuit (et vero in rebus magni momenti non semel lapsus est) decreta omnia pugnaciter defendere, ac mordicus tenere, et quasi tempestare delatos, ad eius doctrinam, tanquam ad saxum aliquod adhaerescere? Quid foedius?'

[98] Cf. Toletus, *Physica*, praef.: 'Usus praeterea est corrupto Aristotelis libro, et pluribus in locis depravato; id quod eius scripta prae se ferunt. Graecis fere omnibus explanatoribus caruit; Latinis etiam, qui nec dum extabant, destitutus fuit': cf. Pererius, *De communibus*, praef.: 'Sint ista ut dicunt: negari tamen non potest, Averroem, interpretando Aristotelem, ob ignorantiam linguae Graecae, mendososque codices, et bonorum interpretum penuriam, multifariam hallucinatum esse'.

[99] Cf. Toletus, *Physica*, praef.: 'Adde fuisse Mahumetanum, et (quod ipsa scriptura facile declarant) conceptum animo adversus Christianam religionem odium semper habuisse; ut necesse sit, sua eum sordissima secta, scripta quoque philosophica infecisse non parum'.

[100] Translated in George E. Ganss, *Saint Ignatius' Idea of a Jesuit University. A Study in the History of Catholic Education, Including Part Four of the Constitutions of the Society of Jesus*

Ledesma also highlights Averroes' reliance on a 'corrupted book of Aristotle' and his lack of knowledge of almost all Greek commentators (and indeed any of the Latin commentators) —an accusation against the reliability of the Arabic philosopher.[101] Yet, Ledesma concedes, 'wherever Averroes was right, we will not reject him, wherever he was wrong, we will prefer other interpreters, wherever he was impious, we will condemn him'.[102]

For Perera, by contrast, a reliance on one individual philosopher is not disgraceful, especially not in the case of Averroes; but it is disgraceful for Christians in general to rely exclusively and regardless of circumstance on one single philosopher, since all philosophers are fallible human beings.[103] The very concept of authority becomes a contested one in this view—in Perera's words, 'I owe much to Plato, more to Aristotle, but most to reason'.[104] Moreover, Averroes' lacking knowledge of Greek and his faulty sources are raised not as an accusation but rather as an excuse for the mistakes Averroes made when he interpreted Aristotle relying on his own linguistic abilities and on available texts. To sum up, Perera concedes two types of error: firstly, errors which arise from the limited capacity of human understanding and the human condition, which is to err; and secondly, errors which are due to contingent factors of textual transmission, language faculties, and philological issues.

Perera's conception of a pious Christian philosophy which also rests on philological issues derives from these ideas. For Perera, an awareness

(Milwaukee, 1954), 326. Latin in MSPI i. 297: 'Quamvis liber suspicione, malae doctrinae vacet, cum tamen suspectus est auctor, legi eum non convenit. Solet enim opus in causa esse ut, qui legit; ad auctorem afficiatur; et auctoritas, quam apud ipsum habet in iis quae bene dicit; posset postmodum aliquid persuadere ex iis quae male dicit. Rarum est etiam aliquid veneni non admisceri in iis, quae a pectore veneni pleno egrediuntur'.

[101] Cf. Toletus, *Physica*, praef.: 'Usus praeterea est corrupto Aristotelis libro, et pluribus in locis depravato; id quod eius scripta prae se ferunt. Graecis fere omnibus explanatoribus caruit; Latinis etiam, qui nec dum extabant, destitutus fuit: ut necesse sit, in eo nec gravem, nec securam inesse doctrinam, nam et si acutum quiddam raro, exile tamen dicendi, et philosophandi genus, in eo reperitur; est tamen illud obscurum, inusitatum, et saepe ab Aristotelis sensu intelligentiaque alienum, quod recta interpretatione, ac versione Aristotelis, aliorumque interpretum luce caruerit'.

[102] Cf. Ibid. 'Nos igitur, ubi quidpiam recti dixerit, non aspernabimur: ubi secus, alios ei longe doctiores anteponemus, et ipsum impietatis, ubi tale quid dixerit, condemnabimus'. See also Sander, 'The Debate', 45–6, for Alfonso Salmerón's similar attitude.

[103] See also Sander, 'The Debate', 45–6, for Alfonso Salmerón's similar attitude.

[104] Cf. Pererius, *De communibus*, praef.: 'Ego multum Platoni tribui, plus Aristoteli, sed rationem plurimum'. Cf. also MPSI ii. 671: 'Aristotelicum illud in omni studiorum ratione servandum est: Amicus Socrates, amicus Plato, sed magis amica veritas'. On this passage see Ulrich G. Leinsle, 'Delectus opinionum. Traditionsbildung durch Auswahl in der frühen Jesuitentheologie', in Georg Schmuttermayr, Wolfgang Beinert and Heinrich Petri (eds.), *Im Spannungsfeld von Tradition und Innovation: Festschrift für Joseph Kardinal Ratzinger* (Regensburg, 1997), 116 n. 32; Blum, *Aristotelianism*, 143; Sander, 'The Debate', 44 n. 66; 46 n. 76.

of how reliable a text may be is a prerequisite for any judgement on philosophical doctrines. Moreover, it enables scholars to defend some authors and explains why some philosophical tenets seem to contradict the truth of Christian faith. Perera's study plan from the *Documenta* provides an impressive picture of such an approach. Philological and historical scholarship was meant to support his programme of propaedeutics in three ways: (a) a brief reconstruction of the textual transmission and its consequences, and a scholarly review of extant editions of translations of, and commentaries on, Aristotle; (b) an awareness of topics peripheral to a strictly philosophical curriculum of Jesuit universities; and (c) an emphasis on a mindful reading of doxographical accounts.

However, these features are supplemented by the more epistemological insight that the human intellect is fallible by nature, and the metaphysical belief that a true argument in philosophy can never, in principle, contradict a doctrine of faith. A science of true, immutable things—and both philosophy and theology fall into this category—nevertheless needs to cope with factors such as fallible human individuals, their textual heritage, and also fallible human readers with their own sets of language skills and textual backgrounds. In Perera's view, a reflection on both the philological and epistemic factors for human error ensures an erudite and pious groundwork for Jesuit philosophy. Additionally, Perera's efforts here also redeemed Ignatius of Loyola's overarching attempt to establish a Jesuit learning that mirrored the principle of *pietas et eruditio*, a combination of thorough education and religious dedication.[105] Perera did so in his own way, and integrated different trends of Aristotelian philosophy into his own, even including approaches that were considered impious by some of his fellow Jesuits. Perera fitted these approaches into a strictly Christian philosophy curriculum.

Cristiano Casalini
Boston College
18 Wade Street
Boston, Massachusetts
U.S.A.
casalini@bc.edu

Christoph Sander
Technische Universität Berlin
Sekr. H 23
Straße des 17. Juni 135
10623 Berlin
Germany
c-sander@heimat.de

---

[105] John W. O'Malley, 'How Humanistic Is the Jesuit Tradition? From the 1599 Ratio Studiorum to Now', in Martin R. Tripole (ed.), *Jesuit Education 21: Conference Proceedings on the Future of Jesuit Higher Education, 25–29 June 1999* (Philadelphia, 2000), 189–201; Peter Hans Kolvenbach, 'Pietas et eruditio', *Gregorianum* 85 (2004), 6–19.

Edition

Criteria of edition

The treatise entitled *Documenta quaedam perutilia iis qui / in studiis philosophiae cum fructu / et sine ullo errore versari / student*, is preserved in manuscript at the Biblioteca Ambrosiana in Milan under the shelf mark D496 inf. (ff. 25r–31v). It is in good condition and the high quality of the reproduction narrows the range of possible errors of reading to a few lines at the top of the ff. 27r and 27v, where the ink passed through the sides of the sheet. The document shows a few corrections and one major insertion, which we have marked between asterisks ['*'] (f. 26r).

Concerning the editing style, the document presents numerous contracted words and abbreviations that we decided to expand in this edition, since the author traced clear and coherent signs for missing syllables and letters. We respected the author's capitalizations and punctuation, correcting them only when this was evidently due to the author's incoherence.

Documenta quaedam perutilia iis qui in studiis philosophiae cum fructu et sine ullo errore versari student:

Primum Documentum

5   Meminerint philosophiam subiectam esse debere fidei, & religioni Christianae, ita ut quicquid fides docet verissimum et certissimum habeant, quamquam vel repugnet Aristoteli vel ad eius cognitionem philosophia aspirare non possit. Etenim magis quam Aristoteli credendum est Deo, qui auctor est fidei nostrae, et cui libuit plurimas et maximas res abscondere a sapien-

10 tibus, & prudentibus & eas revelare parvulis, & cum philosophia sit opus humani ingenij secundum mensuram eius definita, non est mirandum eam, immensae Divinitatis auxilia atque misteria non posse comprehendere. Itaque semper in memoria et ante oculos habeant illas sententias non plus sapere quam oportet sapere, sed sapere ad sobrietatem, et item scruta-

15 tor maiestatis opprimetur a gloria, & quemadmodum serpens primos parentes humani generis perniciose deceperit inani pollicitatione scientiae boni & mali.

Secundum Documentum

Licet in ijs quae docet fides christiana perspicuum sit quaedam esse quae non possunt lumine naturae scientifice comprehendi, aut demonstratione 20 probari, cuiusmodi sunt ea quae traduntur de creatione hominis, de primaeva integritate, atque innocentia, de Ultimo fine eius, de resurrectione mortuorum & alia horum similia. Ea tamen sunt eiusmodi ut qui negent facile redargui queant, & adduci in multa & gravia incommoda, demonstrando quae praedictis fidei decretis contraria sunt falsa & absurda esse. 25 Omnia igitur nostrae religionis dogmata verissima & certissima sunt. Sed eorum quaedam lumine naturae cognosci & probari possunt, quaedam autem minime omnia tamen eiusmodi sunt, ut quae illis utentur adversari, facile etiam rationibus physicis refelli atque coargui possint.

Tertium documentum

30

Quemadmodum philosophia diligenter addiscenda est propterea quod earum rerum cognitionem continet [25r] quae maxime digna est homine [sic!] Ingenuo, sic etiam Theologia: quae tradit doctrinam earum rerum quae necessariae sunt ad bene beateque vivendum cognoscenda est. Quocirca convenit eos qui in Philosophia sine ullo errore versari cupiunt, 35 si non se totos dederint ad perdiscendas & pertractandas res Theologicas, saltem ad eas cognoscendas et quasi degustandas aliquid opere studijque conferre. Siquidem magnopere decet philosophum Christianum habere notum et exploratum et quid agere, & quo pacto de rebus Divinis bene sentire & loqui debeat.

40

Quartum documentum

Caveant imitari consuetudinem loquendi eorum philosophorum, qui in explicandis controversijs philosophiae ita loqui consueverint. Hoc v.g. mundum esse aeternum, verum etiam et teneri debet secundum philosophiam, at secundum fidem Christianam falsum esse, nam cum verum 45 semper vero consonet, fides autem nostra vera sit, et item philosophia si quidem est scientia quae in rebus veris et immutabilibus, necesse fieri non potest ut dogmata fidei adversentur decretis philosophiae. Quare sic potius loquendum est, hoc scilicet mundum esse de novo factum, pro vero et certo habendum est secundum fidem. Sed Aristoteles putavit esse falsum 50 et impossibile. Itaque licet sit consentaneum fidei: tamen est repugnans doctrinae Aristotelis, neque hoc mirum et absurdum videri debet, nam cum Aristoteles more aliorum hominum, et potuerit errare et interdum erraverit, tum in hoc tum in alijs rebus, non est mirandum veritatem fidei

55 pugnare cum erroribus Aristotelis. Vel alterum etiam loqui possumus hoc
    v.g. Deum esse trinum & unum: verissimum est secundum fidem, sed nec
    lumine naturae, nec rationibus philosophicis cognosci et ostendi potest, non
    igitur dicendum est esse contra philosophiam, sed supra philosophiam.

Quintum documentum

60 Turpe est philosophari non amore veritatis, & sapientiae, sed praecipue
    honoris et lucri cupiditate: turpius est philosophiam quae docet fugienda
    esse vitia magis etiam quam pestem et mortem, scelerum et vitiorum sor-
    dibus inquinare: sed longe turpius est odio vel gratia cuiusquam, aut ob
    aliquam causam simulare, dissimulare aut celare veritatem, earumque
65 rerum, quas nobis exploratum est falsas esse, patrocinium et defensionem
    suscipere. [25v]

Sextum documentum

    Quatuor sunt quae magnopere conducunt: tum ad bene perficiendum
    studijs philosophiae, tum etiam ad perfectam eius scientiam comparandam.
70 Primum, lectio tum speculatio, postea disputatio, ad extremum scriptio.

Septimum documentum

    Aristoteles imprimis (quandoquidem eum omnes sequuntur tanquam
    principem & ducem philosophiae) studiose, diligenter, & assidue legendus
    est, sed in eius lectione multa sunt animadvertenda:

75   1° modus philosophandi, quod est valde consentiens naturae nostri
          intellectus, procedit enim quantum fieri potest ex propriis non ex
          rationibus aut alienis, ex sensibusque experientiis, ex ijs quae eviden-
          tiam, et certitudinem habent, aut ex naturali lumine intellectus, aut
          ex iudicio sensu, nec more aliorum philosophorum involuit philoso-
80   phiam fabulis, aenigmatibus, allegorijs, & metaphoris.

      2° ordo & methodus qui in Aristotele singularis fuit & ab omnibus
          mirifice commendatur, et fere est vel resolutionis, vel compositionis,
          sed ea in dispositione principalium partium scientiae atque libro-
          rum clarius elucet, in singulis autem capitibus et disputationibus
85   interdum obscurior et perturbatior existit - - - nam illam angustiam
          non perpetuo tenere sed interdum negligere summae artis est.

      3° genus orationis quod est maxime pressum, adstrictum, concisum, et
          plerumque obscurum, maxime in scriptis dialecticis, physicis, &

metaphysicis, nam in Rhetoricis Ethicis et politicis, nec ubertas, nec perspicuitas, nec suavitas orationis desiderari potest. Illam autem 90 obscuritatem Aristotelis igitur res magna ex parte minuet, peritia linguae graecae, usque graecorum interpretum habere notas & exploratas voces et phrases, quae sunt quasi propriae Aristotelis & ab eo non semper uno modo sed varijs in locis varie usurpantur. Postremo crebra et accurata lectio & consideratio scriptorum 95 Aristotelis et eorum inter se comparatio.

4° genus probationis quod in quaestionibus speculativis et gravibus est (quoad eius fieri potest) dummodo vel propter quid vel quia, nam interdum propter summam difficultatem rerum cogitur. Tummodo uti rationibus probabilibus, ut cum de rebus caelestibus et Divinis 100 agitur. In his autem rebus quae non sunt valde obscurae, nec gravi confirmatione indigent, utitur divisionibus, sillogismis hipoteticis, inductionibus et exemplis, at in rebus moralibus adhibet [26r] testimonia aliorum sententias, historias, inductiones, et similitudines. Sed illud maxime animadvertendum est num Aristoteles cum de re 105 aliqua tractat; agat de ea populariter an philosophice, probabiliter tum et dialectice ut minuat difficultatem nihil decernendo, an serio demonstratione suas profitendo sententias, num obiter, et propter aliud, an ex professo et pro se, num ex sua sententia an ex opinione aliorum nam qui hoc non animadvertit, putabit in dictis Aristotelis 110 multas esse repugnantias cum eadem de re varijs in locis varie sentire videatur. Exemplorum aut illius non semper est requirenda veritas, quippe cum non ad confirmandum sed ad declarandum solum adhibeatur. Germana item sententia Aristotelis non est eruenda, ex his locis in quibus obiter et aliud agens de re ipsa disputat, sed ex his in 115 quibus serio pro se et ex professo agit.

5° Commemoratio aliorum philosophorum quam Aristoteles in aditu fere cuiuslibet gravis & arduae dispositionis praeponere consuevit magna ex parte nobis est difficilis ad intelligendum, propterea quod illorum scripta non habemus, ex quibus aperte cognosci, et pro certo 120 affirmari possit, quod illi senserint, quocirca multum proderit antiquitatis & veterum historiarum scientem atque peritum esse et tenere quod Diogenes Laertique, Plutarcus, Plinius aliique scriptores de dictis factis decretisque veterum philosophorum memoriae prodiderunt, quam autem apud Aristotelem crebro est mentis Democriti 125 cuius doctrinam, quod eadem propemodum esset quam Epicuri, copiose prosecuto est Lucretiuque: Eius lectio non parvam lucem afferet ad intelligenda multa loca Aristotelis.

In tali autem enarratione opinionum considerare oportet num fide-
130   liter referat opiniones aliorum, num bene refellat, num alij easdem
opiniones alio modo acceperint et exposuerint, num non tam sententias eorum oppugnet quam emendet verba, et modum loquendi
*corrigat. Simplicius enim autor est Platonem saepe numero repre-
hendi ab Aristotele et in iis rebus, in quibus recte sensit, et idem
135   sensit quod Aristotelis non propter sententiam & doctrinam, quam
ille veram esse non ignorabat, sed propter modum loquendi* impro-
prium, inusitatum, & minime philosophicum, ne umquam is prae-
beret aliis errandi occasionem.

6° assidue legere Aristotelem non vaganti errantique animo, et sine
140   defectu sed cum attentione animadversione et ordine, incredibilem
affert utilitatem ad bene philosophandum. Quocirca recte sentiunt,
qui suadent nullum diem intermittendum esse, quin legatur aliquid
Aristotelis, sed in eo legendo animadvertendum est, an in aliis locis
scriptum relinquit, aut idem aut simile, aut contrarius, et quo pacto
145   talis repugnantia tollenda sit: an is locus quem legimus vel aperte vel
occulte [26v] an faveat aut repugnet alicui earum opinionum quae
iactantur inter philosophos an contineatur praeclaram aliquam sententiam quae ad alia res philosophicas tractandas accomodari possint,
an pariat graves aliquas difficultates quae perscrutatione indigeant.

150   7° ediscere omnia verba Aristotelis & singulos textus memoriae man-
dare, nec facile est & utitur esse magis onerosum quam utile, at ea
loca in quibus praecipuas philosophiae materias tractat animo iac-
tare, & quaecumque ad idem pertinent in unum colligere, eiusque
sententias & rationes quibus utitur sine in confirmando sine in
155   refellendo memoria tenere, atque haec omnia sic habere expendita
et numerata ut quoties cunque res postulat, aut nobis libuerit, in
usum proferre possimus, uberrimum fructum habet in philosophia.
Quamobrem utile conscribere locos omnes et praecipuis materiis et
questionibus philosophicis, primum de loquendis tum de physicis
160   postea de metaphysicis ad extremum de moralibus et aethicis, in quibus locis quaequnque ad singulas materias pertinent ex variis locis
Aristotelis collecta & diligenter notata reponenda sunt. Nam licet
hoc aliqua ex parte peti possit ex tabulis seu indicibus qui satis locu-
pletes et copiosi in Libris Aristotelis scripti sunt, tum cum hoc fit
165   studio, opera & industria nostra, maiori et cum fructu & voluptate fit.

8° nihil praestabilius est atque fructuosius quam Aristoteles: quoad
eius fieri possit proposuisset Aristotelis & intelligere & interpretari
hoc est unum locum pro alia loca eiusdem explanare, saepenumero
enim usu venit ut quod uno loco dictum est ab eo breviter obscure

& ambigue idem alijs locis uberius, apertius & accuratius explica- 170
tus fuerit.

9° diligenter considerare & tenere optima ea quae sunt quasi fundamenta & principia disciplinae Aristotelis quibus vel tota vel magna
ex pote doctrina eius nititur et continetur. Voco autem fundamenta
& principia generales sententias et decreta quibus saepe utitur ad 175
multas & varias res philosophicas pertractandas cuiusmodi sunt,
aeternitas mundi & motus, quicquid fit ex subiecto & pro motum
fieri, quicquid incipit esse, desinit esse, & contra naturam agere
propter finem cum ordine, atque expositionibus quod est melius,
atque alia huius generis promulta quae non inutiliter faceret quod 180
ex libris eius in unum colligens seorsim descripta & exposita
haberet, propendendum autem est an huiusmodi principia sint
absoluta, an falsa, & contra fidem nostram; si falsa fuerint, an
eorum falsitas lumine naturae ostendi et refelli [27r] & quae illis
contraria suscepit philosophice comprobari queant, quae dogmata 185
ex talibus principiis pendeant, & ab Aristotele deducta fuerint,
quae alia deduci valeant. Comparanda item sunt principia philosophica Aristotelica, cum principiis philosophiae Platonicae, &
videnda an sint eadem, an quaedam discrepent verbis ne, an etiam
rebus et utra sint probabiliora vel magis philosophica.   190

10° qui graece sciunt graece legant Aristotelem, non modo ut melius
percipiant doctrinam eius, sed etiam ut orationis eius candorem,
proprietatem, venustatem, et quasi sobrietatem, quandam frugali-
tatem, maiori cum voluptate degustent. Qui autem graeca non
intelligunt, aut commodius latine legent, querant optimas & proba- 195
tissimas versiones librorum eius, quas autem ego ex his quae passim
nunc extant tales esse putem breviter subijceram. In scriptis logicis
& physicis maxime omium probatur mihi translatio vetus quae
nuper emendata fuit, & recens excussa parvis voluminibus circumfertur, nam etsi nonnunquam importuna quadam superstitione, 200
singula verba Aristotelis eo quo greco sunt ordine, quasi numerata
latine reddens, & formulas graece linguae proprias totidem verbis
latinis satis barbare, & insulse exprimens faciat nobis Aristotelem
obscurum & ferreum quendam scriptorem, tum contra vere et fideliter (quod imprimis requirendum est ab interprete) sensum eius – 205
representat caeteris versionibus (quas adhuc vidi) praeferendam
iudico – Demum in Metaphisicis probo versionem Bessarionis: in
hisque de animalibus Theodori Gazae; in Ethicis Lambini, vel etiam
Argiropuli; in politicis Johannis Sepulvedae, in Rhetoricis Caroli
Sygonii, in poetica Petri Victorii. Esse legatiores autem versiones 210

Aristotelis, quae multis additis et immutatis faciunt Aristotelem non
modo suo, sed latine loquentem longe retroque ponendas censeo.

11°   Aristotelis libros multis annis in fossa quadam subterranea sepul-
      cros iacuisse Strabo in 13° libro suae geographiae auctor est, quos
215   postea multifariam corrosos a tineis cum emendandos suscepisset
      Appellion quidam Teius multa detrahens, supplens, & immutans,
      corrupisse magis quam correxisse dicitur. Deinde mendose a librariis
      imperitis saepius descripti, atque in diversas linguas perverse trans-
      lati sunt. Quamobrem nec dubitandum, nec mirandum est: nos
220   [27v] pluribus locis Aristoteles habere mutilum, mendosum, &
      corruptum, sed ad hoc diiudicandum opus est acerrimo iudicio,
      eoque in stilo & doctrina Aristotelis exercitatissimo, an autem
      aliquus locus corruptus sit nec ne, hoc modo cognosci poterit.
      Primum, consideratur idem locus in aliis exemplaribus tam grecis
225   quam latinis, tam vetustis quam recentioribus, & quod in pluribus
      & maioris fidei auctoritatisque codicibus: eiusmodi sunt graeci, et
      antiquiores repertum fuerit, verisimile est id proprius accedere ad
      verum sensum Aristotelis. Deinde idem iudicari debet ex aliis locis
      Aristotelis, in quibus idem scriptum fuerit apertius & sine ullius
230   errati suspicione. Praeterea ex proprio modo Aristotelis loquendi,
      sentiendi & philosophandi ad haec si locus aut nullam aut falsam
      & absurdam, aut maximo repugnantem doctrinae Aristotelis sen-
      tentias continet mendosus & corruptus iudicari debet. Postremo ex
      interpretatione grecorum expositorum quibus propter nativam grae-
235   cae linguae cognitionem, et summam in scriptis Aristotelis exerci-
      tationem plurimum in hoc genere tribuendum est.

12°   Quoniam in lectione et intelligentia Aristotelis magna pars
      acquirendae philosophiae consistit tum in praecipiendo studii &
      operae quisque collocabit quantum in philosophia proficere volu-
240   erit, tum autem se in philosophia proficisse intelligat, quantum ei
      Aristoteles placuerit, in eius scriptis. Tanta omnis doctrinae subtili-
      tas et ubertas abdita & abstrusa est, ut quemadmodum veteri pro-
      verbio Aphrica dicitur semper aliquid novi afferre, sic Aristoteles
      his a quibus studiose & accurate legitur & colitur, semper aliquid
245   novi & praeclari affert ad philosophandum.

Octavum documentum

Deinde legendi sunt interpretes Aristotelis qui suis commentariis verba
eiusque explanando sententias, amplificando & confirmando, & omnes
difficultates solvendo: Aristotelem nobis ad intelligendum planiorem, ube-
250 riorem locupletiorem & nervosiorem reddiderunt. Horum alii sunt

antiquiores, alii recentiores: illos tres quasi classes facimus: unam graecorum, alteram Arabum, 3^am Latinorum. In prima Alexandrum Themistium Simplicium & Philoponum, in media Avicennam & Averroem, in extrema Albertum & D. Thomam numeramus: de quorum singulis iudicium nunc breviter aperiendum est. 255

Alexander merito praeferendus est caeteris expositoribus, propter auc- toritatem antiquitatis [28r] diligentiam interpretandi gravitatemque doc- trinae, primus enim scriptis Aristotelis lucem, fidem, honorem addidit, suisque commentariis effecit ut Aristoteles ab omnibus legi, amari, & reli- quis philosophis anteponi coeperit. Huius oratio priscam philosophorum 260 brevitatem referens pressa & adstricta est, continens magnam vim senten- tiarum & multam, variam, gravem, solidamque eruditionem: nemo melius errata quae in libris Aristotelis latent, aut deprehendit, aut emendavit: nemo occulta sensu eius, & obscuras dubiasque sententias certius divinavit, clarius illustravit, & firmius communivit, cuius tanta fuit olim auctoritas ut 265 (quemadmodum refert Averroes) nemo Aristoteleus haberetur qui non esset Alexandreus. Huius igitur commentarii omnes qui nunc extant (uti- nam autem extarent omnes) singulari studio legendi & colendi sunt, max- ime vero quatuor libri eius naturalium quaestionum, unus liber de fato ad Severinum & Antoninum Imperatores, duo de anima et disputatio de 270 mixtione. De Themistio pauca dicenda sunt, cuius summa brevitas, maxima perspicuitas, singularis elegantia, paraphrases eius in Aristotelem amabiles & claras omnibus reddiderunt, quod nihil aliud continent, quam purissi- mum succum eruditionis libatum, & haustum ex commentariis Alexandri. Simplicius qui propter magnitudinem ingenii atque doctrinae merito cog- 275 nomentum magni adeptus est, multa reliquit egregiae eruditionis moni- menta, sed ego praecipue laudo, amplector, & admiror commentarios eius in octo libros physicos Aristotelis, nihil enim illis subtilius, uberius, lima- tius, eruditius, & accuratius desiderari potest quorum prolixitas solet offen- dere & ab eorum lectione reijcere minutos quosdam et plebeos philosophos, 280 qui laboris impatientes philosophicis institutionibus tingi modo non autem penitus imbui, & informari volunt, sed ea prolixitas cumulatissime com- pensatur ingenti fructu eruditionis: quae ex illis capi potest. Eandem plane laudem obtinerent, quos scripsit in libros de caelo nisi & graece multis locis corrupti essent, & in Latinum sermonem perversissime translati fuissent. 285 Opus autem eius in libros de anima valde dissimile est reliquorum scripto- rum, continet enim doctrinam brevem ieiunam involutam & Platonicam, potius quam peripateticam, cuius operis auctor quicunque fuit (nam multi putant non esse Simplicii) ita se gerit [28v] ut non tam Aristotelem expli- care quam varias quasdam contemplationes Jamblici sequeri & declarare 290 voluisse videatur. Commentarius eius in Categorias Aristotelis magnam habet utilitatem propter diligentem & amplam explicationem earum

opinionum quae fuerunt apud veteres philosophos de quibus nos nihil
praeter ea quae refert Simplicius cogitationi Hermogenis. Commentariolo in
295   Epictetum propter sanctitatem gravitatemque doctrinae moralis plane aur-
eus est nec tum legendus sed etiam quodammodo ediscendus est. Philoponi
oratio facilis, elegans et copiosa est, ingenium saepe acutum & faecundum,
sed iudicium plerumque infirmum, leve, etiam puerile atque sophisticum,
valde enim delectatur & crebro utitur rationibus popularibus & dialecticis
300   & cavillis sophisticis, ut non sine causa saepe numero reprehendatur &
rideatur a Simplicio in 8° Physico inter commentarios eius propter caeteros
probo eos quos in libros de generatione & anima conscripsit. Opus autem
illius contra praelum de aeternitate mundi legendum est, continet enim
multa scitu digna. Hoc autem de graecis etiam universe dici potest, eos in
305   explanatione verborum & sentientiarum Aristotelis longe praeferendos esse
caeteris expositoribus. Itaque ex illis praecipue quod Aristoteles senserit
quodve his aut aliis verbis significare voluerit petendum & cognoscendum
est. Sed veniamque ad Arabes, Avicennam quanto in medicina aliis omnibus (Hippocratem et Galenum his non numero) superior fuit tanto in
310   philosophia et se ipso & aliis quorum plurimis inferior extitit. Itaque quemadmodum scripta eius quae pertinent ad medicinam libenter legerem, ita
quae spectant ad philosophiam, legere non magnopere curaverim, nisi ea de
causa forte legenda sint quod is saepe reprehendatur ab Averroe, & a quibusdam Latinis philosophis in praetio habeatur, atque frequenter citetur.
315   Opus eius philosophicum, Logicam, physicam, et metaphysicam complectens in laude est apud multos philosophos, sed in eo tametsi nonnunquam subtilis est tum semper obscurus, perplexus, horridus, dissimilis
peripateticorum et ab Aristotelica philosophandi ratione longissime remotus est. Aliud item opus eius de anima, & quod Arabice inscribitur Almahad,
320   hoc est de loco animarum post mortem nec paucos nec parvos errores
continet, et quod in eo vera sunt, non tractantur physice, sed vel historice,
vel etiam fabulose nec ullis, aut necessariis aut verisimilibus argumentis
confirmantur. Sed libet hic opponere iudicium Averrois de Avicenna quem
ille pluribus locis suis quasi coloribus [29r] pulchre depinxit. Quodam igi-
325   tur loco ita ait Avicennae sermo semper medius est inter peripateticos et
loquentes, his enim admisisset suam Metaphysicam cum his quae traduntur secundum leges & alibi quae Avicenna transtulit ex Aristotele pro
aspectu eo Aristoteles utitur. Sed re vera nihil minus sunt, quarum illius
libri potius faciunt homines discendere a sapientia quam ipsam largiantur
330   & alibi Avicenna non est imitatus Aristoteles nisi in Dialoga sed in aliis
erravit, & maxime in Metaphysica & hoc ideo qua incepit quasi a se, &
alibi Avicennam fecit errare multa confidentia in proprio ingenio, & parva
exercitatio in Logica.

Averroes fuit singularis decus, gloria & praesidium lycaei, cui uni (Alexandrum et Simplicium excipio) ausim dicere plus debere disciplinam 335 peripateticam quam omnibus aliis simul expositoribus. Hic omnes proprie libros Aristotelis amplissimis & doctissimis commentariis illustravit. Quamobrem nomen etiam commentatoris katà tèn exokèn promeruit hic. Aristotelem a calumniis aliorum egregie vindicavit, hic decreta eius mordicus semper tenuit, & pugnaciter ac pro illis tamquam pro ariis & fociis 340 contra omnes fortiter dimicavit. Hic tantum roboris & dignitatis scriptis Aristotelis adiunxit ut nomen eius non minus quam ipsius Aristotelis ab optimis quibusquam philosophis in sermonibus, disputationibus, & scriptis ipsorum magna cum laude usurpetur atque celebretur. Hic amatur & colitur ab omnibus philosophiae studiosis: nisi ab his a quibus vel non 345 legitur, vel non intelligitur, & qui nocticae similes ob infirmam ingeniorum aciem, non possunt eum cernere et sustinere clarissimum philosophiae peripateticum splendorem commentarii eius in Aristotelem qui excellunt caeteros & praecipue legi debent sunt hi magna commentaria in libros posteriorum: in libros physicos, in de caelo, in de anima, in secun- 350 dum & dodicesimum metaphysicae, paraphrases eius in parva naturalia, in libros de partibus & generatione naturalium in libros de caelo et in metaphysicas paraphrases studiosis philosophiae valde probatas & commendatas esse velim nihil enim illis brevius, apertius, venustius, & politius optari potest. Sunt etiam alia opera eius philosophica immortali laude 355 digna ut libellus de substantia orbis. Primum libri colliget in quibus universam medicinae scientiam breviter et dilucide exposuit. Eximium est illud opus quod appellatur destructio destructionum in quo summum ingenii acumen, acerrimam vim iudicii, & subtilem atque copiosam multarum rerum scientiam cernere & admirari licet. Iam vero digressiones 360 multae et variae quae in commentariis eius: quae tamquam stellae in caelo mirabiliter [29v] collucent, auream continent philosophiae doctrinam. Itaque mihi persuasum esse eum qui huiusmodi digressiones praeceptas, cognitas, & animo ac memoria comprehensas teneat magnam partem philosophiae prospectam & exploratam habere. Constat tamen Averroim 365 in explanatione verborum Aristotelis nonnumquam lapsum & hallucinatum esse propterea quod mendosam & corruptam versionem Aristotelis haberet, quod ipse non aut semel traduerit & conqueritur, sed quantum in eo fuit semper graecos interpretes sequutus & imitatus est, porro obscuritas et perplexitas orationis quam in commentariis eius apparet, tota provenit 370 ex translatione Latina, nam cum lingua Arabica & Latina maximo intervallo disiunctae sint quod mirum est id quod Arabice scriptum fuit si verbum e verbo Latine reddatur, obscurum horridum, & insulsum existere. Sed ad superandas hasce difficultates magnopere conferet diu multumque

375 versatum et exercitatum esse non modo in scriptis Averrois, sed etiam
     Averroistarum qui verba & sententias Averrois diligenter explanarunt
     quorum tante princeps est Zimara qui in solutionibus contradictionum in
     theorematibus quos conscripsit magnam lucem dedit nobis ad intelligen-
     dum Aristotelem. Sed de Averroe pluram non dicam, illud solum hoc
380 loco: quasi clausulam huius sermonis memorabo, quod dictum fuit a
     quodam clarissimo philosopho. Is enim cum doceret publice philosophiam
     saepe numero dicere solebat, neminem unquam fore bonum Aristotelicum
     qui non esset perfectus Averroista.
         Restat ut deinceps de Latinis expositoribus dicamque. Quemadmodum
385 inter graecos Simplicius sic Albertus inter Latinos cognomentum Magni
     consequutus est, fuit vir magno, gravi, excelsoque ingenio, et praestanti
     cognitione rerum naturalium est abditissimarum atque minutissimarum
     primus Latinorum: doctrinam Aristotelis multis in id conscriptis libris dili-
     genter & copiose pertractavit. Cuius librorum duo sunt genera: unum
390 eorum in quibus Aristotelis interpretatus est non quaedam sigillatim
     explanans, sed quae ab eo tradita fuerant in Logica, Physica, Metaphysica
     eodem pene servato ordine latius et accuratius exponens, in quibus libris
     sunt plurimae digressiones refertae varia & gravi eruditionem. Alterum
     genus est eorum librorum, in quibus nec verbis nec ordini Aristotelis
395 adstricti materias phylosophicas per se, ac modo suo tractandas suscepit: in
     his multi primas deferunt ei operi quod dicitur Quatuor Coequevis et quod
     appellatur Summa de Homine, sed ego maxime omnium laudo & probo
     librum quod inscribitur de Apprehensione modo dialogi compositum,
     cuius libri doctrina quaedam & sententiae sine dubio sunt Alberti stili vero
400 apertior, completior atque [30r] politior est: quasi ut credere possim auc-
     torem eius fuisset Albertum. Hunc librum equidem cupio omnibus phylo-
     sophicae studiosis per quem notum & familiarem esse, nam quecunque
     pertinent omni ex parte ita breviter, perspicue, diligenter et accurate
     declarat, ut in eo genere nihil amplius requiri posse videatur. Sed quicquo-
405 rum in Alberto cuncta fere laudanda sunt: illud tamen vitiosum & dignum
     reprehensione videri potest quod in modo philosophandi nimis obscurus
     & horridus sit, et non tamen peripateticos quam Arabes, & Platonicos
     sequi & imitari studuerit, cum enim de rebus arduis & gravibus disputat:
     plerumque totam disputationem refert atque revocat ad Metaphysicam,
410 abstractiones, & nescio quas libras intelligentia, atque luces quasdam intel-
     lectuales, quas ego admirari quaedam possum: intelligere vero aut etiam
     credere vix possum. Deinde in his quae scripsit de metallis, animalibus &
     plantis valde accusatur a viris earum rerum doctissimis & peritissmis aiunt
     enim eum quaecunque ab aliis accepisset: ea quasi certissima naturae orac-
415 ula posteritati tradidisse in quibus tum multa sunt et experientiae contraria,
     penitus falsa, fabulosa et absurda. Quamobrem quaedam dixisse fertur: duo

fuisse philosophos Latinos qui in scribenda historia rerum naturalium egregie mentiti fuerunt sed unum eleganter alterum barbarum extitisse. Plinium veterem et Albertum significans.

D. Thomae multum profecto detur Aristotelis non modo propter com- 420 mentarios quibus omnia pene scripta eius mirifice illustravit, sed etiam propterea quod auctorem suae sanctitatis tantam dignitatem & auctoritatem tribuit Aristoteli, ut eius potissimum eam apud christianos unus praeter ceteros philosophos Aristotelis legatur, discatur, colatur, publice doceatur, putereturque ad sacrae theologiae scientiam capessendam pluri- 425 mum adiumenti conferre posset, nemo enim Christianorum est paulo cultiori & politiori ingenio, que non D. Thomae exemplo suo vehementer inflammavit ad philosophandum, nemo enim quantumvis religiosus et sanctus quem iam pudeat Aristotelem discere publice profiteri in eoque docendo & interpretando etiam totam vitam consumeret: multa in D. 430 Thomae fuerunt eaque praeclara magno ingenii, claritas, gravitas, firmitasque iudicii magna philosophiae scientia, cum incredibili divinarum rerum cognitione coniuncta innumerabilia quoque propemodum humanae & divinae philosophiae monumenta, singularis etiam modestia in refellendis aliorum opinionibus, primum enim [30v] quoad eis fieri potest eos 435 qui videri errasse conatur excusare & bene interpretari verum: si id commode fieri non potest: ita reprehendit ut videatur non personam insectari: sed eius solum errata confutare voluisse. Itaque in omnibus scriptis eius excellens doctrina, venerabilis quaedam gravitas, et amabilis est quaedam sanctitas mirabiliter splendit porro doctrina philosophiae: quae in eo fuit 440 amplissima non tantum petenda est ex commentariis eius in Aristotelem quos ille breves & succinctos esse voluit, ut ultimas sententias Aristotelis breviter & dilucide exponeret non ut ostentaret subtilitatem & copiam eruditionis; sed ea potissimum cognosci & iudicari debet ex scriptis theologicis maxime vero ex quadripartita summa theologiae: cuius prima pars 445 partim est metaphysica partim physica. Prima vero 1^{ae} tota pene moralis est. Ex summa etiam contra gentiles, quod opus viri docti magnopere laudant, & admirantur quamquam nonnullis videatur esse nimis Metaphysicum cui profecto si varietas et ornatus quaedam politioris eruditionis accessisset nihil in eo desiderari potuisset: libellus item de ente et essentia 450 cum nonnullis aliis opusculis physicis non parva legentibus utilitatem afferre possunt.

Commentarii eius in librum perihermeneias & libros de caelo, quos iam senex etate & philosophandi exercitatione conscripsit, inter alios perspicuam laudem obtinet, in quibus sequutus est graecos interpretes in illis 455 quidem Ammonium in his vero Simplicium quod si in aliis commentariis itidem fecisset (non potuit autem ut opinor quod graecorum scripta tum non dum reperta essent, aut Latinitatem donata) si tum fecisset scripta

460 eius commentariis graecorum non modo conferri sed et preferri potuis-
sent. Non desunt tamen qui vituperent in commentariis eius minutas
divisiones & partitiones verborum Aristotelis, quas inculcat in principio
fere cuiuslibet commenti, aiunt enim eas plurimum officere memoriae &
intelligentiae, & legentibus valde importunas atque molestas esse. Verum
haec minora & leviora sunt: quam ut gloria tanti viri aliqua ex parte violare
465 & minuere possint. Obruuntur enim & obscurantur multitudine mag-
nitidineque ac splendore virtutum ac laudum eius, ita ut si quae in eo vitia
fuerunt, ea profecto tanta luce penitus offuscata minime appareat. Sed de
gravioribus, & antiquioribus Aristotelis expositoribus satis dictum sit. [31r]
     Si quod autem in libris eorum quos ante memoravimus erratum inest
470 contra philosophiam & christianam veritatem, id nobis continua nulla vel
dignitatis vel auctoritatis eorum habita ratione improbandum, reiiciendum
& execrandum est, ut in Alexandro Deum non esse causam efficientem
omnium rerum, nec eorum quae sunt infra lunam explicatam, cogitationes
curam & providentiam habere animos huius nativos & mortales esse. In
475 Averroe suam, cuiusque hominum formam, unam cum corpore nasci &
occidere, intellectum autem quod immortalis est; unum numero assistere
cunctis homnibus; vim & potestate Dei finita, & circumscriptam esse ut
nec de novo quicquid facere, nec aliquid ex nihilo moliri queat, & alia huius
generis figmenta monstra & portenta, futilitatis & impietatis plenissima,
480 neque vero mirandum est hos viros caeterosque sapientes tam graviter &
absurde lapsos & deceptos fusse, homines enim fuerunt, quorum errant
fallaces, sensus, angusta ingenia, infirma iudicia, vitae multis flagitiis ingenerata, mens humanae inscitiae tenebris circumfusa, & celesti destituta
luminem. Nos igitur immortales gratias Deo immortali agamus, eumque
485 pie & caste semper colamus, atque veneremur, quod singulari beneficio
suo: pro Christum senatorem, & doctorem humani generis: ea nobis clarissime patefecit, quae acutissimis doctissimisque philosophis obscura &
occulta esse voluit, nec tamen in iis qui philosophiam tradit quod sequendum, aut fugiendum, quod ite probandum aut interpretandum nobis esset
490 iudicavit. Sed etiam earum rerum: quae omnem intelligentiam vim atque
facultatem, infinitis partibus superant, cognitionem liberaliter impertivit.
Sed revertamur ad institutam tractationem.

'Origenian Platonisme' in Interregnum Cambridge: Three Academic Texts by George Rust, 1656 and 1658

Marilyn A. Lewis, Davide A. Secci, and Christian Hengstermann, with assistance from John H. Lewis, and Benjamin Williams[*]

The Cambridge Platonist scholar Sarah Hutton has argued that '[t]he years 1658–1662 could be described as an Origenist moment in English theology'. She notes that these years saw the publication of William Spencer's Greek/ Latin edition of Origen's *Contra Celsum* (1658); of Henry More's *The Immortality of the Soul* (1659), *An Explanation of the Grand Mystery of Godliness* (1660), and *A Collection of Several Philosophical Writings*, especially its 'Preface General' (1662); of *A Letter of Resolution concerning Origen* (1661), usually thought to have been written by George Rust; and of Joseph Glanvill's *Lux Orientalis* (1662).[1] While the philosophical-theological circle to which More, Rust, and Glanvill belonged has been, since the late nineteenth century, denoted the 'Cambridge Platonists', recent research has stressed the Origenian quality of their Platonism, so much so that scholars at the Westfälische Wilhelms-Universität, Münster, refer to them as the 'Cambridge Origenists'.[2] Perhaps the term 'Origenian Platonisme',

[*] The authors are grateful to the editor for his constant encouragement and patience and to the anonymous reviewers for their helpful criticisms and suggestions. Marilyn Lewis thanks the other authors for their valuable contributions but takes full responsibility for any errors.

[1] Sarah Hutton, 'Henry More and Anne Conway on Preexistence and Universal Salvation', in Marialuisa Baldi (ed.), *"Mind Senior to the World": Stoicismo e Origenismo nella Filosofia Platonica del Seicento Inglese* (Milan, 1996), 113–25 on 113.

[2] John Tulloch, *Rational Theology and Christian Philosophy in England in the Seventeenth Century*, 2 vols. (Edinburgh & London, 1872), invented the term 'Cambridge Platonists', using it as the title for vol. 2; Alfons Fürst and Christian Hengstermann (eds), *Die Cambridge Origenists: George Rusts Letter of Resolution concerning Origen and the Chief of his Opinions*, *Adamantiana* 4 (Münster, 2013); see also <http://www.uni-muenster.de/FB2/origenes/>.

coined by John Beale in 1666, best describes the richness of the Platonic, neo-Platonist (including Origenian and Plotinian) and Renaissance Platonist texts on which the circle drew.[3] This article adds substantial detail to our knowledge of what we might then call the 'Origenian Platonist moment', by presenting English translations of three Latin academic texts, with annotations to the two longer ones, written by George Rust in 1656 and 1658 while he was a fellow of Christ's College, Cambridge.

The first text, *Messias in S. Scriptura promissus olim venit* (The Messiah promised in the Holy Scripture came a long time ago) should be assigned to Rust's fulfilment in 1656 of the requirement to dispute in the Divinity Schools in the University of Cambridge in order to qualify for the degree of Bachelor of Divinity (BD).[4] It is remarkable for its dependence on the teaching of Ralph Cudworth and confirms Rust's general adherence to what might be described as the 'Origenian Platonist' party at Christ's during the 1650s. Further, it suggests a lively awareness of a current political issue—the question of the readmission of the Jews—within the academic context of a Cambridge Divinity disputation. The second and third texts were presented at the annual University of Cambridge Commencement Day in 1658, when Rust incepted BD. The first of these was Rust's Act Verses, a souvenir printed broadsheet containing poems on the two theses prepared by the respondent, which was distributed to the audience before the public disputation. It contained two poems, *Resurrectionem e mortuis Scriptura docet nec refragatur Ratio* (Scripture teaches the resurrection from the dead, and reason does not contradict this) and *Anima separata non dormit* (The soul, separated from the body, does not sleep).[5] The final text, *Resurrectionem è Mortuis S. Scriptura tradit, nec refragatur Ratio* (The Holy Scripture tells of the Resurrection of the dead, nor does reason oppose it) was the discourse which Rust defended in the disputation.[6] Not only are these two 1658 texts important additions to the writings constituting the Origenian Platonist moment, but a reconstruction of the Commencement on 5 and 6 July will show that they formed part of what was perhaps the most public exposition and celebration of Origenian Platonist doctrines in Interregnum Cambridge.

[3] Rhodri Lewis, 'Of "Origenian Platonisme": Joseph Glanvill on the Pre-existence of Souls', *Huntington Library Quarterly* 69 (2006), 267–300 on 267.

[4] *The Remains of that Reverend and Learned Prelate, Dr George Rust*, ed. Henry Hallywell (London, 1686), 47–79.

[5] Bodleian Library, Oxford, Wood 276a (CCCCLXIV), single printed broadsheet; J. J. Hall, *Cambridge Act and Tripos Verses, 1565–1894* (Cambridge, 2009), 7–19, 154–5.

[6] MSS and transcriptions at http://www.hrionline.ac.uk/hartlib/, search on 27/24 and 55/13.

'Origenian Platonisme' at Christ's College, Cambridge

Henry More, elected to a fellowship at Christ's in 1641, and Ralph Cudworth, who became master of the college 1654,[7] were able to create and develop an Origenian Platonist ethos at Christ's during the 1640s and '50s through their attraction of like-minded younger men to the college. Christ's had suffered badly during the Earl of Manchester's purge of the University in 1644: ten royalist fellows had been ejected out of a total fellowship of thirteen. Nine rather undistinguished Puritan fellows were intruded, but they had all vacated their fellowships by the time Cudworth became master in 1654.[8] Their resignations created the opportunity first for More, and then also for Cudworth, to attract suitable Master of Arts (MA) candidates from other colleges for election to fellowships. Rust, who had graduated Bachelor of Arts (BA) from St Catharine's College in 1647, was elected to a Christ's College fellowship in 1649; he retained it for a decade, proceeding MA in 1650 and incepting BD in 1658.[9] He and the other new fellows transmitted their opinions to their own pupils, thereby enabling Christ's to flourish as a centre of broadly defined Origenian Platonism. By the second half of the 1650s, young men sympathetic to More's and Cudworth's theology made up the majority of the fellowship of Christ's College.[10] After the Restoration, Ralph Widdrington, a Christ's fellow who bitterly opposed More and Cudworth, would characterize the college as 'a seminary of Heretics'.[11]

The Origenian Platonism of Christ's College was essentially an irenic version of ethical Christianity which rejected materialism, atheism, predestinarianism, and enthusiasm. More, Cudworth, and the young fellows whom they attracted to Christ's can be broadly characterized by a desire

---

[7] John Peile, *Biographical Register of Christ's College Cambridge, 1505–1905, and of the Earlier Foundation, God's House, 1448–1505,* 2 vols. (Cambridge, 1910–1913), 1: 414, 465.

[8] John Peile, *Christ's College* (London, 1900), 164–5.

[9] For Rust, see Tulloch, *Rational Theology,* 2: 433–7; Peile, *Biographical Register,* 1: 486–7; William C. De Pauley, *The Candle of the Lord: Studies in the Cambridge Platonists* (London, 1937), 176–85; Sarah Hutton, 'Rust, George (d.1670)', in Andrew Pyle (ed.), *The Dictionary of Seventeenth-Century British Philosophers,* 2 vols. (Bristol, 2000), 2: 700; Jon Parkin, 'Rust, George (c.1628–1670)', in *Oxford Dictionary of National Biography* (hereafter ODNB), ed. Henry C. G. Matthew and Brian Harrison (60 vols. Oxford, 2004); Sarah Day, 'George Rust and Intellectual Life in 1650s Cambridge', unpublished M.Phil. thesis, Cambridge, 2010: Seeley Historical Library, classmark 9.10.38.

[10] For further detail, see Marilyn A. Lewis, 'The Making of a Platonic Fellowship at Christ's College, Cambridge, 1648–1669', forthcoming.

[11] Marjorie H. Nicolson, 'Christ's College and the Latitude-Men', *Modern Philology* 27 (1929), 35–53; eadem (ed.), *The Conway Letters: The Correspondence of Anne, Viscountess Conway, Henry More, and their Friends, 1642–1684* (London, 1930; rev. Sarah Hutton, Oxford, 1992), 242 (quotation).

to combat what they saw as the materialism and atheism of Hobbes, and to some extent Descartes, in contradistinction to which they strongly affirmed the existence and immaterial substantiality of spirit, in reference to both God and the human soul. They also opposed the divine voluntarism of both Hobbes and the Calvinists by affirming human free will and by rebutting the doctrine of predestination with its corollary of divine tyranny. On the contrary, they stressed the goodness of God, whose promises of rewards and threats of punishments followed rationally from his commandments. Against the enthusiasm which they saw in sectarian claims to special inspiration, with its resultant antinomianism, they cherished the God-given rational faculty in humankind, the 'Candle of the Lord' (Proverbs 20:27), which gave human beings dignity and enabled them to moderate their habits and personal relationships according to the pattern of the life of Jesus. They consequently insisted on the soteriological and epistemological necessity of 'deiformity', the moulding of the human soul in godlikeness, in order to enter into relationship with and to know God.

Having studied the influence of More and Cudworth on a wide sample of Christ's students' writings and careers,[12] I would suggest that a distinction should be drawn between this broad Origenian Platonist ethos at Christ's, on the one hand, and the acceptance and public expression of some of the more controversial Plotinian and Origenian doctrines, on the other. A broadly based Origenian Platonist understanding of God and the human soul, which rebutted the prevailing Augustinian Calvinism of Interregnum Cambridge, was held by a large and loosely inclusive party within the college, but there is much less evidence of adherence to doctrines which might have appeared to be more dangerous, like the pre-existence of the soul. There is a paucity of evidence that pre-existence was generally held by the Origenian Platonist party at Christ's, and Cudworth overtly rejected it.[13] When *A Letter of Resolution concerning Origen* was published anonymously in 1661, it was censured by Theophilus Dillingham, vice chancellor of the University of Cambridge, and later attacked in print by Samuel Parker, the Archbishop of Canterbury's censor of books.[14] The

---

[12] Marilyn A. Lewis, ' "Educational Influence": A New Model for Understanding Tutorial Relationships in Seventeenth-Century Oxbridge', *History of Universities*, 27/2 (2013), 70–115.

[13] Ralph Cudworth, *The True Intellectual System of the Universe* (London, 1678), 1.1.34 on 43–4.

[14] Samuel Parker, *An Account of the Nature and Extent of the Divine Dominion and Goodnesse* (Oxford, 1666), 44–111; Nicolson (ed.), *Conway Letters*, 194. Josef Lössl, 'George Rusts Darstellung der Geschichte des ersten Origenismusstreits im *Letter of Resolution*', in Fürst and Hengstermann (eds), *Die Cambridge Origenisten*, 59–83 on 62 n.11, argues that this vice-chancellor was Henry Ferne, for whom see Brian Quintrell, 'Ferne, Henry (1602–1662)', in ODNB, but Joseph R. Tanner, *The Historical Register of the University of Cambridge* (Cambridge, 1917), 25, shows that Dillingham was reinstated on 19 March 1661. For the

public expression of belief in pre-existence clearly carried a degree of risk, and Rust's authorship of *A Letter of Resolution* has never been conclusively proved.[15] But Rust's student Henry Hallywell published three short texts of undoubted Rustian provenance in the 1680s.[16] While this is not the place for an extended critical discussion of these texts from Rust's Cambridge period,[17] a very brief summary of the ideas expressed in them will give us some sense of the intensity of his Origenism and provide some authorial context for his BD discourses.

A Discourse of Truth preceded the two discourses presented in this article. It was preached in Christ's College Chapel in 1651 and again in Great St Mary's, the University Church, in 1655, on which occasion it probably fulfilled the requirement for an aspiring BD candidate to preach once in English in the University Church.[18] Rust argued that truth is not dependent on the arbitrary will of God, but on the 'eternal and immutable' respects and relations between things, which can be known by human beings through Common Notions implanted in their souls by God their creator. Rust refuted the common preaching of 'God's great plot', that most of mankind are predestined to damnation; rather, God's fixed principle is to pardon penitent sinners, an attitude 'very suitable to infinite goodness'.[19] So Rust's adherence to the general programme of Origenian Platonism was made clear, and his Platonist credentials were further confirmed by his reference to truth as conformity to that 'which in God we may call an actual, steady, immovable, eternal Omniformity, as *Plotinus* calls the Divine Intellect'.[20]

---

publication of the work in June 1661, see George Rust, *A Letter of Resolution concerning Origen and the Chief of his Opinions*, ed. Marjorie H. Nicolson (New York, 1933), unpaginated bibliographic note.

[15] For a discussion of Rust's probable authorship of *A Letter of Resolution concerning Origen* (London, 1661), see Lewis, 'Of "Origenian Platonisme"', 274–6.

[16] George Rust, *A Discourse of the Use of Reason in Matters of Religion*, trans. with annotations Henry Hallywell (London, 1683); idem, *Remains*, 1–46; Marilyn A. Lewis, 'Pastoral Platonism in the Writings of Henry Hallywell (1641–1703)', *The Seventeenth Century* 28 (2013), 441–63 on 450–1; eadem, 'Henry Hallywell (1641–1703): A Sussex Platonist', *Sussex Archaeological Collections* 151 (2013), 115–27 on 118, 122.

[17] See Day, 'George Rust', for an excellent discussion of the sources and context of the three discourses mentioned here.

[18] Rust, *Remains*, [sig] A4ᵛ; James Heywood (ed.), *Collection of Statutes for the University and the Colleges of Cambridge* (London, 1840), 291.

[19] George Rust, *A Discourse of Truth*, in *Two Discourses*, ed. Joseph Glanvill (London, 1677), 1ˢᵗ pagination, 1–34; reprinted in *Two Choice and Useful Treatises* [ed. Henry More] (London, 1682), 165–98, annotations paginated separately, 173–271 (by printing this discourse together with Joseph Glanvill's *Lux Orientalis*, More associated it with the doctrine of the pre-existence of souls); reprinted again in *Remains*, 21–46, quotations on 23, 33, 37.

[20] Rust, *Remains*, 37–8.

The second text, *God is Love*, was almost certainly the English sermon at the University Church required of a doctoral candidate after he had incepted BD; it should be assigned to the Michaelmas term of 1658.[21] Here, Rust expressed even more advanced Origenian Platonist ideas. He again took up the theme of God's mercy towards penitent sinners and refuted the Calvinist doctrine of double predestination. He went further in saying that '[a]ll the several Degrees of Individuals of Creatures are like so many Rays, that flow from the inexhaustible Fountain of Light and Being, from whence the farther they go, the weaker and fainter they grow, till at last they reach to the confines of Non-Entity, or rather impossibility of Existence', thus echoing More's endorsement of the Plotinian scheme of being.[22] Rust also quoted Plato's *Symposium* on the nature of love as the 'simple Goodness' which 'is the first Hypostasis in the Platonick Triad', a favourite theme both More and Cudworth.[23] Finally, in a series of theological questions briefly listed toward the end of the sermon, Rust hinted that Origenian responses might be plausible. Most notably, he suggested pre-existence: 'seeing the Souls of Men have so quick a sense of Pleasure and Happiness, why did they not receive their Being in the first moment of Eternity?'[24] Rust's allusion to 'an acute Authour well known among us' whose writings were in process of answering these questions surely pointed towards More, whose *The Immortality of the Soul* would be published in 1659.[25]

The undated *A Discourse of the Use of Reason in Matters of Religion* probably originated as the required Latin sermon at the University Church subsequent to Rust's BD degree, so we might tentatively date it to the Lent term of 1659, just before Rust vacated his fellowship. It was translated into English by Hallywell.[26] Here, Rust again stressed that intellectual conformity to the divine goodness is required for human beings to enter into relationship with God. He agreed that some things in religion are indeed above reason, but urged that faith requires judgement and consent based

[21] Ibid., [sig.] A3ᵛ, 1–20; Heywood (ed.), *Collection of Statutes*, 292.

[22] Rust, *Remains*, 5–7, quotation on 5; Henry More, *Psychodia Platonica* (Cambridge, 1642); idem, *Philosophical Poems* (Cambridge, 1647); idem, *A Platonick Song of the Soul*, ed. Alexander Jacob (Lewisburg & London, 1998), see especially *Psychozoia*, 151–253.

[23] Rust, *Remains*, 9; More, *Psychozoia*; Cudworth, *True Intellectual System* (1678), 1.4.36 on 547–632.

[24] Rust, *Remains*, 15.

[25] Henry More, *The Immortality of the Soul, so farre forth as it is Demonstrable from the Knowledge of Nature and the Light of Reason* (London, 1659); Rust, *Remains*, 17.

[26] Heywood (ed.), *Collection of Statutes*, 292. This sermon was probably the required, *Concio ad Clerum* (address to the clergy); Cambridge University Archives, Grace Book 'Eta', 198, shows that Rust deferred the Latin sermon from the Michaelmas term 1658 until the Lent term 1658/9, on pain of losing his caution money deposited with the university authorities. I owe this reference to Richard Serjeantson. Peile, *Biographical Register* 1: 486, says that 'Rust's last payment was at Lady Day [i.e. 25 March] 1659'; see n.16 above.

on reason; God does not propound anything to be believed that is contradictory to right reason. Human nature was created with a capacity for reason which has not been entirely obscured by the Fall; to the extent that man understands things by the use of reason, he imitates God's immediate understanding.[27] This final discourse from Rust's Cambridge years is perhaps more restrained in its expression of controversial Origenian ideas, but it does nothing to disassociate Rust from the more advanced Origenism of More's and Cudworth's inner circle at Christ's College. On the basis of these three texts, we can certainly include Rust as a contributor to the Origenian Platonist moment, whether or not he wrote *A Letter of Resolution concerning Origen*. This contribution is borne out in the three texts presented in this article, partially in the discourse of 1656 and much more fully in those of 1658.

The Bachelor of Divinity Disputation and the Annual Commencement

According to Hallywell, Rust's *Messias in S. Scriptura promissus olim venit* was '*an Exercise which the Authour performed in the Divinity Schools in the University of* Cambridge *in the Year* 1656'.[28] The Cambridge University statutes of 1570 required a BD candidate 'twice [to] dispute against a bachelor of divinity, and once after the third year . . . [to be] respondent in divinity'.[29] At the public disputation for the BA, MA, and higher degrees, the candidate presented a 'position', a speech in Latin 'responding' to a stated question, setting out the logical grounds for its acceptance as persuasively as he could. Thus, he was known as the 'respondent' or 'answerer'. The respondent was attacked in turn by several 'opponents' holding at least the degree for which he was supplicating, and his task was to rebut them successfully, as adjudicated by the 'Father' of the disputation.[30] *Messias in S. Scriptura* was Rust's position or 'exercise' when he appeared as respondent. The venue will have been the old Divinity School, a building completed in 1400 and forming the northern side of the original Schools Quadrangle of Cambridge University; it still stands to the west of the current Senate House.[31]

---

[27] Rust, *Discourse of Reason*, 35–41. [28] Rust, *Remains*, [sig] [a].

[29] Heywood (ed.), *Collection of Statutes*, 291.

[30] See William T. Costello, *The Scholastic Curriculum at Early Seventeenth-Century Cambridge* (Cambridge, MA, 1958), 14–31; Harris F. Fletcher, *The Intellectual Development of John Milton*, 2 vols. (Urbana, 1956–1961), 2: 219–70.

[31] Robert Willis and John W. Clark, *The Architectural History of the University of Cambridge and of the Colleges of Cambridge and Eton*, 1st edn., 4 vols. (Cambridge, 1886); new

Resurrectionem è Mortuis S. Scriptura tradit, nec refragatur Ratio was the position which Rust defended, as an incepting BD, at the Cambridge Commencement of 1658. In 1665, John Buck, Esquire Beadle of the University of Cambridge, wrote a detailed account of the ceremonial aspects of the disputations for and conferral of academic degrees, or at least of the form that he thought they should have taken.[32] According to Buck, the annual Commencement was a two-day event on the first Tuesday in July and the preceding Monday. The Divinity Acts took place in the University Church, Great St Mary's, where a stage had been erected at the west end. The main event *in Vesperiis Comitiorum* (Commencement Eve) was a disputation in which one of the new Doctors of Divinity (DD) acted as respondent. On the morning of the following day, *in Die Comitiorum* (Commencement Day), there was a disputation in which a new BD was respondent.[33] Earlier, on 11 or 12 June, graces had been passed by the Caput Senatus of the University for higher degrees, including BDs. Those who had 'performed their Acts, or cautioned [i.e. paid a deposit] for them' were admitted to their degrees at that time. Then, 'all the Bac: in Div: newly admitted go into the Divinity school & there choose one of their Company to answer the Divinity Act in Die Comitiorum'. The Commencement Day disputation was thus a showcase performance by the new BD who was most likely to dispute well in public. According to Buck, the BD 'Answerers have usually the favour granted them to choose their Positions Questions', so we may assume that Rust and other new BDs who performed on Commencement Days genuinely held the positions they defended.[34]

Although Rust may have fulfilled the requirements to 'dispute' and 'respond' in time for the annual Commencement of 1656, there was good reason for him to delay incepting as BD until 1658. During the late sixteenth and the first half of the seventeenth century, Calvinists had dominated the Divinity Acts at the annual Commencement. The Commencement had been abandoned in 1641 but reinstated in 1650, since when the prevailing Augustinian Calvinism of Cromwellian Cambridge had been strongly but not invariably represented.[35] In 1656, the vice chancellor was the Calvinist

edn: ed. David J. Watkin, 4 vols. (Cambridge, 1988–2009), 3: 10–11, 16; Richard Newman, *The Old Schools, University of Cambridge: An Archaeological Excavation* (Cambridge, 2009), 2, 21–5.

[32] British Library, London, Add. MS 5843, 'Extracts from Mr. Buck's Book, relating to the Ceremonials of the University of Cambridge, &c.', printed in George Peacock, *Observations on the Statutes of the University of Cambridge* (London, 1841), Appendix B, pp. liv–xci on pp. lxxix–xci; Hall, *Act and Tripos Verses*, 2–8.

[33] Buck's Book, pp. lxxix–lxxxvii; Hall, *Act and Tripos Verses*, 7–8.

[34] Buck's Book, pp. lxxviii–lxxix.

[35] [John Worthington?], 'The Life of the Reverend and most Learned Joseph Mede, B.D.', in *The Works of the Pious and Profoundly-Learned Joseph Mede, B.D.*, ed. John Worthington

Theophilus Dillingham, master of Clare Hall in succession to Cudworth.[36] Anthony Tuckney, equally Calvinistic, had just been appointed Regius professor of Divinity and presided over the Divinity Act.[37] The DD respondent, John Boylston of Jesus College, will not have offended the Origenian Platonist party by defending the position 'The Sacrament of the Eucharist is salutary and is of perpetual use in the church of Christ';[38] but the BD respondent, John Frost of St John's College, where Tuckney had been master since 1653, will have done so. He preached the sermon on the Commencement Eve, denouncing Arminians, whose doctrine of natural light and universalism made a mockery of the scriptural doctrine of the salvation of the predestined elect by the death of Christ, and he disputed the next day on the position 'Faith justifies by functioning in the manner of an instrument', 'to the admiration of all Auditors, and abundant satisfaction of the whole University'.[39] In 1657, Dillingham was vice chancellor for a second term, and the DD respondent, Samuel Gardiner of Corpus Christi College, defended the position that 'Without the grace of Christ, a free power of decision for spiritual good does not exist in fallen man',[40]

(London, 1672), pp. i–xlv on p. xix; Nicholas Tyacke, *Anti-Calvinists: The Rise of English Arminianism, c.1590–1640* (Oxford, 1991), 33, 39; Jeffrey K. Jue, *Heaven upon Earth: Joseph Mede (1586–1638) and the Legacy of Millenarianism* (Dordrecht, 2006), 27; Hall, *Act and Tripos Verses*, 22–4, 146–52. The author is grateful to Richard Serjeantson for allowing her to see his unpublished paper, 'The Theory and Practice of Rebellion in Confessional Europe: The Case of John Knight (1622)', which provides useful context at 23–4, 26–9.

[36] British Library, London, MS Harley, 7038, a list of degrees of Doctors, Masters of Arts, etc., in the University of Cambridge, 1500–1658, drawn up by William Dillingham, transcribed by Thomas Baker, fols 33–112 at fol. 111, for 1556 [*sic* for 1656]; for this MS see Hall, *Act and Tripos Verses*, 13. For Dillingham, see J.R. Wardale, *Clare College* (London, 1899), 113; Tanner, *Historical Register*, 25; John and John A. Venn, *Alumni Cantabrigienses: From the Earliest Times to 1751* (hereafter Venn, *AC*), 4 vols. (Cambridge, 1922–1924), *s.v.* Dillingham, Theophilus (1629); John Gascoigne, 'Dillingham, Theophilus (1613–1678)', in ODNB.

[37] British Library, MS Harley, 7038, fol. 111; Tanner, *Historical Register*, 75; Venn, *AC*, *s.v.* Tuckney, Anthony (1613); Patrick Collinson, 'Tuckney, Anthony (1599–1670)', in ODNB. For Tuckney's criticism of Whichcote's Platonism, see 'Eight Letters of Dr. Antony Tuckney and Dr. Benjamin Whichcote', in Benjamin Whichcote, *Moral and Religious Aphorisms*, ed. Samuel Salter (London, 1753), separately paginated 1–134; Tod E. Jones (ed.), *The Cambridge Platonists: A Brief Introduction* (Dallas, 2005), 51–156.

[38] British Library, MS Harley, 7038, fol. 111; John Boylston, *Sacramentum eucharistiae est salutaris & perpetui usus in ecclesia Christi* (Cambridge, single sheet, 1656); Venn, *AC*, s.v. Boylston, John (1626); Hall, *Act and Tripos Verses*, 152–3.

[39] John Frost, *Fides justificat sub ratione instrumenti* (Cambridge, single sheet, 1656); idem, *Select Sermons Preached upon Special Occasions* (Cambridge, 1658), full Latin text of his position on 41–58, Commencement sermon on 59–85; for Frost's BD 'exercise', *De tota Christi justitia credentibus imputata*, dedicated to the Calvinist John Arrowsmith, see [sig.] B–17; Zachary Crofton, *The Peoples Need of a Living Pastor* (London, 1657), 47–8, quotation on 48; Venn, *AC*, *s.v.* Frost, John (1644); Gordon Goodwin, rev. Stephen Wright, 'Frost, John (1625/6–1656)', in ODNB; Hall, *Act and Tripos Verses*, 152–3.

[40] British Library, MS Harley 7038, fol. 111; Samuel Gardiner, *Supremus magistratus habet summam potestatem circa sacra* and *Sine gratia Christi non datur in homine lapso liberum*

while the BD respondent, Josiah Lamplugh, also of Corpus Christi, argued either that 'New revelations, apart from Scripture, are not to be expected' or that 'Good works do not deserve eternal life'.[41] The Calvinist tone of these two Commencement Divinity Acts was unmistakable.

By 1658, however, Dillingham had been replaced as vice chancellor by John Worthington, and a brief opportunity had been created, on 5 and 6 July, for the Origenian Platonist party to appear as the public face of Cambridge.[42] Rust was now able to take his place in the Commencement which marked the apex of their influence within the University. Worthington, master of Jesus College, was a member of the Origenian Platonist circle through theological conviction as well as friendship with its leading figures and marriage to Benjamin Whichcote's niece Mary.[43] In 1660, Worthington would publish his edition of John Smith's *Select Discourses*, one of the foundational documents of Cambridge Origenian Platonism.[44] The 1658 DD respondent, who also preached on the Commencement Eve, was Worthington's close friend Nathaniel Ingelo, an Edinburgh graduate who had become a fellow of Queens' College in 1644, at the same time as John Smith, but was now a fellow of Eton College.[45] Ingelo's sermon, preached within a few weeks of the publication of William Spencer's edition of

arbitrium ad bonum spirituale (Cambridge, single sheet, 1657); idem, *De efficacia gratiae convertentis, ejúsque agendi modo* (Cambridge, 1660), gives the full Latin text of the second position, presumably indicating that this was the position he defended; Tanner, *Historical Register*, 25; Venn, *AC, s.v.* Gardiner, Samuel (1636); Hall, *Act and Tripos Verses*, 153.

[41]   British Library, MS Harley 7038, fol. 111; [Josiah] Lamplugh, *Novae revelationes extra Scripturam sacram non sunt expectandae* and *Bona opera non merentur vitam aeternam* (Cambridge, single sheet, 1657); Venn, *AC, s.v.* Lamplugh, Josiah (1642); Hall, *Act and Tripos Verses*, 153–4.

[42]   Worthington himself seems to have presided over the Divinity Act. Buck's Book, p. lxxxiii, says that the Lady Margaret Professor of Divinity usually moderated the Divinity Act on Commencement Day, but the name of the incumbent, Richard Love, does not appear in British Library, MS Harley 7038, fol. 112. For Love, see Tanner, *Historical Register*, 73; Venn, *AC, s.v.* Love, Richard (1611), E.T. Bradley, rev. S.L. Sadler, 'Love, Richard (1596–1661)', in ODNB.

[43]   Tanner, *Historical Register*, 25; Venn, *AC, s.v.* Worthington, John (1632); *The Diary and Correspondence of Dr. J. Worthington*, (ed.) James Crossley and Richard C. Christie (Chetham Society, 13 = i., 36 = ii. Part 1, 114 = ii. Part 2, 1844–86), i. 111–14; John T. Young, 'Worthington, John (*bap.* 1618, *d.* 1671)', in ODNB.

[44]   John Smith, *Select Discourses*, ed. John Worthington (London, 1660).

[45]   Cambridge University Archives, Grace Book 'Eta', 174, I owe this reference to Richard Serjeantson; British Library, MS Harley 7038, fol. 112; Nathaniel Ingelo, *The Perfection, Authority, and Credibility of the Holy Scriptures* (London, 1659; 2nd edn, 1659: 'October 1658' in MS on title page); *Worthington Correspondence*, i. 112; for Ingelo's and Worthington's friendship, see i. 36–7, 119, 244–5; ii. Part 1, 66, 140, 168, 170–1, 190, 204, 229–33, 245–8; ii. Part 2, pp. vii–ix, 269–70, 336–40, 356, 363; Venn, *AC, s.v.* Ingelo, Nathaniel (1644); Jackson I. Cope, '"The Cupri-Cosmits": Glanvill on Latitudinarian Anti-Enthusiasm', *Huntington Library Quarterly* 17, (1953), 269–86 on 283 n.36; Ian W. McLellan, 'Ingelo, Nathaniel (1620/21–1683)', in ODNB; Hall, *Act and Tripos Verses*, 154.

Contra Celsum, openly approved of Origen as a defender of the use of true philosophy in the service of Christianity.[46] At the Restoration, Ingelo would publish *Bentivolio and Urania*, in which the quest for deiformity and the return of the pre-existent soul to her divine habitat were described in a romance largely based on More's *Platonick Song of the Soul*.[47] At Ingelo's request, his friend Benjamin Rogers received the degree of Bachelor of Music, conducting a performance of his setting of Ingelo's text *Hymnus Eucharisticus* (Hymn of Thanksgiving) for twelve voices.[48]

There were three new BDs in addition to Rust: Thomas Rolt, Samuel Jacombe, and Symon Patrick.[49] If the pattern described by Buck was followed, the other three will have chosen Rust to represent them on the Commencement Day. It is probably impossible to discover Rolt's precise opinions; a fellow of Sidney Sussex College, he published nothing, but the fact that he was rector of Wilden in Bedfordshire from 1657 until his death in 1695 suggests flexibility.[50] Jacombe and Patrick were both fellows of Ingelo's Queens' and close friends who shared Latitudinarian principles and friendliness toward the Origenian Platonists.[51] Patrick had preached

[46] Ingelo, *Perfection of Holy Scriptures* (2nd edn), 67–8, 87–95, 121, 157–9. Origen, *Contra Celsum*, ed. William Spencer (Cambridge, 1658), dedication, [sig.] A2, dated 1 July 1658, but the exact date of publication is unknown. Ingelo, in his Epistle Dedicatory to John Worthington, [sig.] (a 8ᵛ), dated 16 August 1658, said, [sig.] A2ᵛ, that he had included some things in the printed version of his sermon for which he had not had time in the sermon as delivered, so it is possible that he had added the references to Origen during the six weeks following the Commencement.

[47] Nathaniel Ingelo, *Bentivolio and Urania* (London, 1660); idem, *Bentilvolio and Urania, the Second Part* (London, 1664), both reprinted many times; McLellan, 'Ingelo, Nathaniel'.

[48] British Library, MS Harley 7038, fol. 112; Anthony Wood, *Athenae Oxonienses* 2 vols. (London, 1691–1692), 2: 847–8; Joseph Foster, *Alumni Oxonienses, 1500–1714* 4 vols. (Oxford, 1891), s.v. Rogers, Benjamin (1658); Venn, *AC*, s.v. Rogers, Benjamin (1658); Lydia M. Middleton, rev. Peter Lynan, 'Rogers, Benjamin (1613/14–1698)', in ODNB. Ingelo's 'text', as recorded in *Worthington Correspondence*, i. 112–13, is a compilation of verses from Psalm 32 and other psalms; for an English translation by Ingelo, see Bodleian Library, Wood 398 (13–14) [in a collection of single printed broadsheets collected by Anthony Wood], on the verso of which there is a MS note giving the circumstances of another performance of this work at the Guildhall, London, on 12 July 1660 before the king and court; the Latin and English texts were printed on broadsheets and distributed among the audience. Another text by Ingelo, confusingly also known as *Hymnus Eucharisticus* and also set to music by Rogers, is the Magdalen College, Oxford, hymn; Rogers was Informator Choristarum at Magdalen 1665–85. This text, more properly known as 'Te Deum Patrem colimus', is sung on Magdalen tower on May morning; it was produced on an audio CD, *Music for a May Morning* (Cantoris Records, 1992), with sleeve notes by Mark Heather.

[49] Cambridge University Archives, Grace Book 'Eta', 174; I owe this reference to Richard Serjeantson.

[50] Venn, *AC*, s.v. Rolt, George (1644).

[51] Simon Patrick, *The Hypocritical Nation Described* (London, 1657), Epistle to the Reader by Samuel Jacombe, [sig.] A2ʳ⁻ᵛ; Patrick, *Divine Arithmetic, or the Right Art of Numbring our Dayes* (London, 1659), 62–4; idem, *Autobiography*, in *The Works of Symon Patrick, D.D.*, ed. Alexander Taylor, 9 vols. (Oxford, 1858), 9: 405–569, on 426, 428; Venn, *AC*, s.v. Jacombe,

John Smith's funeral sermon in 1652 and would perform the same office for Jacombe in 1659.[52] He would soon publish, *A Brief Account of the New Sect of Latitude-Men*, which largely coincided with the broad philosophical/theological position of the Origenian Platonist party.[53] Patrick, Jacombe, Ingelo, and Rust were all included among Joseph Glanvill's 'Cupri-Cosmits', a mythical portrait gallery in 'Bensalem' which displayed pictures, of 'the "latitudinarian" divines who', according to Jackson I. Cope, 'are credited with providing the central force in the movement toward toleration which came from within the Restoration Church of England'.[54]

The Messiah Promised in the Holy Scripture Came a Long Time Ago

In *Messias in S. Scriptura promissus olim venit*, Rust was responding to a contemporary religious and political issue which was being debated with much passion during 1655–6. By attempting to prove that the Jews were mistaken to continue looking for the coming of the Messiah, he was rejecting current Jewish messianic expectations of a saviour to deliver European Jewry from persecution. The foremost Jewish messianist, Rabbi Menasseh Ben Israel, had accepted Lord Protector Cromwell's invitation to travel from Amsterdam to England in the autumn of 1655, and Cromwell had appointed the Whitehall Conference to consider Menasseh's petition for Jewish readmission to England, a projected reversal of the forcible expulsion of Anglo-Jewry in 1290. Menasseh's hope was that the readmission of the Jews would complete the Jewish Diaspora in all the nations of the earth,

Samuel (1644), Patrick, Simon (1644); Neil H. Keeble, 'Jacombe, Thomas (1623/4–1687)', Jon Parkin, 'Patrick, Simon [Symon] (1626–1707)', both in ODNB.

[52] Patrick, *Divine Arithmetic*; idem, *A Sermon Preached at the Funeral of Mr John Smith*, in Smith, *Select Discourses*, 481–526; Jacombe published only *A Short and Plain Catechism* (London, 1657; 7th edn, London, 1694) and *Moses his Death* (London, 1656), a funeral sermon for Edward Bright, a fellow of Emmanuel College, Cambridge.

[53] S. P., *A Brief Account of the New Sect of Latitude-Men* (Cambridge, 1662); ed. T. A. Birrell (Los Angeles, 1963), pp. i–iv, argues for Patrick's authorship.

[54] Cope, 'Cupri-Cosmits', quotation on 270, see 275–6 (Patrick), 276–8 (Rust), 283–4 (Ingelo); also included are Cudworth, Whichcote, Outram, Smith, More, Tillotson, and Stillingfleet. Cope's article is an edition of University of Chicago Library, MS 913, Joseph Glanvill, 'Bensalem, being a Description of a Catholick & Free Spirit both in Religion & Learning, in a Continuation of the Story of the Lord Bacon's New Atlantis'; Cope omitted material on 56–7, where 'Jcambo' (Samuel Jacombe) and 'Cardo' (Samuel Cradock?) are described. I am grateful for the kind assistance of Thomas Whittaker of the Special Collections Research Center, for providing scanned copies and transcriptions of the omitted sections. See also Richard Ward, *The Life of Henry More, Parts 1 and 2*, ed. Sarah Hutton, Cecil Courtney, Michelle Courtney, Robert Crocker, and Rupert Hall (Dordrecht, 2000), p. xxiii n.2.

a necessary preliminary to the coming of the Messiah. The deliberations of the Whitehall Conference were inconclusive, but throughout 1656 Menasseh and his philo-Semitic sympathizers continued to hope that the Protector would issue a formal proclamation on readmission. This question was of direct relevance to the Origenian Platonists as both Whichcote and Cudworth were members of the Whitehall Conference, although it remains an open question whether or not they favoured readmission.[55]

Rust constructed his exercise using well-worn arguments from Genesis 49:10, Haggai 2:6–9 with Malachi 3:1, and Daniel 9:24–6. All of these texts were used to support his contention that the Messiah must have come before the destruction of the Second Temple and the city of Jerusalem by the Romans in AD 70. From Genesis, he argued that the Sceptre (Jewish rule of the Hebrew people, however circumscribed) would not depart from the Tribe of Judah (the most powerful of the twelve tribes of Israel) until the coming of Shiloh (the Messiah), but, since the Sceptre had been decisively lost in AD 70, the Messiah must have come before that date. From Haggai and Malachi, he argued that the Messiah must have come before the destruction of the Second Temple, and from Daniel, he argued that a correct computation of the Seventy Weeks brought one accurately to the dates of Jesus of Nazareth's life, death, and resurrection.

In Rust's rebuttal of Jewish messianism, he adhered closely to Cudworth, whose lectures as Regius professor of Hebrew in 1656–8 would attempt to prove that the Messiah had already come at the time indicated by a correct understanding of Old Testament chronology.[56] Further, although Rust's discourse did not mention Origen, it must be seen to echo the Alexandrian Father's rebuttal of the alleged Jewish arguments in *Contra Celsum*. As James Bellamy's English translation of *Contra Celsum* would later put it succinctly, '[t]o conclude, without Doubt, our SAVIOUR is already come, who was expresly foretold, ev'n by the *Jewish* Prophets'.[57] The case for

---

[55] See Marilyn A. Lewis, ' "The Messiah Promised in the Sacred Scripture came a Long Time Ago": The Cambridge Platonists' Attitudes towards the Readmission of the Jews, 1655–1656', *Jewish Historical Studies* 45 (2013), 41–61.

[56] British Library, London, Add. MSS 4986–4987, Ralph Cudworth, Commentary on the Seventy Weeks of Daniel; Thomas Birch, 'An Account of the Life and Writings of Ralph Cudworth, D.D.', in Ralph Cudworth, *The True Intellectual System of the Universe*, ed. Thomas Birch 2nd edn, 2 vols. (London, 1743), 1: pp. vi–xxi on x–xi; see Lewis, 'Messiah Promised', 55, on the problems associated with identifying these MSS with Cudworth's professorial lectures.

[57] *Origen against Celsus: Translated from the Original into English*, trans. James Bellamy (London, *c.*1710), 2.39, second pagination, on 202; Bellamy translated only the first two books. ESTC errs in assigning the first edition of this work to 1660: see Hengstermann in Fürst and Hengstermann, *Die Cambridge Origenists*, 14 n.11, 326 n.1. See also, Henry R. Plomer, *A Dictionary of the Printers and Booksellers who were at Work in England, Scotland and Ireland from 1668 to 1725* (London, 1922), 256, for the dates during which the bookseller Jonathan

Cudworth's supervision is further strengthened when we consider Rust's access to books. Of the seventeen works which Rust can be said definitely to have used, three are now held in the Old Library at Christ's College and were probably there in Rust's time, but twelve appeared in the bookseller's catalogue of Cudworth's library when it was sold at auction in February 1691.[58] While it is possible that some of the books cited by Rust might have been acquired by Cudworth after Rust's preparation of his exercise, it seems highly likely that Cudworth allowed Rust to use his personal library in 1656.[59]

Cudworth's close supervision of Rust during the preparation of *Messias in S. Scriptura* is further suggested by the fact that he made extensive use of Christian Hebraist sources. The Cambridge University statutes required that a BD candidate should have attended daily lectures in Hebrew for five years,[60] and it would seem that Cudworth was trying to encourage Rust as a budding Hebraist. Rust's underlying argument was that Christians, who were now able to exercise competent Hebrew scholarship in reading the Old Testament,[61] were better placed to interpret prophecies of the time when the Messiah should come than were Jews, whose reliance on the rabbinic literature collected in the Talmud often led them to accept false, or even ridiculous, interpretations of Scripture. Cudworth was an excellent Hebraist,[62] but, despite his own study and Cudworth's encouragement, Rust's Hebrew seems to have been limited. There is no evidence that he read the Hebrew Bible or the Talmud himself; rather, he worked entirely

Robinson was active. For the full version of this section, see Origen, *Contra Celsum*, ed. Spencer, 110–11; Origen, *Contra Celsum*, trans. Henry Chadwick (Cambridge, 1980), 2.79 on 127–8.

[58] Edward Millington, *Bibliotheca Cudworthiana* (London, 1691).

[59] Rust is unlikely to have had much money for the purchase of his own books. Peile, *Christ's*, 160–4, 174–5, notes the financial difficulties of the college during the Interregnum. There is no extant evidence that Rust, who had been a sizar at St Catharine's (see Day, 'George Rust', 4), had any source of income other than his fellowship. Morgan, 'Tutors and Students', in Victor Morgan and Christopher Brooke, *A History of the University of Cambridge*, ii: *1546–1750* (Cambridge, 2004), 314–42 on 325, notes that 'the private relationship between a tutor and his aristocratic students was also a supplementary source of earnings'; in 1656, Rust was tutor to two fellow commoners, George Fell and Richard Pettus, for whom see Peile, *Biographical Register*, 1: 569, 571, but nothing is known of his relationship with these students' families. Sarah Hutton has kindly shared with me her notes on Huntington Library, San Marino, CA, Hastings MS 14505, a letter from Edward Lord Conway to George Rawdon, which reports Henry Stubbe's comment that, at Rust's death in 1670, his library consisted chiefly of Socinian books which were not valuable as they had been reprinted.

[60] Heywood (ed.), *Collection of Statutes*, 291.

[61] See Stephen G. Burnett, *Christian Hebraism in the Reformation Era (1500–1660): Authors, Books, and the Transmission of Jewish Learning* (Leiden, 2012).

[62] David S. Katz, 'The Abendana Brothers and the Christian Hebraists of Seventeenth-Century England', *Journal of Ecclesiastical History* 40 (1989), 28–52, on 40–1.

from books containing Latin explanations of the meaning and context of Hebrew words. Cudworth owned a number of works by Johannes Buxtorf the elder, professor of Hebrew at the University of Basel from 1591 to 1629, the Christian Hebraist who probably did more than any other scholar to make it possible for Christians to learn Hebrew without the aid of a Jewish teacher, but his *Lexicon Hebraicum et Chaldaicum* of 1607 seems to account for Rust's references. Rust also used Buxtorf's violently anti-Jewish *Synagoga Judaica* of 1641.[63]

Rust drew his material mainly from the polemical writings of Christian Hebraists, composed for the purpose of exposing Jewish errors. Several of the works Rust used contained Hebrew texts with Latin translations and commentaries. The oldest of these was *Pugio Fidei* (The Dagger of Faith) by the thirteenth-century Dominican Friar Raymundus Martini, a massively learned handbook containing passages from the Talmud with Latin translations and highly critical commentary, designed for the use of Christian preachers tasked with converting Iberian Jews. Although *Pugio Fidei* had long circulated influentially in manuscript, Rust used the printed edition of 1651, with annotations by the Catholic Joseph de Voisin of the Sorbonne.[64] Rust also drew on the annotated translations from Hebrew to Latin of the Dutch Calvinist Constantijn L'Empereur, professor of Hebrew at the University of Leiden from 1627 to 1646. His commentary on the *Itinerary* of Benjamin of Tudela, a Spanish traveller of the twelfth century, and his super-commentary on the paraphrase of Daniel by Joseph ben David ibn Yahya, a sixteenth-century Italian grammarian and philosopher, both published in 1633, were designed to show the errors of these Jewish writers.[65]

---

[63] Johannes Buxtorf, *Lexicon Hebraicum et Chaldaicum* (Basel, 1607), reprinted many times—Cudworth owned the 1631 edn, for which see Millington, *Bibliotheca*, 19; idem, *Synagoga Judaica* (Basel, 1603), also reprinted many times—Cudworth owned the 1641 edn; Millington *Bibliotheca*, 7. Millington lists other works by Buxtorf on 1, 3, 7, 12, 17, 19, 21, and 24. For Buxtorf, see Stephen G. Burnett, *From Christian Hebraism to Jewish Studies: Johannes Buxtorf (1564–1629) and Hebrew Learning in the Seventeenth Century* (Leiden, 1996).

[64] Raymundus Martini, *Pugio Fidei adversus Mauros et Judaeos*, ed. Joseph de Voisin (Paris, 1651); Millington, *Bibliotheca*, 1. For Martini, see Robert Chazan, *Daggers of Faith: Thirteenth-Century Christian Missionizing and Jewish Response* (Berkeley, 1989), esp. 115–36.

[65] Constantijn L'Empereur, *Masa'ot shel Rabi Binyamin; Itinerarium D. Beniaminis* (Leiden, 1633); Millington, *Bibliotheca*, 7, says Cudworth owned the 1634 edn. but I have not found this; English translations, *The Itinerary of Rabbi Benjamin of Tudela*, trans and ed. Adolf Asher 2 vols. (London & Berlin, 1840); *The World of Benjamin of Tudela: A Medieval Mediterranean Travelogue*, trans. and ed. Sandra Benjamin (Rutherford, NJ & London, 1995). Constantijn L'Empereur, *Perush Don Yosef Ibn Yahya 'al Daniyel; Paraphrasis Dn. Iosephi Iachiadae in Danielem* (Amsterdam, 1633); Millington, *Bibliotheca*, 4, says Cudworth owned the 1643 edn, but I have not found this. For L'Empereur, see Peter T. van Rooden, 'Constantijn L'Empereur's Contacts with the Amsterdam Jews and his Confutation of

Rust used *De Bello Judaico* (The Jewish War) and *Antiquitates Judaicae* (Jewish Antiquities) by the first-century Jewish historian Flavius Josephus in a Greek/Latin edition,[66] but the only modern Jewish writer consulted by Rust was Menasseh Ben Israel, whom Cudworth and More both met personally sometime between September 1655 and October 1657.[67] Rust referred to him as a 'praiseworthy author' and accepted some of his expositions of Hebrew words, but he was also quite critical of his interpretations of prophecy. Menasseh's *Conciliator*, heavily used by Rust, was an attempt to reconcile apparently divergent passages in the Old Testament; it was originally written in Spanish for Menasseh's Sephardic community in Amsterdam but was widely known from the Latin translation by Dionysius Vossius, published in Amsterdam in 1633.[68] Without mentioning the title, Rust used Menasseh's Latin *De Resurrectione Mortuorum* (The Resurrection of the Dead), published in 1636, also in Amsterdam.[69] Rust also cited Menasseh's *Humble Addresses* to the Lord Protector, published in English in 1655 while the rabbi was hoping that Cromwell would make a formal proclamation to readmit the Jews.[70]

Judaism', in J. van den Berg and Ernestine G.E. van der Wall (eds), *Jewish-Christian Relations in the Seventeenth Century: Studies and Documents* (Dordrecht, 1988), 51–72; idem, *Theology, Biblical Scholarship, and Rabbinical Studies in the Seventeenth Century: Constantijn L'Empereur (1591–1648), Professor of Hebrew Theology at Leiden* (Leiden, 1989); Marvin J. Heller, *The Seventeenth-Century Hebrew Book: An Abridged Thesaurus*, 2 vols. (Leiden, 2011), 1: 505, 524–5.

[66] Flavius Josephus, *Hierosolymitani Sacerdotis: Opera quae exstant* (Geneva, 1634), *Antiquitates Judaicae*, 1–703, *De Bello Judaico*, 705–1032; Millington, *Bibliotheca*, 2; English translation, *Josephus*, trans. Louis H. Feldman, Henry St J. Thackray, and Allen Paul Wikgren, 9 vols. (London, 1958–1965), 2–3. for *Jewish War*, 4–9. for *Jewish Antiquities*.

[67] *Two Choice and Useful Treatises* [ed. More], annotations to *Lux Orientalis*, 27; Richard Kidder, *A Demonstration of the Messias*, 3 vols. (London 1684–1700), 2: [sig] A4, 3: pp. iii–iv; Jan van den Berg, 'Menasseh Ben Israel, Henry More and Johannes Hoornbeeck on the Pre-existence of the Soul', in Yosef Kaplan, Henry Méchoulan, and Richard H. Popkin (eds), *Menasseh Ben Israel and his World* (Leiden, 1989), 98–116 on 98; David S. Katz, 'Henry More and the Jews', in Sarah Hutton (ed.), *Henry More (1614–1687): Tercentenary Studies* (Dordrecht, 1990), 173–88 on 178, 187 nn.33–4.

[68] Menasseh Ben Israel, *Conciliator, sive de convenientia locorum S. Scripturae, quae pugnare inter se videntur* (Amsterdam, 1633); English translation, *The Conciliator of R. Manasseh* [sic] *Ben Israel*, trans. E. H. Lindo, 2 vols. (London, 1842); Millington, *Bibliotheca*, 5 lists the 1632 edn, but this was the Spanish edn, and Millington gives the Latin title; for this quotation, see *Messias in S. Scriptura promissus olim venit*, 78 below. For Menasseh Ben Israel, see Kaplan et al., *Menasseh Ben Israel*; Sina Rauschenbach, 'Mediating Jewish Knowledge: Menasseh Ben Israel and the Christian Respublica Litteraria', *Jewish Quarterly Review* 102 (2012), 561–88.

[69] Menasseh Ben Israel, *De Resurrectione Mortuorum* (Amsterdam, 1636); Millington, *Bibliotheca*, 9.

[70] Menasseh Ben Israel, *To His Highnesse the Lord Protector of the Common-Wealth of England, Scotland, and Ireland* (London, 1655), 9; Millington, *Bibliotheca*, does not list this pamphlet.

Rust consulted other books published in the Netherlands. Not surprisingly, he read Hugo Grotius' *De Veritate Religionis Christianae* (The Truth of the Christian Religion) of 1640, a work by the Dutch Arminian jurist whose commitment to religious toleration resonated with the thinking of the Origenian Platonists, although, like them, he strongly refuted Judaism.[71] Although Rust did not specifically mention Simon Episcopius, the Dutch Remonstrant who systematized the theology of Jacobus Arminius, he definitely used the first volume of his *Opera Theologica*, published posthumously in Amsterdam in 1650. Episcopius' section on the Messiah in his *Institutiones Theologicae* contains three successive chapters which discuss Rust's three Old Testament texts in the same order as Rust presented them, and Rust drew on these chapters very heavily, including the copying of several distinctive quotations. But he once assigned an Episcopius quotation to Raymundus Martini and kept quiet about using this source, perhaps because the theology of Episcopius was so abhorrent to the Calvinists who dominated the Cambridge Divinity School in 1656. None of Rust's use of Episcopius is particularly Arminian; but the mention of his name might have seriously jeopardized the success of Rust's exercise. Cudworth later acquired the 1675 London edition of Episcopius' works, but the 1650 first volume in the Christ's College Old Library might well be the very copy used by Rust.[72]

Rust also used the works of two Dutch Calvinists, Antonius Hulsius and Joannes Hoornbeek, both of whom wrote to refute the arguments of Menasseh Ben Israel concerning the timing of the Messiah. *Riv Adonai 'im Yehudah, sive Theologiae Iudaicae pars prima de Messia* (The Lord's Contention with Judah, or Jewish Theology, part one, of the Messiah), published by Hulsius in 1653, some years before he became professor of Theology and Hebrew at the University of Leiden in 1676, contained a good deal of Hebrew text translated into Latin.[73] Hoornbeek's *Teshuvat Yehudah, sive,*

[71] Hugo Grotius, *De Veritate Religionis Christianae* (Leiden, 1640), bk 5 refutes Judaism; Millington, *Bibliotheca*, 8. This was the first edn containing Grotius' extensive notes; although there were several earlier translations of the main text, the first English translation containing the notes was *The Truth of the Christian Religion*, trans. John Clarke (London, 1711). For Grotius, see Jan-Paul Heering, *Hugo Grotius as Apologist for the Christian Religion: A Study of his Work De Veritate Religionis Christianae (1640)* (Leiden, 2004), 144–55 for the Jews, 236 for Clarke's translation.

[72] Simon Episcopius, *Opera Theologica,* 2 vols. (Amsterdam, 1650–1665), 1: *Institutiones Theologicae*, 3.4.6–8 on 163–71; Christ's College Old Library, classmark B.7.6: no information available as to when this volume was acquired; Millington, *Bibliotheca*, 1; for Rust's erroneous assignment of an Episcopius reference to Martini, see *Messias in S. Scriptura promissus olim venit*, 63 below. For Episcopius, see Frederick Calder, *Memoirs of Simon Episcopius* (New York, 1837).

[73] Antonius Hulsius, *Riv Adonai 'im Yehudah, sive Theologiae Iudaicae pars prima de Messia* (Breda, 1653); Millington, *Bibliotheca*, 4; for Hulsius, see *Nieuw Nederlandsch Biografisch*

Pro Convincendis et Convertendis Judaeis (The Repentance of Judah, or, To Refute and Convert the Jews), mainly a Latin text, was published in 1655, a year after he became professor of Theology at Leiden.[74] Two English works apparently not owned by Cudworth were *Daniels Weeks* (1643) and *Diatribae* (1648) by Joseph Mede, a fellow of Christ's from 1613 to 1638; Rust might well have used the copies which still remain in the Christ's College Old Library. Mede had been the foremost scholarly millenarian of his day; while he never declared himself to be an Arminian, he was firmly opposed to the Calvinist doctrine of double predestination.[75] Neither did Cudworth own the Latin *De Templo* (1592) by the Spanish Jesuit Francisco Ribera, who was primarily known for his futurist interpretation of the Book of Revelation, although this book recalls the subject of Cudworth's earliest lectures as Regius professor of Hebrew in 1645 on the Temple of Jerusalem.[76] Finally, the only work published in England except for those of Mede, but one which Cudworth did own, was the Latin *Annales* of the Calvinist Archbishop of Armagh James Ussher, published in two parts in 1650 and 1654. Ussher, who famously dated the creation of the world to 4004BC, assembled a universal chronology synchronizing biblical and pagan sources, culminating in the coming of the Messiah, Jesus Christ, at the correct time.[77]

This reading list shows that Rust used books by Roman Catholic, Calvinist, and Arminian authors impartially: all were useful in refuting

Woordenboek 10 vols. (Leiden, 1911–1937), 8: 888–9: < http://resources.huygens.knaw.nl/ retroboeken/nnbw/#page=0&accessor=accessor_index&view=homePane>; Burnett, *Christian Hebraism*, 130, 288.

[74] Joannes Hoornbeek, *Teshuvat Yehudah, sive, pro convincendis et convertendis Judaeis* (Leiden, 1655); Millington, *Bibliotheca*, 4, indicates that Cudworth owned the 1645 edn, certainly an error. For Hoornbeek, see *Nieuw Nederlandsch Biografisch Woordenboek*, 8: 843 (see n.73 above for website); van den Berg, 'Pre-existence of the Soul', 112–16; Burnett, *Christian Hebraism*, 130, 288.

[75] Joseph Mede, *Daniels Weeks: an Interpretation of part of the Prophecy of Daniel* (London, 1643), 139–76, Christ's College Old Library, classmark A7.29 (viii); idem, *Diatribae. Discourses on Divers Texts of Scripture* (London, 1648), Genesis 49:10, 100–107, Christ's College Old Library, classmark C.15.30 (two other copies were donated later). For Mede, see [Worthington?], 'Life', in *Works*, pp. i–xlv, especially pp. xviii–xix; Jue, *Heaven upon Earth,* especially pp. 25–30, 44–57.

[76] Francisco Ribera, *De Templo, & de iis quae ad Templum pertinent* (Salamanca, 1591; Leiden, 1592; Antwerp, 1602), this book does not appear in Millington, *Bibliotheca*, nor is it held in the Old Library at Christ's College. For Ribera, see Jean-Robert Armogathe, 'Interpretations of the Revelation of John: 1500–1800', in Bernard McGinn (ed.), *The Encyclopedia of Apocalypticism*, 3 vols. (New York & London, 2000), 2: 185–203 on 189–90. For Cudworth's lectures, see Birch, 'Life and Writings of Cudworth', p. vii.

[77] James Ussher, *Annales*, 2 vols. (London, 1650–1654); Millington, *Bibliotheca*, 11; English version, by the author, *The Annals of the World* (London, 1658); for Ussher, see James Barr, 'Why the World was Created in 4004 B.C.: Archbishop Ussher and Biblical Chronology', *Bulletin of the John Rylands University Library of Manchester* 67 (1985), 575–608; Graham Parry, *Trophies of Time: English Antiquarians of the Seventeenth Century* (Oxford, 1995), 130–56.

Jewish objections to the Christian claim that Jesus of Nazareth was the Messiah. The catholicity of his reading is reinforced by the fact that continental books outnumbered those published in England, with books published in the Netherlands heavily represented. And Rust's reading was up to date: about a third of the books he used were published from 1650 onwards, namely Episcopius's works, de Voisin's edition of Martini, and the books by Hulsius and Hoornbeek, all of which he drew upon substantially. But to what extent can this exercise be classified as an Origenian text? The argument from Genesis 49:10 appears early in the *Philocalia* of Origen and in *Contra Celsum* but receives much more extensive treatment in several of the works mentioned above, as the annotations to Rust's text below will show.[78] *Messias in S. Scriptura* is not, in itself, a deeply Origenian text. Its Origenian significance lies in Cudworth's influence, which allowed Rust to present a safely orthodox argument while avoiding confrontation with the prevailing Calvinism of the University of Cambridge in 1656.

The Holy Scripture Tells of the Resurrection from the Dead, nor does Reason Oppose It

Two years later, when explicit public support for Origen was briefly possible, Rust made a significant contribution to the Origenian Platonist moment in both his Act verses and his discourse *Resurrectionem è Mortuis S. Scriptura tradit, nec refragatur Ratio*. The Act verses, distributed to the audience immediately before the BD disputation on Commencement Day, served as poetic souvenirs of the two theses on which Rust was prepared to dispute.[79] The argument of the first, 'Scripture teaches the resurrection from the dead, and reason does not contradict this', coincided with his discourse, to be discussed in this section. The second, 'The soul, separated from the body, does not sleep', was a refutation of psychopannychism—the doctrine that the soul sleeps at the death of the body—and mortalism—the doctrine that the soul dies with the body—to be awakened or revivified for reunification with the resurrected body at the final judgement.[80] While there is no extant writing of Origen on these doctrines, Eusebius of Caesarea reported that Origen was able to restore to orthodox belief some

---

[78] *Origenis Philocalia*, ed. Jean Tarin (Paris, 1618), ch. 1 on 5–6; Millington, *Bibliotheca*, 5; *The Philocalia of Origen*, trans. George Lewis (Edinburgh, 1911), 1.3 on 3–4; Origen, *Contra Celsum*, trans. Chadwick, 1.53 on 49; 5.32 on 289 n.5.

[79] Buck's Book, p. lxxxii; Hall, *Act and Tripos Verses*, 3–8, 154–5.

[80] For psychopannychism and mortalism, see Brian W. Young, '"The Soul-Sleeping System": Politics and Heresy in Eighteenth-Century England', *Journal of Ecclesiastical History* 45 (1994), 64–81 on 69–74; Bryan W. Ball, *The Soul Sleepers: Christian Mortalism from Wycliffe to Priestley* (Cambridge 2008), 19–21.

'Arabians' who mistakenly believed that 'the human soul dies for a while in this present time, along with our bodies, at their death, and with them turns to corruption; but that hereafter, at the time of the resurrection, it will come to life again along with them'.[81] I have discussed elsewhere the anti-Hobbist and anti-Calvinist implications of the Origenian Platonist rejection of psychopannychism and mortalism.[82] More, Cudworth, and later Henry Hallywell all refuted these doctrines as incompatible with an Origenian understanding of the naturally immortal, immaterial soul, which journeys, fully alive and conscious, in successive vehicles towards its divine goal.[83]

While Cudworth's encouragement can still be discerned in the preparation of Rust's position *Resurrectionem è Mortuis*, the more immediate influence on him in 1658 was More. Rust drew on material from More's *Conjectura Cabbalistica* of 1653 and his *Enthusiasmus Triumphatus* of 1656,[84] but there is strong evidence that he also had access to More's as yet unpublished *The Immortality of the Soul* of 1659 and *An Explanation of the Grand Mystery of Godliness* of 1660. In *The Immortality of the Soul*, More set out, on the basis of reason, his belief in the pre-existence of the soul, its fall into a terrestrial body, and its afterlife in first an aerial and then an etherial body on its return to its divine source. In the explicitly Christian *Grand Mystery of Godliness*, More discussed belief in the resurrection of the dead.[85] Many strong similarities between Rust's text and these deeply Origenian works demonstrate that he must have discussed their contents with More. But Cudworth, too, would later discuss the journey of the soul in an Origenian manner. Indeed, resemblances between Rust's 1658 discourse and Cudworth's *The True Intellectual System of the Universe*, completed in 1671 but not published until 1678, suggest that Rust also consulted him while preparing his text.[86]

Resurrectionem è Mortuis was an exposition of I Corinthians 15, St Paul's discussion of the resurrection body, to which Rust gave a definite Origenian

[81] Eusebius, *The Ecclesiastical History*, trans. J.E.L. Oulton and H.J. Lawlor, 2 vols. (Cambridge, MA, 1926–1942), 2: 6.37 on 90–1.

[82] Marilyn A. Lewis, 'Expanding the Origenist Moment: Nathaniel Ingelo, George Rust and Henry Hallywell', *Adamantiana* 11 (Münster, forthcoming).

[83] Henry More, *Antipsychopannychia* in *Platonick Song*, ed. Jacob, 439–86; idem, *Immortality* of the Soul [sig] b^v; idem, *An Explanation of the Grand Mystery of Godliness* (London, 1660), 1.6–10 on 15–30; Cudworth, *True Intellectual System* (1678), 1.5.3 on 799–800; [Henry Hallywell], *A Private Letter of Satisfaction to a Friend* (n.p., 1667), 2–31.

[84] Henry More, *Conjectura Cabbalistica. Or, A Conjectural Essay of Interpreting the Minde of Moses, according to the Threefold Cabbala* (London, 1653); idem, *Enthusiasmus Triumphatus, or, a Discourse of the Nature, Causes, Kinds, and Cure, of Enthusiasme* (London, 1656).

[85] More, *Immortality of the Soul*; idem, *Grand Mystery of Godliness*, 1.6.6–10 on 15–30, 6.3.3–6 on 221–30.

[86] Cudworth, *True Intellectual System* (1678), 1.5.3 on 785–806.

cast. He asked whether the resurrection body will be the terrestrial body restored to life and healed of all corruption or whether it will be a new body which nevertheless retains personal identity. He then argued that it will not consist of matter numerically identical to that of the terrestrial body, but that a new aerial body will maintain personal identity by its vital connection to the same soul. The soul must always be united to some kind of matter, but to insist on the resurrection of the terrestrial body only exposed the Christian religion to derision. Origen had stated that 'Neither we nor the divine scriptures maintain that those long dead will rise up from the earth and live in the same bodies without undergoing any change for the better', and he identified that necessary change as the clothing of the immaterial soul with an aerial vehicle.[87] More, in his *Grand Mystery of Godliness*, challenged those who believed 'That the Mysterie of the *Resurrection* implies *the resuscitation of the same numerical body*'. He affirmed that 'as God gives to the blades of corn grains quite distinct from that which was sown, so at the Resurrection he will give the Soul a Body quite different from that which was buried'.[88] Twenty years later, Cudworth's version of this argument was 'that *the Christian Mystery, of the Resurrection of Life*, consisteth not in the Souls being reunited to these Vile Rags of Mortality, these *Gross Bodies* of ours (such as now they are) but in having them *Changed into the Likeness of Christ's Glorious Body*, and in this *Mortal's putting on Immortality*'.[89]

While Rust's insistence on the soul as an 'incorporeal substance' was surely a refutation of the materialism of Thomas Hobbes,[90] he was also pursuing an anti-Calvinist agenda. In his *Institutes of the Christian Religion*, Calvin had condemned 'the error of those who imagine that the souls will not receive the same bodies with which they are now clothed but will be furnished with new and different ones'. He had asserted that 'Scripture [does not] define anything more clearly than the resurrection of the flesh that we now bear', although 'the quality [of that flesh] will be different'.[91]

---

[87] Origen discusses the resurrection body in *Contra Celsum*, trans. Chadwick, 5.17–19 on 277–9, quotation on 277, 5.23 on 281, 7.32 on 420–1, 8.49–50 on 488–9; idem, *On First Principles*, trans. G.W. Butterworth (Gloucester MA, 1973), 2.10.1–3 on 138–41, 2.11.6 on 152, 3.6.4–7 on 249–53.

[88] More, *Grand Mystery of Godliness*, 6.4.3 on 224.

[89] Cudworth, *True Intellectual System* (1678), 1.5.3 on 795–9, quotation on 799; See Lloyd Strickland, 'The Doctrine of "The Resurrection of the Same Body" in Early Modern Thought', *Religious Studies*, 46 (2010), 163–83, on 164, 180 n.10, for More and Cudworth.

[90] Jon Parkin, *Taming the Leviathan: The Reception of the Political and Religious Ideas of Thomas Hobbes in England 1640–1700* (Cambridge, 2007), 92, 119; Richard W. Serjeantson, 'The Soul', in Desmond M. Clarke and Catherine Wilson (eds), *The Oxford Handbook of Philosophy in Early Modern Europe* (Oxford, 2011), 119–41 on 135–6.

[91] Calvin, *Institutes of the Christian Religion*, ed. John T. McNeill, trans. Ford Lewis Battles, 2 vols. (London, 1960), 2: 3.25.7–8 on 998–1003, quotations on 999, 1002.

Thus, Rust's 1658 discourse was an attack on Calvinism and will have been understood as such by his auditors. While Rust did not explicitly cite the Arminian Thomas Jackson's *Maran atha: or Dominus veniet* of 1657, this commentary on the clause in the Apostle's Creed on the 'resurrection of the body' was extensively used in Rust's discourse.[92] Jackson stated that the '*Identity or unitie of matter* is less needfull unto the numerical unitie or Identitie of mans body, because the soul of man, amongst all other vegetables, is only immortal, and remaineth the same it was after it be severed from the body'; therefore, the resurrection body maintains personal identity rather than requiring material exactitude.[93] Rust's use of Jackson is particularly significant, in that little evidence of the Cambridge Origenian Platonists' reading of Jackson has yet been identified.[94] Rust did, however, acknowledge in this discourse his use of the writings of Simon Episcopius, although he casually located his reference as 'somewhere in Episcopius'.[95]

Rust's classical and patristic references represent sources beloved of his Origenian Platonist mentors.[96] From classical Greek sources, Rust cited Homer's *Iliad* on the incorporeal nature of the gods, the *Golden Verses* of Pythagoras on the immortal aerial body, Hippocrates' treatise *Heart* on the 'pure and luminous bath' from a distillation of the blood which nourishes human intelligence, and Diogenes Laertius' *Lives of the Eminent Philosophers* on the fine and delicate substance of the soul.[97] Rust also referred to Hermes Trismegistus on the aerial vehicle of the soul; this was an essential source for More and Cudworth, despite Isaac Causabon's unmasking of

[92] Thomas Jackson, *Maran atha or Dominus veniet: Commentaries upon these Articles of the Creed never before Printed* (London, 1657), section 4, 'Of the Resurrection of the Dead', 3421–3467, quotation at 11.15.7 on 3451. This is vol. 11 of 12 vols of commentaries upon the creed, published with separate titles 1613–57, although Jackson had died in 1640. For Jackson, see Sarah Hutton, 'Thomas Jackson, Oxford Platonist, and William Twisse, Aristotelian', *Journal of the History of Ideas* 39 (1978), 635–52; eadem, 'Plato in the Tudor Academies', in Francis Ames-Lewis (ed.), *Sir Thomas Gresham and Gresham College* (Aldershot, 1999), 106–24 on 115–18; A. J. Hegarty, 'Jackson, Thomas (*bap.* 1578, *d.* 1640)', in ODNB; James Bryson, *The Christian Platonism of Thomas Jackson* (Leuven, 2016).

[93] Jackson, *Maran atha*, 11.15.8 on 3451.

[94] See Bryson, *Christian Platonism*, 3.

[95] Episcopius, *Opera Theologica*, 1; for quotation, see *Resurrectionem è Mortuis S. Scriptura tradit*, 27/24/2B below.

[96] Here, no effort has been made to identify the particular editions Rust used; rather, the annotations to his text below will identify the influence of More, Cudworth, and Jackson on Rust's choice of quotations.

[97] Homer, *Iliad: Books 1–12*, trans A. T. Murray, rev. William F. Wyatt 2 vols., 2nd edn (Cambridge, MA, 1999), 2: 5.341 on 230–1; *The Pythagorean Golden Verses*, trans. and ed. Johan C. Thom (Leiden, 1995), verses 70–1 on 98–9; *Hippocrates*, trans. and ed. Paul Potter 10 vols. (Cambridge, MA, 1923–2010), 'Heart', 9: 58–69, at ch. 11 on 67; Diogenes Laertius, *Lives of the Eminent Philosophers*, trans. Robert D. Hicks 2 vols. (Cambridge, MA, 1958–9), 2: 7.157 on 260–1, 9.19 on 426–7, 10.63 (Epicurus) on 592–3.

the *Corpus Hermeticum* as a Greek text from the early Christian era rather than an ancient Egyptian text.[98] Rust again used Josephus's *Jewish War*.[99] His classical Latin sources were Cicero's *Dream of Scipio*, a vision of immortality, and book six of Virgil's *Aeneid*, the journey of Aeneas to Hades.[100] The patristic writers cited by Rust were Tertullian and Augustine. Although Rust referred explicitly only once to Tertullian's *On the Resurrection of the Flesh*, he seems to have known this work well.[101] He occasionally agreed with it but more frequently attempted to confute Tertullian's contention that the soul itself is corporeal and that the resurrection body will be constituted of the same numerical flesh as the terrestrial body, despite having 'put on incorruptibility'. His quotation from Augustine came from the exposition of I Corinthians 15 in his *Answer to Adimantus*.[102] Rust's philological interests had largely shifted from the Hebrew of his earlier discourse to the Greek of the New Testament and the Septuagint, although he briefly cited Menasseh Ben Israel's *De Resurrectione Mortuorum* on several Old Testament passages.[103]

While this is not the place to engage in a lengthy discussion of the authorship of *A Letter of Resolution concerning Origen*, I would suggest that *Resurrectionem è Mortuis* proves only that Rust was an important member of More's and Cudworth's Origenian Platonist circle at Christ's College, not that he was the author of the *Letter*. While the long section at the end of the *Letter* concerning the resurrection body contains some arguments very similar to those of Rust's position, they have been handled rather differently: references in the annotations to *Resurrectionem è Mortuis* below will enable the reader to compare the two texts closely. Further, the style of the *Letter* suggests a different author from that of Rust's two English texts from his Cambridge years, *A Discourse of Truth* and *God is Love*, and from the two English sermons from his subsequent time in Ireland, *A Sermon*

---

[98] *Hermetica: The Ancient Greek and Latin Writings which contain Religious or Philosophic Teachings ascribed to Hermes Trismegistus*, trans. and ed. Walter Scott 4 vols. (Oxford, 1924–1936), 1: 12.14a on 230–1. For Isaac Casaubon on the *Corpus Hermetica*, see Anthony Grafton, Joanna Weinberg, and Alastair Hamilton, *'I have always loved the holy tongue': Isaac Casaubon, the Jews, and a Forgotten Chapter in Renaissance Scholarship* (Cambridge, MA, 2011), 30–42.

[99] *Josephus*, trans. Thackray, *Jewish War*, 3: 6.199–213 on 434–7.

[100] Cicero, *Laelius, on Friendship & the Dream of Scipio*, trans. and ed. J.G.F. Powell, (Warminster, 1990), *Somnium Scipionis*, sect. 8 on 144–5; *Virgil*, trans. H. Rushton Fairclough, rev. George P. Goold, 2 vols. (Cambridge, MA, 2004), 1: *Aeneid*, 6.714–15 and 730–4 on 582–3, 6.745–7 on 584–5.

[101] *The Writings of Quintus Sept. Flor. Tertullianus*, trans. Peter Holmes 2 vols. (Edinburgh, 1870–1872), *On the Resurrection of the Flesh*, 2: 215–332.

[102] Augustine, *The Manichean Debate*, ed. Roland Teske and Boniface Ramsey (New York, 2006), *Answer to Adimantus, a Disciple of Mani*, ch. 12 on 190–4.

[103] See n.69 above.

preached at New-Town and *A Funeral Sermon preached at the Obsequies of… Jeremy [Taylor]*.[104] *A Sermon preached at New-Town* contains a defence of the immortality of the soul, while the funeral sermon for Taylor discusses life in heaven, making them the natural successors to Rust's 1658 position, within the pastoral context of a funeral address. *A Private Letter of Satisfaction to a Friend*, published anonymously by Hallywell in 1667,[105] definitely reflects Rust's influence and should be included within this closely related family of texts, so references to this work also appear in the notes to *Resurrectionem è Mortuis* below.

Provenance of the Texts and Editorial Principles

Messias in S. Scriptura promissus olim venit was published in Latin in 1686 in Henry Hallywell's edition of Rust's *Remains*.[106] Hallywell said nothing of the provenance of this text, the manuscript of which is no longer extant, so we do not know whether he had a Rust holograph or a complete copy or perhaps the notes of someone who was present at the oral exercise. Hallywell was not admitted to Christ's College until 11 May 1657, so any notes from which he might have written up the exercise were unlikely to have been his own.[107] Hallywell gave no indication as to why he did not translate this exercise into English, as he had done with Rust's *Discourse of the Use of Reason*. It seems likely that he thought that it would not be of interest to the general reader, while the academically trained reader would find no linguistic barrier in the Latin text. Hallywell's introductory notes contain his own thinking on why God has allowed the Jews to remain opposed to Christian belief, rather than comments on Rust's text.[108]

Rust's Act verses, *Resurrectionem e mortuis Scriptura docet nec refragatur Ratio* and *Anima separata non dormit*, are apparently extant only in the printed broadsheet which was distributed as Rust stood up to dispute at the University of Cambridge Commencement Day Divinity Act. To the best of my knowledge, only one copy survives, in the collection of such

---

[104] Rust, *Remains*, 1–46; idem, *A Sermon preached at New-Town the 29 of Octob. 1663. At the Funeral of the Right Honourable Hugh Earl of Mount-Alexander* (Dublin, 1664); idem, *A Funeral Sermon, preached at the Obsequies of the Right Reverend Father in God, Jeremy Lord Bishop of Down: Who deceased at Lysburne, August 13th 1667* (London, 1668).

[105] See n.83 above.

[106] Rust, *Remains*, 47–80; digital images at Early English Books Online, < http://eebo.chadwyck.com>.

[107] Peile, *Biographical Register*, 1: 577.

[108] Rust, *Remains*, [sigs] [a-a 4]; Lewis, 'Messiah Promised', 59–60.

verses assembled by the antiquary Anthony Wood, now kept in the Bodleian Library in Oxford. The Latin verses are printed in two columns, with 'Julii 6. 1658. *In die Com. Respond.* Georgio Rust, *B.D. Coll.* Christi *Socio.*' at the foot of the page.[109] Marilyn Lewis transcribed these verses, and Christian Hengstermann translated them into English. Hengstermann is also preparing a corrected Latin version and a German translation, both of which will be published in Germany.[110]

Two manuscript copies of Rust's position, *Resurrectionem è Mortuis S. Scriptura tradit, nec refragatur Ratio*, are contained in the Hartlib Papers (MS 61) in Special Collections, Western Bank Library, at the University of Sheffield, at folios 27/24/1A-14B and 55/18/1A-13B.[111] The first of these is translated from the Latin and printed here. When he published Rust's *Remains* in 1686, Hallywell could not find this discourse, and he appealed to any reader who might have a copy to send it to the printer, Miles Flesher, or the bookseller, Walter Kettilby, promising its safe return.[112] Apparently none ever did, but the inclusion of the document among the Hartlib Papers can be explained. On 7 June 1659, Samuel Hartlib wrote to John Worthington that 'I shall speedily, God willing, return Mr Rust's Position, after it is once more perused to you', indicating that Worthington had sent it to the London 'intelligencer'.[113] The two copies of the discourse in the Hartlib Papers are both in the same scribal hand.[114] They do not differ significantly, except that the first (27/24) has annotations in the hand of the mathematician Nicolaus Mercator, a friend and regular correspondent of Hartlib.[115] As these are limited to corrections in the text, they have been

---

[109] Bodleian Library, Oxford, Wood 276a (CCCCLXIV), also mentioned in British Library, MS Harley, 7038, fol. 112; Hall, *Act and Tripos Verses*, 154–5.

[110] *A Letter of Resolution Concerning Origen and the Chief of His Opinions/Ein klärender Brief über Origenes und seine Hauptlehren. Einleitung, Text und Übersetzung*, trans. and ed. Christian Hengstermann, *Adamantiana* 9 (Münster, forthcoming).

[111] MSS and transcriptions at <http://www.hrionline.ac.uk/hartlib>, search on 27/24 and 55/13. I am grateful to Mary Sackett of the University of Sheffield Library for arranging access to digital images of these MSS before they were freely available online.

[112] Rust, *Remains*, title page, [sig.] [a 4]ᵛ.

[113] *Worthington Correspondence*, 1: 134; Richard W. Serjeantson, 'Herbert of Cherbury before Deism: The Early Reception of the *De Veritate*', *The Seventeenth Century* 16 (2001), 235 n.70; for Hartlib, see Mark Greengrass, 'Hartlib, Samuel (*c.*1600–1662)', in ODNB.

[114] For Hartlib's use of scribes, see <http://www.shef.ac.uk/library/special/hartlib>; for Rust's hand, see *State Papers Online I–IV: The Tudors, Stuarts and Commonwealth 1509–1714*, SP 63/324, fol. 22; SP 63/327, fol. 155, at <http://gale.cengage.co.uk/state-papers-online-15091714.aspx>; for Rust's signature, see British Library, London, Add. MS 22910, fol. 6, an attestation, dated 17 November 1655, that Cudworth was 'lawfully chosen' master of Christ's on 29 October 1654, signed by Rust and 6 other fellows.

[115] For Mercator, see D.T. Whiteside, 'Mercator, Nicolaus (Kauffman, Niklaus)', in *Complete Dictionary of Scientific Biography* (2008), Encyclopedia.com, at <http://www.

silently incorporated into this edition; their importance lies in the fact that Mercator read the text with care.

For the two discourses, our aim has been to produce a readable English text in which the sense of Rust's arguments can be clearly discerned. The technical quality of discourses prepared for academic disputation has made this particularly challenging, and the reader must understand that their intrinsic nature will always make the texts difficult and perhaps somewhat unattractive. Davide Secci initially supplied a literal translation of Rust's Latin, which Marilyn Lewis then edited as an English text. At a later stage, Hengstermann checked Lewis's English version against the Latin, to make sure that her English rendering had not strayed from the sense of Rust's original. Hengstermann also read and helpfully commented on an earlier draft of this introduction. The Greek and Hebrew words used by Rust presented particular problems. Their presence was required by Rust's need to prove his skill as a philologist, and much of his argument depended on their precise meaning. For this reason, we have retained them, adding English translations (where the meaning was not clear from the immediate context) in square brackets. While this might seem cumbersome, it will enable the reader who lacks knowledge of these languages to see what Rust was attempting to do with these words. Benjamin Williams transcribed and translated Rust's Hebrew. This was particularly difficult in the 1658 discourse, as the scribe who copied the Hebrew passages apparently did not know Hebrew and drew an approximation of the characters, working from left to right. Many of the Greek words in the 1658 discourse were faultily transliterated in the Sheffield transcription. Their correction and translation was the joint work of Secci, John Lewis, and Hengstermann. Most biblical references have been expanded in the texts or given in full in the notes; all quotations are from the Authorized Version, unless the Septuagint is specified.

The annotations are the work of Marilyn Lewis, with the identification of several classical references by Secci. They attempt to show which books Rust drew upon and how he combined material from a number of sources in constructing his own arguments. While he may well have been working on this material for some time, the topicality of both positions suggests a period of intense work immediately before their presentation. The titles of works and their authors' names cited by Rust, abbreviations of which were embedded in his texts, have been expanded for easy recognition. These works have then been searched for further correspondences with Rust's texts, and references to the pages and/or sections upon which he drew are

encyclopedia.com/doc/1G2-2830902917.html>; for Mercator's friendship with Hartlib, see <http://www.hrionline.ac.uk/hartlib/>, search on 'Mercator'.

given in the notes. Comparison of Rust's texts with these references builds up a picture of Rust working with two sets of books, under the close supervision of first Cudworth and then More, giving us a much clearer sense of how a BD candidate at Christ's College in the second half of the 1650s developed into a fully fledged Cambridge Origenian Platonist.

M. A. L.

Marilyn A. Lewis, independent scholar, 54 Sparrow Way, Greater Leys, Oxford, OX4 7GE, United Kingdom

Davide A. Secci, independent scholar
Christian Hengstermann, Research Associate, Faculty of Divinity, University of Cambridge

John H. Lewis, retired priest, Church of England
Benjamin Williams, Leverhulme Early Career Fellow, Department of Theology & Religious Studies, King's College London

The Messiah Promised in the Holy Scripture Came a Long Time Ago

[*The Remains of that Reverend and Learned Prelate, Dr George Rust*, ed. Henry Hallywell (London, 1686), page 47]

If the Holy Spirit had deemed it opportune to provide a full account of the conversation, narrated by the Evangelists, that our Saviour had with two disciples on the way to Emmaus after he had been raised from the dead,[1] how successfully could we have disentangled the present discussion, and with how little trouble could we have proved not only that the Messiah came, but also that he was Jesus of Nazareth himself! And furthermore, if the Jews' obstinacy had not required this apology, I might seem to be wasting time pointlessly in reinforcing the fact that the Messiah came, after the holy life, the celestial doctrine, the divine deeds, the glorious Resurrection of our Jesus, with all of which, and with other most certain arguments, he publicly proved that he himself was that promised and long-awaited Messiah. But since there is such a breed of worthless men who are so blinded by prejudice that in the light of noonday they would dare to deny that it is daytime, I considered demonstrating that our Jesus himself was the promised Messiah, since it is an accepted fact among liberal and judicious men that the stubborn incredulity of the Jews and their sworn hatred towards God's Christ cannot be justified by any means. In truth, considering this subject on a higher level, I easily persuaded myself that it required a longer disquisition than either your patience or the nature of this exercise could stand. So I digressed to that issue which is right in front of me, with the same wisdom and, as I hope, with the same success. In fact, since it was proved in the thesis that the Messiah came, I believe there will not be such a great dispute about it in the hypothesis. Having thus first given the explanation of the terms and of the issue (which are clear by themselves), I will establish our claim in what follows.

---

[1] Luke 24:13–35; this story does not appear in the other three Gospels.

Truly, it would not be out of place to make a preliminary attempt with a few arguments, especially since these, which should be presented as a prelude,

[page 48]

can bear some weight, at least among the Jews.

In the Talmud Tract *Sanhedrin* (as Raymundus Martini quotes in *Pugio Fidei*), the Rabbi says כלו כל הקיצין that all the marks are complete, that is, for the coming of the Messiah: there we find a discussion of that name.[2] In the same codex, chapter *Chelek*,[3] is found the lauded and celebrated saying of Elias, a Rabbi who was held in such honour among the Jews that by examining his words carefully they study them no less than the text of the Holy Scripture itself. 'Two thousand years confusion', he says, 'two thousand years the Law, two thousand years the Messiah', and the world is destroyed in one year. So, according to the tradition from the calculation of the Jews, the fourteen centuries destined for the coming and duration of the Messiah have already passed.[4] Furthermore, the great Hugo Grotius, in book five of *De Veritate Religionis Christianae*, a work worthy of such an author, says that a certain Hebrew scholar, Nehumias, who preceded Jesus by fifty years, had already openly said that the time of the Messiah prophesied by Daniel could not extend beyond those fifty years.[5] In the same Talmud Codex *Sanhedrin*, another certain Elias says to Rabbi Jehuda that 'the world will last not less than eighty-five Jubilees, and in the last Jubilee the son of David will come'. It is well known that the Jubilee is composed of fifty years, and, because of this, eighty-five Jubilees together provide a total of 4,250 years. Thus he was supposed to come at the beginning of the fifth millennium. In the same place the Rabbi says 'the son of David will not come until the wicked reign of Edom (i.e. of the Romans) has lasted

---

[2] Raymundus Martini, *Pugio Fidei adversus Mauros et Judaeos, cum observationibus Iosephi de Voisin* (Paris, 1651), de Voisin, 2.2 on 214–15.

[3] *Chelek* = portion; it occurs among the first words of the eleventh chapter.

[4] See *The Babylonian Talmud*, ed. Jacob Shachter, Harry Freedman, and Isidore Epstein, 35 vols, (London, 1935–1948), 23: *Sanhedrin*, 97a–b on 657. Rust could have found comments on this passage in: Menasseh Ben Israel, *De Resurrectione Mortuorum* (Amsterdam, 1636), 3.3–4 on 263–77; Johann Buxtorf, *Synagoga Judaica* (Basel, 1641), 439; *The Jewish Synagogue*, trans. A. B. (London, 1657), 314; Simon Episcopius, *Opera Theologica*, 2 vols. (Amsterdam, 1650–1665), *Institutiones Theologicae*, 1: 3.4.2 on 157; Martini, *Pugio Fidei*, 2.10.1–2 on 315–16; Joannes Hoornbeek, *Teshuvat Yehudah, sive Pro convincendis et convertendis Judaeis* (Leiden, 1655), 2.1 on 180. Rust simply copies names of rabbis and their sayings from his secondary sources, so no attempt has been made in this edition to identify them; for the difficulties involved in identifying rabbis, see Hermann L. Strack and Günter Stemberger, *Introduction to the Talmud and Midrash*, trans. Markus Bockmuehl (Edinburgh, 1991), 62–110.

[5] Hugo Grotius, *De Veritate Religionis Christianae* (Leiden, 1640), bk 5 on 261–2; *The Truth of Christian Religion*, trans. John Clarke (London 1711), 5.14 on 235; Episcopius, *Institutiones Theologicae*, 1: 3.4.2 on 157.

in Israel for nine months', but from that time as many centuries as these nine months have gone past.[6] We also learn from the lauded book of Talmud that the Messiah was born on the day when the Temple was burned by Titus, and he would sit among poor people and lepers at the gates of Rome, or, as the Talmudic gloss interprets it, in that part of the garden of Eden which faces the gates of Rome.[7] Whatever that is, we know for certain that about that time there was great expectation of the coming of the Messiah, if we trust either evangelical history or the secular writers. For Suetonius (and also Tacitus, with almost the same words, in the *Life of Vespasian*)

[page 49]

says that 'there had spread over all the Orient an old and established belief that it was fated at the time for men coming from Judaea to rule the world'.[8] And Josephus, in *De Bello Judaico* book 7, chapter 12, says 'what more than all else incited them to the war was an ambiguous oracle, likewise found in their sacred scriptures, to the effect that at that time one from their country would become ruler of the world'. He says that they accepted that as if it were their own, and many wise men were deceived by the interpretation. This response clearly designated the empire of Vespasian, who was created emperor while he was among the Jews. He says these things, whence it can be seen how the belief that a Messiah would come had such deep roots in men's minds then that those among them who became enlightened with the highest knowledge preferred to refer the predictions and oracles which talked of this king to a secular and heathen leader, rather than accept that those predictions were not related to their own age.[9] And the Jews nowadays do the same. Indeed, the Jews around that time gave credibility to this fact by their actions themselves, some of them by following Herod as a Messiah, others Judas Gaulonites, or by an especially memorable deceit following Bar Kochba as their leader, whom all the wise men of that time, and the great Doctor Rabbi Akiva among

---

[6] Hoornbeek, *Pro convertendis Judaeis*, 2.1. on 189. For the Jubilee, see Leviticus 25; *Sanhedrin*, 97b on 658; Franciscus Ribera, *De Templo*, (Salamanca, 1591), 5.24–5 on 219–22; Martini, *Pugio Fidei*, de Voisin, Prooemium on 31.

[7] Buxtorf, *Synagoga Judaica*, 442–3; A. B. trans., 316; Hoornbeek, *Pro convertendis Judaeis*, 2.1 on 120; see *Sanhedrin*, 98a on 664; the city of Jerusalem and the Second Temple were destroyed by the Romans in AD 70.

[8] Suetonius, *Vespasian*, ed. Brian W. Jones (Bristol, 2000), 4.5.1 on 2, 35; '*The Annals' and 'The Histories' [of] Tacitus*, trans. John A. Church and William J. Brodribb, ed. Hugh Lloyd-Jones (London, 1966), *Histories*, 5.13 on 455 (this translation used for quotation).

[9] Flavius Josephus, *Hierosolymitani Sacerdotis: Opera quae exstant* (Geneva, 1634), *De Bello Judaico*, 7.12 on 960–2; *Josephus*, trans. H. St. J. Thackray, 9 vols. (London 1956), 3: *The Jewish War, Books IV–VII*, places this passage at 6.312 on 466–7 (this translation used for quotation). See also Episcopius, *Institutiones Theologicae*, 1: 3.4.2 on 157–8; Hoornbeek, *Pro convertendis Judaeis*, 3.1 on 218–9.

them, accepted as a Messiah.[10] Having erred and been wrong so often, the Jews then fixed the terms for the coming of the Messiah. Finally, a curse made them wary of calculating the time: 'perish the Spirit of those who estimate the end of time'.[11] However, neither did the blind curiosity of the Jews stop here, but others did the same thing in relation to other times. Each one set the period of the coming of a pseudo-Messiah according to the limitations of his own mind. These things are described by the author of *Schalshelet Hakabbalah* [The Chain of Tradition]. Some assigned it to the year 5335 from the creation of the world, which occurred in AD 1575. Others the year 5337 [1577]. Others 5360 [1600]. Rabbi Gedaliah 5358 [1598]. Abravanel in his *Commentaries on Isaiah and Jeremiah* the year 5263 [1503] or 5294 [1534]. In truth Rabbi Saadia says that Rabbi Solomon Jarchi, Rabbi Levi Ben Gerson, Rabbi Moses Ben Nachman, and Rabbi Bechai, all being of the same mind, established that the Messiah would come in the year of the World 5118 [1458]. Zohar actually postponed it to year 5408, which occurred in AD 1648.[12]

[page 50]

Finally, after all these figments [of imagination] had been proved wrong, they relegated their pseudo-Messiah to the very end of the sixth millennium, linking his coming to the resurrection of the dead, so that Menasseh Ben Israel does not consider it fit to concede forty years of duration to his reign, which is said to be eternal by the holy prophet's predictions.[13] But setting aside what are in part dreams, in part ravings of the Jews, let us see on what foundations our thesis is based.

---

[10] Buxtorf, *Synagoga Judaica*, 441; A. B. Trans., 315; Grotius, *De Veritate*, bk 5 on 265, 272; Clarke trans., 5.14 on 237–8, 5.16 on 243; Martini, *Pugio Fidei*, de Voisin, 2.2 on 212, 2.4.14–20 on 256–8, 2.4.23 on 261–2, 3.16 on 679; Antonius Hulsius, *Riv Adonai 'im Yehudah, sive Theologiae Iudaicae pars prima de Messia* (Breda, 1653), 1.2 on 414; Hoornbeek, *Pro convertendis Judaeis*, 2.1 on 152–3, 3.1 on 209–10. Bar Kochba's revolt against Roman rule occurred in AD 132–5.

[11] Buxtorf, *Synagoga Judaica*, 442; A.B. trans., 316; Hoornbeek, *Pro convertendis Judaeis*, 2.1 on 125; see *Sanhedrin*, 97b on 659.

[12] Martini, *Pugio Fidei*, de Voisin, Prooemium on 57–62; Hulsius, *Theologiae Iudaicae*, 1.1 on 134–5; Hoornbeek, *Pro convertendis Judaeis*, 2.1 on 182–3, 190–1; these sources do not contain all of the dates given by Rust, but a more complete source has not been found among the books which Rust definitely used. Rust refers to Gedaliah ben Joseph ibn Yahya, *Schalshelet Hakabbalah* (Venice, 1586–1587; Krakow, 1596) and to Isaac Abravanel, *Commentarius . . . super Iesaiam, Ieremiam, Iehazkelem, et prophetas XIII minores* (Amsterdam, 1642, 1647); he was unlikely to have been able to read these works, which were entirely in Hebrew, but he saw references to them in the secondary sources listed above. British Library, London, Add. MSS 4986–4987, Ralph Cudworth, Commentary on the Seventy Weeks of Daniel, contains many messianic dates, which Cudworth may well have discussed with Rust. For Abravanel's calculation of 1503, see Benzion Natanyahu, *Don Isaac Abravanel: Statesman & Philosopher*, 5th edn., (Ithaca & London, 1998), 216–26.

[13] Ben Israel, *Resurrectione Mortuorum*, 3.2.6 on 262–3; see *Sanhedrin* 99a on 668–9.

Argument I. Thus we borrow the first argument from Genesis 49:10. 'The Sceptre shall not depart from Judah (Targum, or the Aramaic paraphrase Onkelos, who, as the author of *Sepher Ikkarim* relates, received the oral law from Shemayah and Abtalyon, whose translation of it holds so much authority among the Jews, that it is a sin to go against it, interprets the word שבט [*shevet*] as 'exerting the power' עביד שולטן. The Targum of Jerusalem translates it as מלכין 'kings'; The Targum of Jonathan translates מלכין ושלטנין as 'kings and princes'), nor the lawgiver from between his feet until (Jonathan translates it as 'until that time when') Shiloh comes', or 'Messiah', or the 'King Messiah', as all the Targumists take it, 'and he will bring about the union and obedience of peoples'.[14]

Before I derive the argument from this, it should be noted that the Sceptre is the emblem of the Lord, and thus when any people distinct and separated from others is governed by its own laws, among them there is the Sceptre and the majesty of power, so that the Sceptre went first to Judah when, after the defection of the ten tribes, Judah ended up as a kingdom.[15] However, after the Babylonian Captivity, those who ruled it were sometimes of the tribe of Levi, sometimes strangers like Herod and others. Nevertheless, later the kingdom of the Jews remained the same, and so, therefore, did the majesty of the Jewish people and the command. The meaning of the prophecy appears thus: that there will be some day when the tribe of Judah receives that honour and prerogative, so that the kingdom of God will remain under Judah's control, and God had different

---

[14] See Joseph Albo, *Sefer Ha-'Ikkarim: Book of Principles*, trans. and ed. Isaac Husik, 4 vols. (Philadelphia, 1929–1930), 4: 423; *Pirke Aboth: The Ethics of the Talmud: Sayings of the Fathers*, trans. and ed. R. Travers Herford (New York, 1964), 30–1. These texts are commented on in: Johann Buxtorf, *Lexicon Hebraicum et Chaldaicum* (Basel, 1631), 766–7, 811–12, 846; Constantijn L'Empereur, *Masa'ot shel Rabi Binyamin; Itinerarium D. Beniaminis* (Leiden, 1633), [sigs] *6, **8; Menasseh Ben Israel, *Conciliator, sive de convenientia locorum S. Scripturae, quae pugnare inter se videntur* (Amsterdam, 1633), Genes. Quaest 45, 87–92; *The Conciliator of R. Manasseh* [sic] *Ben Israel*, trans. E. H. Lindo, 2 vols. (London, 1842), Genesis Question 68, 1: 93–9; Grotius, *De Veritate*, bk 5 on 274; Clarke trans., 5.18 on 245; Joseph Mede, *Diatribae. Discourses on Divers Texts of Scripture* (London, 1648), Gen. 49.10 on 100–104; Episcopius, *Institutiones Theologicae*, 1: 3.4.6 on 163; James Ussher, *Annales* (London, 1650), 41; *The Annals of the World*, trans. the author (London, 1658), 28; Martini, *Pugio Fidei*, 2.4.1 on 250–1, 2.7.9 on 277, de Voisin, 2.4 on 265–6; Hoornbeek, *Pro convertendis Judaeis*, 2.1 on 127, 131, 3.1 on 214. See also *Origenis Philocalia*, ed. Jean Tarin (Paris, 1618), ch. 1 on 5–6; Edward Millington, *Bibliotheca Cudworthiana* (London, 1691), 5; *The Philocalia of Origen*, trans. George Lewis (Edinburgh, 1911), 1.3 on 3–4; Origen, *Contra Celsum*, trans. Henry Chadwick (Cambridge, 1980), 1.53 on 49; 5.32 on 289 n.5.

[15] Mede, *Diatribae*, 103. *Res publica* means 'state', but 'kingdom' has been preferred here and elsewhere below as it clearly refers to the kingdom of Judah.

plans for Judah than for the other ten tribes, despite the fact that they were going to take the Sceptre in due course.

[page 51]

Nevertheless the Sceptre would leave them for some centuries before the coming of the Messiah. Judah, however, would be a kingdom with its own kings, military leaders, princes, governors, whoever and whatever they were, until the times of the Messiah.[16]

Having said this, I argue from this passage that the Sceptre was not to be removed from Judah before the coming of the Messiah, that is, the Messiah would come while the kingdom was still standing. Therefore, the removal of the Sceptre, which already happened 1,500 years ago and more, necessarily proves that the Messiah has come.[17]

The Jews take many exceptions against this argument, but they can actually be reduced to these three sections. Namely:

1. There are some who, while understanding 'Messiah' by Shiloh, do not understand שבט [*shevet*] as 'reign'.

2. Others take שבט as 'reign', but by Shiloh they do not understand Messiah.

3. Finally, others understand *shevet* and Shiloh in the same sense we do, but they do not recognize the force of the argument.[18]

First Exception: It is not שבט that will be removed, i.e. a staff, or a rod, the support of Judah, and lawgiver, etc., before the coming of the Messiah; i.e. the Jews in their captivity will never lack any support, and lawgivers, who will look after them and will spur them to fight against adversaries. Thus says Menasseh Ben Israel in *Quaestiones supra Genesin* [Questions on Genesis] and in a book recently published in our language.[19]

Reply. First, truly, *shevet* used in an absolute sense nowhere means 'support through advice and help'. Second, to what end should the patriarch have promised comfort only to his son Judah, even though the other ones were going to suffer not lesser, but greater evils?[20]

---

[16] Ben Israel, *Conciliator*, 89–92; Lindo trans., 1: 95–9; Mede, *Diatribae*, 105–6; Episcopius, *Institutiones Theologicae*, 1: 3.4.6 on 166; Hoornbeek, *Pro convertendis Judaeis*, 2.1. on 129–30.

[17] Hoornbeek, *Pro convertendis Judaeis*, 2.1 on 129–30, 143.

[18] Ben Israel, *Conciliator*, 88–9; Lindo trans., 94–5; Episcopius, *Institutiones Theologicae*, 1: 3.4.6 on 163; Martini, *Pugio Fidei*, 2.4.1 on 251, 2.7.9 on 277; see *Sanhedrin*, 98b on 667.

[19] Ben Israel, *Conciliator*, 87–92; Lindo trans., 1: 93–9; idem, *To His Highnesse the Lord Protector of the Common-Wealth of England, Scotland, and Ireland* (London, 1655), 9.

[20] Ben Israel, *Conciliator*, 89; Lindo trans., 1: 94; Episcopius, *Institutiones Theologicae*, 1: 3.4.6 on 165.

Second exception: שבט will not be taken away, i.e. the reproof is not taken away from Judah, and the lawgiver from between his feet, i.e. there will always be enemies at their doors, as it were, who will impose laws on them, until the Messiah comes. Thus says Rabbi Joel Ben Soeb.[21]

Reply. This exposition is not tenable at all. First, there is good reason to doubt whether *shevet*, when found anywhere else, can be taken as 'reproof'.

[page 52]

Especially, second, it is linked to the word מחקק [lawgiver] which has a more positive meaning everywhere.[22] Third, whoever either considers what is added by Moses at Genesis 49:28—'All these are the twelve tribes of Israel, this it is that their father spake unto them, and blessed them; everyone according to his blessing he blessed them'—or, above all, pays close attention to the whole speech of the patriarch to his son Judah, will easily understand that he invoked all good and fortunate things.[23] Fourth, from David to Hezekiah, the reign of Judah enjoyed prosperity and opulence, and therefore it is not true at all that the Sceptre had departed from him.[24] Why should the aforementioned afflictions be restricted to Judah, given that the remaining descendants of Jacob also underwent most of them?[25]

Third exception: שבט i.e. the tribe will not be taken away from Judah nor will the lawgiver; this is the view of the patriarch. Although the king of the Assyrians was going to take the ten tribes into lands unknown to us, the tribe of Judah would nevertheless never cease to exist; i.e. it would not be removed from the sight and activities and notice of men, but it would always have lawgivers, i.e. wise men by whom it would be taught until the coming of the Messiah.[26]

---

[21] Ben Israel, *Conciliator*, 91; Lindo trans., 1: 97; see also Mede, *Diatribae*, 104.

[22] Ben Israel, *Conciliator*, 88; Lindo trans., 1: 94; Hoornbeek, *Pro convertendis Judæis*, 2.1 on 144.

[23] Episcopius, *Institutiones Theologicae*, i. 3.4.6 on 165; Ben Israel, *Conciliator*, 91; Lindo trans., 1: 97.

[24] Rust says 'had *not* departed from him' (my italics), but this must be an error.

[25] Hoornbeek, *Pro convertendis Judaeis*, 2.1. on 137–9; see *Sanhedrin*, 99a on 669.

[26] Buxtorf, *Lexicon*, 766–7; Ben Israel, *Conciliator*, 91–2; Lindo trans., 1: 97–8; Episcopius, *Institutiones Theologicae*, 1: 3.4.6 on 165. In Hallywell's printed edn, a marginal note here indicates that 'Junius' and 'Tremel' translated שבט [*shevet*] as 'tribe'; this is a reference to a Latin translation of the Old Testament from the Hebrew and the Syriac by Immanuel Tremellius, an Italian Jewish convert to Christianity, who served as Regius Professor of Hebrew at Cambridge 1549–53, and his son-in-law, Franciscus Junius the elder. Millington, *Bibliotheca*, 1, lists the Hanover, 1596, edn. I have consulted *Biblia Sacra sive Testamentum Vetus. Ab Im. Tremellio et Fr. Iunio* (Amsterdam, 1633), Genesis 49:10, 28 on 38; it is not clear whether Rust or Hallywell added this note.

Reply. The point of this exception is that the tribe of Judah would not become extinct before the Messiah's coming; but this interpretation, that the tribe would not depart from Judah, would be like saying that Judah would not be separated from himself. This Judah is undoubtedly understood not as the Patriarch Judah himself, but as his descendants, and the tribe of Judah, just as the other sons of Jacob are understood as their tribes, as Moses teaches us at Genesis 49:28, 'all these are the tribes of Israel', etc. This will be clear to anyone who pays diligent attention to the blessings of the single tribes. Furthermore, there has been some confusion about all the tribes and the families of around 1600 years ago; even the Jews themselves do not deny this.[27]

Fourth Exception: לא יסור שבט [the rod shall not depart] i.e. no matter how the ten tribes are separated from the house of David, nevertheless the tribe of Benjamin will not be separated from Judah, etc.[28]

[page 53]

Reply. Truly, this is not worthy of such a solemn prophecy at all! Certainly God himself, when he threatens the splitting of Solomon's kingdom, promises that he will give to the son a single tribe. And there is Ahijah's prophecy to Jeroboam: 'Solomon', he says, 'will have one tribe'.[29] And at I Kings 12:20 we read clearly that after the defection of the ten tribes 'there was none that followed the house of David, but the tribe of Judah only'. The link of Benjamin with Judah's tribe was so insignificant that the Holy Spirit did not even deign to make any mention of him. Nevertheless (to point this out), if there was a time in which Judah's tribe could be called great, that was certainly when the Jews' kingdom was standing and the tribe of Benjamin was subject to the authority of Judah. How ridiculous it is to say that instead of receiving a blessing, Judah's brother Benjamin would be subjected with him to the same yoke of slavery and tyranny until the coming of the Messiah.[30]

To this particular refutation of the single exceptions, I will add three general arguments about why שבט should not be given any other meaning than 'Sceptre'.

---

[27] Ben Israel, *Conciliator*, 88, Lindo trans., 1: 94; Hoornbeek, *Pro convertendis Judaeis*, 2.1 on 149–50.

[28] Hoornbeek, *Pro convertendis Judaeis*, 2.1 on 149–50.

[29] 1 Kings 11:30: And Ahijah caught the new garment that was on him, and rent it in twelve pieces: 31: And he said to Jeroboam, Take thee ten pieces: for thus saith the Lord, the God of Israel, Behold, I will rend the kingdom out of the hand of Solomon, and will give ten tribes to thee: 32: (But he shall have one tribe for my servant David's sake, and for Jerusalem's sake, the city which I have chosen out of all the tribes of Israel.)

[30] Episcopius, *Institutiones Theologicae*, 1: 3.4.6 on 164; Hoornbeek, *Pro convertendis Judaeis*, 2.1 on 144.

1. Which is the argument *ad hominem*:[31] It was interpreted as 'domination' by all the Targumists, the Talmudic Doctors, Rabbi Hadarschan, the other old Rabbis and most of the more recent ones.

2. Because it is joined with מחקק, [lawgiver], which is never understood in any other sense than a forensic one.[32] However, it is the custom of the Scripture to repeat the same thing with different words. All the proper rules of exposition dictate that when two expressions occur together, and they have a similar meaning, we derive the interpretation of each from the other. We are not so naïve as to ascribe to one a meaning which is in strong opposition to the meaning of the other with which it is paired.

3. If, in this passage, the Sceptre is not said to have been promised to Judah, then there will not be any promise of it within that blessing. And who would believe that God would not reveal a matter of such importance at such a moment to an old man who was about to die, or that it should be omitted by him, while he provides even more minute details about the other sons and even about Judah himself?[33] And thus we have already moved to the second kind of exceptions, which deny that 'Messiah' should be understood by Shiloh.

[page 54]

Here, then, is the fifth exception. The Sceptre will not be taken away from Judah until Shiloh comes, i.e. Moses. Then the reign of Judah will be taken and handed over to Moses of the tribe of Levi. Thus Rabbi Bechai about that passage.[34]

Reply. But what a poor attempt to escape! How could it have been the Sceptre of the Israelites, let alone of Judah while they were dwelling in Egypt? They were barely a people, under somebody else's sceptre and labouring miserably under the yoke of tyranny. Nor is it an effective argument, that it is likely that there was no mention of their first redemption from the Egyptian captivity. It had already been predicted by Abraham, so there was no need of a new revelation.[35]

Sixth exception. The Sceptre will not be taken away from Judah until Shiloh comes, i.e. David. Thus Aben Ezra and Rabbi Levi Ben Gerson.[36]

---

[31] Here, an appeal to the authority of particular persons.
[32] Hoornbeek, *Pro convertendis Judaeis*, 2.1 on 143–4.
[33] Episcopius, *Institutiones Theologicae*, 1: 3.4.6 on 165.
[34] Ben Israel, *Conciliator*, 90–1; Lindo trans., 1: 97; Martini, *Pugio Fidei*, de Voisin, 2.4 on 266.
[35] Martini, *Pugio Fidei*, de Voisin, 2.4 on 266–7.
[36] Ben Israel, *Conciliator*, 90; Lindo trans., 1: 96.

Reply. But how it can be said that Judah had the Sceptre before David's time? It should not be denied that the prerogative of the firstborn was given by God to Judah over Reuben, Simeon, Levi, and the first and most honoured place in the moving of the encampment, in the offerings of gifts, in the distribution of land, and in receiving the petitions of the people was always assigned to Judah. Truly, this was not the honour granted to Judah by the Sceptre and the command, but only by the prerogative of the first-born.[37]

Seventh exception. לא יסור שבט מיהודה, the Sceptre will not be brought to Judah, עד כי יבוא שילה, until it is laid down, i.e. until the Tabernacle is destroyed, Shiloh. In fact, this occurred at the same time when it was destroyed, and Samuel came and anointed David as a king. This is also the exposition of Rabbi Bechai.[38]

Reply. But in truth סור means 'to go back', 'to decline', 'to turn away', but in no way 'to gather in', and even less so when it is joined with the preposition מן which always means 'motion to a place'. Shiloh, when it means 'the place', is spelt differently in the text and without י in the middle; nor does בא [to come] ever mean 'to be laid low', unless we are talking about the sun, which appears to go under the earth and the ocean.[39]

[page 55]

Apart from these grammatical impediments, 'David' would have to be inserted as well, so that the meaning is consistent, viz. 'the Sceptre will be gathered in until Shiloh is forsaken, and David comes, to whom the people will flock'. Indeed, this entire exposition does such violence to the text that we do not judge it worthy of a refutation.[40]

Eighth exception. The Rule will not be taken away from Judah, nor a lawgiver from between his feet, until Shiloh comes, i.e. until Ahijah the Shilonite divides the robe of Jeroboam into twelve parts. Then also the other tribes will have part of the empire, before then held by Judah alone. Thus says Rabbi Hezekiah, according to Menasseh Ben Israel.[41]

Reply. But the passage with Shiloh, as has already been said, is spelt differently; and where does Shiloh mean Shilonite, and where does it indicate Ahijah? Why should it not indicate Jeroboam instead, to whom the people flocked, since this was predicted of Shiloh? But here it really means neither

---

[37] Buxtorf, *Lexicon*, 766–7; Ben Israel, *Conciliator*, 90, 92; Lindo trans., 1: 96, 98; Episcopius, *Institutiones Theologicae*, 1: 3.4.6 on 165; Martini, *Pugio Fidei*, de Voisin, 2.4 on 265; Hoornbeek, *Pro convertendis Judaeis*, 2.1 on 138–9.

[38] Ben Israel, *Conciliator*, 91; Lindo trans., 1: 97.

[39] Ben Israel, *Conciliator*, 89; Lindo trans., 1: 94–5; Episcopius, *Institutiones Theologicae*, 1: 3.4.6 on 164; Hoornbeek, *Pro convertendis Judaeis*, 2.1 on 141–2.

[40] Genesis 49:10; Hoornbeek, *Pro convertendis Judaeis*, 2.1 on 135–7.

[41] Ben Israel, *Conciliator*, 91; Lindo trans. 1: 97; see n.29 above.

Jeroboam nor Shilonite. In fact, it is wide of the mark to say that the Sceptre departed from Judah when the ten tribes were separated from the house of David. The Sceptre primarily went to Judah, after previously belonging to Israel or the twelve tribes. Nor is it said that David and Solomon were from the tribe of Judah. In fact, along those lines, the Sceptre might as well have been said to belong to Benjamin while Saul was reigning.[42] The state does not belong to the ruler, but the ruler belongs to the state; as it is said that Seneca told Nero.[43]

Ninth exception. The Sceptre will not be separated from Judah until Shiloh, i.e. Nebuchadnezzar, comes, by whom the Jews were taken into captivity.

Reply. First, how is it that Shiloh means Nebuchadnezzar? Second, the meaning of τα [the, plural][44] עמים is broader than merely 'the Jewish people'. Third, יקהת means 'willing adhesion', not 'violent subjection'.[45] Fourth, the Jews in the Babylonian Captivity had their αἰχμαλωτάρχος [spear leader], ראש גלות, head or chief in captivity with martial law and power over life and death, which is what the history of Daniel and Susanna, in the Apocrypha, argues quite clearly. Fifth, this seventy-year-long captivity was not so much the taking away of the Sceptre as an interregnum.

[page 56]

In fact, they later returned to their land and were once more ruled by their own laws.[46] To this particular refutation I will add two arguments, which militate equally against the exceptions of this second kind, by which it is proved that by Shiloh must be understood 'Messiah'.

1. All the Targumists, Bereshit Rabba, Echa Rabbati, or a gloss on Lamentations, the Kabbalists, the Talmudic Doctors, and many more recent authors, understand that the argument is addressed to the Jews about the Messiah. On this point one may consult the *Pugio*

---

[42] Ben Israel, *Conciliator*, 91; Lindo trans., 1: 97; Episcopius, *Institutiones Theologicae*, 1: 3.4.6 on 164, 166; Hoornbeek, *Pro convertendis Judaeis*, 2.1 on 144–5; see I Kings 11:28–42.

[43] Episcopius, *Institutiones Theologicae*, 1: 3.4.6 on 166; see Lucius Annaeus Seneca, *De Clementia*, trans. and ed. Susanna Morton Braund (Oxford, 2011), 1.19.5 on 128–9.

[44] Rust here and in the paragraph below at 2. uses the Greek definite article for maximal grammatical clarity. Latin lacks both the definite and indefinite article, while Hebrew has only one article for both the singular and the plural and also lacks case endings.

[45] Episcopius, *Institutiones Theologicae*, 1: 3.4.6 on 167.

[46] Ibid., 1: 3.4.6 on 164–5. For 'Daniel and Susanna', see *The Septuagint with Apocrypha*, trans. and ed. Lancelot C. L. Brenton (Grand Rapids, 1980), History of Susanna, second pagination, on 134–6, especially verse 5. See also Origen, A Letter to Africanus about the History of Susanna', in *The Ante-Nicene Fathers: Translations of the Writings of the Fathers down to A.D. 325*, trans. and ed. Alexander Roberts and James Donaldson, 10 vols. (Buffalo, 1885–1896), 'A Letter from Origen to Africanus', 4: 783–97, ch. 14 on 795.

Fidei of Raymundus Martini, and Buxtorf on the word שילה [Shiloh].[47]

2. The last words of this passage ('and the peoples will flock to him') are a marker of the Messiah and are the circumlocution of τῳ [to the, singular] Shiloh. If this is not accepted, that is, that το [the, neuter] Shiloh describes these terms, it is not possible to understand what the patriarch means by that Shiloh, on the understanding of which word depends the understanding of the whole prophecy. Let us assess all the interpretations of τῷ [to the, singular] 'Shiloh' that can be made; nevertheless, they do not allow us to conjecture what Jacob had in mind. Take Shiloh as τὰ ἀποκείμενα αὐτῷ [the things stored up for him] as the Septuagint translated it;[48] or as the 'one to whom it has been given back', as the ancient Fathers said; or as *Qui mittendus est* [he who must receive it], as the Vulgate has it, no matter how absurdly; or 'peacemaker', 'fortunate' or 'successful', words derived from שלה; or His Son, as most of the Hebrews take it; so that ו is placed at the end, being a word derived from שליה, *secundina* [afterbirth, placenta], in which the embryo lies and lives, whence שיל son.[49] That is the one to whom the gift is given, from שי, gift, and לו, as Rabbi Solomon says. Take, I say, whichever of these translations you like, who will conjecture what is meant by ἀποκείμενα αὐτῷ [things stored up for him], 'he to whom it is returned', 'peacemaker', 'his son', or 'he to whom it is given as a gift' if we do not accept that these words ('and he will have the obedience of the people') are a circumlocution for the one who is earlier called Shiloh? For then, by means of the surest marker and clue, it is shown who must be understood, for 'all the nations will flock to the Messiah', which was frequently predicted by Isaiah, Micah, and by the other prophets, and which is firmly believed by the Jews themselves.[50]

---

[47] Buxtorf, *Lexicon*, 811–12; Martini, *Pugio Fidei*, 2.4.9–11 on 254, 3.3.3.11 on 531, de Voisin, 2.4 on 265–6.

[48] Buxtorf, *Lexicon*, 811–12; Episcopius, *Institutiones Theologicae*, 1: 3.4.6 on 164; see *Septuagint*, 67, Genesis 49:10.

[49] Episcopius, *Institutiones Theologicae*, 1: 3.4.6 on 164, based on Hugo Grotius, *Annotata ad Vetus Testamentum* 3 vols. (Paris, 1644), 1: Annotata ad Genesin, 49:10 on 53. שיל is not a Hebrew word in itself, but see Ben Israel, *Conciliator*, 89; Lindo trans. 1: 95, for what Rust might have been trying to explain; see also Martini, *Pugio Fidei*, 2.4.11 on 254, de Voisin, Prooemium on 33, 2.4 on 269; Hoornbeek, *Pro convertendis Judaeis*, 2.1 on 128; *Ibn Ezra's Commentary on the Pentateuch: Genesis (Bereshit)*, trans. H. Norman Strickman and Arthur M. Silver (New York, 1988), 430–1.

[50] Buxtorf, *Lexicon*, 811; Ben Israel, *Conciliator*, 89; Lindo trans. 1: 95; Mede, *Diatribae*, 105.

Let us move on to the third kind of exceptions, that is the one of those who take

[page 57]

shevet and Shiloh in the same sense as we do, yet denying that from this passage it can be proved that the Messiah has come. Let it be thus.

Tenth exception. 'The Sceptre shall not be taken away from Judah', i.e. so that it is transferred to one of his brothers. Hence, it is not predicted here that the Israelites will always have a king or the Sanhedrin, but that when they do he will be from the tribe of Judah. Thus say Bereschit Rabba, Rabbi Moses of Gerona, Rabbi Obadiah Sphorno, Rabbi Bechai, as we are taught by Menasseh Ben Israel and by Joseph de Voisin in his Observations on Raymundus Martini.[51]

Reply. First, what would become of that blessing, of the promise to Judah that he will not serve his brothers, but that nevertheless he will undergo a foreign tyranny? Second, and this must be considered above all, this prophecy will be completely meaningless if you interpret it in this sense. In fact, if, immediately after the Sceptre went to Judah, he had to depart with his brothers under a foreign yoke and he stayed there until the coming of the Messiah, this prophecy would nevertheless have been fulfilled.[52]

Eleventh exception. The words to be analysed in this way are לא יסור שבט מבין רגליו עד־כי יבוא שילה,[53] so that the sense is that the Sceptre will not be taken away forever after the Messiah has come. Thus say Bereshith Rabba and Rabbi Bechai, who also note that the translation of Onkelos says the same in the corrected codices. Hence they try to bolster this claim by adding to עד the Jethib accent, which (if we agree with Menasseh) marks and separates the periods.

Reply. עד certainly means 'eternity' or 'eternal time', but only at the end of the phrase. In the middle it means 'always', 'throughout': and with כי it means 'as far as'. כי actually means 'because', or 'which', or 'if', or 'but', certainly not 'when' or 'where', as the experts in Hebrew teach us. And Jethib does not distinguish and separate periods, as can be seen in that passage itself and in the verse immediately following it.

But the *athnach* determines the *colon* and the breathing, and we find that accent in the word רגליו immediately before עד, so that

[page 58]

---

[51] Ben Israel, *Conciliator*, 89–91; Lindo trans., 1: 95–7; Martini, *Pugio Fidei*, de Voisin, 2.12 on 351.

[52] Episcopius, *Institutiones Theologicae*, 1: 3.4.6 on 165.

[53] Genesis 49:10.

עד כי must necessarily begin the sentence.[54] But setting aside these grammatical objections, which nevertheless do turn this interpretation upside down, how futile, ludicrous, and ridiculous this exposition would make the prophecy! The patriarch is introduced as predicting that after 4,000 years the Sceptre will not depart from Judah for a generation, i.e. a space of 40 years. Such an opinion still persists among the Jews, that the coming of the Messiah will be close to the end of the world, and Menasseh says that perhaps the coming of the Messiah and the resurrection of the dead will be in the same year and day.[55]

Twelfth and last exception. שבט [*Shevet*] will not be taken away', i.e. no matter how slight the command and jurisdiction were over the tribes of Israel, etc., Judah was undoubtedly always the chief of his brothers. And in the exile in Spain and France the chiefs of Israel were always of the race and house of David; thus says Abravanel.[56]

Reply. If it all boils down to this in the end, clearly next to nothing is promised in this prophecy. What about the chiefs of the families with kings and princes among them? *Shevet* means jurisdiction, but in a political sense, which a people can only lay claim to if it is a nation distinct and separate from the others and ruled by its own laws. This points to that honorific status which Benjamin of Tudela extolled in his *Itinerary* 500 years ago, when in Baghdad he saw with his own eyes a great number of Israelites, as he reports it, following at a certain time that prince whom they believed to be from David's race, cheering him while he went by in his chariot with the words 'make way for the son of David', and similar expressions. But that author has already been found by learned men, and above all by Constantijn L'Empereur, to be guilty of fairy tales and falsehood, compromising his reliability with sensible men.[57] Hence, I do not consider this exception to be worth an arduous refutation. Anyway, the frequent exchanges which had already been taking place for a long time between parts of Europe and almost all the nations and places in the world abundantly refuted the dreams and creations of that kind.

---

[54] Ben Israel, *Conciliator*, 89–90; Lindo trans., 1: 94–6; Episcopius, *Institutiones Theologicae*, 1: 3.4.6 on 166; Hoornbeek, *Pro convertendis Judaeis*, 2.1 on 135–6. The *athnach* is a Hebrew accent marking the division of a verse; *colon* is a single line of poetry.

[55] Ben Israel, *Resurrectione Mortuorum*, 2.21 on 236–7, 3.2 on 251–63, 3.5.7 on 296; Hoornbeek, *Pro convertendis Judaeis*, 2.1 on 117–18.

[56] Ben Israel, *Conciliator*, 91–2; Lindo trans., 1: 97–8; Episcopius, *Institutiones Theologicae*, 1: 3.4.6 on 167; Hoornbeek, *Pro convertendis Judaeis*, 2.1 on 144–5.

[57] L'Empereur, *Itinerarium D. Beniaminis* [sigs] *4ᵛ, **5-**7ᵛ, 70–5; *The Itinerary of Rabbi Benjamin of Tudela*, trans. Adolph Asher, 2 vols. (London & Berlin, 1840), 1: 100–105; see also Menasseh, *Conciliator*, 92; Lindo trans., 1: 98; Episcopius, *Institutiones Theologicae*, 1: 3.4.6 on 167; Hoornbeek, *Pro convertendis Judaeis*, 2.1 on 139, 145–6, 210. Benjamin of Tudela's visit to Baghdad took place c.1170.

[page 59]

And thus we have, as briefly as possible, gone through all those refutations which the Jews oppose to our argument in favour of the coming of the Messiah on the basis of the prophecy of the Patriarch Jacob. However, there are three arguments which I thought should be added to what I have already said by way of an appendix:

1. It should not be surprising at all that the Jews have come up with some means of escape, with which they endeavour to elude other passages of the Holy Scripture. In fact, it seems virtually impossible, no matter how much we plough through the Scripture, that men's cunning should not give it ever different meanings. Words scarcely occur which do not have various meanings, nor phrases which cannot support different constructions, nor parts of speech which cannot be divided and defined in different ways.[58] Truly, if the prophecies were conceived with words so eloquent and distinct that only one meaning could be given to them, the Jews would have to admit that the Messiah came in the past and that he was Jesus of Nazareth himself.

2. There is no reason to expect anything else from God than that he takes sufficient care of the instruction of a sincere and upright soul who will immediately embrace a sufficiently clear truth. Truly, for anyone who does not assent that the meaning of Scripture is that which is more likely, and who would, if it were possible, make up another meaning for the words, there would not be any believable meaning of Scripture left. For if someone believes that the meaning of Scripture is the one to which the words can be dragged and twisted in any way possible, then he will be right to believe any meaning of Scripture he wants. A judicious and sincere mind will recognize the meaning of Scripture that the words themselves, not twisted by force, so easily express.[59]

3. For an argument, these exceptions bear no weight, and the same applies to those which satisfy the Jews, since the number of their arguments is so great. If they were satisfied with one in particular, they would not labour so much in resorting to the others.

We derive the second argument, by which it is proved that the Messiah has already come, from Haggai 2:6–9: 'For thus saith the Lord of hosts; Yet once, it is a little while, and I will shake the heavens, and the earth,

---

[58] Ben Israel, *Conciliator*, 92; Lindo trans., 1: 99.
[59] Cf. Ben Israel, *Conciliator*, 88; Lindo trans., 1: 93.

[page 60]

and the sea, and the dry land; and I will shake the nations, and the desire of all nations shall come: and I will fill this house with glory, saith the Lord of hosts.... The glory of this latter house shall be greater than of the former, saith the Lord of hosts: and in this place will I give peace, saith the Lord of hosts'.[60] To this passage I add a related one, Malachi 3:1: 'Behold, I will send my messenger, and he shall prepare the way before me: and the Lord, whom ye seek, shall suddenly come to his temple'. From these passages I argue as follows: The Messiah was to come while the Second Temple was still in existence. Therefore, once the Second Temple had been destroyed, it necessarily follows that the Messiah had come.[61]

The Jews make these exceptions: First, in the passage from Haggai there is no mention of the Messiah, nor any indication that 'the desire of all nations' can be understood as the Messiah, nor that the presence of the Messiah is 'the glory of this latter house', which is greater than the glory of the former. Thus they have established two interpretations of this passage.[62]

The earlier one is by Rabbi David Kimchi, Rabbi Azariaha-adomi, and the Talmud in the codex *Baba Bathra*, who place the glory of the Second above that of the previous one, (1) in the structure and ornamentation with which Herod provided it from the ruins of the old one; (2) in duration, the First Temple did not last more than 410 years, but the Second Temple 420. And according to this exposition, 'the desire of all nations' does not mean anything other than gold, silver, gems, and pearls, which are things the people most desired, who nevertheless, with God guiding their hearts, were destined to contribute to the ornate building of the Temple.[63]

Reply. Truly, according to this reasoning, the glory of the Second Temple was in no way greater than the glory of the former; in fact (1) the glory of the structure, ornamentation, and duration is clearly not at all worthy of

---

[60] Episcopius, *Institutiones Theologicae*, 1: 3.4.7 on 168; Martini, *Pugio Fidei*, 2.9.7 on 303; Hulsius, *Theologiae Iudaicae*, 1.2 on 515–28; Hoornbeek, *Pro convertendis Judaeis*, 2.1 on 112, 150; see *Sanhedrin*, 97b on 659; Origen, *Contra Celsum*, trans. Chadwick, 7.30 on 419.

[61] Grotius, *De Veritate*, bk 5 on 264–5; Clarke trans., 5.14 on 237; Episcopius, *Institutiones Theologicae*, 1: 3.4.7 on 168; Martini, *Pugio Fidei*, 2.9.10 on 304; Hulsius, *Theologiae Iudaicae*, 1.1 on 24; 1.2 on 279–94; Hoornbeek, *Pro convertendis Judaeis*, 2.1 on 112, 178–80; see *Sanhedrin*, 99a on 669.

[62] Episcopius, *Institutiones Theologicae*, 1: 3.4.7 on 168; Hoornbeek, *Pro convertendis Judaeis*, 2.1 on 178–80.

[63] Hulsius, *Theologiae Iudaicae*, 2.1 on 515–25; Episcopius, *Institutiones Theologicae*, 1: 3.4.7 on 169; Hoornbeek, *Pro convertendis Judaeis*, 2.1 on 153. See *Babylonian Talmud*, 21: *Baba Bathra*, 3a on 7–8; for Rabbi Azariaha-adomi, see Joanna Weinberg, *Azariah de' Rossi's Observations on the Syriac New Testament: a Critique of the Vulgate by a Sixteenth-Century Jew* (London, 2005).

such a prophesy. 2. Still, although they were to be considered of no account, let us look at these five things which the Jews say were in the previous Temple, but certainly not in the second. They are (1) Urim and Thummim; [page 61] (2) The Ark of the Covenant, in which were stored the Tablets of the Law, the Staff of Aaron and the Urn of Manna; (3) Celestial fire; (4) Schechina, or the Divine Presence; and (5) the Spirit of Prophecy.[64] Others list them differently. The author of *Meor Enajim*, Rabbi Azarias, says 'the Presence of the Divine Power and those five precious things which were in the former Temple did not enhance it to inestimable honour in the second one'.[65] And there are certainly learned men who grudgingly agree with Josephus (the other authors shine thanks to his authority alone) that the Temple was destroyed by Herod and then built again, but only some of the external ornaments were added. Ecchius and others mention those parts of the Temple, but they always rely on Josephus.[66]

2. Nevertheless the Temple of Herod (the Jews call the Second Temple either 'of Zorobabel' or 'of Herod') was not to be compared to the Temple of Solomon in terms of structure and ornamentation, no matter what Joseph ben Gorion (an author some hundreds of years more recent than he claims to be),[67] I say, no matter what he says, that nothing of like beauty was ever seen. In fact, (1) Herod in his oration to the Jews, according to the writer Flavius Josephus, resolved to supply the Second Temple with what it lacked to make it equal to the Temple of Solomon. Because it was 60 cubits lower he resolved to make it reach the same height, without considering proportion of length and width. So it seems likely that where Josephus writes that he put the old foundations under the Second Temple, this meant only that he made those foundations, which necessarily had to be different in order to make the building higher,

---

[64] Episcopius, *Institutiones Theologicae*, 1: 3.4.7 on 168–9; Hulsius, *Theologiae Iudaicae*, 1.1 on 49, 152, 158; Hoornbeek, *Pro convertendis Judaeis*, 2.1 on 156.

[65] Hoornbeek, *Pro convertendis Judaeis*, 2.1 on 157.

[66] Episcopius, *Institutiones Theologicae*, 1: 3.4.7 on 169; Hoornbeek, *Pro convertendis Judaeis*, 2.1 on 155–6, 165. 'Ecchius' is possibly a reference to Johannes Eck, *Ains Judenbüechlins Verlegung* [Against the Defence of the Jews] (Ingolstadt, 1541), ch. 3 on [sig.] C ii[v], but there is no other evidence that Rust would have been able to read this virulently anti-Semitic work in German; it does not appear in Millington, *Bibliotheca*.

[67] Martini, *Pugio Fidei*, 2.4.22 on 260–1; Hulsius, *Theologiae Iudaicae*, 1.1 on 122–9; 1.2 on 518, 523–6; Hoornbeek, *Pro convertendis Judaeis*, 2.1 on 155–6. Joseph Ben Gorion was the author of the *Sefer Yosippon*, which is presented as a work of Flavius Josephus but really dates from the middle of the ninth century. Rust might have seen *The Wonderful, and most Deplorable History of the Latter Times of the Jews, and of the City of Hierusalem* (London, 1652), translated from Hebrew to English by Peter Morwyn in the mid sixteenth century and attributed to Joseph Ben Gorion, on 2; for Herod's rebuilding of the Temple, see ch. 3 on 53 (error for 79) – 83; this work does not appear in Millington, *Bibliotheca*.

while preserving the other elements of the structure. A man of great culture, Johannes Hoornbeek, made the same comment about this phrase in his book *Pro convincendis et convertendis Judaeis*, published recently. This seems even more likely, because Josephus himself was witness to the fact that Herod employed 1,000 priests for not more than half a year in the Nαῷ [Temple] itself, i.e. the building of the roof, and that he finished the rest of the building in eight years, employing 11,000 workers, when on the other hand

[page 62]

Solomon employed 143,000 for seven years: see Francisco Ribera *De Templo*, book 1 chap. 28.[68] Second, the Temple of Herod was not equal or similar in ornamentation to Solomon's, as will be clear from II Chronicles 3:4, 6–7.[69] It was covered with gold inside and adorned with precious gems, and its vases were all made of gold, differently from those in the Second Temple, which the Jews themselves say were of bronze, not to mention the most glorious columns of Jachin and Boaz, or the enormous lake of molten bronze, which the Temple of Herod lacked.[70]

Thus, we have said three things here. First, the Temple of Herod was inferior to Solomon's in terms of the extension and the mass of the building. Second, it was even more inferior in terms of splendour and ornamentation, since silver and bronze were used instead of gold and pearls. Third, which is paramount, the five things mentioned above, which Herod's Temple lacked, were part of the First Temple, and their absence could be compensated for by nothing other than the coming of the Messiah. Obviously, it is clear how little the Jews rely on this exception, because they added that futile one about the duration, 'like master like man'.[71] Can they think that God, many centuries earlier, would predict that he would move sea and desert land, and move all the nations, so that he could make

---

[68] Ribera, *De Templo*, 1.28 on 46–7; Hulsius, *Theologiae Iudaicae*, 1.1 on 179–82; Hoornbeek, *Pro convertendis Judaeis*, 2.1 on 155–6, 164. For Herod's oration to the Jews and rebuilding of the Temple, see Josephus, *Hierosolymitani Sacerdotis, Antiquitates Judaicae*, 15.14 on 542–6; *De Bello Judaico*, 6.6 on 915–19; *Josephus*, trans. Thackray, *Jewish War*, 3. 15.184–247 on 255–77; *Jewish Antiquities*, trans. Ralph Marcus and Allen Wikgren, 8: 15.11.380–425 on 189–207.

[69] II Chronicles 3:4: And the porch that was in the front of the house, the length of it was according to the breadth of the house, twenty cubits, and the height was an hundred and twenty: and he overlaid it within with pure gold. 6: And he garnished the house with precious stones for beauty: and the gold was gold of Parvaim. 7: He overlaid also the house, the beams, the posts, and the walls thereof, and the doors thereof, with gold; and graved cherubims on the walls.

[70] See II Chronicles 3:17, 4:2.

[71] '*dignum patella operculum*', a common Latin tag, for which see John Clarke, *Phraseologia Puerilis, Anglo-Latina in ususm tyrocinii Scholastici* (London, 1638), [sig.] A7ᵛ.

the glory of the Second Temple greater than that of the first, because it will last ten whole years longer than the first one?[72]

Besides, the subsequent events should not be neglected (and in this passage I will settle the issue), namely that the Jews, far from reaching peace after the restoration of the Temple by Herod, were enslaved by the Romans and became their tributaries, and not much later they were destroyed together with the Temple.[73]

In giving these warnings Abravanel, the wisest of the Jews, takes another path. At Haggai 2:6 he introduces God when he talks about this Second Temple, which they were already building, and God calls it small and little, and he threatens that he will move all the nations (i.e. he will spur the Romans on towards destroying it). At verse 7 he consoles the Jews with

[page 63]

the promise of the third Temple which they will build after their return from the long captivity, by which they are now oppressed, and that he will fill this Temple with his glory, which will be greater than that of the Temple of Solomon. This is the main point and the whole paraphrase of the passage, see Antonius Hulsius in *Theologiae Iudaicae*.[74]

Reply. This house הבית הזה at verse 3 is undeniably understood as the second house, and Abravanel himself, verse 6, talks about the same one. How could anyone convince himself that the same words used again at verses 7 and 9 are to be understood as the building of the Temple after many centuries, that is, some thousands of years, without there being a change of subject nor any hint or trace of that change? What remains of this passage is, therefore, that the aforementioned glory of the Second Temple compared to that of the first one is nothing other than the Messiah who will enter it. For he is the glory of Israel, and the glory of the God of Israel, by whom sky and earth, sea and desert would be moved, and all nations will tremble. He is Urim and Thummin from which springs the revelation of the divine will.[75] He is the Ark of Covenant and the propitiation by his own blood. He baptises with Spirit and fire; he receives the Spirit without limit, and in him is the bodily fullness of divinity.[76] Hence, the body and substance of these shadows, which were the glory of the First Temple, are restored through the Messiah. Rabbi Akiva, who was in so much honour among the Jews that Rabbi Eliezer said of him that 'to me

---

[72] Episcopius, *Institutiones Theologicae* 1: 3.4.7 on 169.

[73] Hoornbeek, *Pro convertendis Judaeis*, Prolegomena on 9.

[74] Haggai 2:6–7; Hulsius, *Theologiae Iudaicae*, 1.2 on 514–28; Hoornbeek, *Pro convertendis Judaeis*, 2.1 on 155–6.

[75] Hulsius, *Theologiae Iudaicae*, 1.1 on 49; Hoornbeek, *Pro convertendis Judaeis*, 2.1 on 130–1, 149, 156–7. For Urim and Thummim, see also Ribera, *De Templo*, 3.12 on 122–8.

[76] Colossians 2:9.

all the wise men of Israel are worth as much as the outer layer of garlic apart from this bald one' (i.e. Rabbi Akiva who was bald, and above him they say that the Holy Spirit rested as above the seventy elders), this Doctor Mishnicus interprets this passage as referring to the days of the Messiah, as Raymundus Martini teaches us.[77] And the man above all praise, Hugo Grotius, very learned in the writings of the Jews, says about this passage that all the Jews who lived before the massacre believed that the Messiah would appear in the Second Temple.[78]

[page 64]

Further, 'desire of the nations' is a proper and familiar circumlocution for the Messiah, to whom all the peoples will flock, as is predicted everywhere by the prophets. This overturns either exception equally, as does another passage, Malachi 3:1,[79] which nevertheless the Jews twist into another meaning. Rabbi Solomon understands by the message and the messenger of the covenant the Angel of Death, whom God sends to destroy the impious and call them to judgment. But Abravanel rightly rejects this exposition. This certainly did not require a particular prophecy, being already known to everybody; and the judgment in the passage is not particular and private, but universal and public. Nor did the prophets utter threats of spiritual evils, but rather of corporeal and earthly ones, such as the destruction of the City and the Temple. Nor can it be easily explained why God should be said to enter his Temple when he afflicts the soul with infernal punishments. Hence, Abravanel and Kimchi and Aben Ezra (though both have their own commentaries, which you can see are all rejected in Hulsius' *Theologiae Iudaicae*) nevertheless all agree about this, that this prophecy will be fulfilled when the Jewish people have returned from captivity and when all their enemies have been defeated. Then God will build the Temple once more, and will fill it with the majesty of his divine presence.[80]

But, first, anyone who carefully considers the aim of the prophecy will see what a miserable attempt to escape this is. In all the passages about the First and Second Temples the Jews are reproached for all the horrendous sins which they committed again after their return from the Babylonian captivity, of which the most notable were the defiling of sacrifices, the

[77] Rust has mistaken or misrepresented the source of this reference, which is not found in Martini, *Pugio Fidei*, but which does appear in Episcopius, *Institutiones Theologicae*, 1: 3.4.7 on 168. See *Babylonian Talmud*, 31: *Bekoroth*, 58a on 396.

[78] Grotius, *De Veritate*, bk 5 on 264–5; Clarke trans., 5.14 on 237; perhaps half a million Jews were massacred by Rome following Bar Kochba's revolt against Roman rule in AD 132–5, and survivors were driven from their homeland, initiating the modern Diaspora of the Jews.

[79] Episcopius, *Institutiones Theologicae*, 1: 3.4.7 on 168; for Malachi 3:1, see p. 60 above.

[80] Hulsius, *Theologiae Iudaicae*, 1.2 on 279–94.

repudiation of legitimate wives in order to enter into other marriages with foreign women, and shameless murmuring against God. To this impiety, in Malachi chapters 3 and 4, God utters threats of the Day of Judgement and revenge. Yet, mitigated by God's customary goodness, this day will be deadly to the impious and the source of salvation for the pious and God-fearing. It is evident that these threats of judgement extend to the Jews who lived in the time of the Second Temple, which also clearly points to

[page 73][81]

the fact that the day of his coming must not be postponed beyond the duration of the Second Temple. Second, this is especially true if we consider that Jews today consider themselves innocent of those sins which, in the prophet's writings, elicit the divine wrath.[82] Third, that the time is imminent is shown by the many emphatic words which occur in the text: הנה behold!, which is a note of something in the near future; פתאם will come promptly; בוא comes. We cannot find words that indicate the brevity of time so emphatically, when these things of which the passage talks are going to happen after two, and even more, thousands of years, as the Jews now dream. We have already proved that the time of the fulfilment of this prophecy already passed a long time ago. The Jews (not even the later ones) do not deny that the passage is about the days of the Messiah. The passage itself evidently refers to the Messiah. He is the only lord whom they asked and waited for; who will have someone to precede him in order to prepare the way before him,[83] who is the herald of the covenant which they desire, he who above in the aforementioned prophecy of Haggai was called 'the desire of all nations'. To sum up, the Messiah was going to come while the Second Temple was still in existence. But the Second Temple had already been destroyed many centuries before, therefore it necessarily follows that the Messiah came long ago.[84]

Third and last we derive an argumentation from the Holy Scripture, from Daniel 9:24–26. 'Seventy weeks are determined upon thy people and upon thy holy city', etc.[85] Thus it must be known and understood that

---

[81] There is no actual gap between 64 and 73: this is simply an error in pagination.

[82] Episcopius, *Institutiones Theologicae*, 1: 3.4.4 on 161.

[83] Rust would have believed that this aspect of the prophecy was fulfilled in John the Baptist.

[84] Episcopius, *Institutiones Theologicae*, 1: 3.4.7 on 170.

[85] Daniel 9:24: Seventy weeks are determined upon thy people and upon thy holy city, to finish the transgression, and to make an end of sins, and to make reconciliation for iniquity, and to bring in everlasting righteousness, and to seal up the vision and prophecy, and to anoint the most Holy. 25: Know therefore and understand that from the going forth of the commandment to restore and to build Jerusalem unto the Messiah the Prince shall be seven weeks and threescore and two weeks: the street shall be built again, and the wall, even in troublous times. 26: And after threescore and two weeks shall Messiah be cut off, but not for himself: and the people of the prince that shall come shall destroy the city and the

from the announcement of the return of the people and of the rebuilding of Jerusalem until the Prince Messiah there will be seventy weeks and sixty-two weeks. After those sixty-two weeks, the Messiah will be cut off. From this passage I argue that, before the City and the Temple were destroyed, the Messiah was to be cut off, therefore the destruction of these, which plainly happened some centuries before, most certainly proves that the Messiah has come.[86]

Nor can the Jews deny that this argument will be valid if this passage actually refers to the Messiah. But by 'the Messiah' at verse 25 they pretend to understand either Cyrus, as Rabbi Solomon Jachiadis and Menasseh Ben Israel say;

[page 74]

or Nehemiah, as Aben Ezra says; or Joshua the Priest, as Rabbi Levi Ben Gerson says; or Zorobabel, as Abravanel and most of the modern authors say. Or at verse 26 by 'Messiah' they understand Agrippa, the last of those kings (who they say was killed in Rome by the Emperor Vespasian together with his son Mombasus three and a half years before the destruction of the Temple, if the chronologies of these men are to be trusted), as Rabbi Sol Arab. Menasseh says; or the high priest, or the anointed priest, as Rabbi Saadia Gaon says; or the Temple itself, as Jachiades says.[87] However, we shall easily refute these comments by determining the time when these seventy weeks must start according to the Jews. For either way (even though the learned men take a different view, not without reason, the seventy weeks have to finish with the death of Christ, but this is what the Jews find hardest to swallow at the present time), it is to be conceded that they have to finish with the destruction of the City and the Temple. Most of the ancient and modern Jews have these seventy weeks start with the destruction of the First Temple, and from that time up to Cyrus or Joshua, or Zorobabel, they count seven times seven or forty-nine years. But Rabbi Aben Ezra sets their beginning at the time of Darius II, whom the passage at Daniel 9:1 is about,[88] and from then he counts seven times seven or

---

sanctuary: and the end thereof shall be with a flood, and unto the end of the war desolations are determined. Episcopius, *Institutiones Theologicae*, 1: 3.4.8 on 170; Hoornbeek, *Pro convertendis Judaeis*, 2.1 on 171, links this verse to Genesis 49:10. Martini, *Pugio Fidei*, de Voisin, 2.4 on 267.

[86] Joseph Mede, *Daniels Weeks: an Interpretation of part of the Prophecy of Daniel* (London, 1643), 139–76; Episcopius, *Institutiones Theologicae*, 1: 3.4.8 on 171; Hulsius, *Theologiae Iudaicae*, Appendix: Abarb. De 70 Vaticiniis Dan. on 544–73.

[87] Episcopius, *Institutiones Theologicae*, 1: 3.4.8 on 171; Hulsius, *Theologiae Iudaicae*, Appendix on 553–4; Hoornbeek, *Pro convertendis Judaeis*, 2.1 on 158, 168–74.

[88] Daniel 9:1: In the first year of Darius the son of Ahasuerus, of the seed of the Medes, which was made king over the realm of the Chaldeans. Hoornbeek, *Pro convertendis Judaeis*, 2.1 on 168–70.

forty-nine years up to Nehemiah. But by accepting either calculation we would go against all historical credibility. From the third year of Darius the Illegitimate (between him and the destruction of the First Temple, apart from the captivity of seventy years, the ages of many rulers went by, and between him and Darius the Mede the successions of the princes which the Holy Scripture mentions are not agreed), I say, nevertheless, that from the third year of Darius the Illegitimate to the destruction of Jerusalem, 490 years went by.[89] The third year of Darius the Illegitimate, as is clear from Diodorus, occurred in the third year of the 89th Olympic games, or in the 355th Olympic year. The destruction of Jerusalem by Titus took place in the 845th Olympic year, which is a generally acknowledged fact.

[page 75]

The precise difference between these two points is 490 years. The same thing is evident from the Astronomical Canon by Ptolemy: the first year of Darius the Illegitimate in the Canon of Ptolemy matches the 325th of Nabonassar. Therefore the third year of Darius occurs simultaneously with the 327th of Nabonassar. The last year, that is the death of Nero, is the 815th of Nabonassar. Therefore the destruction of the Temple is two years later, in the 817th year of Nabonassar. Thus the difference is 490 years. We owe these calculations to that most successful interpreter of the prophetic writings, Joseph Mede, an ornament not only of Christ's College but also of the University of Cambridge.[90] So that Cyrus, Cambises, Smerdis, Darius Hystaspis, Xerxes, Artaxerxes, most of whom are listed in the Holy Scripture, but occur individually in the secular writers, would be mere phantoms of history, if any trust was put in the calculation of the Jews. Really, it can appear surprising to one who considers into what a short stretch of time the Jews compress the duration of the monarchy of the Persian prophet, which (so that they can escape the strength of this, and fill their heads with delusions) they claim lasted not more than fifty-two years. They easily ascribe the remaining 382 years to the domination of Greece and Rome, which completes the sixty-two weeks, and according to Aben Ezra only forty-nine years have to be added to those.[91] Nevertheless, if Herodotus, Thucydides, Xenophon, Diodorus Siculus, and others are to be trusted, we would necessarily reach at least 200 years. The *Annales* of the Most Reverend James Ussher, Archbishop of Armagh, a man most learned in all

---

[89] Episcopius, *Institutiones Theologicae*, 1: 3.5.2 on 218; Hulsius, *Theologiae Iudaicae*, Appendix on 548–56.

[90] Mede, *Daniels Weeks*, 140–5.

[91] Constantijn L'Empereur, *Perush Don Yosef Ibn Yahya 'al Dani'el; Paraphrasis Dn. Iosephi Iachiadæ in Danielem* (Amsterdam, 1633), (reverse pagination) [sig.] ***3ʳ&ᵛ; Episcopius, *Institutiones Theologicae*, 1: 3.4.7 on 169; Hulsius, *Theologiae Iudaicae*, Appendix on 551; Hoornbeek, *Pro convertendis Judaeis*, 2.1 on 168–70.

historical and especially in chronological writings, notes this.[92] Then, they recognize four Persian kings, against all the consensus of secular history which shows us fourteen, and they impudently claim that almost all of them are listed in the Holy Scripture, as Constantijn L'Empereur demonstrated by induction in the discourse to the reader which precedes his edition of Joseph Jachiada's *Paraphrasis in Danielem*.[93]

Therefore, the 'Messiah' at verse 25 cannot be said to be the one quoted by the Jews. To which considerations, I add that it is without foundation to suppose that Daniel's verse 25 is about one Messiah, and verse 26 about another one.[94] But for the same reason just mentioned he cannot be the Temple in verse 26,

[page 76]

for it is clear that something different is meant by the same word in the previous verse. We never read of the Temple being called 'Messiah'. Nor does verse 26 indicate by Messiah 'the anointed priest', or the high priest of those times, because of the reasons already mentioned, since the Jews say there was no anointed priest through the entire duration of the Second Temple. See Raymundus Martini, *Pugio Fidei*, and the *Observations* of Joseph de Voisin about that passage.[95] Nor can Agrippa be understood as the Messiah, since the Messiah was to be killed after sixty-two weeks, before the destruction of the City and the Temple. The history of those times narrates that Agrippa was dragged to Rome by Vespasian and lived many years after the destruction of Jerusalem.[96] Therefore in this passage we must see the Messiah himself. Thus it is clear that he to whom this passage refers is simply and absolutely called משיח [Messiah] and משיח נגיד [Prince Messiah], since elsewhere this term is not applied to anyone, be it a king or a priest, or to anyone else, without the addition either of 'lord' or of an added or proper name, as will be clear to one who examines all the passages, which are not many. Nor could we find 'Messiah' in an absolute usage in the entire Holy Writ, apart from this single passage in Daniel, which argues for the fact that the Jews read this as a prophecy of the

---

[92] L'Empereur, *Paraphrasis in Danielem*, [sig.] ***2ᵛ; Ussher, *Annales*, 324–5; *Annals*, 231, and the preceding discussion of the Persian Monarchy; Hulsius, *Theologiae Iudaicae*, 1.2 on 289.

[93] L'Empereur, *Paraphrasis in Danielem*, (reverse pagination) [sigs] **-*4ᵛ , see especially ***3ᵛ, see also 184–182; Episcopius, *Institutiones Theologicae*, 1: 3.4.8 on 171.

[94] Mede, *Daniels Weeks* 147; Episcopius, *Institutiones Theologicae*, 1: 3.4.8 on 170.

[95] Martini, *Pugio Fidei*, 2.3.28 on 233; de Voisin, 2.3 on 246.

[96] Episcopius, *Institutiones Theologicae*, 1: 3.4.8 on 171; a marginal note, perhaps added by Hallywell, refers to Joseph Scaliger, *Thesaurus Temporum Eusebii Pamphilii* (Leiden, 1606), within which see Scarliger's *Animadversiones in Chronologica Eusebii*, 176, 182, for the years 2061 and 2086, respectively. This book does not appear in Millington, *Bibliotheca*.

Messiah long ago, and hence they attached that name to their king, for whom they were waiting.[97]

We are left with the only the exception by the Jews which, if it has any weight at all, will fell with a single blow the whole structure of the arguments which have been so far presented in favour of the coming of the Messiah. Therefore it is necessary to treat it in a brief, yet satisfactory, way. They say that the promise about the Messiah depends on certain conditions and that, therefore, his coming may be postponed by their sins. But this exception would have a greater semblance of probability, if, in the time determined for the coming of the Messiah, our Jesus had not appeared, Jesus who proved by means of evident and most certain signs and indications that he was the very Messiah promised so many times.[98]

[page 77]

However, after noting this, let us first consider that the Jews conveniently convince themselves that our Jesus, who took on the name of Messiah, was killed in a noble deed. Nor should it be denied that, if he had falsely promoted himself as Messiah, they would have provided God with a most welcome sacrifice when they crucified a deceiver of the people. And since Jesus is accepted as the Messiah almost everywhere, deceiving, as they hold, the entire world, this cannot but make them greatly pleasing to God as they resist a rebellion, as they call it, without regard for their own freedom, fortunes, and dangers for their lives. So, if this is not a fault, then it is a great virtue; and thanks to this God cannot but turn a blind eye to the many other sins of the Jews. If things are thus, there is no reason at all why the coming of the Messiah should be postponed, rather it should be precipitated.[99]

Second, this exception is opposed by the text which the Jews call the 'Exposition of Isaiah', chapter 53, along these lines. They interpret this passage as referring to the Jewish people (while we interpret it as a reference to the Messiah), when they dream that the Gentiles who believe in the innocence of the Jews nevertheless recognize that they suffered this hard and long captivity, not because of their own sins but because of the sins of the Gentiles.[100]

Third, what, then, are the sins of the Jewish people (it is not an issue about the sins of single individuals, whoever they might be) that set an

---

[97] Mede, *Daniels Weeks*, 147; Episcopius, *Institutiones Theologicae*, 1: 3.4.8 on 170–1.

[98] Grotius, *De Veritate*, bk 5 on 271; Clarke trans., 5.16 on 242; Episcopius, *Institutiones Theologicae*, 1: 3.4.4 on 162, 3.4.8 on 170.

[99] Grotius, *De Veritate*, bk 5 on 271; Clarke trans., 5.16 on 242; Episcopius, *Institutiones Theologicae*, 1: 3.4.4 on 160.

[100] Hulsius, *Theologiae Iudaicae*, contains a long collection of glosses on Isaiah 53 by a number of rabbis, 324–410, 482–533, which are indexed in his Brevarium, 581–4.

obstacle to the coming of the Messiah? These offences are not against the Law, neither the ritual nor the judicial one. For these laws almost exclusively related to the Temple and the Holy Land. And if there are rites which also apply outside the boundaries of Palestine, the Jews are most diligent in observing them. Nor are they offences against the first or second Table of the Law, since they are followers of the one God, the fiercest enemies of any idolatry, and they hold the name of God in such great reverence that they dare not utter the Tetragrammaton.[101] They observe the Sabbath accurately, and they are far removed from the sins of their fathers, who sacrificed their sons to Moloch and nevertheless received only seventy years of captivity as a punishment for these crimes. 'And we do not sin as seriously as our ancestors did',

[page 78]

says Menasseh Ben Israel, 'and we should probably not have been driven from our land, if we were not already banished from it'. Why, then, would it be that the Messiah should delay his coming? 'Because of the sins of our ancestors', says the praiseworthy author.[102] But who would be such an unfair judge of things that he would think that God would so harshly condemn the descendants to 1600 years of captivity because of the sins of their ancestors, God, who already long ago warned the Jews against saying any longer 'the fathers have eaten sour grapes and their children's teeth are set on edge', but instead each one will atone for his own injustice, and those who ate sour grapes would have their own teeth set on edge. Besides, how is it that those who prophesied about the coming of the Messiah after these sins were committed, nevertheless set down the time of his coming?[103]

Fourth, in the same way it cannot be said that the coming of the Messiah is postponed because of the sins of the Jews, since it was predicted with eloquent words that, because of the serious crimes of the people, the City and the Temple were to be destroyed after the coming of the Messiah, Daniel 9:26.[104]

Fifth, how can this promise be said to be conditional on something and therefore uncertain, when it is set according to a fixed time, namely seventy weeks?

---

[101] The technical term for the four-letter Hebrew name of God, which Jews did not utter because of its sacred character, usually substituting 'Adonai', the Lord; see Episcopius, *Institutiones Theologicae*, 1: 4.4.1 on 280–1; *Sanhedrin*, 90a on 602.

[102] Ben Israel, *Conciliator*, Genes. Quaest 43 on 65; Lindo trans., Question 46 on 1: 68–9 (this translation used for quotation); see *Sanhedrin*, 97a on 657. See also Episcopius, *Institutiones Theologicae*, 1: 3.4.4. on 159–62.

[103] Jeremiah 31:29; Ezekiel 18:2; Hulsius, *Theologiae Iudaicae*, 1.2 on 287; Hoornbeek, *Pro convertendis Judaeis*, 2.1 on 199–203.

[104] Episcopius, *Institutiones Theologicae*, 1: 3.4.9 on 170.

Sixth, against this stand the testimonies of the old Rabbis and doctors of the Talmud, whom you can see praised by Raymundus Martini in *Pugio Fidei*. They wrote that 'in the Times of the Messiah, Men would have the Impudence of Dogs, the Stubbornness of an Ass, and the Cruelty of a wild Beast', and that the Messiah would come when the condition of the Jewish people became criminal and despicable.[105] But it is consistent neither with right reason nor with the Holy Scripture that the coming of the Messiah should be delayed by the sins of the people. He was going to come exactly to that end that the human race could be led to a proper sobriety, awareness, and knowledge of God; Jeremiah 31:31–32, and Malachi 1:4–6.[106] Thus the sins of the Jews, which up to this day have provided fuel and nourishment for the divine wrath, are nothing other than the fact that they turned away (and still do) and that they crucified our Jesus, blessed by God forever; all this in spite of the fact that

[page 79]

he proved that he was the true Messiah with his life, doctrine, resurrection, and miracles.

And so by means of arguments drawn from the Holy Scripture, we have defended our arguments from the Holy Scriptures from all the objections raised by the Jews.

4. I establish the fourth and last argument from reason in the following way. Is the Messiah that prophet whom Moses predicted that God was going to raise, he who likewise the prophets teach and the Jews believe will be the great doctor of the Gentiles, and in whose days God promised that a new covenant with the house of Israel would be made? Is the Messiah, I say, the one who had to abrogate Moses's law, which is not the question in our present times, but I do know for certain that the Law had to last until the coming of the Messiah, and the Jews are commanded to remember this

---

[105] This reference is not found in Martini, *Pugio Fidei*, but it does appear in Grotius, *De Veritate*, bk 5 on 290; Clarke trans., 5.20 on 255 (this translation used for quotation); see *Sanhedrin*, 97a on 656; see also Episcopius, *Institutiones Theologicae*, 1: 3.4.4 on 161.

[106] Jeremiah 31:31: Behold, the days come, saith the Lord, that I will make a new covenant with the house of Israel, and with the house of Judah. 32: Not according to the covenant that I made with their fathers in the day that I took them by the hand to bring them out of the land of Egypt; which my covenant they brake, although I was an husband unto them, saith the Lord. Malachi 1:4: Whereas Edom saith, We are impoverished, but we will return and build the desolate places; thus saith the Lord of hosts, They shall build but I will throw down; and they shall call them, The border of wickedness, and, The people against whom the Lord hath indignation for ever. 5: And your eyes shall see, and ye shall say, The Lord will be magnified from the border of Israel. 6: A son honoureth his father and a servant his master, if then I be a father, where is mine honour? and if I be a master, where is my fear? saith the Lord of hosts unto you O priests, that despise my name. And ye say, Wherein have we despised thy name? Episcopius, *Institutiones Theologicae*, 1: 3.4.4. on 160, 3.4.8 on 171.

by their last prophet, Malachi?[107] Thus since God abundantly demon-strated his intention to abolish the Law and cult of Moses, it is most cer-tain proof that the Messiah came to establish another Law, to which all the world is to be subject. Whether this Law be jurisdictional or ceremonial, no judgment of the divine will in abolishing that Law can be more satisfy-ing than the disappearance of this state and people to which these judicial laws were directed, and the destruction of the City and the Temple, from which most, and the most important part as well, of the ceremonies depends. So, that which was peculiar to the cult of Moses for about 1600 years was offered as a sacrifice.[108]

And in this way God showed his own mind so openly that not only Chrysostom and Sozomen, but also Ammianus Marcellinus, who was not Christian at all, writes that the Jews were hindered by globes of flames exploding against the foundations in the construction of the Temple, which they started under the auspices of Julian.[109] Nothing could be said about the will of Heaven which would be more significant than this, that God did not want this Jewish cult to be revived, and likewise the Messiah had already come. I could put this forth in a fifth argument, that there was once among the Jews one through whom all prophecies and predictions which concerned the Messiah were completely fulfilled. But since such a disquisition should rightly be granted an entire dissertation, I set it aside, and I conclude from the things I have already said, that 'The Messiah promised in the Holy Scripture came a long time ago'.

---

[107] Malachi 4:4: Remember ye the law of Moses my servant, which I commanded unto him in Horeb for all Israel, with the statutes and judgements.

[108] Hulsius, *Theologiae Iudaicae*, 1.1 on 103.

[109] *The Homilies of S. John Chrysostom on the Gospel of St. Matthew*, trans. George Prevost, 2 vols. (Oxford 1852), Homily 4, 1: 43–65, on 44–5; *The Ecclesiastical History of Sozomen, comprising A History of the Church, from A.D. 324 to A.D. 440*, trans. Edward Walford (London, 1855), 5.22 on 240–2; *Ammianus Marcellinus*, trans. John Carew Rolfe, 3 vols. (Cambridge, MA, 1950–1952), 2: 23.1 on 310–11. Cudworth does not appear to have owned edns of these works, but they would have been a standard part of Rust's theological reading at Cambridge. Grotius, *De Veritate*, bk 5 on 268; Clarke trans., 5.15 on 240, cites Ammianus Marcellinus.

George Rust, University of Cambridge Commencement Day Divinity Act Verses

6 July 1658

Scripture Teaches the Resurrection from the Dead, and Reason docs not Contradict This

Whoever is guided by God and reason, the mind's two eyes, sails safely like the one whose course follows the light of the twin stars, Castor and Pollux. Such a one consults oracles more potent than the sacred Delphi, the rock of Cumae or some mumbling cave. We call upon these two lights as our two sacred witnesses that human souls, separated from their earthly burden, will not therefore be perpetually cast about naked once they have put off their body and material covering. When, however, so many centuries have passed according to the law of fate and the stars have completed so many orbits in their fixed order, which the omnipotent Father has prescribed to worldly time, the fiery mind will put on an ethereal coat radiant with rays of light. Loathing its erstwhile rags, the clothing of its body now cast off, it shines as though it wore the Golden Fleece or a garment rich in Tyrian purple.

Surely, it is the fate of mortals that sometime the final day will come, when the scheme of things dissolves in the world's molten lime. The Orcus will exhale and the sky will rain fire. Mount Etna will from its lowest entrails vomit forth bombs of raging fire, exploding its furnaces, and the whole scattered landscape will be nothing but one Etna. Wherever you turn your eyes, black clouds of smoke and a fiery mass hovering above will pervade the lightless void. Imagine that the face of the earth and the sky look like this when, finally, mounting from above his ivory throne, Jesus appears in the clouds amidst his angelic hosts. And the gates of death, opened at the sound of the trumpet, set fearful mankind before his tribunal. Here, as soon as each mind has been subjected to the judge's impartial law, the innocent and pure souls will be given a radiant body, starry, brandishing its shiny hair, as they join the blessed King and fly to their shining houses and heavenly homes where, taken upon the Deity's caring lap, they will rest in eternal peace.

Dare you complain, reason, that bodies, once made dust, cannot regain their form? You are ignorant! Have you not heard of the Assyrian bird, returning to life from the ashes, its body consumed by flames? Have you never seen the ashes of a burned flower, arranged by art, beautifully resume that erstwhile form? Does not the spirit like every little grain of ash visibly occupy its former seat, hastening to restore its effigy and arranging into order all its fleeting particles? Seeing these miracles of nature and of art, those imitations and copies of our life to come, will you not believe that the boundless God who governs the world with a nod can restore our ruins?

No matter how this will come to pass, lest we believe the mind to sleep and be devoid of all perception of things as it lives on, stripped of its body, I follow the guidance of the divine oracle and the light of reason, attributing to the soul a life after the final demise as follows: Freed from earthly dirt and all the savagery of fate and a stranger to any death and danger, it aspires to God's own lot. Related to the higher orders of things, it shines, crowned with a coronet of ether and a subtle fiery vehicle.

The soul, separated from the body, does not sleep

I have seen animals, their limbs numb with cold, fall asleep in a sharp winter of stiffening cold. However, when the spring returned, the air warming the fields with its mild west winds, life returned and thrived in their body. This same story will be told about us. It is the lot of our soul, as it is freed from its limbs and flees them. Bereft of its clothes and incapacitated by death's cold torpor, it lies numb, imprisoned, as it were, in Niobe's marble, until the long day softens the rigid souls with fire, when the fabric of the world is dissolved and the final trumpet, grim as thunder, rouses them from their sleep, both poles reverberating with its noise.

Do tell me, can the inebriation, the cause of this slumber, persist? Can the mind, gorged on the pleasures of the flesh in the sprawling foam of its evil sense-induced drunkenness, snore and hide in the dark for a thousand millennia? Oh, you most wholesome sleep of the gods, gently take hold of the sleeping shades and protect them in your lap. Put flowers upon their pillows and feathers into the mattresses of their beds, I pray, and send them pleasant dreams in their sleep. Send them, I pray, refreshing streams of water and soft buzzing sounds. Send them, I pray, the murmurs of dropping water, the shades of Elysium, the pastures of the Thessalian valley and the quivering voice which the nightingale brings forth. If you give me these pleasures and dear silence, oh sleep, I, for my part, shall not ask to be woken at all. Well done, then, my mind, your forehead bound with poppy flowers, glide safely into God's quiet lap! You will celebrate a long-lasting peace and long quiet and drink from cups filled with Lethe's water.

Yet the poets, I remember, imagine Rhadamanthus to be severe to whom the laws of the infernal place are entrusted. And on departing from its icy limbs into the air, the mind receives its reward or punishment from this judge's mouth at once. Or are you sleeping, Prometheus, hated by the gods, while the bird is gnawing at your entrails in Scythia's mountains? And you, sorcerer Sisyphus, is it sleep or the stone that lies so heavy on you? And you, Ixion, are you being moved in a cradle or on a wheel? I marvel at all those many who, even while being tormented with the Eumenides' savage blows, quite enjoy their rest and quiet! Indeed, one even tends to count virtuous heroines and men of high birth amongst the gods and rightly so. Slaying a monster, protecting a city with a strong hand or routing the foe in battle—will they gain such resounding glory and great triumph to snore more strongly and lie more softly? No, those very fates await the souls right upon their death which Nemesis will assign them according to their desert: The pure mind will exult on the summit of Olympus, free from sleep and joining the angelic choirs. Having shaken off its heavy burden and donned a lighter garment, the mind's living power and new life shines. The impure and guilty soul is tormented by its own Erinys, wide awake, being relentlessly beset by its own Furies.

Christian Hengstermann,
Research Associate, Faculty of Divinity, University of Cambridge

The Holy Scripture Tells of the Resurrection from the Dead, nor does Reason Oppose It: The soul Separated does not Sleep

[Sheffield University Library, MS 61, folio 27/24/2A]

Among all the extravagant opinions that commonly plague the Church, it has always seemed to me that those which cause the downfall of a pious and holy life and of good habits are most to be feared. Among them, we should especially notice the denial of the fundamental article of our faith, the resurrection of the dead.[1] While shedding light on that, and at the same time touching on the other subject,[2] we will labour to remove all the obstacles, proving our case by carefully following fine distinctions. But let us not spend more time on this introduction; let us tackle the facts.

First, there are some things that should be mentioned about the word 'resurrection'. It should be observed that ἀνάστασις [resurrection] and ἀνάστασις τῶν νεκρῶν [resurrection from the dead] and ἔγερσις [rising, awaking] properly mean 'conservation of the thing in being', or 'the condition of the life exceeding and beyond this mortal one'. Thus, it is said of Pharaoh at Romans 9:17, εἰς αὐτὸ τοῦτο ἐξέγειρά σε [even for this same purpose have I raised thee up]. In Hebrew it is העמ[ד]תיך [I raised you up]

---

[1] Tertullian, *On the Resurrection of the Flesh*, trans. Peter Holmes, in *The Writings of Quintus Sept. Flor. Tertullianus*, 2 vols. (Edinburgh, 1870), 2: 215–332, ch. 1 on 215; Thomas Jackson, *Maran atha or Dominus Veniet: Commentaries upon these Articles of the Creed never before Printed* (London, 1657), 11.13.1 on 3422, 11.16.11 on 3465–6.

[2] 'The soul separated does not sleep' was the other position on which Rust was prepared to dispute, but no text is extant. See his Act verses at Bodleian Library, Oxford, Wood 276A (CCCCLXIV); Christian Hengstermann's English translation immediately precedes this text. Rust's Act verses are also mentioned in British Library, MS Harley, 7038, fol. 112 J. J. Hall, *Cambridge Act and Tripos Verses, 1565–1894* (Cambridge, 2009), 154–5. See also Henry More, *An Explanation of the Grand Mystery of Godliness* (London, 1660), 1.6–10 on 15–30.

'I made you stay', which the Septuagint translates διετηρήθης [conservation], 'you are spared from those ills, which destroyed your people'.[3] And concentrating on the noun does not reveal anything else. Στάσις is its position or stand, and accordingly ἀνάστασις νεκρῶν [resurrection of the dead] is the new status of men or standing firm again. Ἀνάστασις [resurrection], then, and ἔγερσις [rising, awaking], have almost the same meaning as διατήρησις [preservation], since in death we seem to sink either into nothingness or at least into a very deep slumber. In this case, the divine preservation is rightly called ἀνάστασις [resurrection], as if rising to our feet, and ἔγερσις [rising, awaking], as if awaking from sleep, since it seems that in death we will lose all vital functions.[4]

[27/24/2B]

Thus the Septuagint translated the Hebrew יקום [living creature] at Genesis 7:4, 23,[5] as ἀνάστημα, 'thing remaining and living on the earth', and, in that version, ἀνίστημι [to raise] matches the word חיה [to preserve alive] which they also translate with ζωοποιέω [to make alive] and ζωογονέω [to preserve alive] even when it simply means 'I let somebody live', as at Exodus 1:17,[6] Nehemiah 9:6,[7] and in a great many other passages. So it should not seem surprising that ἀνίστημι [to raise] is understood as meaning the same thing. It also corresponds to קום [to arise], 'to remain', 'to stand', 'I act so that something should stand', 'that something should stand that would otherwise dangle and fall', from which it is clear that ἀνάστασις [rising] and ἔγερσις [rising, awaking] mean neither rising from dust, nor awaking from sleep, but simply the condition of life after the trial of death. However, we note in passing that the prophets love to speak in a way that strikes the minds of their audience forcefully. Accordingly, they use the kind of language which will make their message sound most

---

[3] *The Septuagint with Apocrypha*, trans. and ed. Lancelot C. L. Brenton (Grand Rapids, 1980), 81: Exodus 9:16: And for this purpose hast thou been preserved, that I might display in thee my strength, and that my name might be published in all the earth; More, *Grand Mystery of Godliness*, 1.6.5 on 17.

[4] More, *Grand Mystery of Godliness*, 1.6.5 on 17, 6.4.4 on 225.

[5] *Septuagint*, 8–9: Genesis 7:4: For yet seven days having passed I bring rain upon the earth forty days and forty nights, and I will blot out every offspring which I have made from the face of all the earth. 23: And God blotted out every offspring which was upon the face of the earth, both man and beast, and reptiles, and birds of the sky, and they were blotted out from the earth, and Noe was left alone, and those with him in the ark; More, *Grand Mystery of Godliness*, 6.4.4 on 225.

[6] *Septuagint*, 70: Exodus 1:17: But the midwives feared God, and did not as the king of Egypt appointed them; and they saved the male children alive.

[7] *Septuagint*, 642: Nehemiah 9:6: And Esdras said, Thou art the only true Lord; thou madest the heaven and the heaven of heavens, and all their array, the earth, and all things that are in it, the seas, and all things in them; and thou quickenest all things, and the hosts of heaven worship thee.

impressive.[8] Thus, they express the act of bringing back from captivity with 'to revive the dead, to resurrect bodies, to stir up and to open the sepulchres', as in Isaiah 26:19,[9] Ezekiel 37,[10] etc.

Even if Menasseh Ben Israel and his Jews make an effort to infer the resurrection from these passages, they nevertheless grudgingly admit that they are to be regarded as referring to a temporary salvation, as the thing itself shows. So the resurrection cannot be demonstrated from them without resorting to the Kabbalah, as is related somewhere in Episcopius. Menasseh himself admitted as much when he was questioned on the subject.[11] Clearly, then, such a way of speaking is mostly used in a figurative sense, especially among holy authors who are inspired from heaven. We should not inspect every subtle and original shade of meaning to ascertain an author's intention. Ἀνίστημι [to raise] in both profane and sacred authors is used as much as possible about things which were not previously expressed in words with certainty. Acts 5:36–7; 7:18, 20, 30,[12] disclose that ἀνίσταναι usually means simply 'to rise', or rather 'to appear'.

[27/24/3A]

Second, ἀνάστασις [rising] sometimes is synonymous with the Hebrew תחיה [revival, resurrection], or with 'eternal life' and 'blessed immortality', as in Luke 20:35, 36.[13] Sometimes it is expressed with the addition of

---

[8] Simon Episcopius, *Opera Theologica* 2 vols. (Amsterdam, 1650–1665), *Institutiones Theologicae*, 1: 3.4.24 on 215 More, *Grand Mystery of Godliness*, 1.6.3–4 on 16.

[9] Isaiah 26:19: Thy dead men shall live, together with my dead body shall they arise. Awake and sing, ye that dwell in dust: for thy dew is as the dew of herbs, and the earth shall cast out the dead.

[10] Ezekiel 37 is the vision in which the prophet is commanded by God to prophesy to the dry bones; at verse 11 these are identified as 'the whole house of Israel'; Jackson, *Maran atha*, 11.13.ch. heading on 3421.

[11] Menasseh Ben Israel, *De Resurrectione Mortuorum* (Amsterdam, 1636), Isaiah 26:19: 1.2.2 on 15–16, 1.6.1 on 37, 2.14 (no section numbers in book 2) on 196–8, 2.15 on 204–5; Ezekiel 37: 1.2.2 on 16, 1.2.4 on 22–3, 1.6.1 on 37, 2.1 on 140–2, 2.2 on 146, 2.7 on 175–6, 2.11 on 188–90, 2.15 on 204–6, 2.16 on 207–8; Kabbalah: 1.12.17 on 88, 3.9 (no section numbers in book 3) on 326. Episcopius, *Institutiones Theologicae*, 1: 3.4.17 on 192, 3.4.24 on 215, 3.5.5 on 224.

[12] Acts 5:36: For before these days rose up Theudas, boasting himself to be somebody; to whom a number of men, about four hundred, joined themselves: who was slain; and all, as many as obeyed him, were scattered, and brought to nought. 37: After this man rose up Judas of Galilee in the days of the taxing, and drew away much people after him: he also perished; and all, even as many as obeyed him, were dispersed. 7:18: Till another king arose, which knew not Joseph. 20: In which time Moses was born, and was exceeding fair, and nourished up in his father's house three months. 30: And when forty years were expired, there appeared to him in the wilderness of mount Sinai an angel of the Lord in a flame of fire in a bush.

[13] Luke 20:35: But they which shall be accounted worthy to obtain that world, and the resurrection from the dead, neither marry, nor are given in marriage: 36: Neither can they die any more: for they are equal unto the angels, and are the children of God, being the children of the resurrection.

ἀνάστασις ζωῆς [awaking of life] and ἀνάστασις τῶν δικαίων [the rising of the just]. Strictly speaking, the meaning of that word is restricted to the resurrection of the dead clothed with their own bodies, as we currently understand it.

Having explained these things, let us proceed to examine our question, both from the Scriptures and from reason. As for the first main part, I shall discuss only I Corinthians 15 without delay.[14] But before we turn to the Apostle's argument, we should be warned. The City of Corinth was rich and opulent and, as the proverb has it, wallowing in luxury and pleasure. Nothing serves as much to obscure the meaning and understanding of divine things, which leads to the extinguishing of hope for a future life.[15] Take the example of the Gnostics and Valentinians, and recently the followers of David Joris, and an excessive number of enthusiasts who have indulged in the pleasures of the flesh, in the past as well as in the current century. They believed, along with Hymenaeus and Philetus, that τὴν ἀνάστασιν ἤδη γεγονέναι [the resurrection has already happened]. They turned this whole article of faith into an allegory, believing that the height of resurrection is to be without mundane concerns, especially marriage, and, following the example of the unmarried Essenes, to give oneself to meditation.[16] Because of this, they had, so to speak, a new life, compared to which their previous life looked like death. Therefore they called the former death, and the latter resurrection. This fabrication took hold of them so easily, since the Stoics, the Peripatetics, and Epicureans among them very likely objected to the stupidity and impossibility of resurrection.[17] It is clear that for the Corinthians this was a similar stumbling block. But the Apostle properly foresaw that, while they were outstandingly spiritual and undermined the status of the greatest mysteries and even the principles and foundations of the Christian religion with their allegories, the lowest depravities of lustful

---

[14] Jackson, *Maran atha*, 11.16.ch. heading on 3455.

[15] The proverb referred to is *Non est cuiuslibet Corinthum appellere*, 'It is not given to everyone to land at Corinth'. Erasmus, in his *Adagiorum Chiliades* (Venice, 1508, and often reprinted) explained that Strabo's *Geography* had assigned the origin of the proverb to 'the luxury of Corinth and its courtesans', see *The Collected Works of Erasmus: Adages Ii1 to Iv100*, trans. Margaret Mann Phillips, annotated Roger A. B. Mynors (Toronto and London, 1974–), 31: 317–19.

[16] Tertullian, *Resurrection of the Flesh*, chs 19–22 on 247–54; Henry More, *Conjectura Cabbalistica* (London, 1653), 244–5, 247; idem, *Enthusiasmus Triumphatus* (London, 1656), 22, 30–7; idem, *Grand Mystery of Godliness*, 1.6.2, 6 on 16–17, 5.8.3 on 153, 5.9.9 on 158, 5.11.1 on 161, 6.2.1 on 218, 6.3.2 on 221, 6.12.5 on 249, 6.16.3 on 265, 6.16.4 on 267, 6.17.3 on 269, 6.19.1 on 274; Ralph Cudworth, *The True Intellectual System of the Universe* (London, 1678), 1.5.3 on 795; for Hymenaeus and Philetus, see I Timothy 1:20, II Timothy 2:17–18.

[17] Tertullian, *Resurrection of the Flesh*, ch. 19, on 247–8; Jackson, *Maran atha*, 11.13.2 on 3423.

pleasure would easily have thrown them into the blindest impiety, which was in fact what happened.[18]

[27/24/3B]

Those enthusiasts and the Corinthians themselves had started to shape their habits according to this doctrine. Therefore, the Apostle considers it to be of the highest importance firmly to establish this truth, the foundation of our whole religion.[19] In treating this subject, we should issue a warning: the Apostle had to deal with those who denied not only the resurrection of the body, but also the future life, which are both denoted ἀνάστασις [resurrection] and ἔγερσις [rising, awaking], as we have already said. Besides, it should be noticed that the prophetic style, and that of men who are divinely inspired, need not be subjected to the rules of scholastic and ordinary writers. Nor should they be expected always to adhere to only one term. But since they are pregnant with many things, it is necessary that they give birth to their words in starts, as it were, touching on many things only in passing, as the Spirit working within them suggests.[20] Therefore we should not expect that the apostolic discourses will be limited to defending the resurrection of the body. If they only prove blessed immortality, that will suffice. These points are just as important as those which follow in proving our position, namely, that we are unable to attain the highest happiness and blessedness until the moment when we are clothed in celestial bodies. Both alike have been called into question, even though, as will become apparent later, we are in reality incapable of the highest happiness and felicity until we are clothed in heavenly garments.[21] By demonstrating the former point, we will simultaneously overcome objections to the latter.

After these prefatory remarks, I will briefly touch on some of the apostolic arguments that occur in this chapter. First, to those things which the Corinthians doubted, it seems appropriate to add the applicability of Christ's resurrection to us. First, however, he seems to give reasons for the possibility of this matter which the Corinthians doubted, as is seen in verses 35 and 36.[22] It implies no contradiction that that which has happened in the past may happen again now. The antecedent is proved with a great many arguments of the *reductio ad absurdum* variety.[23] Since they are

---

[18]   More, *Grand Mystery of Godliness*, 1.6.6 on 17.

[19]   Jackson, *Maran atha*, 11.11.13.2 on 3423.

[20]   Episcopius, *Institutiones Theologicae* 1: 3.4.24 on 215; More, *Grand Mystery of Godliness*.

[21]   More, *Grand Mystery of Godliness*, 6.5.2–3 on 226–7.

[22]   I Corinthians 15: 35: But some man will say, How are the dead raised up? And with what body do they come? 36: Thou fool, that which thou sowest is not quickened, except it die; Jackson, *Maran atha*, 11.14.1 on 3434; [George Rust?], *A Letter of Resolution concerning Origen* (London, 1661), 61; Cudworth, *True Intellectual System*, 1.5.3 on 796.

[23]   The 'antecedent' is a statement contained in the 'if' clause of a conditional proposition, here, if Christ was not raised from the dead. *Reductio ad absurdum* is a method of

sufficiently evident by themselves, and fully explained by others, we need not quote them. Be it sufficient to say that Jesus openly declared that he was going to rise on the third day, and, if events had not confirmed his words, Christ's doctrine would be undone and his constancy in willingly accepting death would prove only stubbornness and folly.

[27/24/4A]

Secondly, Christ's resurrection proves not only that our resurrection is possible, but also that it will indeed take place.[24] Christ arisen is ἀπαρχὴ τῶν κεκοιμημένων ἐγένετο; ['the first-fruits of them that slept'].[25] This metaphor, pointing to the fact that Christ rose first to blessed immortality, and to a heavenly body, also shows the manner in which the first-fruits, or the first bundle reaped from the crops, consecrated the whole harvest. Thus also Christ, in his resurrection, marked all who partake of his nature for the joyous harvest and a similar resurrection.[26] Truly, the connection between Christ's resurrection and ours is intimate. So it is clear that the founder and leader of our religion commanded us to tread in his footsteps. By setting out on that road, he promised that we will be the heirs of his glory and, as his companions, will be where he is. Therefore, since he has attained eternal life and a glorified body, it follows, according to the faith we have received, that we who follow his example will also reach the same state. Furthermore, divine goodness and even divine equity require that those who imitate him, to some degree, in life and endurance should obtain the appropriate reward of blessedness.

The other argument comes from the same apostolic passage. It is found in verses 30, 31, and 32: 'And why stand we in jeopardy every hour? I protest by your rejoicing which I have in Christ Jesus our Lord, I die daily. If after the manner of men I fought with beasts at Ephesus, what advantageth it me, if the dead rise not? Let us eat and drink, for tomorrow we die'.[27] The sum of these things is that Paul and the remaining apostles could not legitimately be considered mad and having taken leave of their senses, nor of lacking understanding of either pain or pleasure. Neither does it appear likely that they would have exposed themselves to so many miseries, afflictions, dangers, and deaths without some serious reason.

proving the falsity of a premiss by showing that the logical consequence is absurd; see Jackson, *Maran atha*, 11.16.1 on 3456–7.

[24] More, *Grand Mystery of Godliness*, 1.6.7 on 17; George Rust, *A Sermon preached at New-Town the 29 of Octob. 1663. At the Funeral of the Right Honourable Hugh Earl of Mount-Alexander* (Dublin, 1664), 28; [Henry Hallywell], *A Private Letter of Satisfaction to a Friend* (n.p., 1667), 23–4.

[25] I Corinthians 15:20; Jackson, *Maran atha*, 11.16.1 on 3457, 11.16.9 on 3464.

[26] Jackson, *Maran atha*, 11.16.9 on 3464; More, *Grand Mystery of Godliness*, 6.6.6 on 229–30.

[27] More, *Grand Mystery of Godliness*, 1.6.2 on 16.

[27/24/4B]

But it is impossible that a moderate and conscientious soul, among so many evils of the present life, would have the strength to endure with so much equanimity, patience, and joy, except for the hope of blessed immortality, the highest perfection of which could not be touched, were it not for the spiritual and celestial body. Our Saviour demonstrates the resurrection of the dead with this argument against the Sadducees: 'I am the God of Abraham, Isaac, and Jacob',[28] that is, I will be their special εὐεργέτης [benefactor]. This is the meaning of this expression, as the author of the Letter to the Hebrews explains: Διὸ οὐκ ἐπαισχύνεται αὐτοὺς ὁ Θεὸς ἐπικαλεῖσθαι αὐτῶν. Ἡτοίμασεν γὰρ αὐτοῖς πόλιν; [wherefore God is not ashamed to be called their God: for he hath prepared for them a city].[29] Therefore as the Jews noted, in the Holy Scripture God is not called the God of anyone while he is still leading this mortal life.[30] So, since it is certain that an excellent reward awaits those whom God claims in such a particular manner, it is necessary that after death there should be a life and that this life should be most blessed. One life cannot be without the body, nor can the other be without the celestial body, as will be shortly demonstrated.

In order further to elucidate this point and the apostolic argument, we believe that the following theorems, as the props and struts of both issues, should be set out. Nevertheless we should first remind ourselves that today we are only dealing with two kinds of men—enthusiasts and philosophers. Against the former we have thus far argued from the Holy Scriptures. I will now confront the philosophers who allege that the resurrection is folly.[31] No one should find it either extraordinary or unpleasant if we adapt our method to theirs to some extent.

First, the soul cannot function independently from matter.[32] I will prove this through the following steps. Without doubt, the divine fecundity can do anything that is not inconsistent with itself. Next, the essential properties of things are so closely linked to the things themselves that it cannot be explained any further. Nevertheless, although every substance is ingenerate and incorruptible, and even though it does not depend upon another

---

[28] Mark 12:26; Jackson, *Maran atha*, 11.13.6 on 3426, 11.16.1 on 3456; Episcopius, *Institutiones Theologicae*, 1: 3.4.1 on 156; More, *Grand Mystery of Godliness*, 1.6.10 on 18.

[29] Hebrews 11:16.

[30] This circumlocution of Mark 12:27 (He is not the God of the dead, but the God of the living) fits the purpose of Rust's argument; cf. Jackson, *Maran atha*, 11.13.5 on 3426; [Hallywell], *Private Letter*, 25.

[31] Jackson, *Maran atha*, 11.13.2 on 3423.

[32] *Origen: On First Principles*, trans. G. W. Butterworth (Gloucester MA, 1973), 1.1.6 on 11, 1.6.4 on 58; More, *Immortality of the Soul*, 3.1.1–2 on 328–30, 3.18.10 on 532; idem, *Grand Mystery of Godliness*, 6.5.1 on 226; [Hallywell], *Private Letter*, 18.

substance, it is still possible that a substance may be such that it cannot exercise its functions without an intimate connection with matter.[33]

[27/24/5A]

Furthermore, when some excellent reasons persuade us that this or that is a certain way, there is no reason why the fact that it is a mere possibility should, by contrast, prevent our giving it our assent. The soul is the kind of substance which cannot function if it is not vitally linked with matter. From this it can be seen, but not demonstrated, that it will have a close union with this body, so unrefined and earthly, but its most intellectual operations will depend to a high degree on the appropriate mixture of animal spirits. It seems inconsistent that a substance of that kind, once separated from this bond, will be free and naked, and will operate independently from any matter whatsoever. Rather, it should be believed that the nature of the soul necessarily implies association with a body of some kind, otherwise it will be unable to exercise its faculties and vital functions.[34]

Second, in this earthly body, the spirit's proper instruments are movement, sense and reason. There is no reason for us to waste time in trying to prove this proposition, It is indeed καθαρὰ καὶ φωτοειδὴς περιουσία as Hippocrates says, a certain 'pure and luminous substance' that provides sustenance and nourishment to the soul, and on that all the physicians and philosophers are of the same opinion.[35] This relationship with the external air, which we perceive when our thoughts are clear or confused on account of the sky, whether it be clear or cloudy, demonstrates abundantly that the soul's matter, which shares many qualities with the air, the changes of which easily effect changes in matter itself, acts as a handmaid for the soul in perceiving things. Otherwise, the balance of the external air would neither help nor hinder the processes of our minds at all.[36] Facial expressions, which seem nothing but a certain moistening of the eyes and of the remaining parts of the face by the animal spirits, are not a lesser proof.

[27/24/5B]

It follows that, apart from the face, all the features and proportions hint at the current state of the mind, which must result from the kinship between these spirits and the soul itself.[37] The same can be proved by considering

---

[33] Jackson, *Maran atha*, 11.15.2 on 3445.

[34] Cudworth, *True Intellectual System*, 1.5.3 on 785–810, *passim*, see especially 771 (error for 793), 800.

[35] *Hippocrates*, ed. and trans. Paul Potter, 10 vols. (Cambridge, MA, 1923–2010), 'Heart', 9: 58–69, ch. 11 on 67, 'a pure and luminous bath'; More, *Immortality of the Soul*, 2.8.3 on 201, 2.17.8 on 308.

[36] More, *Immortality of the Soul*, 2.8.4 on 201, 2.17.8 on 308; [Hallywell], *Private Letter*, 57–8.

[37] More, *Immortality of the Soul*, 2.8.8 on 203–4, 2.8.11–12 on 207.

vertigo, the paralysis of a limb, lipothymia,[38] and other arguments, on which it is useless for me to insist, since it is generally acknowledged among those who have the least experience of either philosophy or medicine.[39]

Third, the purer the spirits, the better the soul exercises its functions. This follows from what has been said. If the spirits are the instrument of the soul, then the more impurities have been removed from them, the easier and freer those functions whose instruments they are will be. It can be ascertained from experience that drunkenness and luxury cloud the intellect, and that a purer climate of the region and of the sky considerably augments the clarity and cleverness of the mind. The masters of piety and wisdom usually encourage moderation and purification of the spirit, in order to reach the true and right understanding of things.[40]

Fourth, the soul which has escaped from this earthly prison is clothed in an aerial ὄχημα [vehicle].[41] This is the next step up. There are not usually leaps or voids in nature, but everything is fashioned in steps and gradients of appropriate quality or shape.[42] Certainly, a few souls which are purified beyond measure and greatly devoted to the glory of God and the good of mankind will have, once their earthly dwelling has been destroyed, a building in heaven that comes from God, an eternal house not built by human hands, οἰκοδομὴ Θεοῦ ἀχειροποίητος αἰώνιος ἐν τοῖς οὐρανοῖς [house not made with hands, eternal in the heavens],[43] to which Saint Paul aspired. They will rise εἰς τὴν ἐξανάστασιν τῶν νεκρῶν [to the resurrection from the dead], to which he aspired, although he had not yet attained it.[44]

---

[38] Sudden faintness without losing consciousness.

[39] More, *Immortality of the Soul*, 2.9.6 on 213.

[40] Ibid., 2.11.3 on 228, 3.1.9 on 337–8, 3.14.7 on 477; idem, *Grand Mystery of Godliness*, 6.6.3 on 228; [Rust?], *Letter of Resolution*, 60; Rust, *Sermon preached at New-Town*, 12–13; [Hallywell], *Private Letter*, 8, 28; Cudworth, *True Intellectual System*, 1.5.3 on 786–7.

[41] ὄχημα = support, carriage, chariot, but the English word the Cambridge Platonists used for the material clothing of the soul was 'vehicle', see e.g., More, *Conjectura Cabbalistica*, 41, 170; idem, *Immortality of the Soul*, 2.14 on 257–67, 3.1 on 326–40; idem, *Grand Mystery of Godliness*, 1.6.9 on 18, 1.7.1 on 19, 6.5.2 on 226, 6.5.6 on 227; Cudworth, *True Intellectual System*, 1.5.3 on 785, 778 (error for 788), 789, 792, 771 (error for 793); cf. Tertullian, *Resurrection of the Flesh*, ch. 35 on 275, which condemns those who propose 'some body of a subtle, secret nature'.

[42] Origen, *First Principles*, 3.6.6 on 251; More, *Immortality of the Soul*, 3.1.5 on 333, 3.3.1, on 352; Rust, *Sermon preached at New-Town*, 31; [Hallywell], *Private Letter*, 3.

[43] II Corinthians, 5:1; Tertullian, *Resurrection of the Flesh*, ch. 41 on 286–7; Origen, *Contra Celsum*, ed. William Spencer (Cambridge, 1658), ch. 7 on 353; *Origen: Contra Celsum*, trans. Henry Chadwick (Cambridge, 1980), 7.32 on 420–1; Origen, *First Principles*, 3.6.4 on 249–50; More, *Grand Mystery of Godliness* 1.7.1–4 on 19–20; [Rust?], *Letter of Resolution*, 63.

[44] Philippians 3:11: If by any means I might attain unto the resurrection of the dead. 12: Not as though I had already attained, either were already perfect: but I follow after, if I may apprehend that for which also I am apprehended of Christ Jesus; More, *Grand Mystery of Godliness*, 1.7.5 on 21.

In truth these should be considered as ἅπαξ λεγόμενα [*hapax legomena*]⁴⁵
and singular instances and extremely rare examples.

[27/24/6A]

So the soul, once it has broken the bars of this prison, is immersed in
an immense ocean of air,⁴⁶ with which it can vitally merge even more
effectively than with this earthly body. It is clear that, as I have said, the
animal spirits, which are related to air, are the proper instruments of all
the soul's functions even under this corporeal burden. And those which
we call corporeal organs do not contribute to any function, as clearly
results from their mechanical structure, other than to transmit the motions
and the impressions of external things to the centre of the soul and the
seat of perceptions. Thus, for instance, the eyes are provided with various
fluids because of the refraction of rays, so that more of them can be collected in the central point, so that the impression is stronger and more
easily transmitted to the Common Sense.⁴⁷ The same can be said of the
ears and the other bodily organs. We learn from anatomists that bodily
organs are constructed like this, because otherwise it would be difficult,
if not impossible, that the light and rather subtle touch of the objects
could penetrate the firm crust of this earthly body.⁴⁸ For which reason,
the soul in its aerial tabernacle will not require a device of that kind, but
will easily deal with even the very gentle impulses of things, since there
is no thicker barrier that prevents the passage to its inner recesses. If it
pleases, with its imaginative power it can create in that ὄχημα ἀέριον
[aerial vehicle] any organ it likes, in order to achieve an easier perception
of some particular object.⁴⁹

Fifth, even if (thus either by an observing θεία τινι νεμέσει [some divine
nemesis] or by the justice intertwined in the nature of things,⁵⁰ or by the
divine control of the world, which reaches from the highest to the lowest) I
knew for sure that the good are well equipped for the escape of the soul from
the body, the bad otherwise, if the condition of the separated spirits were
evaluated only by the order and laws of nature, it would be necessary for the
good and the bad to be mixed together, as it is now on earth. The same
region, although according to the different purity of souls, the different
habitations, and the different functions, would be their common place of

---

⁴⁵ A word that occurs only once within a text.
⁴⁶ More, *Immortality of the Soul*, 3.1.4 on 332.
⁴⁷ Ibid., 2.8.9 on 204. 2.10.9 on 223–6, 2.4–9 on 155–214.
⁴⁸ Ibid., 3.4.2–6 on 367–70, 3.1.7 on 334–5.
⁴⁹ Ibid., 3.1.10 on 338–9; idem, *Grand Mystery of Godliness*, 6.6.1–2 on 228; [Hallywell],
Private Letter, 5; Cudworth, *True Intellectual System*, 1.5.3 on 787, 789.
⁵⁰ More, *Immortality of the Soul*, 2.18.10 on 323, 3.1.5 on 333, 3.3.3 on 353–4, 3.11.6 on
440, 3.12.11 on 449.

refuge, so that laudable persons would not receive an excellent and superb reward nor would the others their deserved and appropriate punishment.[51]
[27/24/6B]

This would be the state of things, if it were done to us according to nature. At the same time, the Holy Scriptures seem to pass over this inter-mediate state in silence. There, pious or impious things are mentioned, and there is always consideration of the Day of Judgement, when the deeds of each will be simultaneously rewarded. From this, the Church, both primitive and contemporary, has unanimously postponed the great bulk of punishments and rewards to the end of the age. But even the deep silence of St Paul on this subject has provided an opening to the psycho-pannychism of the Socinians,[52] where the souls: 'at the water of Lethe's stream . . . drink the soothing draught and long forgetfulness'.[53]

Sixth, it is especially congruent with divine goodness and rectitude that good men receive the greatest reward. God, out of his long-suffering mercy and kindness, rewards them with the fruit and wages of hardships endured, which they accepted for the sake of God and of the divine life. If God is just, the dead will be raised—thus Tertullian and the Fathers once said.[54] It is right, says the Apostle, for God to give suffering to the impious who torment us, and to give us, who are unjustly tormented, solace in the appearance of Christ with the angels in the flaming fire of his power.[55]

Seventh, the last argument, which follows necessarily from the previous ones. It is appropriate to divine goodness and rectitude that pure, holy souls should be clothed in ethereal bodies,[56] or as the Apostle says, spiritual ones. From them, 'length of days, when time's cycle is complete, has

---

[51] Ibid., 2.18.8–9 on 320–1.

[52] Ibid., preface on [sig.] b^v; idem, *Grand Mystery of Godliness*, 1.6.6–10 on 15–30; [Hallywell], *Private Letter*, 2–3; Cudworth, *True Intellectual System*, 1.5.3 on 795. Psychopannychites believed that the soul slept with the body until the general resurrection and Last Judgement; see n. 2 above.

[53] Virgil, *Aeneid*, trans. H. Rushton Fairclough, rev. George P. Goold, 2 vols. (Cambridge, MA, 2004), 1: 6.714–15 on 582–3; Menasseh Ben Israel, *Conciliator, sive de convenientia locorum S. Scripturae, quae pugnare inter se videntur* (Amsterdam, 1633), Genes. Quaest 18 on 66; *The Conciliator of R. Manasseh* [sic] *Ben Israel*, trans. E. H. Lindo, 2 vols. (London, 1842), Genesis Question 46, 1: 69.

[54] Tertullian, *Resurrection of the Flesh*. Rust gives a brief summary of ch. 14 on 236–8: see also ch. 60 on 327, 'For the judgement-seat of God requires that man be kept entire.'; [Hallywell], *Private Letter*, 32, 76.

[55] II Thessalonians 1:6: Seeing it is a righteous thing with God to recompense tribulation to them that trouble you; 7: And to you who are troubled rest with us, when the Lord Jesus shall be revealed from heaven with his mighty angels, 8: In flaming fire taking vengeance on them that know not God, and that obey not the gospel of our Lord Jesus Christ: 9: Who shall be punished with everlasting destruction from the presence of the Lord, and from the glory of his power.

[56] More, *Immortality of the Soul*, 3.1.4 on 332.

removed the inbred taint'. God will bestow an 'ethereal sense and pure flame of spirit'.[57] The aerial or πνευματικόν [aerial] body is a most appropriate instrument for the soul, ὡς ἄϋλον καὶ ἀΐδιον καὶ παθημάτων καθαρῶν [like a living and eternal body, purified from passions]. The reason is that it is a most pure and refined matter, and most obedient to the commands of the soul, for its most subtle parts can be arranged in any movement or shape with minimal effort.

[27/24/7A]

On the contrary, this earthly mass is demonstrably the highest impediment to the nobler functions of the mind.

> Fiery is the vigour and divine the source of those seeds of life, so far as harmful bodies clog them not, or earthly limbs and frames born to die. Hence their fears and desires, their griefs and joys; nor do they discern the heavenly light, penned as they are in the gloom of their dark dungeon.[58]

The particles of air are neither completely pure nor deprived of any edge or roughness, nor so pliable and malleable that, when critically compressed with great force, they do not spring apart, as a great many experiments make clear.[59] Therefore, this celestial or spiritual matter is a most suitable body for the soul. There is no room for doubt that, just as certain faculties are proper to the terrestrial body, others conform to the aerial one, others to the spiritual one, and the more purified the body is, the nobler the state to which its faculties are awakened. For this reason, it appears to be highly appropriate to divine wisdom and goodness that the soul, when it proves to be obedient and compliant to the supreme will, is roused to more sublime functions, and it rises to higher levels of bliss, divine knowledge, and kindness.

---

[57] Virgil, *Aeneid*, trans. Fairclough and Goold, 1: 6.745–7 on 584–5; Cudworth, *True Intellectual System*, 1.5.3 on 790, quotes the same passage.

[58] Virgil, *Aeneid*, trans. Fairclough and Goold, 1: 6.730–4 on 582–3; More, *Immortality of the Soul*, 3.15.7 on 488–9; Cudworth, *True Intellectual System*, 1.5.3 on 790, quotes lines 735–42, immediately following: Still more! When life's last ray has fled, the wretches are not entirely free from all evil and all the plagues of the body; and it needs must be that many a taint, long ingrained, should in wondrous wise become deeply rooted in their being. Therefore are they schooled with punishments, and pay penance for bygone sins. Some are hung stretched out to the empty winds; from some the stain of guilt is washed away under swirling floods or burned out in fire ..., trans. Fairclough and Goold, on 1: 584–5.

[59] This sentence suggests some familiarity with contemporary discussions of the elasticity of the air, for which see Charles Webster, 'The Discovery of Boyle's Law and the Concept of the Elasticity of the Air in the Seventeenth Century', *Archive for History of Exact Sciences* 2 (1965), 441–502, which is particularly interesting in regard to the experiments of Henry Power (then a medical student, influenced by More) at Christ's College in 1653, on 459–64. More, *Immortality of the Soul*, 3.1.8 on 336, 3.5.3 on 378, mentions experiments with 'Winde-Guns', which he may have read about in Walter Charelton, *Physiologia Epicuro-Gassendo-Charltoniana, or, a Fabrick of Science Natural, upon the Hypothesis of Atoms* (London, 1654), 1.4.2 on 26, 1.5.6 on 55, 3.10.2 on 257, 3.11.2 on 280, 3.14.1 on 329.

Certain Christians relate this Pythagorean verse to this point:

ἢν δ' ἀπολείψας σῶμα ἐς αἰθέρ' ἐλεύθερον ἔλθῃς,
ἔσσεαι ἀθάνατος, θεὸς ἄμβροτος, οὐκέτι θνητός.
[Then, if you leave the body behind and go to the free *aither*,
you will be immortal, an undying god, no longer mortal.][60]

And what Pythagoras calls αἰθέρα [ether] the Apostle calls πνεῦμα [breath,
spirit], which term, even if the schools gave it a very different meaning,
originally does not mean anything other than πνοή [blast] or ἄνεμος
[breath, wind], an indubitably fine and subtle substance. Ψυχὴν πνεῦμα
εἶναι [the soul is breath] affirmed the Stoics.[61] Διὸ καὶ σῶμα εἶναι
[and therefore it is a body], Diogenes Laertius said ἀραιότερον καὶ
λεπτομερέστερον [finer and more delicate].[62] And about this point Hermes
Trismegistus said:

[27/24/7B]

ἔνδυμα εἶναι τοῦ μὲν νοῦ τὴν ψυχὴν, τῆς δὲ ψυχῆς τὸ πνεῦμα [the soul
is a garment of the mind, and the spirit is that of the soul] without doubt
a certain spiritual and celestial matter is the most noble ὄχημα [vehicle]
and garment of the soul.[63]

And thus ἀνάστασις τῶν δικαίων [the rising of the just] or resurrection
to blessed immortality has been demonstrated from the Scripture against
the enthusiasts, and, by reasoning and principles that are clear by their
own light, also against the philosophers who accused it of absurdity. The
reason is that the glorified and spiritual body is requisite in order to achieve
the happiness that belongs to human nature. In the same way, it is particularly fitting to divine goodness that a humble, obedient, and faithful soul
should be made happy.[64]

---

[60] Johan C. Thom, *The Pythagorean Golden Verses: with Introduction and Commentary*
(Leiden, 1995), verses 70–1 on 98–9 ; More, *Immortality of the Soul*, 3.19.10 on 549.

[61] Diogenes Laertius, *Lives of the Eminent Philosophers*, trans. Robert D. Hicks, 2 vols.
(Cambridge, MA, 1925), 2: 7.157 on 260–1, 9.19 on 426–7.

[62] Diogenes Laertius, *Lives*, the closest match to Rust's quotation is probably at 2: 10.63
(Epicurus), on 592–3: 'the soul is a corporeal thing, composed of fine particles, dispersed all
over the frame, most nearly resembling wind with an admixture of heat, in some respects
like wind, in others like heat'.

[63] *Hermetica: The Ancient Greek and Latin Writings which contain Religious or Philosophic
Teachings ascribed to Hermes Trismegistus*, ed. and trans. Walter Scott, 4 vols. (Oxford,
1924–1936), the closest match to Rust's quotation is probably at 1: 12.14a on 230–1: 'The
rarest part of matter then is air; the rarest part of air is soul; the rarest part of soul is mind;
and the rarest part of mind is God'. An earlier translation of this passage appears in Hermes
Mercurius Trismegistus, *The Divine Pymander*, trans. John Everard (London, 1649), 5.49 on
71, 11.70 on 149; (London, 1657), 5.49 on 83, 11.70 on 172.

[64] Origen, *First Principles*, 3.6.4–5 on 250–1; Jackson, *Maran atha*, 11.16.4 on 3459;
More, *Grand Mystery of Godliness*, 6.5.2–3 on 226–7.

But the Scripture also mentions ἀνάστασις κρίσεως [resurrection of damnation][65] and ἀνάστασις δικαίων τε καὶ ἀδίκων [the resurrection of the just and of the unjust],[66] which teaches that all will be raised from the dust and placed in front of Jesus Christ's tribunal, so that they can be judged together according to the things they did while still in the flesh, which is as supremely rational as the Last Judgement itself. The fact that all human beings will visibly appear emphasizes the solemnity and terror of this Day of Judgement.[67]

Even though the resurrection can be shown to be certain from Scripture and reason, someone might still ask πῶς ἐγείρονται οἱ νεκροί; ποίῳ δὲ σώματι ἔρχονται; ['How are the dead raised up? and with what body do they come'],[68] do they rise with the same body or with a different one? This issue is so intertwined with our cause that it would be appropriate to focus on it for a little while. Before we present our proposition, let us hear the arguments of those who say that the resurrection is not the resurrection of the same body at all, or that it makes no difference whether it is or not.[69] First, they say that we certainly do not even have the same body throughout the entire span of our life, so how can we be raised with the same body on the very last day? In fact while we are carried in our mother's womb, weighing half an ounce or less, we do not have even one millionth of the body we have when we reach adulthood and become men.

[27/24/8A]

What about the fact that when we have reached childhood or adolescence, there remain only a small number of atoms from the body with which we were born? The physicians, not without good reason, claim that the whole body changes every seven years. But even assuming that was not true, how could that very tiny part of matter in an embryo individualize the total mass of matter gained by our body later on? And thus our bodies do not remain the same throughout our entire lifespans any more than a stream does which always laps the same banks. Nor is a great vessel filled with rainwater the same as a little drop that sank into it when it first began

---

[65] John 5:29: And shall come forth; they that have done good, unto the resurrection of life; and they that have done evil, unto the resurrection of damnation; Jackson, *Maran atha*, 11.13.ch. heading, on 3421.

[66] Acts 24:15: And have hope toward God, which they themselves also allow, that there shall be a resurrection of the dead, both of the just and of the unjust.

[67] More, *Grand Mystery of Godliness*, 1.7.1 on 19.

[68] I Corinthians 15:35; Origen, *Contra Celsum*, ed. Spencer, ch. 5 on 243; trans. Chadwick, 5.18 on 277–8; Jackson, *Maran atha*, 11.14.1 on 3434, 11.15.6 on 3450, 11.15.9 on 3453; [Rust?], *Letter of Resolution*, 61.

[69] For a review of seventeenth- and early eighteenth-century positions on this question, see Lloyd Strickland, 'The Doctrine of "The Resurrection of the Same Body" in Early Modern Thought', *Religious Studies*, 46 (2010), 163–83.

to fill up. Thus we would have to rise with the body that we had in a specific juncture of life. But why with that one rather than another?[70] However, if there is as strong a reason for the one as for the other, and one of them is unnecessary, then the other is also unnecessary. Hence, neither of them is necessary. Or will we rise with any matter that we have consumed throughout the entire course of our life? But this means that we would not be men but monsters, nor we would rise with the same bodies but with many different ones.

Furthermore, they say, human bodies are dissolved into dust and vapours. They are born anew from the earth as herbs and weeds, the beasts graze on them, men eat the beasts, and this happens by infinite turns.[71] And can we doubt this for any good reason? Can it not be geometrically demonstrated that the whole multitude of men, who have lived since the creation of the world and who will live till the end, is equal to or exceeds the entire earth? Not even one tenth is good for growing food, and that does not provide even one ten-thousandth as nourishment. There is nobody who has reached the age of thirty without having claimed back his mass hundreds of times by eating, if we consider our daily intake of food. From this perspective, we must have absorbed all our ancestors by eating, and will be similarly swallowed by future generations. Thousands of past rivals must lay claim with equal right to one single particle of matter.

[27/24/8B]

This would be so incompatible with the dead emerging from their tombs and the dust of the earth that not even the earth itself would suffice for the bodies to be raised. Besides, most fish are devoured by fish, and, if we substitute men for fish, men are eaten by cannibals, and thus in a series repeated anew 600 times.[72]

Similarly the historiographers narrate that, in the most extreme hunger, mothers ate their infant children, as during the sieges of Jerusalem and Samaria.[73] However, it would be a childish κρησφύγετον [retort] to imagine that this kind of food did not nourish, because in that case nobody would have eaten anything, or that God miraculously satisfied their excessive appetites and renewed their strength. It would be too bold to expect a

---

[70] Jackson, *Maran atha*, 11.15.6–8 on 3449–51, 11.9 on 3453; More, *Grand Mystery of Godliness*, 6.3.6 on 222–3; [Rust?], *Letter of Resolution*, 118; Cudworth, *True Intellectual System*, 1.5.3 on 799.

[71] Jackson, *Maran atha*, 11.15.2 on 3444; More, *Grand Mystery of Godliness*, 6.3.5 on 222.

[72] Jackson, *Maran atha*, 11.14.4 on 3447, 11.15.7 on 3450–1; More, *Grand Mystery of Godliness*, 6.3.4 on 222.

[73] Jackson, *Maran atha*, 11.15.4 on 3448; the reference is to Josephus, *The Jewish War*, for which see Flavii Josephi, *Hierosolymitani Sacerdoti: Opera quae exstant* (Geneva, 1634), *De Bello Judaico*, 7.8 on 954–5; *Josephus*, trans. H. St. J. Thackray, 9 vols. (London, 1956), 3: 6.199–213 on 434–7.

θεὸς ἀπὸ μηχανῆς [*deus ex machina*].[74] For this reason, they say that it cannot be possible that we rise with the same body, since the same matter would necessarily have to belong to so many.

They furthermore claim that the reasons by which this point is upheld are invalid and simply void and verge on the ridiculous. As for a soul's natural inclination towards a body, it is not determined by a certain specific body, as is clear from the first argument. True, it is said that the divine justice requires this for the meting out of rewards and punishments, because if the same body were not resurrected, the man would not be the same. But they cry out in protest with Cicero and the Platonists, the soul is the man.[75] Thus a soul cannot operate separately from the support of the body, but the body is no more essential to the man than the shadow is essential to the body, or the wood-axe to the carpenter. The reason is that, if matter were an essential part of a man, once it is changed, the man would be changed as well. And thus an old man would be different from the infant he once was. Nor does it contribute to the matter that divine justice demands that what participated in pains and labours in religious matters, and what participated in the pleasures of sin, should participate also in happiness or in misery.[76]

[27/24/9A]

It is easily proved through the principles of reasoning and of the sounder kind of philosophy that matter is unable to feel, therefore to feel pleasure or pain, even less to feel vice and virtue, and least of all to feel punishment or rewards.[77]

On top of that, they cry out that nothing has added more insult and derision to the Christian religion among dissolute characters and atheists than the crass but all too frequently accepted interpretation of the glorious article of our religion about the resurrection of the dead, full of so many absurd and contradictory things, and propped up with unskilled reasoning and weak struts.

---

[74] An unexpected power or event saving a seemingly helpless situation.

[75] *The Book of Marcus Tullius Cicero entituled Paradox Stoicorum* (London, 1569), [sig.] f.6; Cicero, *Laelius, on Friendship & the Dream of Scipio*, trans. and ed. J. G. F. Powell (Warminster, 1990), *Somnium Scipionis*, sect. 8 on 144–5; Jackson, *Maran atha*, 11.13.3 on 3424, 11.14.7 on 3439; More, *Immortality of the Soul*, 3.16.5 on 495–6; idem, *Grand Mystery of Godliness*, 6.4.1 on 223–4 (this translation used); [Rust?], *Letter of Resolution*, 128; idem, *Sermon preached at New-Town*, 9, 31; cf. Tertullian, *Resurrection of the Flesh*, ch. 40 on 284, 'now neither the soul by itself alone is "man"…'.

[76] Jackson, *Maran atha*, 11.14.9 on 3441; Cudworth, *True Intellectual System*, 1.5.3 on 801.

[77] More, *Immortality of the Soul*, 2.2.1 on 224; 2.10.8 on 202–3; 3.1.6 on 334; idem, *Grand Mystery of Godliness*, 6.4.1 on 223–4; Cudworth, *True Intellectual System*, 1.5.3 on 786; cf. Tertullian, *Resurrection of the Flesh*, ch. 27 on 243–4, which argues that the soul is corporeal but still requires the flesh to suffer punishment at the Last Judgement; see also ch. 35 on 275–7.

Nor, they say, are the arguments derived from Scripture more compelling. Well, concerning Job 19:25–27,[78] any interpreter, no matter how unskilled, renders it thus: 'For I know that my Redeemer liveth, and that he shall stand at the latter day upon the earth. And though after my skin worms destroy this body, yet in my flesh shall I see God: Whom I shall see for myself and mine eyes shall behold, and not another; though my reins be consumed within me'. The Hebrew nevertheless sounds very different, namely: ואני ידעתי גאלי חי ואחרון על עפר יקום ואחר עורי נקפו זאת ומבשרי אחזה אלוה אשר אני אחזה לי ועיני ראו ולא זר. These words can be properly translated and understood as 'I know that my Redeemer (God, of course, who is quite often distinguished by that name) lives and in the end will stand above dust or sand (of course, he will achieve victory in the conflict with my enemies, from which he will save me) even though they (worms, of course, and diseases) consume not only my skin, but also this (as if pointing with the finger to the body or to the fat which is beneath the skin) nevertheless in my flesh I will see God'; and those things which follow.

[27/24/9B]

That most holy man believed that it was possible for God to restore his body, almost destroyed by rot and worms, to its original shape and integrity, which in fact is what happened to him. And what is more, as Menasseh Ben Israel confirms, the Jews without exception understood these words in a similar way, even though they avidly lay claim to all the passages of Scripture which can be used in defence of the resurrection.[79] Nor is it differently interpreted among our own writers, Jean Mercier, Johannes Piscator, Gerardus Vossius, Hugo Grotius, and others.[80]

As for I Corinthians 15:53, 'For this corruptible must put on incorruption, and this mortal must put on immortality',[81] they say, it is not necessary that these words, 'this corruptible one' and 'this mortal one' are restricted to the body itself. In fact, the particle *hoc* [this] by itself does not mean anything else but 'a specific individual', which can be pointed at with a finger. The earthly man is no less corruptible or mortal than the

[78] Jackson, *Maran atha*, 11.13.ch. heading on 3421; More, *Grand Mystery of Godliness*, 6.4.3 on 224.

[79] Menasseh Ben Israel, *Resurrectione Mortuorum*, Job: 1.3.6 on 24–5, 1.16 on 123–33, especially 132–3; Episcopius, *Institutiones Theologicae* 1: 3.6.4 on 224–5; [Rust?], *Letter of Resolution*, 125–8.

[80] Joannes Mercerus, *Commentarii in Librum Iob* (Geneva, 1573), 19.25–7 on 77ᵛ–78ᵛ; Joannes Piscator, *In Librum Jobi Commentarius* (Herborn, 1612), 19:25–7 on 174–6; Hugo Grotius, *Annotata ad Vetus Testamentum*, 3 vols. (Paris, 1644), 1: Annotata ad Librum Job, 19:25–7 on 410–11; Gerardus Vossius, *Theses Theologicae et Historicae* (The Hague, 1658), 12.9 on 177–8. Piscator, Grotius, and Vossius were Arminian commentators; Vossius was a friend of both Menasseh Ben Israel and Grotius.

[81] Origen, *Contra Celsum*, ed. Spencer, ch. 5 on 353; trans. Chadwick, 5.19 on 279; [Rust?], *Letter of Resolution*, 117, 120.

body itself. For this reason, the meaning is simply that we ourselves will be given incorruptibility and immortality at some point, in the manner in which they say that the subject of these phrases, 'sown in corruption, raised in incorruption; sown in dishonour and raised in glory, sown in weakness and raised in power, sown in a natural body and raised in a spiritual one',[82] does not appear to be a body committed to the earth but the man himself. Nor can that which is deprived of all strength be said to be weak, nor that which is not animate a living animal. Nor is a seed which is altogether dead sown, because it would never produce anything. Consequently we are sown into the field of this world when we are first born, and death is the equivalent of the corruption of the seed, which leads to our being clothed in a new body.[83]

[27/24/10A]

However, given that the body is to be understood as τὸ φθαρτὸν τοῦτο [this corruptible one] and τὸ θνητὸν τοῦτο [this mortal one],[84] the identity of the body could not be implied any more strongly. If I said to a beggar that his poor and humble house was being turned into a palace, or his worn and torn clothes into fine purple, it would not follow that his palace and purple would have to be numerically identical to his old house and patched garments. It is, of course, a common way of speaking, and it does not mean anything other than that there will be a great change concerning the person to whom these words refer. Nor, they say, is the argument in any way reinforced by the words ἀνάστασις [resurrection] and ἔγερσις [rising, awaking], apart from the fact that nowhere do they refer to the body, but to the person. You can find the words ἀνιστῆναι [to raise] and ἐγείρειν [to raise, awaken] used about those things, which not only did not die or fall asleep, but which previously did not even exist. Matthew 22:24:[85] καὶ ἀναστήσει σπέρμα τῷ ἀδελφῷ αὐτοῦ [and raise up seed unto his brother]. Acts: 3. 22: προφήτην ὑμῖν ἀναστήσει κύριος ὁ θεός [a prophet shall the Lord your God raise up unto you]. Acts 7:18: ἄχρι οὗ ἀνέστη βασιλεὺς ἕτερος [till another king arose]. Luke 1:69: καὶ ἤγειρεν κέρας σωτηρίας ἡμῖν [and hath raised up an horn of salvation for us] and elsewhere very often. Nor do they feel hard pressed by the Resurrection of Christ, and of his numerical body, in which he communicated with his disciples for forty days. He had not yet ascended to his Father, or as the

---

[82] I Corinthians 15:42–4; Origen, *Contra Celsum*, ed. Spencer, ch. 5 on 243; trans. Chadwick, 5.19 on 278; Origen, *First Principles*, 2.10.1 on 138–9; More, *Grand Mystery of Godliness*, 6.4.3 on 224; [Rust?], *Letter of Resolution*, 110; Cudworth, *True Intellectual System*, 1.5.3 on 796.

[83] [Rust?], *Letter of Resolution*, 61–2; Cudworth, *True Intellectual System*, 1.5.3 on 796.

[84] I Corinthians 15:53.

[85] MS erroneously gives Matthew 20:24; More, *Grand Mystery of Godliness*, 6.4.4 on 225.

Apostle says, had not yet donned τὸ σῶμα τῆς δόξης [the body of glory].[86] And what is more, if the disciples could not stand the radiance of the now transfigured mortal Christ,[87] and if the just will shine like the sun in the kingdom of his Father, how much more intense must the radiance and light of Christ's glorified body be?

[27/24/10B]

So if he had already begun to shine at his Resurrection, how could the disciples have enjoyed his company? Or why is no mention made of his exceptional glory? Can it be truthfully said that it was hidden from the disciples, their eyes being shut? Why then does Christ call out to their senses—sight, touch—so they could be suitable witnesses of his Resurrection? Besides, the Apostle says with striking words at I Corinthians 15:47: ὁ πρῶτος ἄνθρωπος ἐκ γῆς χοϊκός, ὁ δεύτερος ἄνθρωπος ἐξ οὐρανοῦ. [The first man is of the earth, earthy: the second man is from heaven],[88] where the very ἐναντίωσις [contrast] of the words seems to prove that by ἐξ οὐρανοῦ [from heaven] is to be understood the material cause. And above, at verse 45, the first Adam was created as the first being 'with a living soul', or 'as an earthly living being', as ψυχὴ ζῶσα [living soul] is to be understood in Genesis 1:24[89] and elsewhere, and the last one εἰς πνεῦμα ζῳοποιοῦν, as 'a life-giving Spirit' that lives in such a way that he can keep his life safe and preserve it. But immediately after the Resurrection, our Saviour tries to prove that he is not a ghost, nor, as we, too, will be, akin to the angels, but one who had flesh, bones, etc. Nor is there anything in a living body which we do not find in the body of Christ before he went to heaven, truly not until the mortal quality of his body was changed εἰς αἰθερίαν καὶ θείαν φύσιν [into an etherial and divine nature], as Origen says against Celsus. Indeed, a certain necessity pressed him to appear in the body which had been very recently buried, to give assurance of the truth of his Resurrection and reassure the wavering and unbelieving minds of the disciples. If he had appeared in any other manner, they would not have believed his Resurrection at all, as Thomas demonstrates.[90]

---

[86] Philippians 3:21: Who shall change our vile body, that it may be fashioned like unto his glorious body, according to the working whereby he is able even to subdue all things unto himself; Cudworth, *True Intellectual System*, 1.5.3 on 796, 799.

[87] Cudworth, *True Intellectual System*, 1.5.3 on 799.

[88] Origen, *Contra Celsum*, ed. Spencer, ch. 5 on 243; trans. Chadwick, 5.19 on 278; Cudworth, *True Intellectual System*, 1.5.3 on 797.

[89] *Septuagint*, 2: Genesis 1:24: And God said, let the earth bring forth the living creature according to its kind, quadrupeds and reptiles and wild beasts of the earth according to their kind, and it was so.

[90] John 20: 27: Then he saith to Thomas, Reach hither thy finger, and behold my hands; and reach hither thy hand and thrust it into my side: and be not faithless but believing; Origen, *Contra Celsum*, ed. Spencer, ch. 2 on 97–8; trans. Chadwick, 2.61–2 on 113–14; [Rust?], *Letter of Resolution*, 109, 111–12; Cudworth, *True Intellectual System*, 1.5.3 on 803–4.

[27/24/11A]

There are some other passages by which one can attempt to prove the resurrection of exactly the same body. Since they are usually elusive about such a moot point, they do not seem to make the effort of citing them now worthwhile. Instead let us consider the way in which they [i.e. those who do not accept the resurrection of the same body] try to add substance to their opinion from the Holy Scripture.

The foremost passage is at I Corinthians 15:37: 'And that which thou sowest, thou sowest not that body that shall be, but bare grain, it may chance of wheat, or of some other grain: But God giveth it a body as it hath pleased him'.[91] With these words the Apostle, replying to what is either an objection or a question, but more probably both, ποίῳ δὲ σώματι ἔρχονται; [with what body do they come?], says that it is like the seed committed to the furrows. As we know from first-hand experience, the body which sprouts is not the same but a very different one. So that the discrepancy between the future body and this earthly one would not offend the Corinthians' minds and make them anxious, he showed with many examples, at verses 39, 40, and 41, that there is a great diversity between bodies.[92] Finally, he writes in verse 42: οὕτως καὶ ἡ ἀνάστασις τῶν νεκρῶν. [so also is the resurrection of the dead]. They seek to convince us that these words (as well as the ones before and after them) must refer to the difference between the bodies with which we are now clothed and those with which we shall be clothed at the resurrection one day, and not to the different degrees of dignity and glory of the bodies of different people after they have risen. If this difference were to be observed only in respect of the qualities which do not really pertain to the substance itself, the examples mentioned in these verses would have been inserted by the Apostle inappropriately.[93]

[27/24/11B]

Besides, the vastly different properties that the Apostle attributes to these bodies and the future ones abundantly demonstrate the difference between them. Hence, it should be understood that the identity of the

---

[91] Origen, *Contra Celsum*, ed. Spencer, ch. 5 on 342; trans. Chadwick, 5.18 on 278, 5.23 on 281; Origen, *First Principles*, 2.10.3 on 141; Jackson, *Maran atha*, 11.14.6 on 3439; Cudworth, *True Intellectual System*, 1.5.3 on 796.

[92] I Corinthians 15:39: All flesh is not the same flesh: but there is one kind of flesh of men, another flesh of beasts, another of fishes, and another of birds. 40: There are also celestial bodies and bodies terrestrial: but the glory of the celestial is one, and the glory of the terrestrial is another. 41: There is one glory of the sun and another glory of the moon, and another glory of the stars: for one star differeth from another star in glory; Origen, *First Principles*, 2.10.2 on 139–40; Jackson, *Maran atha*, 11.14.8 on 3440–1; [Rust?], *Letter of Resolution*, 61; Cudworth, *True Intellectual System*, 1.5.3 on 796.

[93] Jackson, *Maran atha*, 11.16.2 on 3457–8.

body cannot be derived only from bare and naked matter, but in the first place from its modifications. In fact, if the numerically identical matter that at some point had constituted a human body, remaining the same in quantity, afterwards were transferred to a plant, none could be so insane or so disregard the common use of language as to believe and say that the body of the man and of the plant are the same. Wherefore anyone who imagines that our bodies will be so pure and luminous that they will imitate the shining of the sun, and so fine, agile, and subtle as to become spiritual, aerial or, even more, ethereal, and nevertheless remain flesh, blood and bones, etc., will inevitably create contradictions and shape chimeras. Likewise, if we supposed a stone to be divided in parts so minuscule that they were as fine as air or celestial matter, but remaining stone at the same time, this would be what they call a *contradictio in adjecto*.[94] In fact, the nature of stone is to be hard, solid, opaque, heavy, etc. If you remove these properties, of course the matter remains, but the stone is lost. At the resurrection, we are going to be made either of different matter or the same. It will definitely be impossible to have the same bodies. Therefore the Apostle, as if summing up the arguments at verse 50, says: 'Now this I say, brethren, (these things up to this point have been said by me) that flesh and blood cannot inherit the kingdom of God; (as though adding the principle on which this assertion is founded), neither doth corruption inherit incorruption'.[95]

[27/24/12A]

Without doubt we will be ἰσάγγελοι [like angels], who, as Homer sings of his own gods,

> οὐ γὰρ σῖτον ἔδουσ' οὐ πίνουσ' αἴθοπα οἶνον
> τοὔνεκ' ἀναίμονές εἰσι καὶ ἀθάνατοι καλέονται[96]
> [for they eat not bread, nor do they drink ruddy wine,
> and so they are bloodless and are called immortals]

The strength of this argument cannot be eluded in any way, nor are we speaking of the carnal behaviours and passions of men, for in that case there would be no connection between this passage and the others before

---

[94] A contradiction between parts of an argument, meaning that a predicate added to a subject contradicts the latter's defining characteristics.

[95] Origen, *Contra Celsum*, ed. Spencer, ch. 5 on 243; trans. Chadwick, 5.19 on 278; Origen, *First Principles*, 2.10.3 on 140; [Rust?], *Letter of Resolution*, 62; cf. Tertullian, *Resurrection of the Flesh*, ch. 48 on 300–3, ch. 51 on 307–9, which argues that, on the analogy of Christ's resurrection, human beings will be raised in the flesh; ch. 50 on 306–7, argues that human beings will be judged not on the substance of their flesh but on their conduct in the flesh.

[96] Homer, *Iliad: Books 1–12*, trans A. T. Murray, rev. William F. Wyatt (2nd edn, Cambridge, MA, 1999), 5.341 on 230–1.

and after it.[97] Paul himself explains his thoughts sufficiently clearly, when he adds, 'nor corruption incorruptibility'. That must be interpreted in the same way as verse 42 above.[98] Nor should we read 'flesh and blood' with the meaning of 'carnal affections' anywhere in the Holy Scripture, as will be clear to one who inspects all of the passages. Those are Matthew 16:17,[99] Galatians 1:16,[100] Ephesians 6:12,[101] and Hebrews 2:14.[102] In fact, σὰρξ καὶ αἷμα [flesh and blood] is a Hebrew expression בשר ודם [flesh and blood, mortal], and it clearly has the same meaning, 'pure genuine earthly man', in which sense it occurs frequently among the Hebraic writers, as an uncommonly learned man among us has observed.[103] In truth, this exposition is rejected by many. Others claim that flesh and blood are to be understood only as corruptibility, and the reign of God as incorruptibility, in the same way as the latter words explain the former ones. Why should the Apostle express his view so obscurely, not to say dangerously, if the denial of that thing creates some danger, in that same passage about the difference between present and future bodies? Besides, if it were possible that flesh and blood were incorruptible, how could they be used synonymously and interchangeably with corruptibility? Saint Augustine appears to support this thesis. In book 12 of *Contra Adimantum* he explicitly says 'there will not be flesh and blood in the resurrection'.[104]

---

[97] For this sentence, the more intelligible reading at MS 55/18/12A has been preferred to that at MS 27/24/12A.

[98] I Corinthians 15:42: So also is the resurrection of the dead. It is sown in corruption; it is raised in incorruption; Cudworth, *True Intellectual System*, 1.5.3 on 796.

[99] Matthew 16:17: And Jesus answered and said unto him, Blessed art thou Simon Barjona: for flesh and blood hath not revealed it unto thee, but my Father which is in heaven.

[100] Galatians 1:16: To reveal his Son in me, that I might preach him among the heathen; immediately I conferred with flesh and blood.

[101] Ephesians 6:12: For we wrestle not against flesh and blood, but against principalities, against powers, against the rulers of the darkness of this world, against spiritual wickedness in high places.

[102] Hebrews 2:14: Are they not all ministering spirits, sent forth to minister for them who shall be heirs of salvation?

[103] John Downame, et al., *Annotations upon all the Books of the Old and New Testament* (London, 1645), s.v. Hebrews 3:14, where Matthew 16:17, Galatians 1:16, and Ephesians 6:12 are cross-referenced. For Downame, a Christ's man, see John Peile, *Biographical Register of Christ's College Cambridge, 1505–1905, and of the Earlier Foundation, God's House, 1448–1505*, 2 vols. (Cambridge, 1910–1913), 1: 196; Paul S. Seaver, 'Downame, John (1571–1652) in *Oxford Dictionary of National Biography*, ed. Henry C. G. Matthew and Brian Harrison, 60 vols. (Oxford, 2004).

[104] Augustine, *The Manichean Debate*, ed. Roland Teske and Boniface Ramsey (New York, 2006), 'Answer to Adimantus, a Disciple of Mani', ch. 12, 190–4; Cudworth, *True Intellectual system*, 1.5.3, on 797. Frances Young, 'Naked or Clothed? Eschatology and the Doctrine of Creation', in Peter Clarke and Tony Claydon (eds), *The Church, the Afterlife and the Fate of the Soul* (Woodbridge, 2009), 1–19, on 18, argues that this was not Augustine's final position: 'later he would speak of spiritual flesh'. [Rust?], *Letter of Resolution*, 62–3, 119.

[27/24/12B]

So far as I know, these are the specific arguments of those who deny the necessity of resurrection of the numerically identical body. It has certainly been difficult to put some restraint on the running quill, but I feel pressed by the restrictions of time—there is very little space to refute each of them separately. Perhaps they will occur more opportunely within the discussion.

Thus we will very briefly devote ourselves to the remaining work of establishing the second part. This article of our faith has always been interpreted as the resurrection of the numerically identical body, apart from certain Socinian innovators. Thus, the things that we have said notwithstanding, I take it as retaining the same meaning through all the ages of the Christian religion, and I believe it should be defended. Well then.

First, any beings which live a sensitive or vegetative life clearly remain the same for the whole span of their life. Thus, we still say that the oak, having reached the age of 500, is the same as when it had just sprung from the earth, not even an inch tall. Second, it is equally clear that all those beings which have a vegetative life and are nourished and grow and lose some part every day, also acquire new parts. They are not made of the same identical matter throughout their whole life, nor could anybody say that there is the same matter within an oak sapling as in an oak tree 600 years old.[105]

[27/24/13A]

Third, it cannot be rightly claimed that the resurrection body is more identical to the body which we have now, than to itself.[106] Fourth, the identity of the body does not require that some parts should not join it during a long interval of time and in a successive process, or simply that its mass should grow gradually. If a new-born infant grew, by means of divine power, directly to the stature of an adult man, we would not say that he had another body, but instead the same and augmented by a miracle. The reasoning by means of which the body is said to be the same throughout the entire span of life should therefore be examined. I could think of only these three reasons: One is that it is always seen under the same exterior appearance, another is that it is unified by the same shape,[107] finally that a certain portion of matter, although very small, forms the base and foundation on which the rest of the body leans for support and is built, or from which the seed is produced.[108] In this sense the Apostle seems to state that the seed which has been sown is the same after the plant or the crop has sprouted. You know, what you sow, he says, will not live again, if it does

---

[105] Jackson, *Maran atha*, 11.15.6 on 3449.
[106] Ibid., 11.13.3 on 3425.   [107] Ibid., *Maran atha*, 11.15.8 on 3451.
[108] See Strickland, 'Resurrection of Same Body', 172–4.

not die.[109] And the experts in natural philosophy know that in any seed there is the plant itself, as can be seen in the seeds of maple, ash, and other trees, although when it has sprouted from the earth with branches and leaves, with the sun warming it, it extends and spreads out wider. Having said that, I say that the resurrection body in the Day of Judgement will be the same as this our body which we now wear, in the same sense, in which the body of any living being can be considered the same for the whole span of its life. In fact, first, it will be seen under the same exterior shape. Second, it will be connected with the same soul.[110]

[27/24/13B]

Third, once the body is dissolved, it is as if the soul takes away with it some kind of seed, i.e. those particles of the body which are finer and more deeply connected with its functions, from which seed God will finally make sprout stem and ear, i.e. it will make the body most glorious.[111] But this will be enough for now. In truth, I believe that a really learned man, deservedly belonging to the Christian community, will be able to demonstrate how much this and other foundations of our religion are supported by reason, hopefully doing it public justice by eventually writing it down.[112] For now I will draw my conclusion from the things I have said.

The Holy Scripture tells of the resurrection from the dead, nor does reason oppose it.

Eternal and omnipotent God, source of light, Father of compassion, you purify the deserving and refresh them with the rays of your clear light and bathe them in the sweetest dew of your love. May your spirit flow into our souls, and guide us to all truths. Be with us, we pray, in this Divinity disputation and resolve the frenzy of disputing and the too-hostile fire into a calm and benign flame of charity, so that 'the earth shall be filled with the knowledge of the glory of the Lord, as the waters cover the sea'.[113]

---

[109] 1 Corinthians 15:36: Thou fool, that which thou sowest is not quickened, except it die; Jackson, *Maran atha*, 11.14.1 on 3434.

[110] Jackson, *Maran atha*, 11.15.7 on 3440, 11.15.7 on 3451; cf. Tertullian, *Resurrection of the Flesh*, ch. 52 on 309–12, which argues (311) that the resurrection body will be 'the same in essence, only more full and perfect; not another, although reappearing in another form'.

[111] Jackson, *Maran atha*, 11.15.9 on 3442.

[112] More, *Grand Mystery of Godliness*, 1.9.1 on 25, refers the reader to idem, *Immortality of the Soul*, 2.16–18 on 286–325 for arguments from reason concerning the resurrection of the body.

[113] Habakkuk 2:14.

John Warren's *Lectures on Anatomy,* 1783–1812

*Mark Somos**

Introduction

This is a transcription of selected passages from a notebook of lectures on anatomy that John Warren (1753–1815), younger brother of the surgeon and revolutionary leader Joseph Warren (1741–75), gave between 1783 and 1812. The manuscript is currently at the Harvard Medical Library in the Francis A. Countway Library of Medicine. Historians of medicine know John Warren for founding the Harvard Medical School (HMS) on September 19, 1782, with Aaron Dexter and Benjamin Waterhouse. The three men served as the School's first professors, with Warren as Professor of Anatomy and Surgery, Waterhouse as Professor of Theory and Practice of Physic, and Dexter as Professor of Chemistry and Materia Medica. Lectures were given in Harvard Hall until the School moved to Boston in 1810.

In 1783 Warren began a series of courses on anatomy that he continued to teach for three decades. At least four notebooks on these courses survive, two or three of them at least partly in Warren's hand. Countway Rare Books H MS b3.13 contains Warren's lecture notes for 1783–5. The last 39 pages of this notebook copy passages from Goldsmith's *Animated Nature,* in a different hand. Another text of substantial length is Countway Rare Books H MS b3.4, which covers Warren's lectures on anatomy from 1783 until 1812, written in various hands, including Warren's. We also have notes on his anatomy lectures surviving on a single leaf (Countway Rare 1.Mw.1784.W). The Countway Library holds another notebook on Warren's lectures with unidentified author and date, probably by a student, under the call number H MS b3.6. Finally, we have Moses Appleton's

* I am grateful to Jack Eckert, Mordechai Feingold, Gaby Mahlberg, Daniel Margócsy, and the staff of the Countway Library for their help, and to Harvey Mansfield for access to Harvard resources. With many thanks to the Alexander von Humboldt Foundation for making the completion of this article possible.

Fig. 3.1. John Warren, *Lectures on Anatomy, 1783–1812*, front cover. Courtesy of Harvard Medical Library, Francis A. Countway Library of Medicine.

notes on lectures by Warren, Waterhouse, and Dexter (H MS b76.1) from 1794 onward. Thanks to this material it is possible to reconstruct Warren's lectures with some fidelity.

Most lectures are, of course, concerned with technical aspects of anatomy, ranging from the structure and parts of the body through characteristics of bones and ligaments to making anatomical preparations. They offer valuable insights into American medical history and progress. While the notes on the technical substance of anatomy are interesting in their own right, the present selection focuses on the history and theory of anatomy that Warren taught as part of his course over the first three decades in the history of HMS.

One of the notebooks, Countway H MS b3.4, the subject of this article, stands out from the body of surviving materials for several reasons. Firstly, unlike the other texts, more than a third of this notebook is taken up by the introductory and concluding lectures of Warren's course. These lectures contain Warren's survey of the history of civilizations, the history of anatomy within that broader history, the utility of anatomy for non-physicians, and the importance of, and early American institutional framework for, the certification of medical professionals, medical ethics, and continuing education.

Here we find Warren telling his students that studying Creation can lead anyone to God through natural religion, without a need for revelation. Pagans came close to being able 'to look through nature up to nature's God', but tended to mistake Nature for God and lapse into idolatry. Christians used to be equally superstitious, according to Warren, who gives a brief historical overview of official prohibitions and public attitudes against dissection, up to and including his own time.

His lecture notes on the utility of anatomy are a *tour de force* of arguments as to why everyone should study anatomy. Prevention, Warren explains, is far more effective than remedial medicine. In our private capacity, a knowledge of anatomy is essential to preventing diseases in ourselves and our families. Warren also makes the case for anatomy's utility for the professions. Sculptors, painters, and musicians should study anatomy both during their training and the pursuit of their craft. Lawyers need only recall the example set by Francis Bacon, and that their fellow citizens' life can depend on their mastery of forensic medicine, to realize that they need to understand nature—human nature in particular—as part of their professional training. Another non-medical profession that should study anatomy is the priesthood. Instead of obstructing the progress of medical sciences, as they have done for millennia, priests should study it because the beauty of the human body is 'so rich a source for argument for the encouragement of morality and religion' that anatomy should be cited and taught from the pulpit. Warren's mistakes and prejudices are as significant as his insights and accomplishments. He argues that little contribution was made to the progress of anatomy in Arabic, or under the papacy.

The second feature that distinguishes this manuscript is that it is the only one that covers more than one or two years of Warren's lectures. Spanning thirty years of his teaching career at HMS, this notebook shows us Warren's revisions over time. For instance, we find a remarkable change in the last version of his introductory lecture. Recounting that courses on anatomy traditionally begin with an historical survey of the discipline, and that HMS has followed this pattern since its foundation, Warren announces that his introduction will, in this exceptional course, survey instead the history of medical education in the United States. He ties this history closely to the experience of a generation of army surgeons who, like himself, served in the War of Independence and made necessity the mother of wartime invention. He further distinguishes American medical history by praising the newly forged country's resistance to the unscientific prejudices entrenched in the Old World. It is only by putting revised and re-revised versions of his lectures side by side that we can appreciate this passionate yet disciplined, defining figure of medical history concluding three decades of teaching with a mould-breaking introductory lecture of proud reflections on the past, and optimism for the future, of American medical practice and training.

Over the lecture series we also see Warren formulate, develop, and promote the argument that a system of medical education and professional licencing must be developed and integrated into interlocking state-wide and national frameworks. Warren uses the lectures to advocate for federal and state investments in this system. He imagines a future when American students will be taught in optimal circumstances, with access to bodies to dissect, reliable and accountable professors and institutionally supported student associations and study groups, and when physicians must regularly return to the university to refresh their skills and learn about the most recent discoveries in order to be allowed to continue their medical practice. Warren gave his first lectures on the history of civilization and anatomy, and on the discipline's utility for everyone in both professional and private capacities, in 1783, the year Britain recognized American independence. His final reflections on the past and future of basic and continuing medical education, and professional ethics and certification in the United States, were delivered in 1812, the year that the US declared war on Britain, and Warren's son, John Collins Warren, launched the *New England Journal of Medicine*. They are fitting bookends for this remarkable document.

The notebook is approximately 25 × 19.5 cm, with around 176 pages of writing, and several inserted pages and slips. Based on comparison with the other texts listed above, Warren's use of subjective pronouns, and rounds of stylistic and substantial revision, it is safe to conclude that most of the notebook is in Warren's handwriting, even though his script deteriorates a little over time. There are a few inserted pages and slips that may have been written by students or assistants. The notebook also contains course outlines in which lectures are titled, numbered, and dated. Warren's revisions follow three guiding principles. Firstly, he updated his lectures in light of new evidence and new Latin, English, and French publications. Secondly, he added a few anecdotes over time to illustrate his points. Finally, he strove for concise and simple expressions, often replacing phrases with shorter ones, or cutting them altogether.

Establishing the sequence in which the notebook's pages were written is not always straightforward. The manuscript is essentially a collection of pages with a leather string run through two holes made in the side of the sheets, and bound together at a later stage. Some sections, such as the first and probably earliest 39 pages, comprise coherent units. Here Warren initially wrote mostly on the recto, right-hand-side pages, and added notes on the left side, the verso of the preceding sheet, during revision. The pages are numbered inconsistently. Sometimes a left-hand-side page has its own page number. Other times it does not. This suggests that Warren added the page numbers to this section not when he started or finalized this section, but between rounds of revision.

The remaining pages of the notebook are unnumbered and often seem haphazardly arranged, although there are several coherent sections. Such sections are formed, for instance, when Warren writes out his final lecture over several years, and strings them together. Even coherent sections do not usually follow each other in any discernible order. A few pages of notes on Warren's 1803 course are followed by notes on several 1804 courses. Then come free-standing notes on an anatomical topic, then outlines for 1799–1802, another thematic discussion, and the 1809 outline. Some pages may be lost. At least the first page of the earliest version of Warren's moving final lecture, now bound between lecture notes for 1804 and 1799, is missing.

The notes to this transcription indicate the section's place in the notebook, as well as interesting revisions, interpolations, and other textual evidence. Punctuation and capitalization have been modernized. I have used paragraph breaks as and when the text's meaning seemed to warrant. Warren usually starts new paragraphs with a sizeable indent. Occasionally he omits or minimizes the indent, for instance in his summary of the importance of Vesalius and Eustachius. These cases consistently suggest a comparatively minor break in thought. For the sake of economy I have often merged minor breaks into one paragraph. Warren's important marginal and interlinear revisions are indicated with <>. Interesting deletions are shown with [[ ]]. The four words I could not transcribe with certainty are set off with {}.

I hope that this partial transcription of the notebook in which John Warren places the study of anatomy into the broader contexts of the history of civilizations, the history of medicine, natural religion, and the history and future of medical education in the United States, will help renew interest in the man and his work, both in and outside the historiography of American medicine.

Alexander von Humboldt Foundation Fellow at the Max Planck Institute for Comparative Public Law and International Law, Heidelberg, and Senior Visiting Research Fellow at Sussex Law School

John Warren, Lectures on Anatomy

It is usual with anatomists previous to entering on a course of actual demonstrations to deliver a history of the origin of, and improvements that have been made in, this very useful branch of medical science. We shall pursue the same method in the course we are now to enter upon, and this in as concise a manner as possible. And it may be observed that in doing this, we shall in fact be giving a general history of the healing art, after having made a few remarks on the importance of this science and the great advantages to be derived from its pursuit by every liberal profession, as well as in some of the mechanical employments of life.

It may not be improper however first to observe that the term made use of to express the object of these lectures is derived from two Greek words, ana & temno, signifying to cut through or into. The term anatomy therefore is properly applied to the dissection of vegetable as well as animal substances, but it is by anatomists generally limited to that division of the parts of an animal body which is made for the purpose of investigating its internal structure.

Lecture 1: Introduction

The arts and sciences have been advancing by various degrees of improvement from the early ages which succeeded the Deluge down through the long tract of time which has intervened between that and the present period. Many interruptions are to be met within almost every branch of arts and literature. The various forms of government, the different systems of religion which have prevailed in the world, have produced a very great fluctuation in the advantages with which pursuits of this kind have been attended. To this we may add the general instability of all human affairs, and the precarious tenure upon which the most flourishing condition of states and kingdoms is possessed and enjoyed.

The inroads of a cruel and relentless enemy may have precipitated a whole people from a state of tranquility and freedom, into all the horrors of slavery and dependence. The minds of men when once reduced to a servile subjection soon lose with the advantages of acquiring the taste for pursuing the more noble employments of a rational mind. A melancholy indifference soon extinguishes every spark of curiosity and ambition, and a total despondency succeeds to their place. An inundation of barbarians

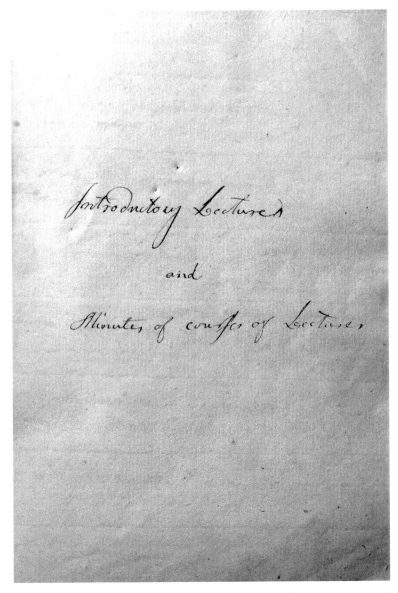

Fig. 3.2. John Warren, *Lectures on Anatomy, 1783–1812,* first page. Courtesy of Harvard Medical Library, Francis A. Countway Library of Medicine.

has often directed that ungovernable rage which usually attends them in the delirium of success to the destruction of those inestimable treasures which many generations have been employed in collecting, and the valuable fruits of accurate observation and faithful experience have fallen the first victims to their stupid frenzy. A striking instance of this is furnished by the fury of the Saracens in the wanton destruction of the Ptolemean Library at Alexandria in 642 when 100,000 Volumes were consign'd to the flames. But when the genius of learning has for some time been slumbering to appearance upon the verge of ruin, some distinguished part of the globe has emerged from ignorance and barbarism, to the immortal honor of these illustrious characters who were born to enlighten and adorn the [[human Mind]] Age.

The luxury, effeminacy and superstition of the Roman Empire had produced a general languishment of the sciences in that part of the world, when by means of the taking of Constantinople by the Turks in the 15th century the Greek philosophers were driven from their native land and fled into Italy, where under their nurture the arts and sciences soon began to recover from their former declension. It is reasonable to suppose that the most important calls of nature were first attended to in the early ages of the world, and we may therefore conclude that after the immediate purposes of supporting life, their next object must have been that of preserving it. The simplicity of their subsistence and their ignorance of the refinement of luxury and effeminacy, it is true, subjected them comparatively to but few diseases. Yet such is the constitution of the human frame, that unavoidable accidents are perpetually threatening it with injury and dissolution. It was therefore necessary to search out such methods as might most efficaciously remove the one and preserve from the other.[1] The art of healing having been thus brought into existence, was more cultivated and improved in proportion to the success and relief resulting from the practice of it, and it is reasonable to suppose that those who were the most respectable for age and experience were most confided in for assistance in these cases, and that they on their part to qualify themselves for the discharge of their duty avail'd themselves of every advantage that offered by enquiring into the structure of the human frame. The bones, doubtless which are the most simple part of anatomy, naturally presented themselves first to this view.

---

[1] Note on opposite page: 'For the Use of those who wish for a more accurate Knowledge of the Matter I would recommend Dr Friend's ingenious History of the Origin and Progress of Physick'. Warren is referring to John Freind, *The history of physick: from the time of Galen, to the beginning of the sixteenth century* (London, 1725–6). The book was translated into Latin and French, and underwent several editions. The copy of the third edition that Warren donated to the Boston Medical Library is now Countway Medicine Rare Books 1.F.67.

The most ready means for accomplishing this end was to repair to their repositories of the dead and examine the structure of the bones, especially those which in any particular instance might chance to be injured. By this way it has happened that anatomy has always preceded physic, having been the earliest and most sensible branch of the healing art. <Homer, when speaking of the plague in the Greek army before Troy, makes a mention of physicians employed in the cure of it, but makes great use of them in healing the wounded.> The priests and elders amongst the Hebrew engross'd the principal knowledge in the art of healing, and it was taught traditionally from father to son and from master to pupil as a most useful branch of ancient philosophy.

Soon after the flood we find enquiries in this branch extending themselves together with monarchy unto the regions about Mesopotamia under a King of Assyria, and thence into Egypt and Chaldea. <Apis, one of the kings of Egypt, is celebrated as the inventor of anatomy and surgery.> The first person who appears to have wrote any thing on anatomy was Mercurius, first King of the Thebans, <who flourished soon after the death of Noah,> according to some who treated on the manner of dissecting bodies. He wrote on a skin a treatise upon the construction of the human body as the basis of five others on the art of healing. From this circumstance the Egyptians lay claim to the invention of the medical art. The Egyptians at that time enjoyed advantages for these researches superior to any other nation in the world. Hermes is said to have written 6 books on medicine, the first of which was on anatomy.

The physician amongst Egyptians was often patriarch priest and king. He was therefore entrusted with the business of cutting and preparing animals for sacrifice. He overlooked the embalming of bodies, which was done with great accuracy and labor, for we are informed that several physicians were employed 40 days in embalming Jacob, a time sufficient to acquire a very considerable insight into the structure of the parts. The embalmers, it is true, as soon as their office was performed, precipitously fled from the subjects on which they had operated, and all who were present pursued them with stones as having incurred the public malediction. Yet it does not appear that they were injured in the process. The Naxan priest had the inspection of the internal parts of animals offered to idols – and to them were committed the care of those who had suffered large wounds, by which much of the situation of the capital parts might be understood.

Amongst the Grecians, according to heathen mythology, Apollo is celebrated for the revival of this art and Asculapius, one of his sons having been an eminent professor of it, was killed by a blast of lightning, and deified by his followers. Little was done toward the improvement of anatomical knowledge for near 500 Years, after which Hippocrates of the

Island of Cos appears to be the first who reduced this, together with the other branches of physic, to a regular system. This great man was born 458 years before the Christian Era. It seems he only once had an opportunity of seeing a human skeleton, but his treatise on fractures is a proof how well he improved it.

The people of Abdera having entertained a conceit that their fellow citizen Democritus was mad because he dissected animals sent for Hippocrates to examine his case; who, finding him employed in this business, readily pronounced him one of the wisest of men. Hippocrates has been justly stiled the Father of Physic and the Prince of Physicians. Aristotle in the year 384, before he established a more philosophical method of pursuing these enquiries <and Alexander his pupil patronized him in his pursuits>, and Herophilus of Alexandria A. Ch. 317 under the reign of Ptolemy Soter, who himself was a man of science, if we may believe Tertullian, undertook the business of dissection in earnest. For not contented with dissecting bodies already dead, because the appearances of the parts were altered by the destruction of the animal functions, he conceived the project of dissecting the living, and under countenance of his master began with the human species. In the prosecution of his plan he is said to have dissected 600 living men in order, as the text expresses, to find out Nature.

Such enormous cruelties, if true, must have brought the art unto disgrace; but the truth of the relation is much to be doubted, especially if we consider the prejudice which have ever existed in the minds of the ignorant who, having been once alarmed, there are scarce any reports, let them be never so groundless, absurd, and in their own nature inconsistent, but what may obtain credit and be propagated with the most surprising exaggerations.

Erasistratus, cotemporary with Herophilus according to the same accounts, seems to have been concerned with him in this bloody pursuit. <Ptolemy Philadelphus, successor to Soter, was the Macaenas of Alexandria and founded a medical school as well as the immense library, afterwards so wantonly destroyed by the barbarians, and Pliny informs us that the kings of Egypt commanded criminals to be dissected.> Alcmaeon, Aretaeus and Praxagoras, to whom Herophilus was a pupil, made some small additions to the system of Hippocrates, but no essential discoveries were made till the days of Galen.

This celebrated physician was born at Pergamus A.D. 131. He was the commentator of Hippocrates, and seems to have made some farther observations from the accidental viewing of skeletons made by carnivorous animals upon the bodies of such as remained unburied, or were contained in sepulchres to which he had access. To this he added the dissection of apes, who in the structure of the parts much resemble the human. He practised in Asia and at Rome, at which latter place he had the advantage of dissecting the bodies of the barbarians that were killed in the battle of Mark Anthony, and were given to the physicians for that purpose. His physiology in his treatise, *De usu partium*, contained the principles which were universally adopted untill the days of the immortal Harvey, whose discoveries in the animal oeconomy furnished a new system of physiology. Next to Galen, Oribassius, professor at Alexandria in the fourth century, seem [sic] to be the most considerable improver of the art.

About the year 600, when the Roman language and Arts had been ruined by the Lombards, and those of the Greeks had much declined in the East, the crafty impostor Mahomet removed the schools of physic which had been established in Alexandria[2] to Hamran and Bagdad AD 721, to be superintended by his own priests and prophets. After extending their conquests over Persia, Arabia, Egypt, Asia, Palestine and Africa, his successors procured to be translated into the Saracen language, or {ruined} Roabic, everything of the sciences that was thought valuable, in the 8th century. They carried their conquests into Spain, and there also obliged the sciences to speak their own language whilst they were in the hands of the Roabs, which continued for 4 or 5 ages. Anatomy received but very little advantage from their cultivation. At the close of the 11th century a Carthaginian by the name of Constanus,[3] having traveled into Arabia for literature, established a school of physic at Salernum in Italy, the earliest medical school in Europe.

The principal revival of anatomy seems to have taken place in Sicily under the Emperor Frederic II in the 13th century, where he made a law that none should be allowed to practise surgery who were not dissectors in anatomy. His physician, Martian, got it established into a public administration every 6 years, at which all physicians and surgeons were obliged to give attendance.

Mundinus in the 14th century became a celebrated anatomist and professor at Bononia <now Boulogne>, and was considered as the standard of anatomical Improvement. Guido de Chauliac, a Man in holy Order in the midst of the same century, made a collection of anatomical and physiological observations from the works of the ancients. The Moorish universities had hitherto been the storekeepers of learning untill it was carried by Arnoldus of Villanova into France and by Peter D'Albano to Padua.

---

[2] Note on opposite page: 'where the celebrated Ptolemean Library was destroyed, consisting of 100,000 volumes had about a century before been wantonly consigned to the flames'.

[3] Constantine the African. Contrary to Warren's description of Constantine as a 'Carthaginian' and his claim that little progress was made in medicine by Muslim physicians, Constantine is described as a 'Saracen' or Muslim in Peter the Deacon's near-contemporary account.

It has been already observed that the luxury of the Roman empire and superstition of the popes were very great discouragements to the sciences in Europe, nor did they flourish there till the year 1459 when the Greek [[Refugees]] were expelled from Constantinople by the Turks, in consequence of which the physicians fled with their manuscripts into Italy, and immediately became the propagators of anatomy and physic.

The art of printing having been discovered a short time previous to this, in AD 1446, every branch of true and useful knowledge was amply diffused throughout Christendom, and most of the ancient writing [sic] were published in various parts of Europe in the same century. <The first anatomical publication in the English language was *The Englishman's Treasures or the true Anatomy of Man's Body* by Thomas Vicary, surgeon in London, which was printed and reprinted 3 or 4 times between the years 1548 and 1633.>

In the beginning of the 16th century lived Andrew Vesalius, who opened the dead body of a nobleman in Spain that he might discover the disease of which he died. He gave public lectures in Louvain <where was established a celebrated university> and Paris at the age of 18, and at 28 wrote a large and valuable book on anatomy. He corrected the mistakes of Galen in his treatise *De corporis humani fabrica*, and his tables were much more accurate than those of any who preceded him. Bartholomeus Eustachius was cotemporary with Vesalius, and a professor at Rome. He was extremely accurate in his tables, and those admirable figures which in the year 1744 were published at Leyden with the explanations of Albinus still continue to be esteemed in the first ranks of anatomical plates.[4]

The principles of natural philosophy which had been established by Roger Bacon of the University of Oxford in the 13th century, and received greater light by Galileo of Florence and the illustrious Francis Lord Verulam, born at London AD 1560, had laid a fondation for ascertaining truth upon only true and incontestible principles of fact and experience. Upon these principles a celebrated genius of the English nation prosecuted an inquiry into the animal oeconomy, and the name of Harvey will forever stand immortal on the page of history as the first discoverer of the circulation of the blood. This great man was born in Kent AD 1576, and the publication of his discovery AD 1628, having entirely changed the face of physiology, may be considered as the true era of medical and anatomical

---

[4] The two relevant copies of this edition, Bernhard S. Albinus, *Explicatio tabularum anatomicarum Bartholomaei Eustachii* (Leiden, 1744), at the Countway Library are Rare Books ff QM25.A143 c.1, and ff QM25.A143 c.3. Copy 1 comes from the Warren collection. Copy 3 contains Warren's autograph, but it is dated 1814. Either Warren inscribed his autograph long after he acquired copy 3, or copy 1 is the one he used when he wrote this passage in his lecture.

disquisition, and seems to have set all Europe at work in the pursuit of so important a subject.

The use of microscopes in anatomical dissections was first adverted to by Harvey, and Lewenhook by the same means and made very great improvements in it. He affirmed that he could discover 3,000,000 of animalcules in a particle of the *semen masculinum*, making only the size of a grain of sand, whose diameter is the 1000th part of such; and by his calculation on the observations he had made upon the scales of the skin which cover the pores, he would make it appear that the minutest grain of sand will cover 125,000 orifices through which the matter of perspiration is perpetually, in a state of health, passing off from the body.

About the same time the ingenious Swammerdam invented the method of using wax injections, whereas Highmore, Glisson and others had only used water and arrived to a very considerable degree of perfection in the art of demonstrating the vessels that contained blood, but unfortunately an excess of religious enthusiasm stopped the progress of his enquiries; and having been so struck with the advances he had made as to have been afraid of rivaling the works of the Almighty, he relinquished the pursuit and communicated the secret to his friend Ruysch, a name highly celebrated for his success in this art. To such a surprising height did this man carry the art of injection, that he attracted the admiration of all Europe by the beauty of his preparations. The English Admiral Berkeley, having been killed in an engagement with the Dutch in the year 1666, Ruysch was ordered by the States General to inject his body, which was accordingly done and it was sent home to his native country in all the apparent bloom of perfect health.

When Peter the First of Muscovy went over to Holland in 1695, he was so struck with the view of Ruysch's collection that he tenderly kissed an injected infant that sparkled with the graces of real life and seemed to smile upon him in all the charms of innocence and beauty. A number of modern luminaries have contributed to the perfection of this science and the discovery of the lympathick, as being independent of the arteries and veins; and truly a system of absorbents is contended for by Dr. Hunter of London and Dr. Munro of Edinburgh.[5]

In last year's introductory lecture I mentioned an extraordinary instance of the preservation of animal bodies from putrefaction, and upon enquiry have since learned that it [is] absolutely an incontestible fact. Instances are indeed recorded of animall bodies preserved from intoxication, and in a great measure retain the original form and proportions, but as this has

---

[5] Warren wrote the next section, from 'In last year's' to 'considerable length of time', on the left-hand-side pages, originally left blank, as a later addition to his lecture.

confessedly taken place upon principles not yet investigated and without any assistance from art, the fact should be improved rather to excite the spirit of inquiry into the operation of Nature by which so extraordinary a change has been produced, and thereby to attempt possessing ourselves of the means of imitating her. Many anatomical advantages might be derived from such a method; and some late observers have attested to the particularity of it by instances it's having been effected. A modern traveller in a letter dated at Bremen in Germany writes as follows, having observed that was it not of such a nature as to be universally examined, he should fear his veracity would be doubted.

"Under the cathedral church in this place, is a vaulted apartment supported on pillars; it is near sixty paces long, and ½ as many broad. The light and air are constantly admitted into it by 3 windows, though it is several feet beneath the level of the ground. Here are 5 large oak coffers rather than coffins, each containing a corpse. I examined them severally for near two hours. The most curious and perfect is that of a woman. Tradition says she was an English countess, who dying here at Bremen ordered her body to be placed in this vault uninterred, in expectation that her relations would cause it to be brought over to her native country. They say it has lain here 250 years.

Though the skin is totally dried in every part yet so little are the features of the face sunk or changed, that nothing is more certain, than, that she was young and even beautiful. It is a small countenance, round in its contour. The cartileges of the nose and the nostrils have undergone no alteration. Her teeth are all firm in their sockets, but the lips are drawn away from over them. The cheeks are shrunk in, but yet less than I ever remember to have seen in embalmed bodies. The hair of her head is at this time more than 18 inches long, very thick and fast that I heaved the corpse out of the coffer by it: the colour is a light brown and is fresh and glossy, as that of a living person. The landlord of the inn who was with me, said he remembered it for 40 years past, during which time there is not the least perceptible alteration in it. In another coffer is the body of a workman who is said to have tumbled off the church, as was killed by the fall. His features evince this most forcibly. Extreme agony is marked in them, his mouth is wide open and his eyelids the same. The eyes are dried up. His breast is unnaturally distended and his whole frame betrays a violent death.

A little child who died of the small pox is still more remarkable. The marks of the pustules which have broken the skin on his hands and head are very discernable; though one should suppose that a body which died of such a distemper must contain in a high degree the seeds of putrefaction. The two other coffers are not less extraordinary. There are in this vault likewise turkeys, hawks, weasels and other animals, which have been hung up here from time immemorial, some very lately, and are in the most complete preservation. The skins, the bills, feather, all unaltered. The cause of this phenomenon is doubtless the dryness of the place when they are laid. The magistrates do not permit that any fresh bodies be brought here, and there is no other subterranean chamber which has the same property."

Captain Cook in the *Account of his Voyages in the Pacific Ocean* gives us an account of a method made use of in the Society Islands for preserving the bodies of their great men, which consist principally in absorbing the moisture as much as possible, and anointing the parts with the oil of the cocoa nut, and by this means they are made to retain some of the features for a very considerable length of time.

It might at the present period be supposed that after so many persons have been employed in inquiries into the structure of the human body and the use of the parts, anatomy must necessarily have arrived to its highest degree of improvement; but this is by no means the case, and a large field is still left open for our inquiry in this branch of science. The extravagant and superstitious veneration for the inanimate remains of the dead have in all ages been an obstacle to anatomical inquiry.

The Mosaic institution considered the touching of a dead body as a disqualifying impurity which subjected such as had been exposed to it to certain very heavy inconveniences, from which they could not relieved untill they had undergone a long and tedious process of purification. The sentiments of the Grecians with regard to this point, though a circumstance not generally adverted to, appears, as observed by Riolan in a passage of Euripides, to have been very similar to those of the Jews.[6] If any one stain his hands with murder, touch a dead body, [[and woman immediately after childbirth,]] the gods discharge him from their altars as injurious and profane.

Use

Having given this brief history of our subject, it may be expected that some observations be made on the use of a knowledge in the structure of the human body.

Considered as a branch of general education, anatomy has many arguments to support its utility. However unobservable may be the manner in which the soul actuates the body, and the nature of that union [[in which consist the perfection of the man]] which constitutes a rational animal, it

---

[6] Jean Riolan the Younger, *Anthropographia et osteologia* (Paris, 1626), i.xiii. Warren may have drawn this reference from Antoine Portal, *Histoire de l'anatomie et de la chirurgie*, 6 vols. (Paris, 1770–1773), 1: 77.

is very certain that the material organs employed as the instruments of the animating principle are more wholly subjected to the cognizance of ourselves. Though it is one of the most difficult sciences to know ourselves in every respect, yet much may be learnt in the material part from an inspection of those organs, the uses of which are so easily deduced from applying the general principles of philosophy to the structure and situation of each. For a man of science to be incapable of giving any account of the system which constitutes a part of himself must certainly be a great deficiency, and deprive him of one very ample source of satisfaction and convenience.

The due performance of the animal functions of so great importance to everyone who considers life and health worth seeking or possessing, may be greatly promoted by a general knowledge of the animal oeconomy. Much depends upon the ability of the physician who is called upon to restore health to the diseased; but it is rarely the case that the physician is or can with conveniency be entrusted with the preventative process. This must greatly rest with each individual, and it is much easier to preserve health than to restore it. [[So much more valuable is it for every individual to acquire a competent knowledge in the structure and uses of the parts that compass the animal system.]] Even in the curative intention, the study of anatomy may not be entirely useless, especially to such as by means of remoteness from medical assistance may frequently stand in immediate need of the most powerful applications, particularly in surgical cases where the success of the means must almost totally depend on anatomical knowledge. Or if we are so fortunate as to meet with those of the profession to whom we may reasonably look up for reliefs, the same qualifications may enable us to determine whether the abilities of the physician are such as we can with safety and contentment rely on for the care of nearest and most dear connexions.

No enquiry whatever can afford more real satisfaction than that which has for its object the residence of a rational and an immortal soul. The philosopher therefore of whatever profession will receive the highest gratification from the scrutiny into that admirable harmony by which the structure of the parts is adapted to the purposes they were intended to subserve. For whatever pleasure may be the result of an examination into natural history, of an investigation of the nature and properties of the various substances produced on the surface or in the bowels of the earth, of the different modes of animate life in birds, beasts, fishes and insects, whatever satisfaction may arise from the researches of astronomy and a survey of the motions, affections and relations of the great though distant bodies of the Universe, and whatever sublime ideas or enlargement of soul the contemplation of beauties of the heavenly bodies may inspire, all those beauties and exquisite proportions are, as it were, concentrated in the little compass of a human body. *Anthropos mikros kosmos*, says a writer of *The Life of Pythagoras*.[7]

That some of the fundamental principles of theology have been confirmed by the survey of the beautiful structure of the parts, the admirable simplicity of their formation, and at the same time the most exquisite harmony and nicely adopted conformity to each other, is what no man who is acquainted with the arguments by which it is enforced can be ignorant of. It was a full sense of the force of them and the strong conviction with which they were attended that forced the devout Psalmist to exclaim, "I will praise thee for I am fearfully and wonderfully made!"[8]

In fact, the history of the pagan nations of the world affords the most convincing arguments for the truth of the assertion that the almighty Architect of the Universe intended his visible work as the only universal lesson by which the rational species of beings were to learn the existence and attributes of the deity. What else is that Light of Nature, which is the sole directory of the moral conduct of so large a proportion of the human race, than that mode of inductive reasoning by which they are taught to look through nature up to nature's God. Obedience to the dictates of a religion founded on these principles without the assistance of any superior lights is so obligatory on the professors of it, that revelation itself seems to have pronounced those who had no other merit but this as deserving of but few stripes. On the other hand, so conspicuous is the wisdom displayed in the various systems which surround us that he who willfully acts in violation of a duty most plainly inferred from the attributes of their Author, as deduced from a survey of that wisdom, is with peculiar emphasis distinguished and reprobated in the expressive language of sinning against the Light of Nature. Indeed, a revelation itself must derive much of its credibility from its correspondence with the fundamental principles of natural religion. Unhappily for a great part of mankind, the veneration paid to the works of the Creator has been carried to such an excess that by a mistaken zeal for the glory of the Author they have been substituted in their religious adorations for the Creator himself. The Persian Sun, the Egyptian Bull, and the Macedonian Son of Jupiter, are instances of a blind devotion to objects which were only the creatures of that power they intended to worship.

We are taught by the best of authority to reverence ourselves, why but because the faculties of the soul and the formation of our bodies are a demonstration of the most exquisite skill and workmanship. The greater

---

[7] In the anonymous *Life of Pythagoras*, preserved in Photius' ninth-century *Bibliotheca*.
[8] Psalms 139:14.

bodies of the Universe are but systems of inanimate matter, by a constant, uninterrupted exertion of omnipotence impelled in the course of their respective destined revolutions. But the human body is a congress of the most beautiful instruments for the use of man, whose faculties and operations are indeed exerted in a manner governed by laws in a very considerable degree subject to the cognizance of our senses.

For a divine then to be totally ignorant of so rich a source of arguments for the encouragement of morality and religion that the knowledge of the animal oeconomy furnishes is certainly inconsistent with that integrity and well grounded confidence in the principles of his profession, which every one for his own happiness should wish to possess.

Before the 16th century, so fully were the people's minds impressed with the sacrilege of dissections, that a consultation was appointed by the Emperor Charles the 5th to be held by the divines of Salamanca, in order to be satisfied whether it were lawful in point of conscience to dissect a dead human carcass. Until very lately, the use of anatomy and skeleton was forbid in Muscovy, the first as inhuman, the latter as subservient to withcraft, and Olearius assures us that one Quirin, a German surgeon, having been found there with a skeleton, hardly escaped with his life; and the skeleton after having been solemnly dragged about the streets was burnt in town.[9]

I shall close this head with the expressive language of the beforementioned physician Galen who, though a heathen, was so fully impressed with the sublime ideas which inspection of the structure of the animal fabric inspired, as to close one of his books on anatomy with a passage full of the most sublime and, we might almost venture to say, divine energy. In writing these books, says he, I compose a true and real hymn to that awful Being who made us all, and in my opinion, true religion does not consist so much in sacrificing many hecatombs on his altars, or in making him rich and costly presents of the most fragrant perfumes, as in being persuaded ourselves and endeavouring to persuade others that he is possessed of unerring wisdom, irresistible power, and all diffusive goodness.

To convince us that the study of anatomy is by no means useless to those who have chosen the law as their profession, we need only advert to the variety of causes of a capital nature which the courts of justice are called to attend. It may often happen that the life of a fellow citizen may depend on so small a circumstance as the slight variation [[of a single Line]] in the direction of an instrument with which a wound has been inflicted. It is the duty of the advocate to point out the distinction between wounds which were in [their] own nature mortal, and such as have become so only by

---

[9] This anecdote also appears in Robert Boyle, *Some Considerations Touching the Usefulnesse of Experimental Naturall Philosophy* 2nd ed. (Oxford, 1664).

neglect and accident. The surgeon, it is true, is usually called upon for his evidence in these cases, but as they seldom admit of any choice, by reason of their suddeness it may often happen that but little confidence ought to be placed in his judgement, and who is the man that would not be struck with horror at the idea of reasoning upon so solemn and important a subject without such information as might enable him in the most intelligible manner to state the circumstances of the case.

A competent knowledge of anatomy must afford the greatest advantages upon such occasion for thriving at the bar, where eloquence and truth should forever attend each other, and where I am confident the applauses of the world can never give such real satisfaction, as when they are attended with a consciousness of having perfectly understood the nature, and having been engaged on the course, of justice. What supreme pleasure then must the recollection of having used those acquirements to the effectual purpose of saving an innocent and perhaps valuable life affords in the calm moments of sober retirement! If but one such instance might happen in an age, it might be well worth the while of every gentleman of that learned profession to dedicate a portion of his life to the pursuit of it.

Some of the most illustrious characters that have shone in the line of the law had an extensive acquaintance with this branch of learning, and I need only mention as an example the name of Bacon whose success and reputation are a sufficient motive to induce the students in that profession to furnish themselves with those means which were so eminently productive of the elevation of that great and useful man.

To the sculptor, the painter, and musician the study of anatomy may also be highly useful, to the two former as it gives them an idea of the true situations and natural appearances of the various attitudes of the body. The admirable figures of Vesalius contained in his second book, of 18 tables on the muscles, have been of great use to the profession of these arts. The first 2, 3, and 4th represent the strong life, and have therefore been particularly selected as their models.

Many of the beautiful and much admired pieces of antiquity have derived their reputation from the skill of the artificer in copying from them by noticing the various appearances produced from the most striking actions and attitudes of nature. The strength of an Hercules with his club would never have been expressed in so lively a manner but by copying nature in the swell of the muscles concerned in the action, with the true and exact position of their several portion learnt by dissection and demonstration.

The various passions which actuate the human breast can never be well express'd without the knowledge of their particular operation on the limbs and features by means of their different effects on the moving powers. This is easily conceived of when we consider that the contraction of some particular muscles is the cause of each of the alterations produced in those external signs which designate the respective affections of the mind.[10] The art of the musician, which in a great measure consists in the invention of sonorous instruments, must undoubtedly be greatly advanced by a thorough understanding of the apparatus of nature in the purpose of conveying sound to the ear, and the perfection of those sounds to be in proportion to the analogy they bear them. To multiply arguments in favour of this study as peculiarly requisite for the physician would be needless.

The structure of the human body, and the particular conformation of the several parts which compose it, are the principles from which result the functions of life; so are the different affections of, or alterations produced upon them, the source of all the diseases to which the human system is incident. However therefore the healing art might in the early ages of the world have suceeded in the hands of such as had no knowledge of these principles, yet is very obvious that those successes must have been derived from observation and experience of the effects of such remedies as happened to present themselves most conveniently for use, and it is as evident that from such experiments the most fatal effects must sometimes have arisen.

The history of physic sufficiently evinces how much the progress of it depended on anatomical investigations, and I believe it may with confidence be asserted, that no man can be a good physician without accurate knowledge of the animal system. But whatever may be thought of the connexion of anatomy with <u>physic</u> – that it is indispensibly necessary to the due discharge of the duty of a surgeon is a point which will be controverted by none, for without it scarcely any manual operation for the relief of those who may call for our assistance can with safety be undertaken, and the daring prescription of those who have ventured on the experiment has often been punished with deserved infamy and disgrace.

Men of honesty therefore will be cautious how they enter upon the practice of surgery, and those who are determined to follow that profession will be indefatigably industrious in their efforts to acquire that knowledge which may qualify them for so important a duty. It is a great advantage attendant on this branch of physic that it is capable of demonstration, subject to no hypothetical reasoning, and so far as it extends must ever exist unalterably the same. It is therefore well adapted to the purpose it

---

[10] Note on opposite page: 'It would be urging their argument too severely by a very great stress upon the new invented science of Mr. Gall in which the influence of the various passions and affections of the mind is supposed to impress certain sensible peculiarities on the structure of the various regions of the human Skull'. Warren is referring to the phrenology of Franz Joseph Gall.

serves, that of a fixed and permanent basis upon which the whole structure of medical knowledge is to be raised.

Direction for Students

As a preparatory to the study of anatomy, a tolerable knowledge in the principles of natural philosophy is undoubtedly requisite for the purpose of understanding the uses of the parts, and a physiological connexion of ideas with each subject of demonstration is the proper method of fixing their structure upon our minds. For a bare inspection of the parts, without deducing their function from their form and situation, would no means produce that permanent impression upon the mind which must greatly depend on the subject's being rendered equally instructive and entertaining. It shall therefore be our business in the demonstration of the parts to intersperse such physiological observations as obviously occur in the description of them.

It may be here observed that no previous medical knowledge is required for the perfect understanding of every part of our subject; and let me inform you that all the most eminent anatomists have given it as their opinion that the reading of authors on this subject previous to dissection is by no means necessary, because books almost universally convey either an imperfect idea of the situation of the parts, or what is frequently the case, lead those who have not attended the demonstrations into such errors as are exceedingly difficult to correct afterwards.

The method I would recommend to students is to be exceedingly attentive to the subject of every lecture, and by no means to quit it until the form and situation is thoroughly comprehended; and that after this the idea of it should be more deeply impressed on the mind by reading the best authors on the same subject and examining the anatomical plates which are the most intelligibly and accurately executed. The best authors on anatomy now extant are Neil, Cheselden, <Fife, John Bell, Charles Bell,> Winslow translated into the English language, and Sabatier, a later author in French not yet translated. Those on physiology are Ray, Haller, Fleming, <Blumenbach> and Boerhave <and Cullen>. These may be consulted with Ruysch, Morgagni, <together with Vicq-d'Azyr and the Anatomia Britannica which completed will consist of 300 plates,> Eustachius and Albinus's *Fables*. On the particular parts the authors who have confined themselves to some single subject as the muscles, Munro on osteology,[11] <and Burke on {muscles}> but after all it will be necessary for every practitioner of physic and surgery to refresh his memory every eight or ten

---

[11] Note on opposite page: 'Withson on the Brain, Portafield, Haller, Linn, Wrisberg on the Eye, Cotunnius, Mechel, Camper and Scarpa on the ear, Walter on the Veins of the head and neck, and Glisson on the liver'.

years by attending a course of anatomical lectures, or dissecting a subject himself. And it would be highly useful for the medical pupils to meet together from time to time for conversation and improvement. The opportunity afforded for this purpose is one of the great advantages resulting from a resort of a large number of students to the schools, where all are at the same time pursuing the same object and advancing by the same path to the temple of medical fame.

An early version of the final lecture

The structure of the body and the faculties of the soul are a full proof of divine skill and attention, and afford an ample field for philosophical inquiry and metaphysical speculation. However fruitless any inquiry may be into the nature of the animating and perceptive principles, yet a full acquaintance with the laws by which their connexion and relations with the body are governed may be rendered highly entertaining and instructive. Whatever may be the nature of the human soul, that its faculties are in a great measure dependent on the configuration of parts is an indisputable fact, for a thousand accidents which take place to alter this form and texture, daily evince it. No sooner are the corporeal organs injured by external or internal violence, especially those which appear to be more immediately connected with what are called the vital parts, than the faculties of the mind become in some measure impaired, and degenerate in proportion to the degree of injury they have sustained in their organization. The same cause continuing to act with violence and without intermission will shortly render it an unfit habitation for the residence of the soul, and being no longer capable of exerting her faculties, she is constrained to quit it and to take her flight from the uncomfortable abode. Indeed so intimate is the relation between the mind and the body that the free exercise of their functions are in a great measure mutually dependent on each other – and the *mens sana* is perhaps to be found only *in corpore sano*, – If such is the importance of [[bodily]] health. If the offence of it is productive not only of corporeal pain and distress, but also of mental imbecility – how [[precious]] sacred is the charge with which the practitioners of the healing art are entrusted. You gentlemen have seen sufficient to convince you that without an adequate knowledge of [[the animal system]] anatomy it will be impossible to obtain any competent idea of the animal oeconomy – and it must be as absurd for one destitute of that qualification to undertake the cure of a disease as for a person [[totally]] unacquainted with the structure of a machine to rectify any derangement.

A multitude however have presumed upon this former, and wickedly sported with the lives of their fellow creatures. It is for you, gentlemen, to determine whether within the compass of your own knowledge there are not to be found practitioners of this description. I know they must be the objects of your contempt and detestation, and that such of you as are determined on the pursuit of the medical profession have ambition and honesty sufficient to induce you to avoid the possibility of ever appearing to others in the light that they do to you. Such as shall in future presume to enter on the profession must, if possible, be more inexcusable than many of those who are new in business in the various parts of the country; – for at that time some of them were students, the advantages for obtaining a knowledge of anatomy and the other branches of medicine in this commonwealth were certainly inferior to what may be derived from a public institution for the purpose. Great prejudice indeed still subsist [sic] in the mind of the vulgar against this method of anatomical inquiry, but happily it is amongst the ignorant and unenlightened only that are to be found. The clouds of superstition are gradually dispersing even amongst these, and the better informed are universally friendly to such institutions [[of the mind]]. It will not, therefore, I trust be long before some regular method should be established for supplying our theatre with subjects for dissection. Till then we must content ourselves with the present uncertain sources of supply, and instead of being furnished with bodies as our occasion require, we must adapt our lectures to opportunity and conveniency.

That these demonstrations may be productive of advantage to such of you gentlemen as have chosen this science for a professional purpose is my most earnest wish and, as if from the deplorable consequences to which I have often been a witness, of ignorance in the profession of the healing [art] and the fatal ends that have ensued, I feel my mind fully impressed with the necessity of the rising generation should be better supplied for the duties of their profession than many of the past. I shall always be happy in affording you any information in my power.

From an undated final lecture, ca. 1800

Gentlemen

We have now arrived at the close of our first course of anatomical lectures under the medical institution of the university in this place. Many disadvantages necessarily attendant on an undertaking so perfectly novel in this part of the Continent have accompanied us in the prosecution of our subject. And far be it from me to assert imperfections from this cause are the only deficiencies that have been apparent in our demonstrations. There are others which I am sensible may with propriety be imputed to causes of a different kind and of a more personal nature. It will however be considered that though the weakness of an institution now in its infancy may not admit of those extensive advantages which the nature of it is calculated to produce, yet that when confirmed by custom and [[strengthened]] maturated by the hand of cultivation, it may be rendered highly useful to the public and a means of promoting inquiries into, and offering knowledge of, the operations of nature in the animal oeconomy. The difficulties attendant on the prosecution of anatomical investigation in this part of the Continent have been so great that nothing but the most determined perseverance will be capable of surmounting them. It is however to be hoped that with the clouds of ignorance and bigotry and those of prejudice and superstition will speedily be dissipated. We may yet hope for the happy day when that profession which has for its object the most [[inestimable Enjoyment of Life]] invaluable blessings will cease to be treated with neglect and indifference, and the means of [medical] education, preparatory to the practice of that profession which regards the lives of our fellow creatures, shall command an attention and countenance at least equal to that which has for its object the precarious tenure of interest and property.

From an undated final lecture, placed after the course outline for 1809

The exquisite harmony and proportion by which the various parts of this complicated system are adapted to each other must fill us all with the most exalted ideas of the skill and wisdom of its Architect. An inquiry into it, and an acknowledgement of it, is a rational tribute to the omnipotent Author. The investigation, by instructing us in the knowledge of ourselves, must evince the position that Man has been the special care of Heaven. The structure of the body and the faculties of the soul are a full proof of divine attention. The consideration must inspire us with sentiments which will naturally be productive of worthy actions.

To prosecute the enquiry then as a branch of natural philosophy is laudable, is useful, and may be productive of effects individually and extensively supremely beneficial. That they may be attended with success by such of you gentlemen as have chosen this profession for the pursuit of your studies and practice is my most sincere wish and belief. Let me recommend to you never to rest satisfied with any present attainments in this Science. Depend upon it, there is an extensive untrodden field for observation, experiment, and improvement. There is every excitement to diligence and perseverance, and believe me, the present is only for laying a sure foundation for a splendid superstructure. If you lose it, you will regret it when it will be too late to profit by the result of your experience. For a thousand obstacles will hereafter present to your view. I cannot wish you a greater happiness than the *mens conscia recti*, ever the fruit of a proper qualification for the grateful office of preserving lives and of relieving the calamities attendant on the diseased and infirmity [sic].

It is a satisfaction that you cannot be deprived of, it is a rational source of real and sublime pleasure. The sensations attending it are an honour to humanity, and stamps an indelible dignity on the character of the physician.

Finis

Final version of the introductory lecture

It has been usual with anatomists to commence a course of lectures on the structure of the human body by a minute history of the origin of their art, and the various discoveries that have in different ages of the world been made in it. We have in this University so far conformed to the general practice in this respect as to give a short account of the authors that have written upon the subject of anatomy; and mentioned the names of those illustrious characters to whom the art of physick, and of anatomy in particular, is most highly indebted. As it will not however be necessary to repeat the history of this branch of medical science at the commencement of every course, I shall in this only advert to the stages of improvement which it has passed through in America, and for a complete view of the subject shall refer such of my hearers, as wish to obtain it, to the ingenious Dr. Friend, who has written largely upon the subject.

It is well known that in the earlier periods of the history of this country it was a pretty general opinion that every thing valuable in the arts and sciences was to be looked for from Great Britain, and particularly in medicine it was thought impossible for any person, however great might be his genius, to acquire proper qualifications for the exercise of his profession without a European education. We accordingly find a very great proportion of the gentlemen who graduated in this University in the first years of its institution seeking abroad those literary advantages and distinctions which were not [to] be obtained in this country. Most of the universities of Europe have been resorted to for this purpose, and if I am not mistaken there was then a much larger proportion of those who exercised the healing art that were regularly educated than what has been the case at some particular period, which might be pointed out subsequent to them.

Our forefathers were acquainted with the great advantage of medical institutions in England, Scotland and Holland, and it is not surprising that they should be deeply impressed with the importance and even necessity of a European education for such as were to be entrusted with the lives and health of their fellow creatures. We accordingly find that soon after the first settlement of this country there were a number of eminent physicians established in it, and we have seen at all times a prevailing disposition to repair to England for the attendance on lectures and hospital practice. The general course of studies was usually commenced under the direction of some gentleman of reputation in places where the extent and variety of business gave him great opportunity for noticing the nature and cure of diseases. After one or two years' attendance in this way, the hospitals on the other side [of] the Atlantic were resorted to, and at least as much time passed in attending the lectures and the public practice of Physic. Such as did not find themselves able to support the expenses of this course commonly placed themselves under the instruction of physicians of large business, and endeavoured to supply the place of more valuable opportunities by this diligence and assiduity. Three or four years of close application in populous situations generally constituted the whole advantages of a candidate for practice.

In more advanced periods, and especially in those approaching more nearly to our own time, we cannot but be sensible that students in Physick and the community at large, and even the established gentlemen of the faculty themselves, had been becoming more and more remiss with respect to medical qualification. In this country and towns throughout this commonwealth it has long been a matter of complaint amongst the discerning part of the people that a very great number of those who professed a competent knowledge of Physick appear'd to be extremely ignorant of the very first principles of theory, and little better than downright injurious.

After months riding with a practitioner and a little acquaintance with technical terms, together with a facility of using them upon all occasions, no matter whether right or wrong, and a few significant gesticulations, were too often the only recommendation with which the young physician set out in the world. The prejudices against opening the bodies of the dead have been so great that all methods have been taken in this part of the continent to prosecute the practice. [[Even in large and populous places the advantages for improvement were sufficiently small. How much more must it have been the case in such parts of the country where this was the pattern of education.]] How was it possible then for students to acquire that information of anatomy without which they must inevitably do much mischief in the practice of Physic? It is reasonable to expect that as society advances in civilization, the follies of superstition will subside. This is undoubtedly a general truth. It may be said that even in the present enlightened age of Europe, strong prejudices subsist with respect to the dissection of dead bodies. Witness the narrow escape of a celebrated English anatomist from the frenzy of an incensed populace but a few years since.

So fearful were the people in the Austrian dominions of disquieting the spirits of the dead by prophaning their reliques that a late edict of the Emperor Joseph anticipating the effects of putrefaction by putting lime into the coffins when about to be buried met with the most violent opposition. The idea of destroying the flesh by the caustic quality of lime was so abominably inhuman; so {rampantly} repugnant to the feelings of animal nature, that all the effects of human modesty were at once roused into action to repel the atrocious insult offered to the species; and though the measure was dictated by the soundest policy, and might, if adopted in populous cities in general, preserve multitudes of their inhabitants from infection and from destruction, yet the wise Emperor was obliged to repeal the law, and add another to the innumerable existing instances of ignorance and superstition over reason and common sense. But notwithstanding all this, the position advanced above is by no means shaken as a general truth – and an attention to the advance of knowledge in general, and of the polite arts in particular, in this country will confirm it as such.

The first proposal for any medical establishment in America originated in a sister state about 30 or 40 years since. The intercourse with strangers which subsisted in the province of Pennsylvania had undoubtedly a tendency to polish and liberalize the inhabitants of Philadelphia especially, which was often resorts of men of all nations and character. We may [note] without disparagement to the other capitals on the Continent [that] all of the progress <cultivation> of sciences was more early attended to than in any other of the provinces. The late Dr John Morgan had the honour of presenting to the Trustees of the College of Philadelphia a plan of the first regular medical establishment in America. This gentleman had received the first part of [his] education in that city. Having completed his pupilship under one of the principal practitioners there, he had been employed in the medical service of the Army for four years of the war before last, during which he had seen a great variety of practice and acquired a deserved reputation in the line of his profession.

Having quitted the Army, he repaired to Europe, where for five years he continued to prosecute his studies under the most celebrated masters. Soon after his return to his native city he was elected Professor of the Theory and Practice of Physick, and in 1765 delivered the first course of lectures on that subject.[12] The present Dr William Shippen had, however, previous to this

---

[12] John Morgan, 'A discourse upon the institution of medical schools in America, delivered at a public anniversary commencement, held in the College of Philadelphia May 30 and 31, 1765. With a preface containing, amongst other things, the author's apology for attempting to introduce the regular mode of practising physic in Philadelphia' (Philadelphia, 1765). Morgan's inscribed presentation copy of his lecture, given to Warren, survives as Countway Medicine Rare Books R745.M82 c.1. The inscription is dated Feb. 27, 1783.

delivered three courses of lectures on anatomy without any connexion with the College, and in a short time after was elected professor of anatomy and surgery in that seminary. A professorship of the Materia Medica was soon after instituted, and to this was added another of Chymistry. Dr Adam Kuhn was elected to the former, and to the latter the present learned and ingenious Dr. Benjamin Rush. Clinical lectures have also been delivered in the hospital of Philadelphia, which is a charitable institution for the attendance of the poor with ample advantages of practical instruction. The fame of this school has been deservedly great, and the name of Morgan is partly entitled to the honour of being mentioned as the founder of it. He is now no more, and it is but a just tribute to his memory to observe that he was a man of great erudition, of indefatigable exertion, and most unimaginable integrity. That to his labours for the promotion of medical science in this country he added the talent of systematizing the plan of education, which had been adopted, and that had it not been for him, it is doubtful whether any regular mode would have been instituted for many years to come.

The utility of the establishment was very soon experienced through the remotest parts of the southern provinces. Medical knowledge was amply diffused through each of them, and a new era in the annals of Physick was constituted by its effects. The lectures on anatomy and surgery are now usually attended by as many as fifty or sixty students in Physick, all emulous of doing honour to their instructor, and of promoting the interests of the healing art in their respective spheres.

In the New England provinces the advantages of pursuing anatomical inquiries by no means kept pace with those of their more southern neighbours. In the town of Boston, however, the prejudices against examining the bodies of such as died with uncommon diseases were gradually abating, and now and then a public execution afforded an opportunity for a cursory examination of a human body.

The chief information of anatomy was still acquired by a laborious examination of books, and how small a degree of knowledge could be obtained in this way is very obvious to every one present. Some few there were who, not satisfied with this kind of pursuit, had the patience to trace out the analogy between the human body and that of brutes for obtaining the requisite information. In this University there were a number of students who formed themselves into a society for this purpose and some small advantages were thought to have attended, but from my own experience I can aver that they were usually inconsistent to the object in view.

Where superior advantages could not be enjoyed, there is no doubt but that such ideas of the animal oeconomy might be obtained from the dissection of brutes as would enable the inquirer to furnish himself with some degree of insight into the pathological part of the science, or that part

which respected the nature of diseases, but would by no means sufficient
to qualify him in the smallest degree for the practice of surgery. The reason
of this is that a great part of the diseases to which the human body is
incidental are such as depend on a derangement of the visceral functions,
or a defect in the {illegible} organs of the body and the viscera are those
parts in which the analogy between brutes and human species is most
conspicuous. Surgery is conversant generally with affections of the limbs
and the external parts of the body, and in those the parts are extremely
dissimilar.

If a limb is [[to be amputated]] operated upon, an artery is avoided in a
human subject. The surgeon who had never seen any other than the dissections of brutes would be as utterly at a loss where to cut as if he had
never seen any at all. Suppose a [[large]] tumour is to be dissected from the
neighbourhood of some of the large blood vessels, or a deep sinus is to be
laid upon for the purpose of giving discharge to confined matter. He
would be as likely to wound the vessel as if he had never studied anatomy
at all, and would therefore be in danger of destroying his patient at every
stroke of the knife. A principal nerve upon which the sensibility of an
important part was dependent might be divided, or the motion of a limb
be utterly destroyed by the cutting of a tendon.

Convinced of these facts, and resolutely determined to surmount every
obstacle that might present itself in the way of anatomical researches, there
were some few who avail'd themselves of means for gratifying their desire
for improvement derived from sources still more arduous and more difficult of access – and these were the utmost limits to which the most fortunate student in the country attained. Many practitioners in the country
had never enjoyed the opportunity [of] seeing a human body opened,
much less of attending any regular description and demonstration of the
parts. He having once or twice opened the body of a cat or a dog for the
purpose of viewing the intestines and inspecting the lungs was as much
many of those could lay claim to who were going forth into the world to
remedy the innumerable diseases to which the complicated structure of a
thousand different organs in the animal system engrieve us.

But the important epoch of the American Revolution, or rather the war
which effected it, is the event to which the science of anatomy and the art
of surgery are indebted for their countenance and promotion. The military
hospitals of the United States afforded the most valuable source of surgical
improvement and anatomical investigation ever enjoyed in this country.
Indeed, few other countries, all things considered, have been circum-
stanced more favourably for these purposes than we were. Even the exigencies of the Army and the necessitous situation of the states were the means
of prompting the invention of the faculty, and of reducing the practice

of Physick in particular, to that degree of simplicity, which at the present day is the boast of our profession, and which in all future ages will doubtless be considered as the test of improvement and of advancement towards perfection in the healing art. Many of the present physicians aver their usefulness to the opportunities derived from this source; and for anatomical and surgical experience no means could possibly be more favorable. For there are no other circumstances that could give the young so complete opportunities of dissecting for himself.

Indeed the American War has been useful in another respect. It has broke down the bars which superstition had erected to the general practice of dissection. It has diffused a spirit of liberality and enlightened policy throughout the New England states, and been the means of exciting the learned to correspondence and association for the advancement of literature. The American Academy of Arts and Sciences would have hardly been instituted at the present period but for these salutary influences, and the establishment of the Massachusetts Medical Society not probably have taken place by many years so early to the sustenance and support of medical improvement in this commonwealth.

The intercourse which it forms between the gentlemen of the faculty throughout the State, and the excitement it produces to application and improvement, and the communications it makes to the public, will doubtless do much good and will probably greatly assist in convincing the world of the importance of education to those into whose hands they are to commit their health and their lives. This Society has made great advances toward instituting a plan of regular education, and nothing is wanting but a little farther assistance from the legislative body to enable them to complete the business. They are by law authorized to examine such candidates for the practice of Physic and Surgery as shall have acquired certain prerequisite qualifications, and to give letters testimonial of their approbation to such as merit them.

Among these prerequisites is a recommendation to students to attend the lectures in the various branches of the profession as taught in universities. A number of other societies are founded and forming in the various counties of the state, and a laudable emulation seems to be generally pervading the United States. In that time after the Charter of the Massachusetts Medical Society had been obtained, the Governors of this University taking into consideration the utter impossibility of the medical pupils being properly instructed by the gentlemen with whom they studied, who were general in large business in all the branches of the profession, were pleased to attach to the University in this place a regular school of Physic, and from the year 1783 the medical lectures of the University of Cambridge have furnished an opportunity to the medical students of their neighbouring states for acquiring that information which a few years past a much heavier expence would not have purchased them. However imperfect may be the present state of anatomical instruction in this University, it must be the wish and hope of every friend to this country that the necessity of repairing to European universities for medical education will shortly be superseded. The heavy expences attending on the numerous objects, which from their novelty must necessarily call off the attention from more solid pursuits, are a strong argument for a preference to an American education.

'Importunity Which Mocked All Denial': The Amherst Charity Fund and the Foundation of Amherst College

Carl I Hammer

1. Introduction: 'Like audacity and presumption'

The story of the Charity Fund, an independent fund which financed the foundation and early growth of Amherst College through designated scholarships and loans, incorporates many elements of the larger American myth. In just one year between May 1818 and May 1819 a small rural community in western Massachusetts numbering only about 1900 inhabitants raised over $50,000, more than $1 million in today's terms, to establish a 'collegiate institution' with the intent to provide 'for the classical education of indigent young men of piety and talents, for the Christian ministry'. They did this in an economy chronically short of cash and credit and during the early stages of the first great economic crisis of the new republic, the Panic of 1819.[1] They then proceeded to erect the first building as a community project, adding contributed materials and their own labour, and they had the confidence to admit the first classes before their

---

[1] The only general study of the Panic is still that by Murray Rothbard, *The Panic of 1819: Reactions and Policies* (New York, 1962), which is primarily concerned with economic remedies proposed and implemented. Massachusetts evidently escaped the worst of the financial crisis which precipitated the Panic, since its banks and government had pursued a relatively restrictive monetary policy; state government's reaction there was consistently *laissez-faire*. Western Massachusetts would not have been immune to the undoubted downturn in the real economy elsewhere, since it was linked commercially to coastal cities such as New Haven and Boston where trade clearly suffered. For possible local repercussions, see below, Part 4, for the funding difficulties with South College.

new institution even had a charter to grant degrees.[2] Professor William S. Tyler in his vigorous and engaging history of the College's first half century— a history enlivened by his own personal experiences as an 1830 graduate and guided by his strong religious convictions—extolled the founding generation 'that they dared to undertake such an enterprise in that age, and not only undertook but achieved it… nothing of the kind had ever been attempted. It was an original idea, and a grand one, and a bold one. It seemed like audacity and presumption… born of the boldness which, in brave and believing souls… knew no such word as fail'.[3]

Here we see ordinary people in an obscure place embracing a dream; a small community practicing self-reliance and self-help but working co-operatively and in harmony with their neighbours; men and women inspired by an ideal to sacrifice themselves selflessly and tirelessly; and who, with pluck and persistence, achieve ultimate success. Like all such historical myths, this myth contains valid historical elements. Indeed, very little of it is demonstrably wrong. Even Tyler's emphasis on the originality of the project is, perhaps, valid for New England, where long-established educational monopolies were still fiercely guarded; in the West especially many new colleges were founded during this period.[4] Tyler was working with the facts as he knew them, probably better than anyone can today. But, like all historical myths, this Amherst myth is necessarily incomplete and its story selective. Tyler's account was clearly restrained by personal sensitivities arising from early disputes over the College which still persisted 50 years later. Moreover, he had to reckon with a changed and more secular world than the strongly evangelical one he had known as a student at early Amherst and with which he clearly sympathized.[5] This required that he present his Providential History, his myth of Amherst's origins, in a slightly secularized form without disowning the religious roots of the

---

[2] Students graduated from the College beginning already in 1822, but it could only confer written testimonials, not academic degrees, before the 1825 charter.

[3] *History of Amherst College during its First Half Century, 1821–1871* (Springfield, 1873), 46. Tyler's celebratory intent was continued in a somewhat less heroic and religious tone by Claude Fuess, *Amherst; The Story of a New England College* (Boston, 1935). See the amusing survey of this historical genre by Joel Rosenthal, 'All Hail the Alma Mater: Writing College Histories in the U.S.', *History of Universities* 27 (2013), 190–222.

[4] For these national developments, see now: Roger L. Geiger, *The History of American Higher Education; Learning and Culture from the Founding to World War II* (Princeton & Oxford, 2015), ch. 5 ('Renaissance of the Colleges, 1820–1840'), 173–214. For financial trends see also Carl Hammer, "Every Tub on its own Bottom'; Financing Higher Education in the United States, 1638–2000', in Rainer C. Schwinges (ed.), *Finanzierung von Universität und Wissenschaft in Vergangenheit und Gegenwart* (Basel, 2005), 271–93, here: 279–81.

[5] For Amherst's relatively tardy accommodation with modernity see Thomas Le Duc, *Piety and Intellect at Amherst College, 1865–1912* (New York, 1946).

College. The story of Amherst's origins was now a triumphal story of Strength of Character.[6]

A fuller and, in some ways more interesting story can be recovered from the surviving historical record which, despite its defects, is still remarkably ample and eloquent. A fire in 1838 destroyed all the records of the Trustees of Amherst Academy and their collegiate successors who were responsible for establishing first the Charity Fund and then the College. In compensation, we have a very complete account of the 'Origin of Amherst College in Massachusetts' published later by Noah Webster who, between 1812 and 1822, was a resident of Amherst and a leading trustee of the Academy until September 1821, when he resigned and the narrative ends.[7] Webster evidently retained copies of several key trustee documents from the period of his incumbency and printed them in his account which, nevertheless, must be read like his other writings as a retrospective piece of skillful special pleading.[8] But the earliest historical account of the Charity Fund and the College is almost contemporary with the events it narrates, since it prefaces the earliest ledger of the Fund which contains the financial records of the first three Financiers or treasurers of the Fund through 1840.[9] The first portion of that ledger appears to have been set up for the initial audit

---

[6] This is much like the historiographical problem which confronted the early nineteenth-century writers on nearby Deerfield's origins: to recast a now unacceptable religious narrative in terms of pioneer character. See Michael Batinski, *Pastkeepers in a Small Place; Five Centuries in Deerfield, Massachusetts* (Amherst, 2004), 96, with further references.

[7] Printed in Webster's posthumous *A Collection of Papers on Political, Literary and Moral Subjects* (New York, 1843), 225–54. It had not been published previously, but Webster had submitted it to Dr William Coggswell, editor of the 'Quarterly Register' of the American Education Society, who had the manuscript in June 1840, 'but he has delayed printing it, by request of Dr. [Heman] Humphrey [President of Amherst, 1823–44] for the purpose of having an addition to it. But I [Webster] do not approve of this – I wish the History, if published at all, to be soon published by itself — & the MS returned to me. It is a part of my family-papers, which I am unwilling to have lying in Boston' (*A Bibliography of the Writings of Noah Webster*, comp. Emily Skeel & Edwin Carpenter (New York, 1958), 354). Presumably, President Humphrey wanted the narrative extended beyond 1821, and Webster was unwilling to chronicle events in which he had not been an active participant. There is no indication of the manuscript's current location, if any.

[8] For Webster's transcripts of Academy records and his selective use of them, see below, Part 4.

[9] Appendix: Amherst College Archives, Early History Collection, Series 2 (hereafter: ACA, EHC 2), Box 5a, 2–8. The history is written in a neat hand at 45 lines per page; the lower section of the first sheet containing pages 2 and 3 is partially missing, entailing the loss of all or substantial parts of lines 28 to 45. This ledger came to the Archives only in 1999 from the College Trustees' office. Its earlier provenance is uncertain, but it probably was in the possession of the College's Controller as a result of the Fund's merger with the endowment of the College in 1941, for which see Stanley King, *A History of the Endowment of Amherst College* (Amherst, 1950), 10–23, here: 23. The current binding is not original, and the individual sheets, of which pages 2 to 93 are written, appear to be uniform, all unlined with a common outer margin.

of the Fund in 1822, and the hand of the historical preface is that of Col. Rufus Graves (1758–1845), another trustee and the first Financier or treasurer of the Fund, who was sworn to that office on 9 July 1819.[10] The hand of the oath agrees closely with that of the historical account and the copy of the Constitution of the Charity Fund which follows it (9–18).

Although Graves's account is shorter than Webster's and shares with it, as we shall see, some of the lexicographer's 'spins', still it offers a very early first-hand account of the Fund by the person most directly active in its establishment, and most probably before the full story of the founding and the completion of the Charity Fund was known. Moreover, it can be supplemented by the much later reminiscences of Graves's son, George Washington, who wrote a lengthy letter to Tyler in 1871 answering the latter's request for information about his father's role in the College's foundation, where the Providential note is still quite prominent.[11] Although his witness must be treated with some caution, both because of his relationship and the late date, still the younger Graves gives evidence largely of events to which he was a personal witness while living with his father in Hanover, NH, and at Amherst where he attended the Academy. Unfortunately, all of these early accounts end with the first College commencement in September 1821, but by combining them with other early narratives and documents and by comparing them with the financial data contained in the Fund ledger, we can reconstruct a relatively complete account of the events which established the Fund and the College through the initial fund-raising period up to the grant of a charter in 1825, an account which differs both in important particulars and in overall conclusions from the established narrative or 'myth'.

2. Beginnings: 'An appeal ... to the Opulent'

Graves's historical narrative in the manuscript ledger apparently begins shortly after his removal in 1815 from Hanover where he was an instructor in chemistry at Dartmouth to a family farm in Leverett, Massachusetts,

---

[10] Graves's oath before Hezekiah Wright Strong, J.P., another Trustee of Amherst Academy, is ACA, EHC 2, Box 5/11.

[11] ACA, William S. Tyler (AC 1830), Biographical File. The first ten pages and most of the eleventh of the letter were printed in 'The Faith of Col. Graves', *Amherst Graduates' Quarterly* 10 (1921), 71–8; the last three, unprinted pages of the manuscript contain additional biographical information. The letter manuscript continues on page eleven: 'I have answered your [Tyler's] enquiries concerning my father's connection with the raising of the $50,000 fund as well as I can from my understanding of what you want. If I have failed in apprehending, you can ask such questions as you wish answered, and I will do the best I can in answering them'.

adjoining his birthplace at Sunderland, and a few miles north of Amherst. In July 1812 Hezekiah Wright Strong, an Amherst lawyer and shopkeeper, had begun to collect money for a secondary school which opened in 1814, and on 13 February 1816 Amherst Academy received its charter. Both Rufus Graves and his brother-in-law, Nathaniel Smith of Sunderland, were amongst the original trustees of the Academy, and this body became the legal entity which subsequently undertook to found the College.

The want of a college within the confines of old Hampshire County, which occupied the entire west-central portion of Massachusetts and until 1811 included Franklin and until 1812 Hampden Counties, was expressed on 10 May 1815 by the Franklin County ministerial association, evidently under the leadership of the Rev. Theophilus Packard of Shelburne, a trustee of Williams College. It was later remembered that Amherst was mentioned by the association members at the time as the most likely place.[12] Both Rufus Graves and Nathaniel Smith were residents of Franklin County and undoubtedly were aware of this ministerial discussion. It must have been about this time that Graves began to consider his involvement in such an undertaking, which he evidently discussed with his more affluent brother-in-law and other members of the Academy board.[13] Graves's historical memoir in the Charity Fund ledger indicates that he first may have undertaken an unofficial solicitation for an 'institution based upon the broad basis of charity', which was discussed and then 'submitted . . . to a number of Judicious and pious individuals, who generally approved the object, but as generally doubted its practicability'. Thereupon, according to Graves:

> To remove [doubts about its practicability] an appeal was made to the Opulent, and many month time and considerable sums of money expended in traveling the Country in quest of an individual or individuals who would found this charity establishment by giving such large sum or sums, as would put the question of practicability forever at rest. But no such individual was found.[14]

---

[12] Tyler, *History*, 24; Frederick Tuckerman, *Amherst Academy; A New England School of the Past, 1814–1861* (Amherst, 1929), 27. Tyler cites an 'Historical Discourse' by the Rev. Theophilus Packard delivered at the centennial of Shelburne in 1868, so this must be the trustee's son who wrote an ecclesiastical history of Franklin County (1854) and had access to the association's records. Packard senior was an original Overseer of the Charity Fund as well as a contributor ($100), and his son was an 1823 graduate of the College.

[13] 'The Faith of Col. Graves', 72, where the younger Graves in 1871 connected this to a remembered solicitation from Amherst, New Hampshire [sic], which had been made to his father while still at Dartmouth in 1812. I can only construe this (probably genuine) memory as a childhood confusion. The year 1812 coincides with Strong's initiation of Amherst Academy solicitations, and after the Amherst, Massachusetts, plan emerged, according to George Washington, '[t]his was the last of New Hamp.'.

[14] Appendix, 2.

His son later recollected that, 'Soon after this he left home to spend a few weeks in this agency in Boston and vicinity... He spent three months and bore his own expenses in the cities and country without having obtained one dollar for the desired object'.[15] Presumably, Graves limited this evidently independent effort with board approval to a few affluent persons of evangelical inclination whom he knew from his previous residence in Boston and eastern Massachusetts where such 'Opulent' were concentrated, but without effect.

It is not entirely clear how Graves's failed initiative among the 'Opulent' relates precisely to the first official act by the Board of Trustees of Amherst Academy cited by Noah Webster which was taken on 18 November 1817 at the annual meeting regarding 'a project formed by Rufus Graves, Esq.'.[16] This, according to Graves's own account, was 'The first proposition, which was the subject of repeated deliberation of the board, [and] was limited to the establishment of a professorship in the Academy for the gratuitous education of pious young men who might be unable to defray the expense'.[17] At that meeting the Board authorized a solicitation to endow a permanent professorship in Classical languages at the Academy for the gratuitous instruction of worthy ministerial candidates and appointed a committee composed of Graves, his brother-in-law Nathaniel Smith, Samuel F. Dickinson of Amherst, and two clergymen, the Rev. Joshua Crosby of Enfield, and the Rev. John Fiske of New Braintree in Worcester County to undertake it'. But Graves tells us that this second effort likewise failed because it 'was a project too limited to engage the patronage of the public', and Webster comments that 'They [the solicitation committee] found that the establishment of a single professorship for the purposes mentioned in the project was too limited an object to induce men to subscribe'.[18]

After this second fundraising failure, Graves led a third effort to reformulate the entire project. According to his son, who conflates his father's first two efforts, Graves persuaded the trustees to authorize him, Nathaniel Smith, and Samuel F. Dickinson to draft a constitution, 'for the raising and governing of the $50,000 fund' to 'establish a Collegiate Institution'.[19] This lengthy and elaborate document was (so his son) composed largely by Graves and published on 23 May 1818 as a general appeal to the 'Christian public' to fund 'the classical education in the [proposed] Institution of

---

[15] 'The Faith of Col. Graves', 73.

[16] Webster, 'Origin', 225–6; complete text from Webster's papers in Tuckerman, *Amherst Academy*, 29–31.

[17] Appendix, 2; unfortunately, the lower section of this page is missing, but the remaining fragments and the text of the following page indicate that it was this Board decision which Graves described in that missing portion.

[18] Appendix, 3; Webster, 'Origin', 226.

[19] 'The Faith of Col. Graves', 73; Webster, 'Origin', 226, does not single out these three from the larger solicitation committee, nor does he ascribe primary authorship to Graves.

indigent young men of piety and talents for the Christian ministry'.[20] The location of that institution was fixed by Article 1 to the town of Amherst. Article 2 of the Constitution specified that the initial sum to be raised by individual subscription for this 'permanent fund' was $50,000, and the whole of that amount had to be raised within one year from 23 May 1818 or the entire fund would be dissolved and the subscribers released from their obligations. How the amount of $50,000 was fixed upon is unknown, but later events indicate that it may have been 'suggested' by representatives of Williams College (see below). Regardless, the specification of a required total amount and a fixed deadline were probably necessary in light of earlier experience to give confidence to potential subscribers in this renewed undertaking. As Article 2 clearly states, this provision was enacted 'with a view to remove all doubt relative to the success of the said object', wording which (somewhat ominously) echoes Graves's account of his first unsuccessful solicitation amongst the 'Opulent'.

This revised scheme as set forth in the Constitution and By-Laws was approved unanimously by the trustees of Amherst Academy with reference to their 'Committee appointed November last' at their Board meeting of 18 August 1818.[21] At the same meeting the newly formed fund committee reported a 'subscription of about six thousand dollars to that fund', as being already in hand,[22] and authorized an enlarged committee of seven worthies now including the newly seated minister of the second Church of Amherst, Nathan Perkins, and the Rev. Winthrop Bailey of neighbouring Pelham, to solicit further subscriptions. But by mid-August the stop-watch had already clicked through one-quarter of the period, and less than one-eighth of the required sum was already secured; six months after initiation, in November 1818 with winter approaching, the Fund was only half subscribed and the quality of some subscriptions was questionable.[23]

3. The Convention: 'Importunity which mocked all denial'

Thus far, the charitable undertaking proposed for Amherst was not highly unusual. Just at this time, in the early nineteenth century, the need for educated ministers to fill empty pulpits not only in New England but, particularly, in new territories now being settled in the West, led to a variety

---

[20] *Amherst College Charity Fund. A Constitution and System of By-Laws* (n.p., 1818); full text copied into the Charity Fund ledger, 9–18. There is an original printed copy in the Archives, ACA, EHC 2, Box 5/8, and the text is also available in Webster, 'Origin', 227–34, and online.
[21] Webster, 'Origin', 226; full text in Tuckerman, *Amherst Academy*, 32.
[22] Appendix, 3.   [23] Webster, 'Origin', 239.

of schemes to enable academic study for young men from modest circumstances who previously had studied only in small numbers at the colonial
colleges.[24] This new influx of largely indigent and often mature students,
the 'infiltration of the poor', into new colleges and academies, quickly
outstripped existing funding sources which were largely local and pater-
nalistic. One important response was the founding of the American
Education Society at Andover and Boston in 1815, which quickly grew to
become a major funder of ministerial students at a variety of academic
institutions through scholarships and loans.[25]

Perhaps it was the initial success of the AES which inspired Graves's
fruitless quests to eastern Massachusetts and to the 'opulent'. But there
was another example closer to home. At about the same time the Hampshire
Education Society was established: in 1815, and in 1817 it began to adver-
tise solicitations in the *Hampshire Gazette* of Northampton in anticipation
of its being incorporated by the state as a charitable institution with a
written constitution in January 1818.[26] At that time this new Society was
supporting six students at Williams College and a seventh to join them
'with a view of being duly prepared for the gospel ministry'. An appeal was
made by the Directors for donations in 'monies, in classical books, in
cloth, in clothing, or in bedding and furniture' for their support. Their
support would benefit, not the residents of Hampshire County themselves, but rather 'our fellow citizens in the new and destitute settlements
of our country who are now famishing for the *bread of life*'. To this end
'Soliciters and Receivers of Donations' were established at seventeen towns
including two at Amherst for the two Congregational churches there.

The modest aims of the Hampshire Education Society contrast sharply
with those embraced in the very same year, 1818, by the trustees of Amherst
Academy. Not only was the financial goal at Amherst much larger, initially
$50,000 or fully ten times the amount of the 'permanent fund' of the
Hampshire Society in 1823 ($4790.78), but the scope of the undertaking

---

[24] The quotation is taken from David Allmendinger's classic account, *Paupers and
Scholars; The Transformation of Student Life in Nineteenth-Century New England* (New York,
1975), 8–27.

[25] Allmendinger, *Paupers and Scholars*, 64–78, recounts the 'strange' history of this novel
institution which reached its peak of influence in the 1830s. The AES was the organization
which had proposed to publish Webster's 'Origin' (see above), perhaps, as a model for
others.

[26] *Hampshire Gazette*, 26 November 1817; *The Constitution of the Hampshire Education
Society and rules of the Directors, &c., A.D. 1818* (Northampton, 1818). The Constitution
states in Article 1 that 'the object of the Society is to receive and manage the Rev. John S.
Schermerhorn's donation and to procure other funds' (5). This is a mistake for the Rev. John
F. Schermerhorn, a native of New York and graduate of Union College, who promoted a
scheme for evangelization in the West. See the very full and interesting historical account of
the Society in the *Hampshire Gazette*, 31 December 1823.

was also incomparably more ambitious. The aim at Amherst was, of course, like that of both the American and the Hampshire Education Societies, to provide learned ministers for empty American pulpits, but the Preamble to the Charity Fund's Constitution stated plainly a much broader objective:

> Taking into consideration the deplorable condition of a large portion of our [human] race who are enveloped in the most profound ignorance, cruel superstition, and gross idolatry; and many of them in a savage state without a written language; together with vast multitudes in Christian countries of which our own affords a lamentable specimen, who are dispersed over extensive territories, as sheep without a shepherd... Under the conviction that the education of pious young men of the first talents in community, is the most sure method of relieving our brethren, by civilizing and evangelizing the world... We the undersigned... do make, constitute and ratify, the following Constitution and system of By-laws...'

Whatever we may think of this today, the trustees' resolve certainly justifies Professor Tyler's assertion that their undertaking was 'an original idea, and a grand one, and a bold one'.

So bold, in fact, that there must have been considerable concern amongst the Amherst trustees that the expanded mission object would be difficult to promote and the substantial financial goal would be difficult to raise within the allotted time. In order to address this concern, the promoters of the Charity Fund conceived a novel scheme to secure acceptance by a broader public and widen substantially the potential subscription base. Although the Hampshire Society had allowed any 'Minister of a Congregational or Presbyterian Church' into its ranks, it had confined its membership primarily to the 'Central Association of Ministers in the County of Hampshire'.[27] On 10 September 1818 the trustees of Amherst Academy authorized a much larger 'convention' of clerical and lay delegates from the Congregational and Presbyterian parishes of Hampshire, Franklin, Hampden, and western Worcester counties along with fund subscribers, to meet at Amherst on 29 September and there discuss and approve the undertaking as described in its constitution.[28] The invitation, like the constitution, emphasized the 'interests of Zion in our own country, and the conversion of the heathen', as 'powerful motives... to supply

---

[27] *Constitution of the Hampshire Education Society*, 5. In fact, it was dominated by clergy from west of the Connecticut River, especially the Rev. Vinson Gould of Southampton (for whose influence see Allmendinger, *Paupers and Scholars*, 14–22), although five of its seventeen depositories for donations were in Franklin County: Leverett, Montague, Sunderland, Wendell, and Whately.

[28] Webster, 'Origin', 234. Text of the invitation in Webster, 'Origin', 234–5; and with an addendum on accommodation in Tuckerman, *Amherst Academy*, 236–7.

missionaries, and furnish destitute churches and people in our own extensive republic'.

Perhaps, the trustees here were also invoking a venerable institution which had been established a century earlier under the leadership of the Rev. Solomon Stoddard of Northampton, the Hampshire Association of Ministers.[29] That association often had been an effective instrument for promoting unity within what Jonathan Edwards was to call the 'neighborhood' of old Hampshire county. The trustees' appeal to this venerable instrument of county harmony and co-operation was, as we shall see, somewhat ironic. But their attempt to reunite this older county entity and its wider population indicates that the new institution was now being promoted as a truly regional project for western Massachusetts and thus worthy of support from a much wider body of subscribers. This object, in keeping with the broad solicitation strategy adopted, was the tenor of the trustees' official letter dated 11 September and signed by Webster, Fiske, and Graves inviting attendance at the west church, that is, the First Church of Amherst, on Tuesday, 29 September at 9am. This invitation did not, however, mention that the location of the contemplated 'seminary' or 'institution' was restricted to Amherst.[30]

The convention duly assembled at Amherst on 29 September, and we are fortunate to have in the College archives a handwritten copy of the convention's official protocol prepared by one of the two Secretaries to the convention, Col. Joseph Billings of Hatfield. It contains a full list of clerical and lay delegates from the parishes but not of the Fund subscribers present. Altogether fifteen clergy and fifteen lay delegates from sixteen parishes in Hampshire county attended; thirteen clergy and thirteen laymen from fourteen parishes in Franklin county; five clergy and one layman from five parishes in Hampden county; and four clergy and three lay delegates from four parishes in western Worcester county—a very respectable turnout on such short notice which demonstrates very high interest in the project indeed. The three clergy Directors of the Hampshire Education Society,

---

[29] Gregory Nobles, *Divisions throughout the Whole: Politics and Society in Hampshire County, Massachusetts, 1740–1775* (Cambridge, 1983), 24–8.

[30] Nor does the Amherst Trustee, Hezekiah Wright Strong, in a diary entry for 29 September: 'Convention of ministers with their delegates, from four counties assemble at Amherst for the purpose of expressing their opinion relative to a contemplated institution for the education of young men for the ministry' ('Diary of H.W. Strong', Pocumtuck Valley Memorial Association, Deerfield, Library, Mss Diaries, Deerfield Families, Strong Family, typescript copy). The original entries, January – December 1818, were evidently made in Strong's copy of the *Massachusetts Register and United States Calendar* for 1818, but there is no indication of the present location of that volume or as to who made the modern transcript. Strong, son of the eminent Judge Simeon Strong, carried on a legal practice in Deerfield as well as Amherst.

the President, the Rev. Dr Joseph Lyman of Hatfield, the Secretary, the Rev. Enoch Hale of Westhampton, and the Rev. Vinson Gould of Southampton, were all in attendance, and Lyman even served as President of the Amherst convention.[31] Perhaps they were looking to glean support for their parallel project? If so, they were quite mistaken.

The protocol is a privileged document not only because of its official status, but also because subsequent developments and the ultimate outcome of the project were both unknown when it was drafted. Graves's, Webster's, and Norton's accounts, of course, did have this benefit of hindsight, and they were partisans of the Amherst project. Still, there is little disagreement amongst these sources about the main line of the proceedings and the main source of contention. Everyone endorsed the establishment of a college in the area, but it was equally clear from the outset that there was no unanimity about its location, a contentious point which the letter of invitation had tactfully (or slyly) avoided, indicating that the Amherst trustees were well aware of opposition to that aspect of their proposal. The constitution of the Charity Fund, which explicitly cited Amherst in Article 1, was referred at the end of the first day to the examination of a select committee of twelve, composed of nine clergy and three lay delegates from fourteen parishes distributed amongst the four counties.[32] In addition, Samuel F. Dickinson of Amherst and Rev Josiah Cannon of Gill in Franklin county were to 'attend' on the committee to assist.

In the event, the committee's report to the convention on the following day, Wednesday, 30 September, made five recommendations, four of which were clearly unfavourable to Amherst. In the most important, the committee recommended the establishment of another, 'disinterested committee' to explore alternative locations in Hampshire county, and there were no explicit references to Amherst elsewhere in the document. Nevertheless, after 'desultory conversation' (so the protocol) the majority of the convention passed a motion by the Rev. Jonathan Grout, a Delegate of Hawley in Franklin county and a subscriber to the Fund, to strike the committee's first and key recommendation for further exploration of alternative locations. Amherst's name was then inserted into the other three recommendations regarding location, the overall responsibility of Amherst

---

[31] The protocol also mentions Samuel F. Dickinson, Esq, of Amherst, and Elisha Billings, Esq, of Conway in official capacities, so they must have been attending as subscribers to the Fund which, indeed, they were. In addition, we have Webster's extensive account of the proceedings which, although he was undoubtedly present, reproduces much information directly from the protocol, and there are also the reminiscences of D.W. Norton, Esq, likewise an observer while still a student at Amherst Academy, which were contained in a later letter to Professor Tyler (*History*, 49).

[32] Heath in Franklin County supplied two members.

Academy's trustees, and the preparation of a site with suitable buildings. But the committee's initial omissions of Amherst were clearly an embarrassment, and both Graves and Webster in their accounts reproduce the recommendations in their final, adopted forms, giving an easily misleading impression of the committee's own conclusions.[33]

Webster says that this final outcome favourable to Amherst was determined 'by a large majority of votes', and Tyler asserts that '[i]t received the sanction of by far the greater part of the Convention' although Graves limits the 'great majority' only to the first and most odious recommendation.[34] This seems to be confirmed by the initial report on the Amherst convention published in the *Hampshire Gazette* of Northampton on 13 October that the margin was 'almost unanimous', which then notes ominously in a asterisked footnote that 'A few gentlemen had left the house before the business was closed'. The protocol itself gives no tally, and we cannot be sure of the margin which may not be meaningful in any event. Since all subscribers to the Fund had been invited to the convention along with the delegates of the parishes, and since their subscriptions had been predicated on an Amherst location, it is quite likely that those favourable to Amherst might dominate in full convention if not in committee. Although the invitation had mentioned the presence of 'subscribers to the fund', it was vague as to their status, since they were neither 'the settled ministers of the gospel' nor their 'lay-delegates'. In this way the convention may have been 'packed', and those favourable to another location may have felt that they had been 'set up'.

That was, indeed, the charge brought subsequently by those who wished to relocate Williams College to Northampton (see below). An open letter written to the *Hampshire Gazette* by a correspondent calling himself 'The Gleaner' and published on 27 October 1818 charges colourfully that 'every mouth [at the convention] which would not say Amherst was sealed, and every arm which would not rise in defence of Amherst [as being a place] "thrown on enchanted ground" was pinioned'. The *Gazette*, a leading supporter of Northampton's cause and no doubt again echoing local sentiment, quickly picked up on this line of foul play and printed an editorial article on 10 November 1818 alleging that, 'the Subscribers to the fund, the Trustees of the Academy, and, in some instances, lay gentlemen who had neither been delegated by church nor people, took their seats as members'.

Moreover, in the same piece the *Gazette* even charged that potential opponents of Amherst had been kept deliberately in the dark about the Amherst Trustees' true plans until the convention itself, so that they would

[33] Webster, 'Origin', 238; Graves's account is even more heavily edited and mentions the 'disinterested committee' (Appendix, 5–6).

[34] Webster, 'Origin', 238; Tyler, *History*, 50; Appendix, 5.

have no time to organize an effective opposition. For that reason, so the *Gazette*, no subscriptions had been solicited 'in Hatfield, nor in Hadley, nor in South Hadley, nor in Northampton, nor, so far as we can learn, in any of the towns in the south or south-western part of the old county of Hampshire', while elsewhere the Amherst Trustees, 'were entering every nook in distant towns and urging their claims for aid and assistance *with an importunity which mocked all denial*' (my italics). Their intent, so the Gazette implied, was to present the unsuspecting convention with a *fait accompli* and demand nothing less than 'unconditional submission' to Amherst. To that end, the *Gazette* also charged that the printing of the deceptive invitation had been removed to far-away Worcester county and dispatch to potential opponents deliberately delayed to catch them unprepared. But, even had opponents been prepared, 'there were Subscribers enough within the shout of a man's voice to have carried every point against them. And these proceedings are, nevertheless, called the decisions of a Convention: a fair expression of the public sentiment! Pshaw – Pshaw'.

The *Gazette's* reporting and editorial comments were clearly partisan, but the *gravamen*, that the Amherst Trustees and the Fund's committee had acted deceptively and in bad faith, have a certain plausibility. If so, even some people sympathetic to Amherst may have resented such tactics. When the convention concluded on Wednesday, it voted its thanks to the two Amherst clergy men 'and the Inhabitants of Amherst, for the hospitality received by the Members'. But the victorious proponents of the Fund and the College may have gained only a Pyrrhic victory. The sparse support for the Fund by the clerical and lay delegates indicates this. Both of the attendants to the committee were subsequently listed as subscribers to the Fund, as were two of the three lay delegates; on the other hand, only three of the nine clergy members of the committee are found amongst the subscribers, and altogether only about 22 invited delegates out of 68 altogether were subsequently listed as contributors to the Fund, barely one-third of the total. This meagre yield seems to confirm broad and continued opposition to the full plan as envisioned by the Amherst Trustees, despite their parliamentary triumph.

4. Ephraimites: 'Not far from the centre of the County of Hampshire'

In fact, there is also a back story, already alluded to, which is necessary to understand these developments at the convention and the subsequent course of the dispute around the Charity Fund. The 'Gleaner's' attack in the *Hampshire Gazette* on 27 October was prefaced there by a report of a meeting on 22 October at the Court House in Northampton 'of a number of gentlemen from various parts of the old county of Hampshire', chaired by the Hon. John Hooker of Springfield. The stated purpose of the meeting was to induce Williams College to relocate 'to some place not far from the centre of the County of Hampshire', and a committee of ten was appointed 'to take such measures as they may deem expedient to carry the foregoing object into effect', enjoining and authorizing them 'to collect such facts, including moral and religious character, as may in their opinion enable the Trustees of Williams College to decide upon the most suitable place, under all circumstances, to which to remove that Institution...'.

Fully six of these ten Northampton committeemen had attended the Amherst convention, and their number included the three clergy Directors of the Hampshire Education Society, the Revs Lyman, Hale, and Gould. They clearly represented the faction, largely from west of the river, which had just been defeated at Amherst. In effect, at Northampton a month later this dissident group took up the rejected recommendation to the convention at Amherst for a 'distinterested committee' to examine alternative locations. Their ostensibly 'disinterested' appeal was a clever appeal to the 'disinterested' public spirit of a broader constituency, and the report of their meeting was to be published in the three principal newspapers covering old Hampshire county. Nevertheless, Hezekiah Wright Strong, an Amherst Trustee and lay delegate at the Amherst convention, noted in a diary entry for 22 October, 'Convention of twelve persons assemble at Northampton for the purpose of defeating the proposed institution at Amherst'.[35] He apparently had no doubt that their true aim was to secure Williams for Northampton rather than Amherst.

Noah Webster's account likewise makes it clear that developments in Amherst were powerfully shaped by decisions being considered at the same time by the trustees of Williams College to remove that college from its remote location in the Berkshires to a more central location in old Hampshire county. Williams's potential student population had been eroded severely by the foundation of Union College (1795) and Middlebury (1802), and enrolment there was in steep decline. A move to a more populous place had first been proposed to the Williams Trustees as early as 2 May 1815 by the Rev. Theophilus Packard of Shelburne.[36] As we saw (above, Part 2), Packard chaired the Franklin county ministerial association meeting eight days later on 10 May where Williams' removal, preferably to Amherst, was endorsed, and he attended the September 1818 Amherst

---

[35] 'Diary of H.W. Strong', PVMA, Library. Eleven persons are named in the *Gazette's* report.

[36] Arthur L. Perry, *Williamstown and Williams College* (New York, 1899), 384–6; Tyler, *History*, 52–3.

convention, served on its select committee, and was a subsequent contributor to the Charity Fund.

It was probably in connection with Packard's early initiative favourable to Amherst that another trustee of Williams, probably the Hon. Joseph Lyman of Northampton, had solicited a letter dated 28 June 1815 from Dr Timothy Dwight, President of Yale (1795–1817) and a Northampton native, on the merits of Williams's relocation rather to Northampton.[37] Dwight rehearsed Northampton's merits at length, and the letter was later printed posthumously on 5 January 1819 by the *Hampshire Gazette* to strengthen Northampton's claim for Williams. In the letter Dwight never mentions Amherst but strongly deprecates the 'absolute error...that a College should be placed in a small town', a remark of course aimed at promoting removal from tiny Williamstown but which also deftly excluded Amherst and all other places in old Hampshire county, with the exception of Springfield which never seems to have been considered seriously.

The relationship of Amherst's founding to the removal of Williams was still a highly sensitive issue in the late nineteenth century when Tyler wrote his *History* of the College and Arthur Latham Perry wrote his great history of Williamstown and the college there; they were both at great pains to downplay any conflict or lingering animosity.[38] However, the constitution of the Charity Fund, itself published in May 1818, had provided explicitly for a joint incorporation of the new college with Amherst Academy, 'and with Williams College also, should it be thought expedient to remove that seminary to the county of Hampshire, and to locate it in the town of Amherst', but leaving the name of the then united institution significantly and tactfully blank (Article 1). Evidently, Williams trustees, possibly including Packard, had visited Amherst to explore such a possibility, and at the meeting of 18 August 1818 when the Charitable Fund and its committee were given official status by the trustees of Amherst Academy, that committee was authorized to contact the Williams trustees.[39]

In the first week of September two 'gentlemen' of Amherst Academy did visit Williams and present the results of their 18 August meeting, but no reply was received from Williams and on 10 September the Amherst trustees resolved, as we have seen, to convene the convention in order to enhance Amherst's claim on Williams as well as to launch further

---

[37] Lyman, who had attended the Amherst convention in September 1818 as a lay delegate from Northampton, was one of the ten committeemen appointed on 22 October 1818 to conduct an independent location search and thus derail the convention's result in favor of Amherst (see above).

[38] Tyler, *History*, 51–61; Perry, *Williamstown*, *e.g.* 415.

[39] Webster, 'Origin', 226, 234.

solicitations.[40] But the apparent disarray at the convention weakened rather than strengthened their case. Nevertheless, on 26 October the trustees of Amherst Academy appointed three persons, Rev. John Fiske, Noah Webster, and Nathaniel Smith, to go again to Williams, and on Tuesday 10 November 1818 they presented the results of the convention to the Williams trustees there but again received no answer.[41] Undoubtedly, the Williams trustees were well aware of the dissension at the convention, since two of their members, the Rev. Packard and the Hon. Joseph Lyman of Northampton, had attended, and they took their cue from the original recommendation to the Amherst convention which had been taken up by the dissident meeting at Northampton on 22 October. They passed a resolution by nine to three, '[t]hat it is expedient to remove Williams College to some more central part of the State', and they authorized their own committee of three distinguished Williams alumni to proceed with a survey of possible new sites for their college in the old county of Hampshire.[42] A week later at their annual meeting on 17 November 1818 the trustees of Amherst Academy authorized an enlarged committee of five, Noah Webster and Nathaniel Smith with three clergy, to meet with the Williams committee during its survey. At this November meeting in Amherst it was also reported to the trustees that the Charitable Fund subscriptions now stood at $25,500.[43]

In the event, because of the difficulties of winter travel, the meeting with the Williams committee of three did not take place until May 1819 when they were finally able to visit several towns in Franklin and Hampshire counties. At Northampton the Amherst trustees' committee made an elaborate presentation evidently composed by Webster and detailing the general advantages of Amherst as a new location for their college.[44] Frederick Tuckerman, in his history of Amherst Academy, fortunately provides additional financial material from their presentation, not printed by Webster but from his manuscript, where it is claimed that the 'inhabitants of Amherst' have already raised $22,000 in 'Contributions' towards

---

[40] Perry, *Williamstown*, 399–400; Webster, 'Origin', 234.
[41] Webster, 'Origin', 238–9.   [42] Perry, *Williamstown*, 400.
[43] The Amherst Trustee, Hezekiah Wright Strong, noted on December 1st, 'Fund for the proposed institution at Amherst, $27,000', but he does not note the decision of the trustees on 17 November, only, 'The Amherst Academical exhibition held in the meeting house', on the evening of the 17th, and that on 10 November the Williams Trustees, 'submitted the question of location to Chancellor Kent, Mr. Payson and Judge Smith' ('Diary of H.W. Strong', PVMA, Library).
[44] Webster, 'Origin', 239–43, contains an elaborate account, possibly composed to counter President Dwight's letter of which he may have been aware, detailing what, 'we suppose to be the most important considerations' regarding the general qualities of an advantageous location before moving on to general financial considerations.

the enterprise including $8,000 for the Charity Fund and an additional $6,000 for the building, with a further $6,000 assured, and that '[t]he whole sum of fifty thousand dollars is subscribed to the charitable fund'.[45] The latter claim regarding the Charity Fund was, as we shall see, certainly not true, and nor was the claim regarding funding for the building. At the same time the offer was renewed to unite the Charity Fund with the continuing operations of a properly relocated Williams. The Williams committee was nevertheless unanimous in selecting Northampton as the place for the relocation.

By then much water had flowed under the bridge and a funding contest between Amherst and Northampton was well underway. In the same issue of the *Gazette* that printed Dr Dwight's letter (5 January 1819), it was reported that the 'main condition [for such a relocation from Williamstown to Northampton] is the procurement of a sufficient fund to justify the measure', and that a local 'committee had been appointed by the inhabitants of this town', which had already 'obtained about $16,000' with the expectation that, 'the aggregate subscription in this town alone will probably be about $20,000'. The Northampton supporters were probably well aware that they were behind Amherst in the race, but they needed to display their greater local financial 'muscle' to regain momentum. Whether they thought $20,000 raised solely in Northampton would be sufficient inducement is unlikely, but their efforts probably were hindered by the same winter weather which delayed the Williams committee.

On 23 June 1819 the Trustees of Williams published their official decision to remove to Northampton. On 1 July Zephaniah Swift Moore, then President of Williams (1815–21) and evidently a partisan of Amherst where he subsequently became the first President of the College (1821–3), sent a letter to the Amherst trustees which Webster does not reproduce, and Perry does not mention.[46] Webster does, however, print the Amherst trustees' response to a later proposal made in November 1819 by the Williams trustees, which shows that the authorities at Williams were still hopeful that a union incorporating the Charity Fund could be effected at Northampton, to which the Amherst trustees replied (correctly) that this would be incompatible with the constitution of the Charity Fund.[47] The

---

[45] Tuckerman, *Amherst Academy*, 237–9. Col. Graves was not a member of the Amherst committee but he may have attended the presentation; his manuscript account of this Northampton meeting is terse, noting only that, 'This [Williams] Committee met in May 1819 and determined that Northampton would be the most suitable place' (Appendix, 6) although he does subsequently claim that the $50,000, 'was subscribed in the term of less than one year next preceeding [sic] the location of Williams College at Northampton by the afore said [Williams] Committee [in May 1819]'.

[46] Webster, 'Origin', 244.   [47] Webster, 'Origin', 244; Perry, *Williamstown*, 402.

lateness of this proposal is surprising because in the early summer of 1819 Northampton proponents had decided to broaden their own solicitation to meet the Charity Fund's falsely claimed $50,000, an amount which the Williams trustees evidently deemed sufficient for their purposes if only it could be got for the right place.

On 28 July 1819 a funding 'convention' was convened in the Court House of Northampton.[48] This Northampton convention was clearly an embarrassment to Tyler because of its membership, and he confined his report of it to an apologetic footnote.[49] It was presided over by President Moore of Williams, and a committee was established to make recommendations. One member of that committee was the Rev Dr Joseph Lyman of Hatfield who had presided at the Amherst convention in the previous autumn but was not a Fund subscriber. No doubt, however, he had learned some practical lessons about effective meeting management there. The purpose of this meeting in Northampton was, as in October 1818, unambiguous: the relocation of Williams College to Northampton. The immediate goal expressed in a resolution was 'to solicit subscriptions for the purpose of raising the sum considered by the Trustees [of Williams] as necessary to indemnify for losses and to ensure the future prosperity and usefulness of the Institution'. In another resolution, it was prescribed that, 'in case the sum of $50,000 should not then [by Wednesday, 25 August] be subscribed, that the General Committee be authorized and requested to take such measures as their wisdom may direct to raise said sum'. Possibly some extraordinary measure was contemplated.

In any event, the example of Amherst's Charity Fund must have been in mind: the precise amount and a particular date were specified at the outset of the enlarged solicitation. Five County committees were then established to solicit in Worcester, Franklin, Hampden, Berkshire, and Hampshire counties. The Rev. Thomas Snell from North Brookfield, who had attended the Amherst convention and subscribed to the Fund, sat on the Worcester committee. Other Amherst convention attendees were the Rev. Sylvester Woodbridge from Greenfield for Franklin county, the Rev. John Keep from Blandford for Hampden county, the Revs Vinson Gould from Southampton and John Woodbridge from Hadley for Hampshire county, and the Hon. Joseph Lyman, a Williams trustee from Northampton on the General committee. The Rev. Heman Humphrey from Pittsfield, who would be Amherst's second president (1823–45), was on the Berkshire County committee. The proceedings were to be published in the relevant county newspapers like the *Gazette*.

---

[48] *Hampshire Gazette*, 3 August 1819; Perry, *Williamstown*, 401.
[49] Tyler, *History*, 58.

On 24 August 1819 the *Hampshire Gazette*, no doubt fearing laggards, reminded its readers that the subscriptions in favour of Northampton were to be presented to the President and trustees at Williams on Commencement Day there on Wednesday, 1 September, and expressed its confidence that, 'the General Court [Legislature] will sanction the removal'. In the same issue, the three Northampton Selectmen, headed by the Hon. Jonathan H. Lyman of the subscription's General Committee, announced a town meeting for Thursday afternoon, 23 September, which would consider, *inter alia*, 'what further measures the town will take in relation to the proposed removal of Williams College'. Obtaining Williams for Northampton had become a civic enterprise. On Tuesday 2 November President Moore made formal petition to the Massachusetts legislature for removal, noting in support that, 'such subscriptions in aid of the College have been made, on condition of its removal to Northampton, fifty thousand dollars having been already subscribed for that object', and more was expected.[50] No Northampton subscription list appears to have survived, and it is unknown how broadly based or well secured it was.

A joint committee of the legislature, chaired by the Hon. Ebenezer Gay, made its report on 1 February 1820 and deemed the proposed removal of Williams to be 'inexpedient'.[51] The joint committee had examined with minute care both the legality and the 'expediency' or necessity of such removal. It discussed at particular length the legality and, possibly echoing the famous Dartmouth College case from the previous year, concluded that Ephraim Williams's original Free School benefaction was inseparable from other funds, and that Williams's continued legal status as a chartered corporation was thus inseparable from its location in Williamstown.[52] On the practical issue of 'expediency' the legislative committee concluded, *contra* President Dwight's earlier arguments, that there was no 'great benefit' inherent in removal to a larger place. The select committee also conducted an interesting *pro forma* financial analysis of both alternatives: remaining in Williamstown and removal to Northampton. The committee evidently accepted the $50,000 Northampton subscription at face value but also pointed out that a (more credible-sounding) amount of $17,681.65 had been subscribed, 'if the Institution be fixed in Williamstown'.

This amount, payable over ten years, had been subscribed following a meeting in Pittsfield in October where resolutions against the removal

---

[50] *Hampshire Gazette*, 23 November 1819; Perry, *Williamstown*, 403–7.
[51] *Hampshire Gazette*, 15 February 1820.
[52] In fact, those in favour of removal proposed to repay only the original amount of the benefaction when implemented in 1785, that is, $9157, ignoring any accrued value in the 35 years since then which would have been 'removed' with the charter.

had been passed; remonstrances were also passed at a town meeting in Williamstown on December 27.[53] The *Berkshire Star* of Stockbridge reported that fully $7,650 of the amount subscribed came from tiny Williamstown alone, a very respectable sum when compared with competing Amherst's $9,210 subscription.[54] Both alternatives, staying and removing, thus appeared to be viable financially, but that was irrelevant. The hopes of attracting Williams held by both Amherst and Northampton were revealed by the legislative joint committee as legally impossible and thus illusory. The *Gazette* vigorously disputed the select committee's conclusion, but the full legislature accepted it by an overwhelming majority in both houses, and the petition for removal was rejected.[55]

Noah Webster was serving out his final term (1819/20) as Amherst's representative in the legislature and was thus very well informed about the course of these proceedings. In fact, on the same day as the committee's report, 1 February, he gave evidence on other pending legislation along with Daniel Noble of Williamstown, also treasurer of Williams College and one of the three dissenting trustees.[56] At that point, on 15 March 1820, the Amherst trustees drew their own consequences and decided to begin establishment of the College and the erection of buildings.[57] Col. Graves reports, 'But the [Williams] petition having fail[e]d of success, the board of trustees of Amherst Academy judged that the way was open for the prosecution of their original design, and determined to put in operation the fund intrusted to their care...'[58] Accordingly, the trustees authorized Col. Graves, the Financier of the Charity Fund 'to procure notes and obligations for the whole amount of the subscriptions and to solicit further subscriptions'. They also moved to set a date for the election by the (presumably certified) subscribers of at least seven Overseers who constituted the board which governed the Charity Fund separate from the College and its finances.[59]

At their next meeting on 10 May 1820 the trustees appointed a committee to secure the property and superintend the erection of the first

[53] Perry, Williamstown, 401–4.

[54] *Star*, 16 December 1819; see also the *Pittsfield Sun* for 8 and 22 December. For Amherst's contribution see the following part and Table 1.

[55] Perry, *Williamstown*, 405. Yet, when Amherst College received its charter in February 1825, the authority, 'to unite Williams and Amherst Colleges into one University, at Amherst' was still reserved to the legislature in Section 7.

[56] *Hampshire Gazette*, 8 February 1819.   [57] Webster, 'Origins', 245.

[58] Appendix, 6.

[59] *Constitution*, Article 6; their minutes have survived from 1822 onwards, ACA, EHC 2, Box 5/12.

building.[60] This was particularly urgent because Col. Elijah Dickinson, who had died earlier that year, had by his will of 15 May 1818 set a term to his Charity Fund gift of three acres in central Amherst with an option to purchase more. His bequest would be void, 'unless the College, University or Institution shall be established at Amherst & located on the premises in three years from this date…'.[61] Apparently, Dickinson's heirs were not sympathetic to his project, and thus the site for the College needed to be improved before the following May 1821. Unfortunately, according to Col. Graves, who was not a member of the building committee, '[i]t was soon found, however, to be impracticable to obtain the means of defraying the expence of such a building, previously to the commencing of the work'. There entailed a frantic scramble to lay the cornerstone on 9 August and to complete the structural work by November before the onset of winter, when 'the bills unpaid and unprovided for, amounted to something short of thirteen hundred dollars'.[62] This was in sharp contrast to the rosy picture which had been presented to the Williams selection committee at Northampton in May 1819, when the trustees maintained that $6,000 had already been pledged for the 'college Edifice…with assurance to contribute as much more'.[63]

5. Accounts: 'Firmly bound and obliged unto the Trustees of Amherst Academy'

We can detect the precise effects of the Amherst convention of 1818 if we now look more closely at the subscription list for the Charity Fund. This subscription list of 1818–19 seems not to have existed in any early redaction. There was, however, such a list printed as an Appendix to Tyler's *History*,

---

[60] Webster, 'Origins', 245–6; Stanley King, '*The Consecrated Eminence*'; *The Story of the Campus and Buildings of Amherst College* (Amherst, 1951), 9–10, 310.

[61] Dickinson's slightly puzzling will is printed in Edward Carpenter, *The History of the Town of Amherst, Massachusetts. 1731–1896* (2 vols, Amherst, 1896), i. 180–3. In the Charity Fund register Dickinson is credited with $600 for land, that is the 3 acres at $200 per acre.

[62] Appendix, 7. Graves's son, who, as a student at Amherst Academy, participated in the building of South College, later provided to Tyler a very colourful and detailed account of his father's efforts to complete the building by the supposed deadline ('The Faith of Col. Graves', 75–8). On 27 June 1820 Noah Webster wrote to Jeremiah Evarts, editor of the *Panoplist*, soliciting money for the building, presumably from evangelical circles in Boston, arguing that despite contributions in kind and labour, 'we cannot proceed without some pecuniary aid. The people in the country have little money – or rather none that they can spare for such an object – and I am apprehensive that the business must stop for want of perhaps a thousand dollars … money we cannot obtain in this region': Harry Warfel (ed.), *Letters of Noah Webster* (New York, 1953), 401–2.

[63] Tuckerman, *Amherst Academy*, 238; this portion of their presentation was omitted by Webster in his 'Origin'.

where he tells us that it was 'arranged by Rufus Graves, Esq., Secretary and Agent of Amherst Academy, and laid before a committee of the Legislature, October 4, 1824', and that Tyler's own exemplar had been 'copied and furnished for this History, at the request of the author, by Lucius Boltwood, Esq', the third Financiar of the Fund.[64] However, as noted in the introduction, there is also an unprinted version of the subscription list in a manuscript register of early Amherst materials now in the College Archives, which is probably Graves's original version. This manuscript also contains a less respectable indication that it must be quite early.[65] It shows that the four largest subscribers, who, by the constitution (Article 10) were entitled each to designate a Fund Overseer, were Rufus Cowls of Amherst ($3,000 value of land in Maine), with Samuel F. Dickinson and Joseph Estabrook both of Amherst, and Oliver Smith of Hadley listed at $1,005 each. This odd latter amount, $1,005, allowed these three to outbid three other subscribers at only $1,000 each, an example of Yankee shrewdness if not of neighbourliness.[66] Indeed, these alterations in the register's amounts must have been made at about the time of the first election of the Overseers, which took place in August 1820.[67] It is likely then that the register's manuscript copy of a master subscription list to the Charity Fund (18–26) was made by Graves, perhaps as early as summer 1820, and was then prefaced

---

[64] Tyler, *History*, 649–54, here: 649. Lucius Boltwood (1792–1872), an 1814 Williams graduate and local lawyer who conducted the first audit of the Charity Fund on 28 August 1822, was the third and a long-serving Financier from 1833 to 1866 (King, *Endowment*, 21–2, 211–13).

[65] ACA, EHC 2, Box 5a, pp.18–26. This manuscript list varies in some minor clerical details from Tyler's printed list which certainly originated with Graves (see above). Tyler's printed list skips the entry for Thomas Moody of Granby, whose name occurs in the manuscript immediately after Azor Moody of Granby, a typical scribal error; and the double entries for two men, the Rev David Parsons of Amherst ($200 in money and $400 in land) and Oliver Smith of Hadley ($500 and another, altered, $505), are combined into one undifferentiated total in Tyler. There are also three small discrepancies in amounts subscribed, none significant for the result. These are trivial variances in an age without mechanical, much less electronic calculators, and Graves may be excused the inclusion of some later subscriptions with the original amount, since they were not material to the outcome.

[66] In each case, the register's entry clearly shows that the amount subscribed by the successful electors was deliberately altered after its entry in the register from 1000 to 1005, that is the final '0' was rewritten to '5' (ACA, EHC 2, Box 5a, 21, 25). But a Wise Providence ensured that this bit of trickery did not go entirely unpunished. The value of Cowls's land was subsequently written down to $700 after exchange for land in Pelham (King, *Endowment*, 216). As of the 1828 Audit, the principal amount Estabrook's note had still not been retired, and his account was $180 or three years in arrears for interest (ibid., 180). By then, Estabrook (1792–1855), a Dartmouth graduate and the College's first professor of Classics and librarian, had long removed himself to the South, in 1824, ostensibly for reasons of ill health. Tyler reports hopefully that Estabrook's subscription was indeed finally honoured, but the odd method described, that it was funded by lottery winnings inspired by a dream, must elicit a certain degree of scepticism (*History*, 10).

[67] Webster, 'Origin', 245.

with his historical account ending in September 1821 (2–8) and the copy of his constitution of 1818 (9–18). The following section, the 'State of the Original Fund' (27–46), which recorded annual payments by the subscribers, was very probably in use a year later by the August 1822 audit, and certainly by 1824 before the legislative inquiry cited by Tyler.[68]

The original subscriptions to the Fund were made over the year between May 1818 and May 1819 at various times and probably recorded on separate sheets, none of which seems to have survived. The unsuccessful successor fund, the so-called $30,000 fund initiated in June 1822, has left some such fragmentary evidences, one of which, printed by Tyler, contains eighteen names grouped under five places.[69] It was probably common for such subscriptions to be solicited town by town although other social groupings such as families also evidently played a role. Presumably, the minister, another leading local worthy, or a visitor from the Fund's committee, particularly Graves, initiated the effort and canvassed locally, recorded the subscriptions, and transmitted them to Amherst, where these individual submissions were consolidated in some way. A running total must have been kept as the year progressed. This is suggested by the interim amount of $25,500 reported to the trustees in November 1818 (above, Part 4), and, as the deadline approached, there must have been further checks to monitor punctual attainment of the $50,000. But this could have been done on an *ad hoc* basis and did not require the creation of a single master register for purposes of internal control.

Indeed, these subscriptions themselves had only a tenuous legal standing whatever their social obligation, much like modern pledges to public broadcasting. That is why Graves was instructed as Financier of the Fund in March 1820 to obtain better security for the amounts, which he evidently did with some success. These securities were duly reported from the third section of the manuscript ledger ('State of the Original Fund', 27–46) in summary form in the first audit conducted by Graves as Financier and Boltwood as Auditor in August 1822.[70] By that time, of the $52,194 which,

---

[68] The audit of 1822 by Lucius Boltwood, the third Financier, was printed by King (*Endowment*, 211–13), from the records of the Overseers of the Fund: ACA, EHC 2, Box 5/12, 1–3. The financial accounts of the Fund which are contained on pages 18 to 46 of the manuscript ledger would have been essential for the audit, since they report not only the original amounts subscribed to the Fund in 1818/19 (18–26) but also annual entries from 1820 to 1826, of their collection, both principal sums and accrued interest for outstanding principal (27–46). The (incorrect) total subscription including $15,000 from the guaranty bond recorded in the register is $52,194 (ACA, EHC 2, Box 5a, 26; cf. Tyler, *History*, 654: $52,244), which is exactly the total amount reported in the first audit of August 1822 (King, *Endowment*, 211), although the sub-totals reported as subscribed after 12 [*recte* 22?] May 1819 vary slightly from that audit (Ms: $110; Audit: $460).

[69] Tyler, *History*, 657–8; ACA, ECH 2, Box 6/1–3, here: 6/1.

[70] King, *Endowment*, 211–12, from ACA, EHC 2, Box 5/12, 1–3. The form of the audit does not follow modern accounting practices and requires some analysis, but the arithmetic is correct.

as recorded in the manuscript, had been subscribed, $7,401 had been paid in cash, $4,555 had been deeded in real estate, and $16,038 was secured by notes of the individual subscribers, $15,000 by a guaranty bond: $43,000 altogether. That left $9,200 of the original amount still unsecured or unaccounted for in 1822, an amount which must be calculated from the data provided in the audit. These accounts agree closely with those presented to the legislature a year later in June 1823, in which it was reported that $44,000 had been paid or secured. The audit also reveals that the Charity Fund was now evidently fulfilling its charge in the constitution (Article 3) which required that five-sixths of income be disbursed in scholarships 'for the classical education of indigent, pious young men'. Altogether $1373.75 had by then been paid to the College Treasurer, John Leland, for scholarships.[71] Immediately thereafter, during the years 1822–3, North College was erected with $10,000 borrowed from the Fund at six per cent.[72]

The total amount of $52,194 of the subscription reported in the August 1822 audit includes a guaranty bond for $15,000 subscribed by nine prominent Amherst residents. This unusual instrument undertook to supply any deficiencies in the total amount of $50,000 stipulated in Article 2 of the constitution for the Charity Fund's success, and these individual subscribers to the bond were 'holden and stand firmly bound and obliged unto the Trustees of Amherst Academy', both jointly and severally, for its fulfilment. The manuscript register contains the names and the amount in its total of $52,194 but does not contain any copy of the bond itself, which apparently survives only in a printed version in Tyler's *History* (654), evidently from a copy made by Rufus Graves. There the bond is dated to 6 July 1818 during the authorized subscription period from May 1818 to May 1819. But this date seems unlikely because the text then refers to 'the Convention holden at Amherst, on the twenty-eighth day of September last', which can only refer to the contentious convention of 29 September 1818 (above, Part 3). Moreover, there would be no way of knowing in the summer of 1818 that the exact amount of the subscription shortfall would be about $15,000, since this could only be determined at the end of the authorized subscription period in May 1819.

It seems likely, therefore, that the date of the bond is, rather, 6 July 1819, well after the end of the authorized subscription period, which was just three days

---

[71] Of that amount $150 was for 'tuition of Beneficiaries in the Academy' and that balance of $1223.75 for 'Beneficiaries in the said [Collegiate] Institution'. If the interest rate obtained by the Fund was six per cent, as seems to have been normally the case, then the payout ratio would amount to five per cent of a fully invested fund, not far from modern guidelines of about four per cent; the remaining one-sixth was to be added to principal.

[72] King, *Consecrated Eminence*, 310; *Endowment*, 214.

before Rufus Graves took his oath as Financier on 9 July (above, Part 1). Webster does not mention the bond in his account but does report that the trustees met on that day and reported that 'the money and other property subscribed amounted, at a fair estimate', to $51,404.[73] This re-dating of the guaranty bond to 1819 also seems to be the sense of the description of the bond by Edward Hitchcock, third President of the College (1845–54), in his reminiscences based upon information provided to him 'by my venerable friend, Hon. John Leland', the first Treasurer of the College and himself a signatory to the bond. Moreover, this conclusion is supported by the legislature's first and unfavourable inquiry into the College's finances in January 1823.[74] Likewise, in 1871 Rufus Graves's son, George Washington, who evidently had no direct knowledge of the bond itself, recollected erroneously that Graves's brother, Benjamin, and his brother-in-law, Nathaniel Smith, 'and some others perhaps' were the signatories after the initial solicitation period.[75]

Presumably, as the trustees' meeting on 9 July approached and as Graves was about to take over his office as Financier, he attempted, after the fact, to fulfil the strict obligation he had set himself in the constitution. He first approached his affluent relatives in Sunderland, both subscribers to the Charity Fund itself, for guarantees, and, when that failed, he finally obtained the necessary instrument from the nine Amherst worthies. Since the year on Tyler's printed copy of the bond is written out as 'eighteen hundred and eighteen' and is, thus, unlikely to be a clerical error, Graves, who provided the exemplar, may well have been responsible for this deliberate backdating which was necessary to legitimatize the entire subscription for public scrutiny. His own account in the Charity Fund register, without mentioning the bond, particularly emphasizes that more than $50,000 'was subscribed in the term of less than one year'.[76]

6. Results: 'Pledges which made the College possible'

Graves arranged his subscription list in rough alphabetical order by name of the subscriber with, for example, all of the 'A's' together, but not grouped in strictly alphabetical order within this section. Places of residence were

[73] Webster, 'Origin', 244.

[74] Edward Hitchcock, *Reminiscences of Amherst College* (Northampton, 1863), 120 2, where the signatory list for the bond differs slightly from Tyler's version; *Hampshire Gazette* from the *Columbian Centinel*, 5 February 1823, where the bond is characterized as 'a new expedient'!

[75] 'The Faith of Col. Graves', 74.

[76] Appendix, 6. We do not know the occasion for Graves's backdated copy of the guaranty bond, but it may have been for the legislative investigation of 1824. However, by then the bond ostensibly had been supplanted by a new solicitation (see below, Part 7).

supplied for each subscriber along with the amount of the subscription, but only in two instances was the security of the subscription indicated, both of them for land. Status of the male subscribers was noted by titles, and wives subscribing were identified when their husbands subscribed as well. The unpublished list in the register also indicates that county of residence was originally noted; this was omitted in Tyler's printed version and may not have been included in Boltwood's later transcription. It is not immediately obvious why Graves took the enormous trouble to prepare this long list in alphabetical order by name from what may have been some very scrappy materials, many of which would already have been grouped by place of residence. And, indeed, arrangement by residence immediately suggests itself as more immediate and practical method for securing and collecting the amounts subscribed. We shall return to this question presently.

Leaving aside the $15,000 guaranty bond described above (Part 5), the manuscript subscription list contains the names of 275 subscribers, 245 men and 30 women (Table 1). The men subscribed $35,081, and the women $2,213, for a total amount of $37,294, $100 more than the manuscript

Table 1: Amherst Charity Fund Summary

Town	Men		Women	
	Number	Amount	Number	Amount
AMHERST*	25	$9,010	2	$200
ASHFIELD	1	200		
ATTLEBORO	11	300	2	45
BELCHERTOWN*	1	50		
BERNARDSTON	7	433	2	100
BILLINGHAM	1	50		
BRAINTREE, NEW*	4	450		
BRIMFIELD	3	700		
BROOKFIELD	4	1350		
BROOKFIELD, NORTH*	2	400		
BUCKLAND*	1	100		
BURLINGTON, VT	1	1000		
CHARLEMONT	3	275		
CHARLTON	3	700		
CONWAY*	12	2325	1	100
CUMMINGTON*	2	600		
DEERFIELD*	7	1075		
EASTON	3	160	1	20
ENFIELD*	3	250		
FOXBORO	5	250		
FRANKLIN	7	475	2	55

GILL*	5	500		
GOSHEN*	1	200		
GRANBY*	11	1050		
GREENWICH	12	1500		
HADLEY*	2	1105		
HADLEY, SOUTH	3	900		
HARDWICK	4	500		
HATFIELD*	1	150		
HAWLEY*	5	900		
HEATH*	10	595	1	10
HOLDEN	1	50		
HOLLISTON	8	345	5	150
HOPKINTON	4	215		
LEOMINSTER	1	200		
LEVERETT*	4	200		
LONGMEADOW	6	445		
MEDWAY	2	75	2	25
MIDDLEFIELD	1	333		
MILLBURY	3	250		
MONTAGUE*	4	300	3	200
NORTHBRIDGE	1	100		
NORTHFIELD	2	50	3	60
PELHAM*	1	100		
SEEKONK, RI	1	50	1	20
SHELBURNE*	7	475		
SHERBORN	1	50		
SHUTESBURY*	1	100		
SOUTHBRIDGE*	5	315	1	10
SPENCER	1	50		
SPRINGFIELD	2	200		
SPRINGFIELD, WEST	1	100		
STURBRIDGE*	1	100		
SUNDERLAND*	14	2375	2	1200
UXBRIDGE	1	100		
WARE*	5	400		
WARWICK	0	0	1	8
WHATELY*	1	200		
WRENTHAM	6	350	1	10
59 TOWNS	245	$35,081	30	$2,213

* = Represented at the 1818 Convention

total which agrees with the 1822 audit. These subscriptions came from 57 Massachusetts towns, from Burlington, Vermont, and from Seekonk, Rhode Island. President King of Amherst was rightly impressed when, in 1950 he wrote:[77]

[77] King, *Endowment*, 11.

All [subscribers] were residents of New England, most from towns in Massachusetts. There were no subscriptions from the residents of Boston or Worcester, the two largest cities in the state; only two from Springfield, of one hundred dollars each. But from Hadley, Sunderland, Conway, Attleboro, Southbridge, Wrentham, Greenwich, Hardwick, Heath, and dozens of other small towns came the pledges which made the College possible.

It appears then at first sight that the Charity Fund garnished very broad popular or, as we would say, 'grass roots' support, and this impression is not entirely incorrect. But it is instructive to look at those towns more closely. In the first place we must note that 25 men and two women (both Dickinsons) of Amherst—a place unmentioned by King—subscribed $9210, about one-quarter of the total amount aside from the guaranty bond and even exceeding the $8,000 claimed before the Williams representatives in May 1819 (above, Part 4). This admittedly included Rufus Cowls's questionable $3000 in Maine real estate, but, even after its write-down to $700, the total would still be an impressive $6910. And those 25 male subscribers included eight of the nine holders of the guaranty bond who were already heavily obligated—only Joseph Church, Jr. is missing. Also missing from the subscribers are the names of two of the leading promoters of the College, Noah Webster and Rufus Graves! Perhaps, they considered their personal contributions in effort, expense, and reputation as sufficient?

The Amherst tax assessment of May 1820 allows some estimate of the financial circumstances of these subscribers.[78] Altogether there were 326 resident and 32 non-resident tax assessments, but in four cases names of residents have been deleted without any indication of the reason. The liability for tax was assessed in three parts: for the number of resident 'polls', that is, males 16 and over; for their improved and unimproved real estate (noted in acres but valued in dollars, presumably at a substantial discount to market or 'true' value); and for the assessed value of their personal property. Altogether these residents of Amherst accounted for 14,940 acres of real property divided between 7,162 acres of improved land and 7,778 unimproved. Thirty-two non-residents accounted for another 832 acres, 566 of which were unimproved. These persons were overwhelmingly men, but five assessments were for widows, including Lucinda Dickinson, a subscriber to the Charity Fund. Seventeen assessments were for the heirs of deceased residents including those of Calvin Merrill, a subscriber and bond guarantor, and Elijah Dickinson, a subscriber and donor of the

---

[78] Digitized images of decennial and other Amherst Tax records for the eighteenth and nineteenth centuries are available from the Jones Library, Amherst, Special Collections, through their website: www.digitalamherst.org.

property for the College, both of whom had died earlier that year. Two, possibly three, assessments were for business associations having property in Amherst. Three grist mills, two tanning mills, 2 fulling mills, one paper mill, and one cotton factory added to the assessed value of real estate.

Altogether 22 subscribers and bond guarantors are listed amongst those assessed, or only about seven per cent of the total, so we are clearly dealing with a very small minority not only of Amherst residents but even of taxpayers.[79] However, they were also clearly amongst the more prosperous. Indeed, four of the five highest total assessments were for Charity Fund subscribers, none of whom, however, signed the guaranty bond.[80] The bond guarantors were each assessed over $100 on their real estate and personal property combined, which also gives a truer contemporary notion of the magnitude of their undertaking. However, these original supporters of the Fund and the College were not the only persons of substance in Amherst. Altogether there were 64 persons assessed at $100 or more, but only 18 of them were early supporters of the College. The only piece of personal property noted by the Assessors, whether the assessed person possessed a carriage, also indicates high social status and some affluence; twenty persons assessed kept a carriage, but only four of them were College supporters: Elijah Boltwood, Rufus Cowls, Samuel F. Dickson, and Dr David Parsons. Participation in the Charity Fund made significant financial demands. Even seemingly modest subscriptions such as $100, which seems to have been the customary minimum for Amherst residents, still represented the equivalent of a substantial assessment. On the other hand, not all Amherst residents who were financially well able to contribute did so. The early supporters of the College were a minority in their own community and even amongst their economic peers, a situation which we shall examine presently.

Very near to Amherst, sixteen persons in Sunderland, the birthplace of Rufus Graves, subscribed $3573, which included very large contributions from two women, Thankful Smith ($700) and Rhoda Graves ($500), the wives of Nathaniel Smith ($1000) and Erastus Graves ($500), who themselves made very substantial subscriptions. These four persons accounted for more than two-thirds of Sunderland's total subscription which reflects the strong local connections by Rufus Graves which we noted above.

---

[79] Two subscribers, the Rev Daniel Clark and Joseph Estabrook, were not assessed. Of the two prominent non-subscribers or guarantors who were instrumental in the foundation of the College, Rufus Graves, a resident of Leverett, was not assessed at Amherst, and Noah Webster was assessed at $108, so he clearly had sufficient funds to make a financial contribution.

[80] John Eastman, $297; Elijah Dickinson's estate, $265; Joseph Cowls, $220; and Jonathan Cowls, $204.

Conway contributed over $2425 from twelve men and one woman, but prosperous Hadley—adjacent to Amherst and singled out by King – supplied only two subscribers, and its large subscription came overwhelmingly from only one man, Oliver Smith (see above). Large numbers of nearby Hampshire subscribers also came from Granby (eleven) and Greenwich (12). Remote Heath (11) in northwestern Franklin County supplied eleven, and another nine subscribers, two of them women, came from Bernardston, also in northern Franklin county as did three women and two men from Northfield there.

Of the 59 places listed, only 26 or fewer than half had a minister subscribing. Both ministers of Amherst's First Church, its early promoter, David Parsons, and his dynamic but controversial successor, Daniel A. Clark, were subscribers. However, one cannot say that clergy in any way dominated the Charity Fund. Aside from the Reverend Parsons, all of the local leaders in the enterprise were laymen like Dickinson and Graves. Nevertheless, clergy as local leaders by virtue of their education and office may have been disproportionately influential and, in a few places, decisive. President King drew attention to Attleboro and Wrentham far to the southeast of Amherst. Indeed, nine towns in southern Middlesex (Sherborn, Holliston, Hopkinton), Norfolk (Franklin, Foxboro, Medway, Wrentham), and Bristol (Attleboro, Easton) counties, places not considered in the founders' initial solicitation strategy, made notable contributions to the Charity Fund to which should be added Seekonk, then in adjacent Rhode Island. And women were particularly notable amongst their subscribers. Here clergy from seven of these towns may have been the key players in soliciting contributions from their congregations, and the apparent strength of women participants may reflect the novel and growing religious activism of women which accompanied the evangelical fervour of the second Great Awakening.[81] These places in southeastern Massachusetts, located between Unitarian Harvard and Baptist Brown, may have sought a theologically acceptable alternative to Yale, which was both more affordable and less susceptible to urban vice than New Haven.

Less surprising are the prominent omissions from western Hampshire County over which King glosses rather quickly. These were foreshadowed as we saw by the debacle at the 1818 convention and the associated hot rivalry in progress between Amherst and Northampton over Williams. No one from Northampton, the county seat, subscribed; nor did anyone from Easthampton, Southampton, Westhampton, or Williamsburg. Hatfield, also on the west bank of the Connecticut River produced only one

---

[81] Daniel Howe, *What Hath God Wrought: The Transformation of America, 1815–1848* (Oxford, 2009), ch. 5, esp. 190–1.

subscription for $150. These towns dominated the Hampshire Education Society, and by their location would have been Northampton's natural allies. More surprisingly there were no subscribers from Greenfield, the seat of Franklin County, although support from other and smaller towns in that county was widespread. Belchertown, then still a larger place than Amherst, sent delegates to the 1818 convention but produced only a single subscription for a modest $50. Various regional rivalries clearly determined financial support for the Charity Fund. The natural desire of the Amherst Trustees to conceal these embarrassing and potentially damaging *lacunae* was possibly a reason for Graves's arrangement of the subscription list by subscriber's name rather than place of residence.

In fact, there was evidently a sharp division within the town of Amherst itself. Neither the Rev. Nathan Perkins of Amherst's Second Church nor his deacon, Nathan Franklin, both of whom had attended the 1818 convention, were contributors to the Charity Fund although Perkins was a trustee of the Academy. This is indicative of pronounced church division within the Amherst community. Lingering Revolutionary political disputes and differences over personal character at the 1782 installation of the Rev. David Parsons, son of the previous minister, led to secession from Amherst's Congregational Church and the incorporation of a second established congregation in the following year. That breach, apparently exacerbated by differing loyalties during Shay's Rebellion in 1786/7 and by Parsons's long tenure, had so hardened by 1819 that an attempted reconciliation failed despite Parsons's resignation from the pulpit of the First Church.[82]

The nineteenth-century historian of the town of Amherst, Edward Carpenter, pointed out that the leaders of the First Church, like the Reverend Parsons, were also the leaders in the establishment of both Amherst Academy and the College.[83] Still, at least three, possibly four, of the subscribers were members of the Second Church and were the College's most affluent, but not most generous, early supporters.[84] Jonathan and

---

[82] See the discussion of the Amherst churches in Leonard Richards, *Shay's Rebellion: The American Revolution's Final Battle* (Philadelphia, 2002), 93–5.

[83] Carpenter, *History* i. 163.

[84] The early records including a membership register from 1810 onwards of the Second Church (now reunited with the First Church) are deposited in Jones Library, Amherst. The relevant membership lists are printed in the *Manual of the Second Congregational Church, Amherst Mass.* (Amherst, 1924), 14–29. The petitioners for secession and other early members are also listed in Carpenter, *History* i. 113. However, as Ronald Formisano points out, church affiliation in this period when the Established Church still existed and dissenting organizations were still discouraged can be difficult to establish, since it could encompass a spectrum of affiliations from committed and full communicant member, through a passive pew renter, to a mere taxable resident of the parish with little religious participation if

Joseph Cowls, who each subscribed $100, had total tax assessments in 1820 over $200, well above Squire Samuel F. Dickinson's $163. And John Eastman, a founding member of the Second Church, who subscribed for $400 in 1818/19 and for another $1000 in 1824 (see below), had the highest tax assessment in the town at $297, and yet he did not join the guarantors of the bond, all of whom had much more modest estates. At the other end of the scale, Joseph Kellog, a member of the Second Church in 1820, made the smallest subscription recorded in Amherst, $50, but on a very modest total estate assessed at only $63. Neither Amherst Congregational church was a monolith, but there were still pronounced differences between them with regard to College support.

Unlike Northampton, where the effort to secure Williams evidently became a civic undertaking, 'The town [of Amherst], as a town, had no part in the enterprise'.[85] That is true in terms of positive support, but the records of the Town Meeting for these years indicate that there was also strong political resistance to Webster, Dickinson, and their allies. This opposition reflected the older church schism, but also more recent political developments.[86] In the May 1819 election for legislative representative, Noah Webster had defeated Dr Timothy J. Gridley, a Yale graduate, recently settled local physician, and son-in-law of the Revolutionary general, Ebenezer Mattoon, a founding member of the Second Church. But in that year Samuel Dickinson ceased to be Town Clerk and Treasurer, a combined position that he had held continuously for many years, and in the following year, 1820, Gridley prevailed over Dickinson for Representative by a margin of 131 to 106, a relatively high turnout which indicates a very sharp contest. This sudden reversal must have been precipitated in some way by the failed reunion of the two parishes, and beginning in May 1820 'the meeting house in the second Parish' began to be used regularly for Town Meetings as well as the traditional site at the First Church.[87]

During all the years of the College's foundation, subscribers to the Charity Fund and the later guaranty bond appeal were a minority amongst the Town's Selectmen, never more than two out of five, and in 1821, 1823, and 1824 not a single Charity Fund subscriber was a Selectman. Similarly, from 1821 through 1824 none was an Assessor, the tax officer whose rolls

any: *The Transformation of Political Culture; Massachusetts Parties, 1790s–1840s* (Oxford, 1983), 156.

[85] Carpenter, *History* i. 163. Town Meeting records between 1815 and 1825 contain no mention of the College (Office of the Town Clerk, Amherst, bound ms. volume: 'Amherst Town Records (1759–1828)', 300–94.

[86] All election results excerpted in Carpenter, *History* ii. 206–13, from 'Amherst Town Records'.

[87] 'Amherst Town Records', 340. The venues are not indicated for all meetings.

as in 1820 also served as voter registration lists. Clearly there had been some sort of political insurrection against the established worthies of the First Church and Trustees of Amherst Academy during this period although we cannot say precisely how much purely local matters and personal animosities weighed against broader religious, political, and academic concerns. Perhaps this permanent local disestablishment of the Amherst Trustees provided additional incentive to Noah Webster for his return to New Haven in 1822?

No Fund supporter was a Representative to the Massachusetts legislature for the crucial years from Gridley's first election in 1820 through his second in 1826. Deacon Franklin of the Second Church prevailed over Dickinson in 1821 (126 to 94), and Aaron Merrick of the same parish, a Democrat, defeated Dickinson (155 to 131) in an exceptionally large turnout for the legislative term 1822/3, the year in which Amherst's first (and disastrously unsuccessful) petition for a charter was introduced to the legislature, unsupported by Merrick.[88] There is little doubt that these political shifts within Amherst reflect the broader political upheaval at precisely this time which led to the speedy demise of the Federalist Party and the fragmentation of the Jeffersonian Democrat-Republican party.[89]

The Trustees of Amherst Academy and the worthies of the First Church were predominately Federalists, as were the majority of voters in Hampshire county and Amherst. A pillar of the Second Church, the father-in-law of Thomas Gridley, was Gen. Ebenezer Mattoon who had served as a Federalist in Congress, so a simple party-political explanation is probably not adequate to account for all local opposition. Rather, what happened in Amherst probably echoed contemporary political developments in Boston, where the continuing commercial exigencies of the economic Panic of 1819 gave rise to a moderate political 'Middling Interest' under the leadership of Josiah Quincy, a regular Federalist, which promoted a more individualist political philosophy in place of traditional Federalist 'organicism and deference'.[90] Even though the local economy in Hampshire

---

[88] Tyler, *History*, 135–54; Carpenter, *History* i. 167–9. This negative result was published in the *Hampshire Gazette* on 5 February 1823 (possibly with some satisfaction) along with an extensive account of the legislative inquiry from the *[Columbian] Centinel* of Boston which underscored the new College's precarious finances as well as the threat to Williams's existence.

[89] Formisano, *Transformation*, 117–70.

[90] Andrew Cayton, 'The Fragmentation of 'A Great Family': The Panic of 1819 and the Rise of a Middling Interest in Boston, 1818–1822', reprinted from the *Journal of the Early Republic* in Ralph Gray & Michael Morrison (eds), *New Perspectives on the Early Republic* (Urbana, 1994), 189–213, here: 209–12. It should be noted, however, that Amherst like many New England 'organic communities' had a well-established heritage of political, social, and religious contention with very little deference, for which see Hugh Bell and Andrew Raymond, 'Early Amherst', in *Essays on Amherst's History* (Amherst, 1978), 3–30;

County was still largely subsistence, if the great merchants of the coast were being squeezed (as they were), they would surely squeeze their business partners inland, who would, in turn, squeeze their local customers and suppliers. The scarcity of credit may explain the relatively high interest rates, normally six per cent, obtained by the Charity Fund from its notes due and its loans.

It is also the case that Amherst was founded during a period of fierce religious polemics instigated by certain 'Orthodox', Calvinist Congregational clergy against their fellow members of the Standing Order, the Unitarian members of the established, Congregational church, who had taken final control of Harvard in 1805.[91] The Orthodox response was to found Andover Seminary in 1809. Noah Webster was closely identified with the periodical, the 'Panoplist', which polemicized aggressively against Unitarianism, and, although Amherst and Andover were not exactly comparable institutions, still the Unitarians, who were particularly influential in Boston and surroundings, were probably unenthusiastic about chartering a second 'orthodox' place of higher learning so quickly, particularly one which might detract from their newly won franchise at Cambridge.[92] And this doctrinal antipathy was, no doubt, accentuated by the explicitly evangelical nature of the new College which formulated and administered its own 'confession of faith' to the new staff in 1821.[93]

Both Congregational church factions, Orthodox and Unitarian, were largely Federalist, and this heated sectarian dispute was aired in the Massachusetts Constitutional Convention of 1820/1 where the Standing Order was only narrowly maintained by skillful parliamentary manoeuvering against Republican assault.[94] Yet, in the 1823 gubernatorial election,

---

and , in the same volume, the pleasantly dyspeptic but not always accurate ruminations by Theodore Baird, 'A Dry and Thirsty Land', 78–138.

[91] Peter Field, *The Crisis of the Standing Order; Clerical Intellectuals and Cultural Authority in Massachusetts, 1780–1833* (Amherst, 1998), 162–71, 210–21.

[92] See the discussion in Formisano, *Transformation*, 121–4.

[93] Webster, 'Origin', 252–3; three clergy including the Rev. Moore were charged by the trustees on 18 September prior to inauguration, 'to report a confession of faith to be subscribed by the president and professors of the collegiate institution previous to their entering on the duties of their respective offices', and at their inauguration that day, '[t]he confession of faith was then read and the gentlemen assented to it'. Graves's account only says that the President and professors 'renewed their answers of acceptance' without further elaboration of a clearly sensitive point (Appendix, 8). The College Charter finally granted by the Legislature in 1825 explicitly forbade that any instructor (but not the President), 'be required by the Trustees to profess any particular religious opinions', and that any student be excluded 'on account of religious opinions' (Section 6).

[94] For an account of the Convention which was dominated by eastern Federalists despite a large Republican delegation see Harlow Sheidley, *Sectional Nationalism: Massachusetts Conservative Leaders and the Transformation of America, 1815–1836* (Boston, 1998), esp. 33–47. Both of the Amherst delegates elected to the Constitutional Convention in October

when the moderate Republican candidate, William Eustis, and his running mate, Levi Lincoln, Jr indicated support for the College charter, they carried a narrow majority of local Amherst voters against the arch-Federalist, Henry Gray Otis, a Boston Unitarian, in their state-wide victory. This startling reversal of the well-established political order in Amherst was evidently secured by a scurrilous whispering campaign against Otis propagated by the College's promoters, who portrayed him as an atheist and a libertine and who thus willingly abandoned their traditional political allegiances by invoking sectarian animosities to advance their educational cause.[95]

However, this new political direction evidently facilitated the renewed bids for a charter in the legislative sessions from 1823 through 1825, and local opposition to the College seems to have abated.[96] Isaac Robbins was elected to both sessions 1823/4 and 1824/5 when the charter petition was twice renewed. He had not been a Charity Fund subscriber, nor was he amongst those who subscribed to relieve the guaranty bond (see below). Still, Dickinson did not oppose him either time, Gridley being Robbin's chief opponent the first time with no significant opponent the second. Robbins, evidently a Baptist although a parishioner at the First Church, was probably a compromise between the warring factions which served to expedite the charter. The sight of so many earnest young men earnestly hoping for degrees after their full course of study in 1825 may also have cooled some passions. The older and relatively weak traditional party

---

1820 were connected to the Second Church: Gen. Ebenezer Mattoon was long-established in Amherst and a founding member of the Second Church, but his fellow Delegate, Israel Scott, a blacksmith, was a native of Whatley. In 1797 at Hadley, he had married the daughter of Eleazar Cowles, Hannah, who joined the Second Church in 1821. In 1820 Scott was only recently returned to Amherst, where he became a business associate of Mattoon and others in the ill-fated Amherst cotton mill. His name appears twice in the 1820 tax assessment: as 'Israel Scott and Co' for a grist and a tanning mill and a cotton factory, all assessed at $295, the second highest in Amherst. As an individual he was assessed at only $50 in personal property and no real estate. It is difficult to perceive his qualifications other than a possible willingness to be subordinate to Mattoon, whose son-in-law, Thomas Gridley, was the newly-elected Representative to the legislature.

[95] Samuel E. Morison, *Harrison Gray Otis, 1765–1848; The Urbane Federalist* (Boston, 1969), 440–1, 544. There is some disagreement over whether the prime culprit in the operation of this rumour-mill was Samuel F. Dickinson, as Morison believed, or, as claimed by Claude Fuess, (*Amherst*, 64–65), his kinsman, the elusive Austin Dickinson from a prominent Second Church family, whose completely undocumented deeds were chronicled much later by Ornan Eastman, *The Rev. Austin Dickinson: his services to Amherst College, in its early history* (New York, 1872), the fantastic claims of which were credited whole by Tyler in a separate section of his *History*, 156–9.

[96] Ralph Waldo Emerson on his visit to Amherst in late August 1823 remarks on the apparently good relations between the students and the townspeople, which he thought unusual: William Gilman, Alfred Ferguson & Merrell Davis (eds), *The Journals and Miscellaneous Notebooks of Ralph Waldo Emerson*, ii: *1822–1826* (Cambridge MA, 1961), 182.

affiliations inherited from the Revolutionary period further evaporated in the so-called 'Era of Good Feelings' under President Monroe (1817–25), which was also marked by Amherst's unopposed and bi-partisan vote for Levi Lincoln, Jr as Governor in April 1825.[97]

7. Relief: 'A select meeting of our friends'

But with regard to funding, these rivalries evidently still had not died away entirely by 1824 when Amherst again sought its charter and prepared for intense financial scrutiny from the Massachusetts legislature. By then the guaranty bond must having been weighing very heavily indeed on its bearers. Calvin Merrill had died in 1820, Jarib White in 1821, and the Reverend Parsons unexpectedly in 1823. This left the remaining six signatories with a substantially increased liability of at least $2500 each which may have been so obviously ruinous as to raise serious reservations amongst the examiners from the legislature. A substitute for the guaranty bond undoubtedly was the prime objective of a new $30,000 fund, undertaken in 1822, of which only a small and undetermined amount was ever paid in.[98] That fund, for which, as we saw, some fragmentary records have survived, aimed to solicit from a 'Christian public' very small amounts between $1 and $10 payable annually for five years and thus well below the general level of the 1818–19 solicitation. It was ridiculed as the 'widow's mite' fund, and such small sums evidently did not repay the costs of soliciting and then collecting them. Moreover, it seems to have included relatively large numbers of women and young people whose small subscriptions were more easily liable to be challenged and discredited before the legislature's investigating committee. Nevertheless, it was still sufficiently credible in June 1823 to be introduced there as evidence of the College's

---

[97] Eustis had died in 1824. The wealthy John Eastman of the Second Church, a Charity Fund subscriber (see above), received a single vote against Levi, evidently as a lone protest, but by whom and on what grounds? In contrast, the election for representative to the legislature in the following month ended with the vote splintered amongst eight men, and it was decided not to send anyone that year, surely an indication of political *stasis* or gridlock (Carpenter, *History* ii. 213; 'Early Amherst Records', 391).

[98] Tyler, *History*, 147, 658–60; King, *Endowment*, 236. The legislative inquiry regarding the first petition for a charter in January 1823 determined that only $2,000 had ever been paid in and that, '[t]hese subscription papers have been carried through the country by young men employed for the purpose, on a salary of $10 per week beside their expenses' (as reported, no doubt with malice, in the *Hampshire Gazette* from the *Columbian Centinel*, 5 February 1823). It is this failed fund for which Ornan Eastman wished to credit the elusive Austin Dickinson: *The Rev. Austin Dickinson*, 2–3.

financial stability; but thereafter whatever funds it finally produced were evidently folded silently into the Charity Fund.[99]

Now in the summer of 1824 it was even more urgently necessary to eliminate the guaranty bond as quickly as possible both to relieve the local Guarantors and to shore up the College's shaky financial credibility with the legislature. Tyler tells us that the trustees, 'after having turned every stone', sent the new President of the College, Heman Humphrey, to Boston where, in President Humphrey's words, he 'laid the case before a select meeting of our friends, and in a few days obtained about half the sum that was needed'.[100] These Boston 'friends' were undoubtedly Orthodox persons of wealth and political influence like the Hon. Samuel Hubbard and S.V.S. Wilder, whose subscriptions of $500 were recorded along with 105 others from fifteen places in a list which this time also recorded the security offered, whether note, bond, or land, along with the amount (Table 2).[101] The total amount pledged slightly exceeded $16,000,

---

[99] Tyler, *History*, 136–7. It is probably to the accounts introduced to the legislature during the second petition for a charter and subsequently circulated by the trustees that Ralph Waldo Emerson refers on the occasion of his visit to the College in late August 1823 when he claims, '[t]he College is supposed to be worth net 85000 dollars' (*Journals* ii. 183).

[100] Tyler, *History*, 145. At the outset of the building of South College, on 27 June 1820, Noah Webster had written to Jeremiah Evarts, editor of the orthodox *Panoplist* to which Webster was a contributor, asking him, 'whether in this exigency we can find a few friends in Boston' who would make financial contributions to the project …' (*Letters of Noah Webster*, 401–2). In the letter Webster mentions the Rev. Sereno Dwight of Park Street Church and 'Mr Hubban', evidently, the Hon. Samuel Hubbard, who did contribute in 1824.

[101] This subscription is recorded in the same register as the Charity Fund (ACA, EHC, 2/5a, 51–58), and is printed by Tyler (*History*, 655–6), possibly also from a transcript by Boltwood. Like the 1818–19 list it is arranged in alphabetical groups by subscriber's name, and the hand, probably Graves's, which produced this redaction is the same as that of the original subscription in the same volume. It seems likewise to have been assembled from a large number of separate documents. Care had been taken this time to obtain written securities in notes and bonds or deeds to land at the time of subscription, and these were probably the exemplars used. Next to four small subscriptions on page 53 is the marginal note: 'Longmeadow, four notes on one sheet, viz.', which explains why these subscriptions from Ely, Bliss, Burt, and Dickinson are grouped with the 'M's. This note probably turned up during transcription after 'B', 'D' and 'E' were finished. On page 55 of the manuscript, another note in the register indicates that John Emerson Strong of Amherst's bond for $100 (69+31; Tyler $200) was a substitute for William Boltwood, that is, for Boltwood's former subscription in 1818–19 which was evidently still outstanding. A further note there records, 'Committees order in favor of William Boltwood'. This is probably the legislative committee rather than the Fund's, and seems to indicate that this substitution was allowed, as was John Leland Jr's for Elijah Upton of Boston, for which Tyler's transcript adds however that, 'For this note – cash advanced by S. V. S. Wilder at the examination before the Legislative Committee' (*History*, 656; cf. 147–8). Thus, it appears that the register's list must have been prepared very soon after the conclusion of the committee's work on 19 October.

Table 2: Contributors to the 1824 Fund for Guaranty Bond Relief Summary

Town	Number	Amount
AMHERST*	23	$8,085
BEVERLY	3	100
BOSTON	51	5663
BRIDGEWATER, NORTH	1	25
DORCHESTER	1	200
HADLEY*	2	250
HARTFORD, CN	1	500
LONGMEADOW*	5	82
MILLBURY*	3	200
PELHAM*	1	100
SALEM	5	175
SOUTHAMPTON	1	50
SPRINGFIELD*	5	450
SPRINGFIELD, WEST*	1	100
WORCESTER	3	150
15 TOWNS	106	$16,130

* = Participants in 1818/19 Charity Fund Subscripton

which was more than sufficient to offset the guaranty bond, and collection appears to have been relatively efficient.[102]

The collection in 1824 differed from that in 1818/19 not only in being more carefully controlled but also in having been more narrowly targeted and more quickly concluded. President Humphrey was correct in emphasizing the importance of Boston for this effort, a place totally unrepresented in 1818/19. No doubt a vital part of the strategy was to enlist political support in the state capital for charter approval as well as to mobilize Boston financial capital. One of the Boston contributors, S.V.S. Wilder, a wealthy merchant and prominent evangelical, was subsequently an original Amherst Trustee, and, in the event, $5663 was subscribed there by 51 men, about one-third of the total amount obtained. But pride of place still went to Amherst where only 23 subscribers accounted for $8085, or half the total of $16,130. Of these two, John Leland, Jr ($1000) and Elijah Boltwood ($500), provided substantial amounts in lieu of their

---

[102] The register concludes with a total amount of $16,338 which differs slightly from Tyler's of $16,230. The arithmetically correct amount after correcting for Strong's bond is $16,130. Collection is recorded by the sheets facing the subscriptions, which are recorded on the verso (left hand side, odd page) with matching annual account columns on the recto from 1825 to 1828, a procedure used for the original Charity Fund. Most of the principal amounts were paid already in 1825 and were recorded in later entries by the same hand, and no entries were made there after 1827.

former guaranty bond liability, and Jay White subscribed another $500, possibly in recognition of his deceased father, Jarib White's, former obligation. John Eastman of the Second Church contributed another $1000 to this solicitation, thus matching Leland as the principal local benefactor of the College. Enos Baker also matched his earlier subscription of $100, and Strong, a new contributor, substituted for Boltwood's $100.

Thus, 20 of the 23 Amherst subscribers in 1824 were entirely new financial supporters including the new President ($500) of the new College which was now a tangible reality rather than an uncertain hope.[103] Still, aside from Eastman, financial support for the College amongst the now dominant group in town government continued to be sparse. Nathan Dickinson, also an original member of the Second Church but much less affluent, contributed only $35, the smallest local amount recorded. Gen Ebenezer Mattoon and Dr Thomas Gridley were once again absent from the contributors, as were Nathan Franklin and Aaron Merrick; nor did Jonathan and Joseph Cowls contribute again as they had in 1818/19. This continued abstinence by such a significant and prosperous segment of the Amherst community underscores President Humphrey's need to seek relief far afield in Boston, previously untapped and the site of Rufus Graves's initial failure.

The balance of contributions came in lesser amounts from thirteen towns, seven of which were previously unrepresented. Aside from a single contributor from Pelham none of the small hill towns of Hampshire and Franklin counties contributed, and the names of Graves and (the now-departed) Webster are once again absent from the subscribers.[104] Of the non-subscribing communities in 1818–19 whose abstention might be attributed to rivalry and pique, only Southampton, with one contributor for a paltry $50, appears in 1824. Did Northampton and its allies west of the Great River still hope that the Amherst venture might yet fade away under the glare of legislative inquisition? The political dissension within Amherst itself may have encouraged such hopes of failure, but the brilliantly successful prosecution of this special solicitation by President Humphrey with its impressive muster of strength in the state capital must have put a final end to them. This solicitation in 1824 also firmly and

---

[103] By his will of 1823 Humphrey's predecessor as President, Zephaniah Swift Moore, left the use of $4000 to his widow for her support, the residue of which was designated for the College after her death (King, *Endowment*, 194–5; see also Emerson, *Journals* ii. 182).

[104] Pelham residents had, however, contributed directly to the construction of South College (see above), and on 28 August 1823 Ralph Waldo Emerson noted along with President Moore's benefaction (see previous note), 'a poor one-legged man [Adam Johnson, a carpenter, who] died last week in Pelham, who was not known to have any property, & left them 4000 dollars to be appropriated to the building of a Chapel' (*Journals* ii. 182–3).

finally established the Charity Fund's viability and, thus appropriately marks the end of its earliest and properly heroic era.

8. Conclusion: 'An infant Hercules'

The College Charter of February 1825 brought a certain loss of local autonomy and a degree of political control by the Massachusetts government. This can be seen in the composition of the seventeen original Trustees of the College, all of whom were named by the legislature as were to be five of their successors. It is notable that two prominent Baptist clergymen and educators were included in the charter, as were two Massachusetts Democrat-Republicans, the plutocrat and former Lieutenant Governor, William Gray, and the Brown alumnus and Lieutenant Governor, Marcus Morton, who signed the charter as Acting Governor but received little political thanks for it in Amherst. Still, there was substantial continuity with nine trustees of the Academy now trustees of the new college. But not a single Amherst resident other than President Humphrey sat amongst the new trustees, and there were only four subscribers to the Charity Fund amongst their number—a bitter price for a sweet victory, and particularly so for the legislature's inclusion of the Rev Dr Joseph Lyman of Hatfield who had worked actively to secure Williams for Northampton. Evidently, some spoils were distributed and some old scores were settled even in this bipartisan 'Era of Good Feelings'. Tyler comments with unusual candour: 'It will not be difficult for the reader to divine the motive for the exclusion of the old trustees when he observes that the persons excluded were among the active agents in the founding of the College, and as such, particularly obnoxious to its enemies'.[105]

What can we usefully conclude about this complex story of Amherst's Charity Fund recovered from the historical record without ourselves lapsing into myth-making? There can be no doubting Tyler's judgment when, from his own perspective in the later nineteenth century, he underscored their achievement. But what drove a relatively small group of men to undertake such a task? All of them had, no doubt, varying motivations beyond improving the standing of their small town: early American 'boosterism'. That probably played a role as did the competitive desire to outdo the nearby county seat, Northampton. And their desire to promote learning and make it more broadly available to those without means— again only to men—was surely genuine as exemplified in the lives of Noah Webster and Samuel F. Dickinson.

[105] Tyler, *History*, 153.

They shared a general vision of a better society with many others, since this was an age characterized by fervent moral and social improvement, much of it resulting from the Second Great Awakening, a broad and non-denominational evangelical Christian revival which animated all of early nineteenth-century America with such plans.[106] But their aim was higher than average. Noah Webster, Rufus Graves, Pastor David Parsons, Samuel F. Dickinson, their companions, and their co-workers knew exactly what they wanted and how to do it. They had a very grand vision and a plan to realize it. The one thing that seems to have unified them all was a desire to improve the entire world. As they expressed it quite clearly in the preamble to the Charity Fund's Constitution, this meant spreading an orthodox Calvinist version of the Christian Gospel—not only within the United States, as was true, for example, of the Hampshire and American Education Societies—but throughout the entire world: 'terras irradient': 'let them [Amherst's graduates] be a light to the world' was their, and still is the College's, motto.

Moreover, they were distinguished by their practical strategy to realize their vision: through a properly chosen, educated, and motivated clergy. Select the right young men without regard to their means but only for their piety and their 'talents', educate them rigorously in the established tradition of Classical learning which had been formulated in Antiquity and proven its worth for more than two millennia, and infuse them through constant worship, Bible study, introspection, and prayer with a strong revivalist, evangelical spirit.[107] It was an energizing formula as even the young Ralph Waldo Emerson noted on his visit to the 'infant Hercules' at the Commencement in August 1823 where, '[n]ever was so much striving, outstretching, & advancing in a literary cause as is exhibited here'.[108] Providing for their education thus became not just a worthy act of charity but a truly noble and great enterprise, and one in which even ordinary persons from the remote hill towns of western Massachusetts could participate.

These founders of the Charity Fund and of Amherst College were, however, no conventional saints. The great historian of Williams, Arthur Latham Perry, notes ruefully, but perhaps enviously, that the Trustees of Amherst

---

[106] Howe, *What Hath God Wrought*, ch. 8, esp. 288–9.

[107] Of the Founders, only Noah Webster had, so far as I know, an articulated educational policy to form the 'Quiet Christian': see Richard Rollins, whose *The Long Journey of Noah Webster* (Philadelphia, 1980) perhaps over-estimates the 'social control' aspect (119–21). Did Webster really desire or expect that, 'students who passed through his school would become obedient and passive' (120)? Those are hardly the qualities of effective parish clergy and missionaries and are quite at odds with Emerson's impression of Amherst students.

[108] Emerson, *Journals* ii. 182.

Academy 'had sufficient self-respect and *esprit de corps* to dictate terms both to their neighbors in Northampton and to their possible coadjutors in Williamstown'.[109] This is not surprising. Noah Webster, a tireless self-promoter and experienced polemicist, was a person with a modest national reputation. Together with the Hon. Joseph Lyman of Northampton, a prominent advocate of Williams's removal there, he had instigated the ill-fated 'Hartford Convention' of 1814/15.[110] It is unlikely that he felt any need for deference to the 'River Gods' of Northampton.

The anonymous 'Gleaner' who wrote in protest against their actions for the *Gazette* on 27 October 1818 likewise implies a certain ruthlessness, citing against them, 'the doctrine of the old school [that] the end never sanctifies the means'. Webster, Graves, and others would, no doubt, have agreed with him. Yet they were quite willing to sacrifice the harmony of their provincial society and to introduce a strong element of political divisiveness to achieve their goal. They conducted their struggle vigorously on three levels: against local opposition and indifference in Amherst, against Hampshire county's Federalist political society under the leadership of Northampton, and even against their fellow orthodox colleagues in the Hampshire clergy as well as powerful elements within the Standing Order of Massachusetts who objected to their theological views. There was no place amongst the Charity Fund's determined advocates for outmoded notions of 'organicism and deference'.

Nor were they above cutting some corners to realize their noble goal. Rufus Graves seems to have taken a leading role here as he did in all aspects of early fund-raising. He apparently back-dated a key document, and we have seen that the value of subscriptions to the Charity Fund could be altered after the fact to enable certain outcomes. We may suspect that some overvaluations of subscriptions like Rufus Cowls's land in Maine were carried on the books and some obviously specious sums like Professor

---

[109] Qualities which Perry attributes (perhaps somewhat doubtfully?) to Scots-Irish influences not shared by their competitors (*Williamstown*, 402–3).

[110] Webster published the relevant documents in his *Collection* of 1843, ch. 18, 311–15, and had probably been instrumental in formulating the 'Amherst Resolutions' of 3 January calling for such an assembly (*Hampshire Gazette*, 19 January 1814). See James Banner, *To the Hartford Convention* (New York, 1970), 314–17, and for additional materials: Emily Skeel (ed.), *Notes on the Life of Noah Webster Compiled by Emily Ellsworth Fowler Ford* (2 vols, New York 1912; rprn New York 1971), ii. 123–8, 497–500. The Convention, called in response to problems caused by the War of 1812, gave rise to exaggerated charges that New England was promoting secession against the federal government, which, ironically, became a severe political liability for its Federalist sponsors. In fact, the first challenge against the First Church establishment occurred in the town's next election for representative to the legislature in May 1815 when Aaron Merrick of the Second Church bested Webster in the first two rounds of voting before being turned back finally in the third (Carpenter, *History* ii. 206; 'Amherst Town Records', 304).

Estabrook's were tolerated well beyond their season. This sort of practice continues in publicly audited accounts today; why not then? The trustees clearly misstated their financial ability to provide for a relocated Williams at Amherst. The first Treasurer of the College, John Leland, Jr, seems to have certified misleading statements about financial assets, particularly about the success of the $30,000 fund, in support of the application to the legislature for a charter in 1823, and solicitors for the Fund may, indeed, have misled some subscribers about the likelihood of Williams's removal to Amherst, as was later charged.[111] This was allegedly the reason why the $1000 subscription from the Rev. Samuel Austin, President of the University of Vermont (1815–21) and former minister of the orthodox First Congregational church in Worcester, was never paid.[112]

The *Gazette's* serious charge that they were not entirely forthcoming about the purpose of their 1818 convention is supported by the wording of their own invitation to it. And their opponents' charge that the proceedings there were rigged to favour Amherst rings, unfortunately, true. Although they were all dedicated Federalists, they were evidently not averse to employing dubious practices to undermine the election of the Federalist candidate for Governor in 1823 so as to secure the office for a Republican more amenable to the Charter. Apparently, the founders of Amherst College were quite willing to use highly divisive practices, splitting old Hampshire County and pitting 'us' against 'them' to pursue their noble goal. Perhaps their opponents in Northampton were equally ruthless? They were, however, also apparently less committed and certainly less adaptable. When the legislature put an end to their undertaking, they apparently abandoned their efforts. But at Amherst this marked the beginning of a new, risky, and ambitious effort. Despite an uncertain outcome and continued opposition or indifference from a large segment of the local population, the founders persisted with determination to achieve their goal. The founders of Amherst College clearly were able to combine their genuine idealism with clarity of strategy, opportunistic pragmatism, and, when required, very hard-nosed practice, indeed bordering on and perhaps even touching the unethical. This is not Tyler's story, although he probably knew much of it, but its tale of devious scheming and bitter strife may be one better suited to our age than his of Strong Character and harmonious community.

Research Associate
University of Pittsburgh

---

[111] Tyler, *History*, 136–40.
[112] Austin's subscription amounted to a full year's salary in Vermont which by 1820, was $3120 in arrears (UVM website), a chronic problem for clergy salaries; perhaps his generous subscription had been made with an eye to securing a softer landing further south?

APPENDIX: Amherst College Archives,
Early History Collection, Series 2, Box 5a, pp. 2–8[113]

The Charitable Institution founded in Amherst for the academic and collegiate education of indigent young men of piety and talents owes its origin to the exertions of certain members of the board of Trustees of Amherst Academy. Those members, in the firm belief that an Institution established on the broad basis of charity for the education of indigent youth of the greatest promise, would meet the approbation and united support of this enlightened Christian community, and would grow to a magnitude beyond an example. – Under these impressions they submitted the proposition to a number of Judicious and pious individuals, who generally approved the object, but as generally doubted its practicability. – To remove which an appeal was made to the Opulent, and many month time and considerable sums of money expended in traveling the Country in quest of an individual or individuals who would found this charity establishment by giving such large sum or sums, as would put the question of practicability forever at rest. – But, no such individual was found.

The first proposition, which was the subject of repeated deliberation of the board, was limited to the establishment of a professorship in the Academy for the gratuitous education of pious young men who might be unable to defray the expense...own education...eighteenth...to attempt...of such a p...of Ruf...[p.3] was a project too limited to engage the patronage of the public. The Committee finding the Christian public well disposed to favour a plan of gratuitous education for pious young men, but on a more extended scale, and having taken the advice of many Clergymen and Laymen of distinction residing in various parts of the Commonwealth, determined to change the plan, and to frame a Constitution for a fund to be the basis of a Charitable Institution, distinct from the Academy.

Such a Constitution was formed and presented to Gentlemen, approved of the plan, and subscribed liberally to the fund which encouraged the Committee that it would meet the generous approbation of the Christian Public. At a meeting of the board of Trustees on the eig[h]teenth day of August 1818 the Committee reported that Constitution to the board with the subscription of about six thousand dollars to the fund, for their consideration and acceptance. On which it was unanimously voted "that we approve of the doings of said Committee and accept their report, and authorize them to take such measures and communicate with such Persons and corporations, they may judge expedient and conducive to the great objects connected with their appointment, and that the Rev. Nathan Perkins and the Rev. Edwards [Whipp]le...be add...mittee."...provides that...be incer-...thought...id County...[p.4] be advantageous to both. The establishment of the Charitable Institution is not made dependent on the removal of the

---

[113] The text follows the orthography and divisions of the manuscript. Manuscript pagination, editorial corrections and notes are indicated by square brackets [ ] and missing text by three dots....

College to Amherst. Both the letter and spirit of the Constitution evince it, and it has always been expected that the institution was to be established whether the College should be removed or not. – In order however to ascertain the probability of such a removal, the board of Trustees of Amherst Academy authorized the Committee by their said vote of August 18th above recited to communicate with the Trustees of Williams College on the subject and two of the Gentlemen waited on them at their meeting in the first week of September next following and presented them with a copy of the Constitution and of the vote above mentioned, together with a letter inviting the union proposed. The board of Trustees of Williams College returned the papers to the Committee without any answer to the application. This silence was considered as a refusal to accede to the proposition; and on the report of the committee to the board of Trustees at Amherst; the said board on the tenth day of September following "Resolved, that it is expedient to invite a convention of Clergy and Laity to approve and patronize the charitable Institution contemplated by the board." In pursuance of this resolve, a circular letter was addressed to the settled congregational and presbyterian clergy in the Counties of Hampshire, Franklin and Hampden and in the western section of the County of Worcester, inviting them, each with a lay delegate, to meet in convention at Amherst on the 29th day of September inst[anter] to deliberate on the subject. A delegate was also invited from each vacant Parish.

On the day appointed there appeared to be represented by the settled ministers, or by lay delegates or by both as follows – in Hampshire County 14 Towns and 16 parishes. In Franklin 12 Towns and 14 parishes. In Hampden 4 Towns and 5 parishes. The whole number of Clergymen present were 37, of delegates 32 total 69. To this respectable con- [p.5] vention the Constitution of the proposed charitable Institution was read and by them committed to a Committee of twelve, to consider and report. In the report, the Committee say, that "The plan of a literary institution founded on the general principles of charity and benevolence to give a classical or collegiate education to indigent pious young men of talents, while it proposes the ordinary advantages to others, is peculiarly suited to the exigencies of the day, and calculated to answer extensively benevolent purposes in relation both to the Church and the world. This plan proposes a literary institution of a pecular [sic] character in no wise hostile to any other in our Country." The Committee further express their approbation of the "constitution, as a legal instrument, executed with skill and judgment, guarding, in the most satisfactory and effectual manner the faithful and appropriate applications of the property consecrated by the donors." On the subject of the location of the institution, the Committee were not united; but they finally concurred in "cordially approving the object of a religious and classical institution on a charitable foundation" – but expressed an opinion that it would best flourish, if it could have " the advantage of that union, which would result from its location by a disinterested Committee appointed by the convention." They also recommended "that suitable measures be adopted by this convention for the establishment of a College in connexion with the charitable Institution."

The report was made to the convention and after debated the proposition for submitting the location of the Institution to a Committee was rejected by a great majority – and the articles of the report being amended were adopted in the following words.

1st. "In this general view of the subject submitted to their consideration, the committee cordially approve the object of a religeous [sic] and classical institution on a charitable foundation in the Town of Amherst and recommend to the convention to give it their united and individual patronage.

2d. "They also recommend that suitable measures be adopted by the Trustees of Amherst Academy for [p.6] the establishment of a College in connexion with the charitable Institution, possessing all the advantages of other Colleges in the commonwealth.

3d. "That it is expected by this convention, that in order to satisfy the public, the people of the Town of Amherst show themselves worthy of such an important privilege by seasonable and liberal aid towards erecting college buildings.

4th. "They also recommend that such preparations and arrangements be made, as will accommodate students at the Institution as soon as possible."–

Soon after these proceedings of the convention were published, the Trustees of Williams College were summoned to meet at Williams Town on the second Tuesday of November then ensuing – and the Trustees of Amherst Academy appointed a Committee consisting of the Rev. John Fiske, Noah Webster and Nathaniel Smith Esquires to repair to Williams Town on that day, and communicate to the board of Trustees of Williams College the result of the convention, with suitable explanations and statements. – This was according done.

At this meeting, the board of Trustees of Williams College resolved that it was expedient to remove the College, on certain conditions – and appointed a Committee of disinterested men to determine the place to which it should be removed. This Commit[t]ee met in May 1819 and determined that Northampton would be the most suitable place.

In consequence of these proceedings of the Corporation of Williams College, the Trustees of Amherst Academy suspended further measures in relation to the charitable Institution; until the event of the application of the Corporation of Williams College to the legislature for an act authorizing a removal of the College should be known. They made no opposition to the application, and took no measures to defeat it. But the petition having faild [sic] of success, the board of Trustees of Amherst Academy judged that the way was open for the prosecution of their original design, and determined to put in operation the fund intrusted [sic] to their care, which according to the subscription list amounted to more than fifty thousand dollars, and was subscribed in the term of less than one year next preceeding [sic] the location of Williams College at Northampton by the afore said Committee.

[p. 7] At a meeting of the board of Trustees of the said Academy on the tenth day of May 1820 a Committee was appointed to solicit donations, contributions and subscriptions for defraying the expense of a College building and to erect the same. It was soon found, however, to be impracticable to obtain the means of defraying the expence of such a building, previously to the commencing of the work.

Encouraged by the success which attended the raising of the fund, and relying on the benevolence of this Christian community under the direction of divine providence, an effort was made to erect a brick edifice for the accommodation of the students, of one hundred feet in length, forty in breadth, and four stories high, to contain thirty two spacious rooms, all partitioned with brick walls from the foundations to the top, with suitable space-ways for entrance, staircases etc, without knowing at the commencement of the work whence a single dollar was to be obtained for defraying the expence.

Some of the stones for the foundation of the Edifice having been collected by voluntary exertion, the ceremony of laying the corner stone was performed with religious solemnities on the ninth day of August then next 1820; the residue of the stones for the building being then in the mountains, the clay for the brick and the stones for the lime, in the earth, and the timber in the forest; but by the united exertions of the benevolent, the walls of the Edifice were completed and the roof raised on the seventh day of November following, which was the ninetieth day from the laying of the corner stone. After the completing of the roof and chimneys, together with a good well of water, the bills unpaid and unprovided for, amounted to something short of thirteen hundred dollars. By a series of like benevolent acts and efforts, the College Edifice was completed and about half the Rooms handsomely furnished, and on the eighteenth day of September 1821 solemly [sic] dedicated.

The exercises were introduced by Noah Webster Esq President of the board of Trustees, giving a concise History of the Institution, and stating the business of the day. A dedicatory prayer was offered by the Rev. Joshua Crosby of Enfield, and an appropriate Sermon from these words, "Upon this Rock will I build my Church, and the gates of Hell shall not prevail against it," delivered by the Rev. Aaron W. Lealand D.D. [p.8] of Charleston S Carolina.

The pleasing solemnities of the occasion were much heigtened [sic] by the inauguration of the Officers of the Institution elect, then present, viz. The Rev. Zeph. Swift Moore D.D. President and Joseph Estabrook AM, Professor of latin and greek languages, who, after having renewed their answers of acceptance, were addressed by the President of the board of Trustees on the subject of their appointment, and the responsibility of their station; and then invested with the charge and government of the Institution, and solemnly inducted to office. After which the President of the Institution delivered an appropriate address in English, and the professor of latin and greek Languages in latin; and the Rev. Thomas Snell of North-Brookfield offered the concluding prayer.

The Rev. Gamaliel S. Olds Professor elect of Mathematics and natural Philosophy, who had accepted his appointment, on account of special exegencies [sic] could not be present. – The Rev. Jonas King Professor elect of Oriental Languages and literature being on his voige [sic] to Europe for the purpose of completing his education was also not present.

The exercises of the day were solemn and interesting, the music chaste and elegant; at the close of which a contribution was taken for the benefit of the Institution; and on the return of the procession from the Church, the ceremony of laying the corner Stone of the Presidents House was performed with religious solemnity; from which stone the Throne of Grace was addressed in an appropriate prayer by the Rev. John Fiske of New Braintree.

The day following viz. September 19th the first term of study commenced. Forty seven young Gentlemen were examined and admitted as members of the Institution, in the respective classes, from the Freshman to the Senior, and entered upon the regular course of collegiate studies.

This study began as a private amusement occasioned by my 50th reunion at Amherst in 2015 and grew from there. Along the way I have accumulated several agreeable debts. The local history librarians at the Forbes Library, Northampton, the Jones Library, Amherst, and the Library of Historic Deerfield and the Pocumtuck Valley Memorial Association were all very helpful as was the Office of the Town Clerk, Amherst. Use of the well-ordered Archives in the Frost Library at Amherst College was a pleasure which was enhanced by the assistance of Peter Nelson, the former Archivist, and, particularly of Margaret Dakin who introduced me to the manuscript register of the Charity Fund (or vice-versa). The late Hugh Hawkins, Professor emeritus of History at Amherst and a certified expert on the history of higher education in America, provided his usual friendly criticism and encouragement. I only wish that I could have shared this published study with him and my old Munich friend, the late Professor Rainer Müller, who first induced me to consider the history of higher-education funding.

From *Studium Generale* to Modern Research University: Eight Hundred Years of Oxford History

Nicholas Tyacke

Laurence W.B. Brockliss, *The University of Oxford. A History.* (Oxford: Oxford University Press, 2016), xl + 871 pp. ISBN: 9780199243563

I

On the completion, in 2000, of the eight-volume *History of the University of Oxford* (hereafter *OU History*), totalling 6,910 pages and involving 138 contributors, it was decided to commission a one-volume distillation by a single author. The choice of Laurence Brockliss, a specialist in the history of early modern French education, turned out in many ways to be a good one, not least because of the welcome comparative perspective which he has been able to bring to the task. Brockliss had already contributed an instructive chapter to volume vi of the *OU History*, discussing inter alia French and German university developments in the period 1789–1850, and had embarked on editing a volume about the history of his own Oxford college, Magdalen, which was published in 2008.[1] He has now produced a finely crafted synthesis which takes the story of Oxford University up to 2015 – whereas the epilogue to volume viii of the *OU History* ended in 1990. The present book is divided into four parts: the 'Catholic University' (*c.*1100–1534), the 'Anglican University' (1534–1845), the 'Imperial University' (1845–1945), and the 'World University' (1945–2015). There are eight maps, eleven tables, and a helpful chronology. The volume is also graced with numerous illustrations, which are provided with commendably full captions. Apropos the marked

---

[1] Laurence W.B. Brockliss, 'The European University in the Age of Revolution, 1789–1850', in Michael G. Brock and Mark C. Curthoys (eds), *The History of the University of Oxford* (hereafter abbreviated as *OU History*), vi: *Nineteenth-Century Oxford, Part 1* (Oxford, 1997), 77–133; idem (ed.), *Magdalen College Oxford. A History* (Oxford, 2008).

fluctuations in the number of students over time, however, one cause for regret is the decision not to reproduce the graph of 'Estimated Annual Freshman Admissions (Decennial Averages) 1500–1909', constructed by Lawrence Stone back in the 1970s.[2] As it stands, Table 1 ('Student Numbers, *c.*1300–2015') is quite difficult to interpret with reference to the early modern period (760).

Given that this book is to a considerable extent a summation of the eight volumes of the *OU History*, it would perhaps be unreasonable to expect Brockliss fundamentally to challenge still prevalent orthodoxies. Certainly in the event his account broadly endorses the view that the four centuries or so between the high middle ages and the Victorian era of reform were a time of decline for Oxford, reaching a nadir under the Hanoverians. Yet this interpretation has been seriously questioned, especially by some of the contributors to volume iv of the *OU History*.[3] Moreover even as regards the eighteenth century not all the authors recruited to volume v of the *OU History* ended up singing from the same song sheet as the editors, Lucy Sutherland and Leslie Mitchell. Here a notable exception was the decidedly upbeat chapter on 'The Physical Sciences', written by Gerard Turner.[4] Since, however, so much of the traditional historiography concerning Oxford University hinges on certain assumptions about the Hanoverian period it is with this that any reappraisal of the big picture has to begin.

Despite distancing themselves from the indictment by Edward Gibbon of Oxford, or at least of Magdalen College, as an institution sunk in sloth, Sutherland and Mitchell did not provide much in the way of a positive alternative.[5] On the contrary readers of volume v of the *OU History* are treated to a double dose of satire from William Hogarth. Thus the frontispiece features 'scholars at a lecture', which Robert Greaves, in his own contribution, describes as a 'savage cartoon of 1737 which pilloried the coarse, bucolic and cunningly stupid faces at the lecture of Henry Fisher, the university registrar'. Also reproduced is Hogarth's own frontispiece to

---

[2] Lawrence Stone (ed.), *The University in Society*, 2 vols. (Oxford, 1975), 1: 6, 91. Stone was strongly of the view that the histories of Oxford and Cambridge should be written in tandem. Such an ambition has since become more feasible with the publication of the four-volume *A History of the University of Cambridge* (Cambridge, 1988–2004), by Christopher Brooke, Damian Leader, Victor Morgan, and Peter Searby. But, with only four authors and at little more than a third of the length, this Cambridge counterpart of the *OU History* is not in the same league.

[3] Mordechai Feingold, 'The Mathematical Sciences and New Philosophies', in Nicholas Tyacke (ed.), *The History of the University of Oxford*, iv: *Seventeenth-Century Oxford*, (Oxford, 1997), 359–448. See also the introduction by the editor.

[4] Gerard L' E. Turner, 'The Physical Sciences', in Lucy S. Sutherland and Leslie G. Mitchell (eds.), *The History of the University of Oxford*, v: *The Eighteenth Century* (Oxford, 1986), 659–81.

[5] *OU History*, v. 476–9, and dust-jacket description of the book.

The Humours of Oxford (1730), a comedy by James Miller, depicting Oxford dons decidedly the worse for wear from drinking port.[6] In addition Mitchell, in his introductory chapter, paraphrases approvingly the claim by another contributor, Gareth Bennett, that 'as long as the precepts of Aristotle and the ancients were unchallenged, and as long as Anglicanism retained its political monopoly, academics were simply required to receive a body of information from their forefathers and to hand it on intact to the next generation'.[7] More generally volume v is replete with the misleading views of Paul Hazard about the 'crisis of the European mind', and of Richard Jones as regards 'ancients and moderns'. For example Stuart Piggott, in his chapter on 'Antiquarian Studies', cites Jones in support of the remarkable accusation that during the eighteenth century not just Oxford University but the English intelligentsia more widely turned their backs on the early-modern scientific revolution.[8]

Unfortunately quite a lot of the foregoing has rubbed off on Brockliss, who writes that 'from the turn of the eighteenth century evidence abounds about the life of the Oxford don, and the testimony is largely negative'. He goes on to attempt a calculation of the excessive quantities of alcohol consumed, albeit exonerating from 'lechery' most of the imbibers concerned and conceding that 'there were limits . . . to the depths to which eighteenth-century dons would sink'. None the less 'indolence', by his account, was the Oxford order of the day (289–92).[9] At the very least, however, such a verdict does serious injustice to the calibre of the professoriate, some of whom were outstanding as well as productive intellects, and, of course,

---

[6] Ibid, 403, 611, Plate XIV, and frontispiece.

[7] Ibid, 3, 359–60, 399–400.

[8] Ibid, 359, 758–9, 771; Paul Hazard, *The European Mind, 1680–1715*, trans. James L. May (London, 1953), *passim*; Richard F. Jones, *The Seventeenth Century. Studies in the History of English Thought and Literatures from Bacon to Pope* (Stanford, 1951), 10–40. The jaundiced view expressed by Piggott stems in part from his study of the antiquary William Stukeley and the latter's alleged succumbing to 'druidical' fantasies as regards Stonehenge and the ancient past more generally: Stuart Piggott, *William Stukeley. An Eighteenth-Century Antiquary* (London, 1950, 2nd edn. London, 1985), 9–12, 79–109, 152–8. For a rebuttal of Piggott's views see David B. Haycock, *William Stukeley. Science, Religion and Archaeology in Eighteenth-Century England* (Woodbridge, 2002), xii–xiii, 6–9, and *passim*.

[9] By way of a palinode, Brockliss, in the preface to his *The University of Oxford. A History* (xii), floats the suggestion that a 'collateral ancestor', one John Brockliss of Sulgrave in Northamptonshire, 'purchased a steam engine', in 1788, 'to run his mill', under the influence of an Oxford-educated duo of squire and parson. Alas, however, for this intriguing hypothesis: the then lord of the manor, John Hodges, does not appear to have studied at either Oxford or Cambridge. The vicar, Richard Wykeham, was indeed an Oxford graduate (BA 1758), but there is no record of his having attended the lectures of James Bradley: Peter Whalley, *The History and Antiquities of Northamptonshire*, 2 vols. (Oxford, 1791), 1: 128–9; Henry I. Longden, *Northamptonshire and Rutland Clergy from 1500–1900*, 16 vols. (Northampton, 1938–1952), 15: 223; Robert W. T. Gunther, *Early Science in Oxford*, 15 vols. (Oxford, 1920–1967), 11: 359–98.

'dons' too. Moreover if only a small minority of Oxford academics, at this period, actually contributed to the *Philosophical Transactions* of the Royal Society, a much larger group of their colleagues read there what they and others had to say, hence furnishing a potential conduit of new knowledge. Some adventurous undergraduates such as John James at Queen's College in the early 1780s even read the *Philosophical Transactions* for themselves.[10] Also the traditional picture of Tory and High Church Oxford, chronicled at length in volume v of the *OU History,* goes largely unquestioned by Brockliss. Yet from the 1730s a statue of Queen Caroline, consort of George II, gazed down onto the High Street from the entrance to Queen's College, as testimony to Whig patronage.[11] At the same time, it must give serious pause for thought that James Bradley, the highly distinguished Savilian professor of astronomy at Oxford from 1721 to 1762, began his career as a chaplain of Bishop Benjamin Hoadly, one of the most notoriously Whig and latitudinarian members of the Hanoverian episcopate. Hoadly had in addition ordained Bradley as priest and presented him to his first living.[12] We should furthermore recall the ultimately unsuccessful attempt to blackball, on grounds of religious heterodoxy, the even more distinguished Edmond Halley, Savilian professor of geometry from 1703 to 1742.[13] On the other hand Edward Bentham, in his inaugural lecture of 1764 as Regius professor of divinity, referred to Isaac Newton as someone in whom theology rejoices, a reminder that natural theology had a significant following at Oxford as well as Cambridge.[14] This in turn raises the neglected but very important topic of Oxford Newtonianism.

Halley, who had begun his astronomical career, voyaging to St Helena, while still an Oxford undergraduate at Queen's College in the mid 1670s, played a crucial role, both editorial and financial, in the publication of the *Principia Mathematica* of Newton in 1687.[15] Provost Timothy Halton of Queen's soon afterwards presented a copy of the book to the taberdars' (senior scholars') library at the college, while his brother, Immanuel Halton, was an early patron of the future Astronomer Royal John Flamsteed.[16]

[10]   Matthew Main, 'What Fellows read, 1677–1712', *Floreat Domus* [Balliol College], 22 (2016), 34; *Letters of Richard Radcliffe and John James of Queen's College, Oxford, 1750–83,* ed. Margaret Evans (Oxford, 1888), 165, 168.

[11]   John R. Magrath, *The Queen's College,* 2 vols. (Oxford, 1921), 2: 91–5.

[12]   *Miscellaneous Works and Correspondence of the Rev. James Bradley, DD, FRS,* ed. Stephen P. Rigaud (Oxford, 1832), vi, viii.

[13]   Colin A. Ronan, *Edmond Halley: genius in eclipse* (London, 1970), 118–22; William R. Albury, 'Halley's Ode on the *Principia* of Newton and the Epicurean Revival in England', *Journal of the History of Ideas* 39 (1978), 24–43.

[14]   Edward Bentham, *De Studiis Theologiciis* (Oxford, 1764), 16.

[15]   Ronan, *Edmond Halley,* 72–3, 80–6.

[16]   *OU History,* iv. 17; Anita McConnell, 'Immanuel Halton (1628–99)', *Oxford Dictionary of National Biography (ODNB),* 24:124.

David Gregory, Savilian professor of astronomy from 1691 to 1708, began propagating Newton's ideas at Oxford almost immediately, as a few years later did John Keill, who succeeded to the astronomy chair in 1712. Gregory and Keill were both episcopalian refugees from Scottish presbyterian persecution, which in turn sheds an interesting light on the relationship between religion and science at the time.[17]

One product of this Oxford Newtonian milieu was James Bradley, who graduated from Balliol in 1714, the college of Gregory and Keill and where two of the most frequently borrowed items from the fellows library were the *Philosophical Transactions* of the Royal Society and its approximate German equivalent the *Acta Eruditorum*.[18] Bradley rightly features prominently in the contribution by Gerard Turner to volume v of the *OU History*, not least due to the great popularity of his lectures on 'experimental philosophy'. Indeed Turner has calculated that over a fifteen year period, between 1746 and 1760, approximately a third of Oxford undergraduates attended these extra curricular lectures.[19] Back in 1729 Bradley had taken over a similar course of lectures delivered by John Whiteside, Keeper of the Ashmolean, from 1714 onwards. After the death of Bradley the lectures were continued by his successor Thomas Hornsby, who in 1785 put on a further course devoted to introducing and proving to his audience, by experiment, the 'principal discoveries' of Joseph Priestly. The normal venue of these lectures was the Ashmolean, which for much of the eighteenth century also hosted courses on chemistry and anatomy. Turner in addition pointed out that Cyril Jackson, dean of Christ Church (1783–1809), was a member of the famous Lunar Society—based in the Midlands and which played a significant part in the genesis of the industrial revolution.[20] Much less well known, however, is that Jackson himself had been elected a fellow of the Royal Society in 1772 and that Matthew Boulton, a leading light of the Lunar Society and a pioneer in the development of steam power, arranged in 1791 for his son Matthew Robinson Boulton to attend the Oxford lectures of Hornsby and Thomas Beddoes.[21] Beddoes, an Edinburgh-trained

[17] David Gregory, *Astronomiae Physicae et Geometricae Elementa* (Oxford, 1702); John Keill, *Introductio ad Veram Physicam* (Oxford, 1701); Anita Guerrini, 'David Gregory (1659–1708)', *ODNB*, 23: 661–4; John Henry, 'John Keill (1671–1721)', *ODNB*, 31:42–5.

[18] Main, 'What Fellows read', 34.

[19] Turner, 'Physical Sciences', 673. He also notes that the eight colleges with the most attendees at Bradley's lectures included the six 'that had their own chemistry laboratories at the beginning of the twentieth century'.

[20] Ibid, 662–8, 672–4; Albert E. Musson and Eric Robinson, *Science and Technology in the Industrial Revolution* (Manchester, 1969), 393–426.

[21] *The Record of the Royal Society of London* (London, 1940), 423; Musson and Robinson, *Science and Technology*, 146. The *ODNB* article on Cyril Jackson, by William R. Ward (29: 470–2), completely ignores his scientific interests: even the election of Jackson as an FRS goes unmentioned.

medic, was lecturing at the time on chemistry. Due to his expressing too open sympathies for the French Revolution, however, the Oxford career of Beddoes was soon after cut short.[22]

What, however, can be said of the Oxford undergraduate curriculum more generally? Writing about early eighteenth-century Cambridge, Christopher Brooke has drawn attention to Daniel Waterland's *Advice to a Young Student*. First published in 1730, although written some decades earlier for students at the sister university, this work's second edition was printed at Oxford in 1755. Covering the four years of the BA degree, Waterland divided up the weekday studies of undergraduates into the two categories of 'philosophical' and 'classical'. The former included works by Gregory and Keill, as well as the *Principia* of Newton and Locke's *Essay concerning Human Understanding*.[23] For a later Oxford adaptation we can turn to the letters of John James, who was studying at Queen's College between 1778 and 1782. James's reading of the *Philosophical Transactions* has already been mentioned, but during his fourth year he also immersed himself in the study of chemistry, attending the university lectures on the subject by Martin Wall—with the encouragement of one of the college fellows, Septimus Collinson, who advised studying chemistry as the 'basis for a compleat skill in naturall philosophy'. Indeed the original plan was for James to have spent a further period at Oxford, attending 'lectures in chemistry, mathematics, and natural philosophy'. This in the event was not to be. Nevertheless, he did find time to make an 'abridgement' of Locke, presumably the *Essay*, and to dip into 'Bayle's Dictionary', the work of an Enlightenment precursor,[24] along with winning the Chancellor's Latin verse prize in 1782 on the set theme of 'Columbus', his entry concluding with a laudatory reference to the subsequent exploits of the '*gens Britonum*'. Two years earlier James had seriously considered entering for this same prize, when the prescribed topic was the 'Death of Cook'.[25]

Clearly the role of Oxford University during the age of the Enlightenment needs much more research. For the present, however, two other instances must suffice. Thus although it has been held against them that the Savilian professors Halley and Bradley were also Astronomers Royal, and as such pluralists (312), this dualism in fact provided Oxford with a valuable window onto the wider world of science and its applications.

[22] Michael Neve, 'Thomas Beddoes (1760–1808)', *ODNB*, 4: 754–6.

[23] Victor Morgan and Christopher Brooke (eds), *A History of the University of Cambridge*, Volume II (Cambridge, 2004), 339–42; Daniel Waterland, *Advice to a Young Student. With a Method of Study for the First Four Years* (Oxford, 1755).

[24] The *Dictionnaire Historique et Critique* of Pierre Bayle, originally published at Rotterdam in 1697, was available in a variety of English translations by the time of John James.

[25] *Letters of ... John James*, ed. Evans, x, 106–7, 112, 122, 126, 148, 164–6, 171–3, 177–8, 203–22, 293. The subject set for the Chancellor's Latin verse prize in 1779 was 'Electricity', about which James did not feel qualified to write: ibid, 66.

Until the construction in the 1770s of the splendid Radcliffe Observatory, with state-of-the-art instruments made by John Bird, Oxford astronomers lacked adequate facilities.[26] As a result of this deficiency, Bradley partly relied on the observatory constructed by George Parker, second earl of Macclesfield, at Shirburn Castle some seventeen miles from Oxford. Macclesfield was himself a keen astronomer and president of the Royal Society (1752–64). One consequence of their liaison was that Bradley came to play a leading role in the reformation of the calendar, which Macclesfield helped steer through parliament in 1751.[27] Britain was thereby at last brought into line with all those other countries which had adopted the Gregorian calendar from the late sixteenth century onwards, overcoming in the process some 150 years of anti-Catholic prejudice.

The second example is in some ways even more striking and virtually unknown until now, concerning as it does Oxford's involvement with all three of the Pacific voyages of Captain James Cook. In this instance the main link was probably provided by Thomas Hornsby, who had succeeded Bradley as Savilian professor of astronomy in 1763 and initially focused much of his attention on the predicted transit of Venus in 1769. Hornsby and his Royal Society colleagues persuaded the Admiralty to provide a ship, captained by Cook, to sail in 1768 to the southern hemisphere in order to observe the transit. As part of the European preparations Hornsby gave a set of lectures in Oxford and arranged for local observers; these in the event were drawn from seven Oxford colleges and halls, as reported by him to the Royal Society.[28] Shortly after the return of Cook, Oxford in 1771 bestowed an honorary DCL on each of the two naturalists who had accompanied the expedition, namely Joseph Banks, a Christ Church alumnus, and his assistant Daniel Solander, pupil of the great Swedish taxonomist Carl Linnaeus. It was, however, the second Pacific voyage of Cook (1772–5) that really seems to have kindled Oxford interest. For reasons that are still unclear members of the university took under their wing the chief naturalist on this second expedition, Johann Reinhold Forster, who had replaced Banks at the last minute. Forster too was awarded an honorary Oxford DCL in 1775 and the following year presented to the Ashmolean Museum a collection of South Sea artefacts.[29]

---

[26] On its completion, the Radcliffe Observatory was described by a visiting Danish astronomer, Thomas Bugge, as 'the best in Europe': Turner, 'Physical Sciences', 681.

[27] Bradley, *Miscellaneous Works*, lxxx–lxxxv, 461. As well as an observatory, Macclesfield built a laboratory at Shirburn: ibid, lxxiv.

[28] John C. Beaglehole, *The Life of Captain James Cook* (London, 1974), 102, 124–7; Ruth Wallis, 'Cross-Currents in Astronomy and Navigation: Thomas Hornsby FRS (1733–1810)', *Annals of Science* 57 (2000), 223–4.

[29] Joseph Foster, *Alumni Oxonienses 1715–1886,* 4 vols. (Oxford, 1888), 1: 57. 2: 479, 4: 1327; Arthur G. MacGregor and Anthony J. Turner, 'the Ashmolean Museum', in *OU History*, v. 657.

Johann Reinhold Forster himself was a product of the University of Halle and had taught for some years at the Warrington dissenter academy in succession to Priestly. When in 1778 Forster published his *Observations made during a Voyage round the World*, 27 of the 85 subscribers were listed as Oxford based. They also comprised eighteen fellows of the Royal Society, including three currently at Oxford (Thomas Hornsby, Cyril Jackson, and Benjamin Kennicott), as well as Banks, shortly to become president, and the secretary of the Admiralty.[30] The advertisement for Forster's *Observations* described the intended audience as consisting especially of the 'friends of humanity'.[31] Apropos Cook's third Pacific voyage (1776–80), Hornsby was instrumental in the appointment of James King to act as an astronomer. King was a naval officer but had spent time at Oxford studying with Hornsby and subsequently was also to join the university ranks of honorary DCLs.[32] As already remarked, the death of Cook during his third voyage, in 1779, was the theme set for the Chancellor's verse prize at Oxford—being won on this occasion by Richard Wellesley, second earl of Mornington.[33]

Forster's son Georg, who had accompanied his father on the second voyage of Cook, published in 1777 a 'philosophical history' of the expedition, which he described as having been undertaken 'from the most liberal motives' and 'by order of an enlightened monarch'. As well as catering to the needs of 'geographers' and 'naturalists', those involved had 'above all' furnished 'the friends of mankind' with evidence of 'various modifications of human nature'. Hornsby apparently had a hand in preparing the English manuscript for publication.[34] A German version followed in 1778, under the title *Reise um die Welt*, and after his return to the continent Georg Forster continued to make accounts of Cook's exploits available in such translations. This culminated with *Des Capitain Jacob Cook dritte*

[30] Michael E. Hoare, *The Tactless Philosopher. Johann Reinhold Forster (1729–98)* (Melbourne, 1976), 9–11, 37–8, 54–64, 183–4; Johann Reinhold Forster, *Observations made during a Voyage round the World, on Physical Geography, Natural History and Ethic Philosophy* (London, 1778), [651]. BL press mark 984.e.1. is the copy of Forster's *Observations* owned by Joseph Banks.

[31] Johann Reinhold Forster, *Observations made during a Voyage round the World*, ed. Nicholas Thomas, Harriet Guest and Michael Dettelbach (Honolulu, 1996), lxxviii.

[32] Hoare, *Tactless Philosopher*, 237–8; John K. Laughton and Andrew C. F. David, 'James King (1750–84)', *ODNB*, 31: 632–3. There is no record of James King in Foster, *Alumni Oxonienses*, but the *Record of the Royal Society* does ascribe an honorary doctorate to him: 429.

[33] Richard Wellesley, 'Viri Eximii et Celeberrimi Navigatoris', in *Primitiae et Reliquiae*, [Part I], (London, 1840), 53–8. For Cook as an 'Enlightenment hero', see Glyn Williams, *The Death of Captain Cook. A Hero made and unmade* (London, 2008), 61–129.

[34] Georg Forster, *A Voyage round the World in his Britannic Majesty's Sloop Resolution, commanded by Captain James Cook* [1772–5] 2 vols. (London, 1777), 1: iii, 14; 2: 605–6; Hoare, *Tactless Philosopher*, 167–8.

Entdeckungs-Reise (1787). By the time of the death of the Emperor Joseph II in 1790, however, Forster was rapidly losing his faith in the ability of enlightened rulers to reform their societies. With Europe now in the throes of the French Revolution, which had broken out the previous year, and a consequent '*crise universelle*', he now set out from Mainz in the company of the young Alexander von Humboldt. Their tour took them down the Rhine, through the Netherlands, across to England, back over the sea to France, arriving at Paris in time for the first anniversary of the fall of the Bastille, and then home again. Travelling through England and visiting the hive of industry represented by Birmingham, Forster notes that due to the '*bizarreries de la constitution anglaise*' this place of sixty thousand inhabitants is without parliamentary representation, prompting the exclamation '*O hommes! O liberté!*' But, both in London and on a visit to Oxford's '*jardin botanique*', he singles out the contribution of his erstwhile patron Joseph Banks to the study of '*histoire naturelle*'.[35] Two years later, French revolutionary forces marched into Mainz and Forster threw in his lot with the Jacobins. The Republic of Mainz, however, barely lasted a year and Forster died in Parisian exile, with a price on his head, in 1794.[36]

Brockliss has drawn attention to the apparent paucity of contemporary Oxford copies of the *Encyclopédie*, with the implication that the eighteenth-century university remained immune to the influence of the *siècle des lumières* (298). But certainly in the guise of the Forsters and *Aufklärung* this was not the case. Moreover, as historians such as John Gascoigne have argued, England had its own version of Enlightenment, drawing on the wellsprings of John Locke and Isaac Newton, and even earlier on Francis Bacon. Paradoxically the traditional ascendancy ascribed to Cambridge mathematics, as epitomized by the tripos examination, contrasting with the greater emphasis on natural history, and especially botany, at Oxford, could be said to have redounded at least in the short term to the favour of the latter. For as Gascoigne has commented, by the late eighteenth century 'Cambridge's mathematical obstinacy...indicated a growing estrangement from the larger English scientific community'. Now 'botany, zoology, chemistry and geology gained more and more followers'. A similar 'change in the scientific climate' is also detectable in France itself, Denis Diderot

---

[35] Georg Forster, *Voyage Philosophique et Pittoresque, sur les Rives du Rhin, à Liège, dans la Flandre, le Brabant, la Hollande, l'Angleterre, la France etc.*, translated from the German by Charles Pougens, 3 vols. (Paris, 'l'an VIII' [1799/1800]), 3: 36–8, 47, 86–7, 162–7. For the complicated relations of the Forsters father and son with Joseph Banks, see *The Banks Letters. A Calendar of the Manuscript Correspondence of Sir Joseph Banks*, ed. Warren R. Dawson (London, 1958), 335–41.

[36] Thomas P. Saine, *Georg Forster* (New York, 1972), 126–56.

proclaiming that 'the reign of mathematics is over'.[37] At the same time 'imperialism' was evidently alive and well in 'Anglican' Oxford, and not just in the form of undergraduate prize poems. Thus Hornsby, in 1765, when urging the scientific merits of dispatching an expedition to the Pacific drew attention as well to the 'commercial' advantages of making a 'settlement' in the region.[38]

II

Misconceptions concerning Hanoverian Oxford have also tended to cast a long shadow over the situation obtaining under the Tudors and Stuarts. Hence conventional wisdom has it that the university's previous age of greatness prior to modern times comprised the thirteenth and fourteenth centuries. Inspired by first-wave humanism and in particular the recovery of the works of Aristotle, Oxford came to vie with Paris, producing a galaxy of international talent in the fields of logic, philosophy, and theology. Names to conjure with in this connection are Duns Scotus, Roger Bacon, and William of Ockham. By contrast not a great deal is known about Oxford University life as a whole at that period. Remarking on this discrepancy, when reviewing volume i of the *OU History*, Linda Colley wrote that the editor, Jeremy Catto, and his then assistant, Ralph Evans, 'have compensated for a paucity of domestic detail by scouring eighteen continental archives and devoting six chapters to the Oxford schools' contribution to European culture'.[39] Volume ii of the *OU History* reveals a similar 'scouring' of foreign archives.[40] This approach is also reflected in the 'chronology' provided by Brockliss, in which Scotus, Bacon, and Ockham all feature, along with five other authors of renown including John Wyclif. He lists two more names under the dates 1498 (Colet) and 1523 (Vives), after which the roll of intellectual honour ceases (731–2). But were this practice of naming famous Oxford men, and latterly women, adopted for later centuries a different picture would emerge. Edmond Halley, whose portrait should by rights feature as the frontispiece of volume v of the *OU History*, has already been mentioned. What, however, of John Locke, who

---

[37] John Gascoigne, *Cambridge and the Enlightenment. Science, Religion and Politics from the Restoration to the French Revolution* (Cambridge, 1989), 1–2, 282–4.

[38] Beaglehole, *Life of Captain James Cook* , 102.

[39] Linda Colley, 'An Obsession with the State', *Times Literary Supplement*, 13 March 1987, p. 261; Jeremy I. Catto (ed., with Ralph Evans), *The History of the University of Oxford*, i: *The Early Oxford Schools* (Oxford, 1984), ix, xxiii–xxxii.

[40] Jeremy I. Catto and Ralph Evans (eds), *The History of the University of Oxford*, ii: *Late Medieval Oxford* (Oxford, 1992), v, xxi–xlii.

despite the sterling efforts of John Yolton, in his contribution to the same volume, still remains a historiographically semi-detached figure as regards Oxford? During the early 1660s, at Christ Church, Locke was already developing some of the philosophical ideas for which later generations came to remember him. Moreover his *Essay concerning Human Understanding* (1690) was abridged in 1696 by an Oxford tutor, John Wynne, for the use of students and with the permission of the author. By 1778 this *Abridgement* had reached a twelfth edition.[41] Clearly, in evaluating the health or otherwise of Oxford University across the centuries a great deal depends on the criteria employed.

It is generally agreed that medieval Oxford was regarded by contemporaries as a source of future clerical administrators in church and state, as well as of parish clergy, and that the university in the main successfully fulfilled that role, the students residing in halls and latterly in colleges. On the other hand some historians, notably Guy Lytle, have also argued that in the late fifteenth century perhaps as many as forty per cent of Oxford students were never ordained, on account of lack of employment opportunities.[42] Brockliss provides an expert summary of the evidence, concluding that 'perhaps many students went home after a few years with their tails between their legs and re-entered the rural elite as bailiffs, reeves, and so on.' Another way of looking at the phenomenon, however, and one which Brockliss also recognises, is to see this as part of the emergence of an educated laity drawn from the ranks of 'small freeholders and affluent tenant farmers'. (31–55) Second-wave humanism, with its new emphasis on rhetoric, also now came increasingly to inform the tuition on offer to the sons of the gentry, who began to flood into Oxford under the Tudors. An alumnus straddling these various worlds was the layman William Worcester, who attended Oxford in the 1430s. Son of a Bristol burgess, Worcester went on to become secretary to Sir John Fastolf as well as acquiring some of the manuscripts of the early English humanist and Oxonian John Free.[43]

At the same time it needs stressing that the harvest of Graeco-Roman literature was compatible with the idea of intellectual progress. This was

---

[41] John Yolton, 'Schoolmen, Logic and Philosophy', in *OU History*, v. 565–91; John Locke, *Essays on the Law of Nature*, ed. Wolfgang von Leyden (Oxford, 1954; 2nd edn Oxford, 1958), 7–15, 30–82, 95–243; John Wynne, *An Abridgment of Mr Locke's Essay concerning Human Understanding* (London, 1696; 12th cdn. Edinburgh, 1778).

[42] Guy F. Lytle, 'The Careers of Oxford Students in the Later Middle Ages', in James M. Kittelson and Pamela J. Transue (eds), *Rebirth, Reform and Resilience: Universities in Transition 1300–1700* (Columbus, OH, 1984), 213–53, 218–20.

[43] Nicholas Orme, 'William Worcester (1415–85)', *ODNB*, 60: 294–5; Roberto Weiss, *Humanism in England during the Fifteenth Century* (Oxford, 1941; 2nd edn, Oxford, 1957), 106–12, 177–8; Jeremy I. Catto, 'Scholars and Studies in Renaissance Oxford', in *OU History*, ii. 769–83, 770, 774–7.

originally formulated in terms of dwarfs standing on the shoulders of giants, but with the overseas discoveries from Columbus onwards the balance of achievement began to swing decisively in favour of the moderns.[44] In this connection one of the missing persons from the pages of Brockliss is Richard Hakluyt, author of three books about the 'voyages' and 'navigations' undertaken by his English compatriots. Hakluyt had spent over ten years at Christ Church, from 1570 onwards, and records that 'in my publike lectures [I] was the first that produced and shewed both the olde imperfectly composed and the new lately reformed mappes, globes, spheares, and other instruments of this art for demonstration in the common schools, to the singular pleasure and generall contentment of my auditory'. Moreover at the same time (1577) he was in contact with the Dutch cartographer Abraham Ortelius, on the subject of the search for the Northwest Passage.[45] Meanwhile, during the reign of Edward VI, Oxford had already been exposed to the bracing message of the continental Reformation, as purveyed by Peter Martyr in his capacity as Regius professor of divinity and marking the approximate inauguration of what Brockliss rather anachronistically calls the 'Anglican University'.[46]

Around the same date that Hakluyt had arrived in Oxford, Henry Savile can be found lecturing there on the *De revolutionibus* of Copernicus.[47] Subsequently it was Savile, together with his friend Thomas Bodley, who came to set a decisive stamp on seventeenth-century Oxford, both in terms of the Savilian professorships of astronomy and geometry, founded in 1619, and the Bodleian Library. Polymath that he was, Savile, in the years 1610–12, also brought to fruition a massive edition of the Greek patristic author John Chrysostom. The first Savilian professor of geometry, Henry Briggs, is another person missing from Brockliss. Like his fellow professor of astronomy, John Bainbridge, Briggs was originally from Cambridge and had held a chair at Gresham College in London, publishing in 1624 his *Arithmetica Logarithmica*. This was followed by his *Trigonometria Britannica* (1633). During the 1630s Bainbridge in turn was instrumental in organizing two astronomical expeditions, one to the Near East and the other to Latin America. A major objective was the establishment of more accurate longitude measurements, and Bainbridge was able to announce in the course of his university lectures that São Luís do Maranhão, in Brazil, was

[44] Richard W. Southern, *Scholastic Humanism and the Unification of Europe*, i: *Foundations* (Oxford, 1995), 33–4, 185–9; John H. Elliott, *The Old World and the New 1492–1650* (Cambridge, 1970, revised edn. Cambridge, 1992), 49–53.

[45] David B. Quinn (ed.), *The Hakluyt Handbook*, 2 vols. (London, 1974), 1: 266–84.

[46] Peter Martyr, *In Epistolam S. Pauli Apostoli ad Romanos* (Zurich, 1559).

[47] Mordechai Feingold, *The Mathematicians' Apprenticeship: Science, Universities and Society in England, 1560–1640* (Cambridge, 1984), 47–8.

approximately 45 degrees west of Oxford. Under the terms of the Laudian statutes the Savilian lectures were built into the university curriculum, as part of the BA and MA programmes. Furthermore a pocket edition of these statutes was issued with a copy of the syllabus—featuring a Copernican motif. By way of replicating such teaching at the college level, Archbishop Laud[48] now set about creating a mathematical library at St John's. Also, in a work of 1640 licensed by the Oxford vice chancellor, John Wilkins assured readers that heliocentricity furnished additional proof of the existence of God. The same year saw the Oxford publication of a handsome folio edition of Francis Bacon's *Advancement and Proficience of Learning.* Oxford medicine too was making strides at this time, the probability of the circulation of the blood being maintained as an Act thesis, in 1633, by Edward Dawson.[49]

Manifestly under the early Stuarts a liberal education at Oxford University comprehended what today we call 'science'. Furthermore this was to remain the case until well into the nineteenth century. The classical inheritance, mediated through a loosely defined framework of the seven liberal arts, furnished a common core, with the possibility of greater specialization thereafter. This also helps to explain the posthumous encomium bestowed on John Gregory, a Christ Church tutor during the 1630s, as being a 'citizen of the world'. Like his colleague Robert Burton, author of the *Anatomy of Melancholy* (1621–41), Gregory included the mathematical sciences among a wide portfolio of interests.[50] Here an illuminating illustration of the nature of the relationship between the various academic components involved comes from the defence of the university mounted in 1654 by Seth Ward, Savilian professor of astronomy. After the English Civil War, Oxford and Cambridge had been attacked in print by radical Puritans who advocated a more utilitarian model of education. In his *Vindiciae Academiarum* of 1654, Ward first refuted the charge that Oxford was opposed to the kind of 'experiments and observations' recommended by Francis Bacon. 'It cannot be denied but this is … the only way to perfect naturall philosophy and medicine, so that whosoever intend to professe the one or the other are to take that course' and 'this way is pursued amongst us'. But, he went on to say, 'our academies are of a more general

---

[48] Laud also arranged for the publication of William Chillingworth's *The Religion of Protestants* (Oxford, 1638), a work which was one of the feeders of Latitudinarianism: Nicholas Tyacke, *Aspects of English Protestantism c. 1530–1700* (Manchester, 2001), 232–3, 279–80, 306.

[49] Tyacke, *Aspects*, 244–61; John Wilkins, *A Discourse Concerning a New Planet* (London, 1640), 237–40. The *ODNB* article on John Bainbridge, by Adam J. Apt (3: 323–4), is woefully inadequate.

[50] John Gregory, *Gregorii Posthuma or Certain Learned Tracts* (London, 1649), sig. (b)ᵛ; Tyacke, *Aspects*, 248, 253–4.

and comprehensive institution, and as there is a provision here made that whosoever will be excellent in any kind, in any art, science, or language, may . . . receive assistance, so is there a provision likewise that men be not forced into particular waies', the aim instead being that of an education 'variously answerable to their genius and designe'.[51] What this meant for many an undergraduate, as Brockliss felicitously puts it, was 'a rich smorgasbord of intellectual delights from which to choose' (245).

At the same time more than accident was at work in the clustering of natural philosophers at Oxford during the upheavals of the mid seventeenth century, which in turn provided one of the springboards of the Royal Society—founded in 1660. The Savile-Gresham professorial axis established in the 1620s had helped to create a critical mass, furthered by the presence in royalist Oxford of William Harvey in the early 1640s, but much more so by the arrival of Robert Boyle in the 1650s and the return of John Wilkins, now as warden of Wadham College, who came to play the role of impresario. Continuity across the Restoration was provided by Christopher Wren, an Oxford product of the 1650s, who after a brief spell at Gresham College was appointed to the Savilian chair of astronomy (1661–73). The great survivor, however, was John Wallis, who served as Savilian professor of geometry from 1649 to 1703. His collected mathematical works, running to three folio volumes, were published at Oxford in the 1690s. But with the return of more settled political times the pull of the metropolis proved irresistible and London became the normal meeting place of the Royal Society.[52] On the other hand such interests remained widespread in the university, as evidenced by the spirited oration delivered in 1693 at the Oxford Act, by Joseph Addison of Magdalen College, in defence of the 'new philosophy'. Addison proudly proclaimed the superiority of the 'moderns', as witnessed by Descartes, Boyle, and Newton.[53]

The brilliant anatomist Thomas Willis, a former member of the Wilkins circle, held the Sedleian chair of natural philosophy at Oxford from 1660 to 1675, while another distinguished figure in the anatomical field was James Keill, brother of John, who can be found lecturing in the university around the turn of the century.[54] Oxford, however, long remained seriously

---

[51] Allen G. Debus, *Science and Education in the Seventeenth Century. The Webster-Ward Debate* (London, 1970), 49–50.

[52] Feingold, *Mathematicians' Apprenticeship*, 122–89; Charles Webster, *The Great Instauration. Science, Medicine and Reform 1626–1660* (London, 1975), 57–67; Robert G. Frank, *Harvey and the Oxford Physiologists* (Berkeley, 1980), 25–30, 45–90; Michael Hunter, *Science and Society in Restoration England* (Cambridge, 1981), 1–86; John Wallis, *Opera Mathematica* (Oxford, 1693–1699).

[53] Feingold, 'Mathematical Sciences', in *OU History*, iv. 396. Addison's oration finds no mention in Brockliss (ed.), *Magdalen College*.

[54] Robert G. Frank, 'Medicine', in *OU History*, iv. 505–58.

outclassed as a medical centre compared with London, Edinburgh, and places further afield. Nevertheless the lack of a teaching hospital eventually began to be rectified with the foundation of the Radcliffe Infirmary in 1770. A sprinkling of Edinburgh-trained medics already existed in Oxford and some of these, such as John Parsons and William Thomson, now became associated with the Radcliffe as honorary physicians. Also the Oxford Botanic Garden, which originated from before Civil War, was attracting medical practitioners to its staff by the 1780s, notably John Sibthorp and his deputy George Shaw, both Edinburgh-trained doctors and in the event founder members of the Linnean Society. (Carl Linnaeus himself had visited Oxford in 1736.)[55] Moreover in 1765, under the terms of the will of Matthew Lee, an anatomy school and readership in the subject had been endowed at Christ Church. The first holder of the post was Parsons, and many of those attending the lectures and demonstrations did so out of general interest rather than with a view to pursuing a career in medicine.[56]

III

While we can debate about the kind of education available in eighteenth-century Oxford, the charge of growing elitism, accompanied by shrinking numbers, is irrefutable. But the reasons for this are less clear. Part of the explanation has to be the development of alternatives, among them the rise of dissenter academies and the increase of private tutoring—sometimes accompanied by foreign travel.[57] On the other hand the student population began to recover from the 1750s,[58] and with the coming of the nineteenth-century age of reform Brockliss really gets into his stride. Aided and abetted by the superb volumes vi and vii of the *OU History*, edited by Michael Brock and Mark Curthoys, he has a fascinating story to tell. Ironically it was an attempt to raise standards, via the new examination statute of 1800, which had the unintended consequence of narrowing the focus of undergraduate study in favour of classics and at the expense of mathematics. By an odd twist of fate, Cyril Jackson, FRS and dean of Christ Church, was the person now singled out for blame, especially at the hands of Edward Tatham, rector of Lincoln College, who accused him of being a diehard Aristotelian. Given what we know about Jackson and not least his enthusiasm for mathematics, the allegation only makes sense, if at

---

[55] Charles Webster, 'The Medical Faculty and Physic Garden', in *OU History*, v. 683–723.
[56] Edward G. W. Bill, *Education at Christ Church Oxford 1600–1800* (Oxford, 1988), 314–18.
[57] Vivian H. H. Green, 'The University and Social Life', in *OU History*, v. 309–14.
[58] Stone, *University in Society*, 1: 6, 91.

all, in the rather narrow confines of a dispute about the teaching of logic—
Tatham claiming somewhat implausibly that the *Organum* of Aristotle
was now being privileged over the *Novum Organum* of Francis Bacon.
Nevertheless this charge of Aristotelianism has tended to muddy the
waters ever since.[59]

A marked change of mood had occurred in the years between the killing
of Captain Cook on a distant Hawaiian strand in 1779 and the guillotin-
ing much nearer home of Louis XVI of France in 1793. Henceforth
European monarchs everywhere, along with their ruling elites, were on
notice to up their game or suffer the consequences, and so too arose the
pressure on Oxford and Cambridge to reform. In the long term making
examinations more demanding meant a greater degree of specialization and
ultimately dividing up the old arts degree into separate parts. Meanwhile
successive changes in the exam system followed on from those of 1800 and
with these there grew a deepening division between the college tutors,
especially the classicists, and the science professors, the latter now thicker
on the ground thanks to recent benefactions. Faced with stiffer tests, students now voted with their feet, increasingly absenting themselves from
lectures deemed irrelevant to exam results. A striking illustration of the
resulting situation is provided by Nicolaas Rupke, in his gem of a chapter
contributed to volume vi of the *OU History*. Rupke provides a bar graph
showing attendance at the lectures of William Buckland, professor of min-
eralogy and reader in geology, whose initial popularity with students was
comparable to that of Bradley in the middle years of the previous century.
Despite a string of discoveries to his name, from about 1830 the annual
numbers present at the lectures of Buckland halved, and the situation was
even worse for some of his colleagues such as Baden Powell, Savilian professor of geometry. Conversely at this very time membership of the
Ashmolean Society, a local Oxford equivalent of the Royal Society and
founded in 1828, was on the rise. Catering for the university seniors, by
1850 this society had about 300 members.[60]

Institutional obstacles to reform were further compounded by the rise
of the Oxford Movement in religion, whose principal spokesman, the future
Cardinal Newman, now emerged as a scourge of Enlightenment values.
Views later to be enshrined in his *The Idea of a University* (1852) and the
notorious 'Theses on Liberalism' in *Apologia pro Vita Sua* (1864), can
already be found present in the sermons which Newman was preaching in
the mid 1820s, condemning what he called 'an irreligious veneration of the

---

[59] Vivian H. H. Green, 'Reformers and Reform in the University', in *OU History*, v. 628–31.
For the continuing interest of Jackson in mathematics, see John Fauvel, Raymond Floud and
Robin Wilson, *Oxford Figures: 800 Years of the Mathematical Sciences* (Oxford, 2000), 162–3

[60] Nicolaas A. Rupke, 'Oxford's Scientific Awakening and the Role of Geology', in *OU History*, vi. 543–62, 547–8.

mere intellectual powers' and warning, as glossed by Michael Brock, 'against the dangers of scientific research'. Newman and his confrères also attacked the vogue for natural theology, thereby putting themselves at odds with the likes of Buckland.[61] What counted in the longer run, however, was a combination of external political pressures and internal academic dissatisfactions, reinforced by an increasing stress on utility. Apropos this last, as Rupke puts it, 'Oxford scientists in the 1830s became caught up in the enthusiasm for linking scientific education and research with agricultural and industrial progress'.[62] Such concerns led the Oxford authorities, in 1850, to create a separate school of natural science, together with another for law and modern history, and to make attendance at professorial lectures obligatory—although this last requirement was soon rescinded. There followed the setting up of a royal commission, on the recommendations of which most closed fellowships and scholarships were thrown open to competition. Furthermore undergraduate subscription to the Thirty-Nine Articles was abolished in 1854 (358–9), spelling an end both to the 'confessional' university and compulsory chapel attendance.[63]

With the opening of the University Museum in 1860, an occasion associated with the historic clash between Thomas Huxley and Bishop Wilberforce concerning the theory of evolution, and the inauguration of the Clarendon Laboratory ten years later, natural science at Oxford, now housed in these two grand new buildings, might seem to have come into its own. Yet as matters transpired, in the arresting words of Robert Fox, the university at this time 'could be seen . . . to have stumbled at the threshold of the modern world'.[64] Part of the problem had to do with some of the personalities involved, such as Henry Acland, the regius professor of medicine, Robert Clifton, professor of experimental philosophy, and William Odling, Waynflete professor of chemistry, none of whom were greatly interested in advancing their subject, but more fundamental perhaps was the still very widely held belief in the virtues of a general education which militated against the establishment of a strong research culture.[65] Allied with this were an ethos of 'service' and the idea of a 'Christian gentleman',

---

[61] Michael G. Brock, 'The Oxford of Peel and Gladstone, 1800–1833', in *OU History*, vi. 7–71, 50–1; Rupke, 'Oxford's Scientific Awakening', 558–9.

[62] Rupke, 'Oxford's Scientific Awakening', 560.

[63] William R. Ward, 'From the Tractarians to the Executive Commission', in *OU History*, vi. 306–336, 314–15, 318–19.

[64] Robert Fox, 'The University Museum and Oxford Science, 1850–1880', in *OU History*, vi. 641–93, 657–9, 691.

[65] Ibid, 686–91. Nevertheless the comparative success story of the Cavendish Laboratory, at Cambridge, suggests that other factors were also involved, especially the traditional emphasis there on mathematics which now seems to have paid dividends: Janet Howarth, '"Oxford for the Arts": the Natural Sciences, 1880–1914', in Michael G. Brock and Mark C. Curthoys (eds), *The History of the University of Oxford*, vii: *Nineteenth-Century Oxford, Part 2*, (Oxford, 2000), 457–97, 484–8.

which permeated every level of what Brockliss dubs the 'imperial university' (345, 396–405). These concepts also had affinities with much older Renaissance thinking about the best way to civilize unruly youth and, in the previous century, 'the Addisonian ethic of politeness' (268). As it transpired, only the impact of World War I served seriously to undermine such shibboleths. Hence the damning verdict of the zoologist Ray Lankester, sometime Oxford professor and friend of Karl Marx, in his Romanes lecture of 1905, that 'traditional education has . . . deprived the well-to-do class of a knowledge of, and interest in, Man's relation to Nature, and of his power and necessity to control natural processes'. The study at Oxford of the ancient literature of Greece and Rome had, he declared, passed its sell-by date, and should give way to 'Physics, Chemistry, Geology and Biology'. As for other arts subjects, 'so-called History' needed replacing by 'Anthropology'. Lankester also praised the recent educational changes introduced in Japan.[66]

Brockliss provides a moving description of the mortality among Oxford men who served in World War I, noting the disproportionately high numbers compared with the nation as a whole. Classicists and public school products proved particularly vulnerable. Among the colleges, Corpus Christi came highest of all with 'a death rate of one in four' (431–2). A possible explanation of this particular statistic, although not one canvassed by Brockliss, is the influence exercised by the writings of that Clifton College and Corpus alumnus Sir Henry Newbolt CH. For Newbolt managed to elevate jingoism into a high art form, with poems such as 'Vitai Lampada' (1892), inspired by the death of General Gordon at Khartoum, which links together sportsmanship and death as exemplified by a schoolboy hero, now grown up, who 'rallies the ranks' of a broken 'square' with an echoing cry across the years: 'Play up! play up! And play the game!'. Fittingly, on the outbreak of hostilities in 1914, Newbolt was recruited to serve in the newly formed War Propaganda Bureau.[67]

Post-war disillusionment with the idea of 'service' helped, at least indirectly, to make research, especially in the sciences, more respectable. As regards undergraduates, however, the now generally agreed mantra was mental training (485, 537–8). New stars in the scientific firmament included the

---

[66] Edwin R. Lankester, *Nature and Man* (Oxford, 1905), 39, 41–4, 48–9. In this same lecture, however, Lankester invoked an earlier period when an Oxford education included the 'knowledge of nature'. 'Our present curriculum is a mere mushroom growth of the last century': ibid, 50–1; Peter J. Bowler, 'Sir (Edwin) Ray Lankester (1847–1929)', *ODNB*, 32: 535–8.

[67] Henry Newbolt, *Collected Poems 1897–1907* (London, [1918]), 131–3; Vanessa F. Jackson, *The Poetry of Henry Newbolt: Patriotism is not Enough* (Greensboro, NC, 1994), 79–84, 196 (fn. 27).

chemist and future Nobel laureate Cyril Hinshelwood,[68] the academic entrepreneur and physicist Frederick Lindeman, and the pathologist and developer of penicillin Howard Florey. Refugees from the continent, fleeing persecution during the 1930s, also made an important contribution. Yet, as Brockliss points out, up to World War II Oxford was still essentially an 'arts university', those graduating in natural science numbering a mere fourteen per cent by 1938 and this despite the blandishments offered by successive governments worried about Britain's lack of competitiveness on the world stage. By contrast graduates in Modern History alone counted for twenty per cent (411–12)[69]. Although the D.Phil. degree had been introduced in 1917, postgraduates remained thin on the ground. Women were admitted as full university members in 1920, but a quota was imposed in 1927 and by the eve of World War II they only comprised seventeen per cent of the undergraduate population. The total number of Oxford students by 1939 was just over 5,000 (740–1, 760). At the same time the university was gradually becoming less elitist, Daniel Greenstein commenting, in his fine contribution to volume viii of the *OU History*, that 'between the wars the proportion of landowners' and gentlemens' sons among the male junior members fell away sharply... while the proportion whose fathers were blue-collar workers, clerks and small shopkeepers simultaneously grew'.[70]

IV

The aftermath of World War II ushered in a second great age of reform. From the point of view of British universities, this was most obviously manifested by the 1963 Robbins Report, which recommended a great expansion of the student population. The government had already agreed to fund student fees and introduce means-tested maintenance grants. About the report as such, Brockliss comments presciently on its evident utilitarianism: 'higher education was [conceived as] first and foremost an economic good'. But this was to be taken much further in the 1996 Dearing Report on universities, which 'reduced the advancement of knowledge to the needs of UK plc'. *A la*

---

[68] Hinshelwood also managed to keep the flag flying for the polymaths, becoming president of the Classical Association and painting pictures—including one of his own laboratory: John Roche, 'The Non-Medical Sciences, 1939–1970', in B. Harrison (ed.), *The History of the University of Oxford*, viii: *The Twentieth Century* (Oxford, 1994), 251–95, 286–9. In this connection Roche has some very pertinent things to say about the 'two cultures' debate, launched by Charles Snow in 1959. For the picture of Hinshelwood's laboratory, see Brockliss, *University of Oxford*, 510.

[69] Jack B. Morrell, 'The Non-Medical Sciences, 1914–1939', in *OU History*, viii. 139–65, 142.

[70] Daniel I. Greenstein, 'The Junior Members, 1900–1990: a Profile', in *OU History*, viii. 45–79, 57.

Dearing, even research in the humanities was now justified partly on the grounds of its contribution to the tourist industry (542–3). This paved the way for reintroducing student charging two years later, and the subsequent abolition of maintenance grants. At the same time numbers of students pursuing 'useful' subjects at post-war Oxford tended to rise in unison. By 2012, forty-five per cent of matriculants were registered in the schools of science and medicine. Postgraduate numbers overall by then approximated to nearly half of the student population, having risen from eleven per cent back in 1939. Already in the 1980s forty per cent of these postgraduates were pursuing a science subject (762–3). This decade also saw the introduction of the 'new "publish or perish" culture' (645) of the Research Assessment Exercise (RAE), whereby academic staff performance, across all subjects, was graded in order to determine levels of government funding. The RAE was replaced in 2014 by the Research Excellence Framework (REF), designed for the same purpose but with special emphasis on 'impact'. By 2013 the annual fees charged to undergraduates had risen to £9,000, although they were still modest by American standards. These were just some of the consequences of what had begun innocently enough in the early 1920s, when Oxford first 'took the king's shilling' (392) via the then University Grants Committee (UGC).

Oxford responded to Robbins by setting up the Franks Commission in 1964. How best to accommodate the projected increase in student numbers, within the confines of the existing college system, soon emerged as a leading concern and in part explains the comparatively modest growth thereafter. Between the mid 1960s and the mid 1980s overall student numbers rose from about 9,500 to just over 13,000 (760). Some discussion also took place concerning the pros and cons of the much vaunted tutorial system. Was it still fit for purpose? Rather more pressing were issues of governance, the diffused Oxford system not complying with the recommended business model. In all these areas the university proved resistant to making major changes. But this did not stand in the way of successfully accessing the unprecedented sums of public funding now becoming available, which in combination with much increased private giving explains the remarkable spate of new building— especially evident in the Science Area abutting the University Parks. The list of academic big hitters, as compiled by Brockliss, was both cause and consequence of this development. Among the older generation were the Nobel prize-winners Hans Krebs, Dorothy Hodgkin, Nikolaas Tinbergen, and Rodney Porter. Thereafter, however, 'much more work came to be undertaken by research teams' and 'it has become harder than ever before to isolate the prince from the attendant lord' (650–3). The new John Radcliffe Hospital, built just outside Oxford at Headington and opened in the late 1970s, finally supplied the previously missing link of a big teaching hospital for the purposes of medical education. Come 2010–11, 'the Medical Division... commanded

60 per cent of Oxford's research money'. The university as a whole now boasted 80 fellows of the Royal Society and 100 fellows of the British Academy (654–5). Marshalled together under the banner of the Department for Business, Innovation and Skills (BIS) from 2009 to 2016, those in the humanities were increasingly encouraged to emulate their colleagues in natural science and medicine. By 2015 the pendulum had swung so far that the chief executive of the British Academy, Alun Evans, instanced 'tackling' the 'challenges' of Ebola, obesity, productivity, and climate change, as 'an example' of what his organization currently sought to achieve by way of research funding. It comes as little surprise that Evans had previously been 'head of strategy' at BIS.[71]

In September 2016, with a student population now approaching 23,000 (760), Oxford came first in the World University Rankings compiled by the *Times Higher Education* magazine.[72] All those of us who have ever spent time studying there can take some reflected pride in this notable achievement. It does, nevertheless, invite the question whether the university is at risk of selling its soul for a crock of government gold. This is one of themes touched on again by Brockliss in the concluding pages of his book, written before victory was in the bag (724). Those who worry about the direction of travel, and would prefer instead a more distant relationship between Oxford and the state, tend to look towards the United States for alternatives. The most obvious way to achieve greater independence is, of course, through private funding, and here Harvard University provides a favourite benchmark. Certainly in recent years Oxford has made strenuous efforts to increase its endowment but still falls very far short of most American rivals (600–4). Brockliss also expresses interest in the possible provision of online degrees, partly as a way of reducing the seemingly inexorable rise in costs (727). There are no easy answers. But in weaving together the myriad findings of the multi-volume *OU History* Brockliss has performed a signal service, and provided in addition a very fitting coda to an enterprise originally conceived by Alan Bullock, in the mid 1960s, as a way of contextualizing the new-look Oxford University ushered in by the Franks Commission. Yet at the same time Brockliss's very able summation alerts us to just how much more there still remains to discover—especially as regards the terra incognita of the eighteenth century.

Department of History,
University College London

---

[71] *Times Higher Education*, 25 June 2015, pp, 22–3.
[72] 'World University Rankings 2016–17', *Times Higher Education*, 22 September 2016, p. 6.

To Bumble or not to Bumble: The Design and Reshaping of Universities in Britain and America Since 1960

Sheldon Rothblatt

David Palfreyman & Ted Tapper, *Reshaping the University, The Rise of the Regulated Market in Higher Education* (Oxford: Oxford University Press, 2014), 307pp. ISBN: 9780199659821; William F. Massy, *Reengineering the University: How to be Mission Centered, Market Smart and Market Conscious* (Baltimore, MD: Johns Hopkins University Press, 2016), 288 pp. ISBN: 9781421418995; Michael M. Crow & William B. Dabars, *Designing the New American University* (Baltimore: Johns Hopkins Press, 2015), 344pp. ISBN: 978142141417233.

All of the works under review are concerned with similar issues, but the first, that by David Palfreyman of Oxford and Ted Tapper of Sussex, analyzes them within the history of policymaking in Britain, mainly England, since about 1960. Its primary thesis is that after much fumbling and experiment, sometimes with and sometimes without academic cooperation, the central British state has up-ended conventional ways of decision-making in universities. What has occurred—and the larger point has been in the literature for some time—is not that central government has taken over the running of the universities but that government has forced higher education institutions to operate under government-influenced market conditions. These are not rigid but loose, calling for more initiative and leadership on the part of institutions to establish their place in a competitive market where state funding is available but never assured at what the dons might consider optimal levels. The authors accept the realities of this situation—they criticize those who remain willing to die in the last ditch—and they note that on the whole the British public has been decently served by the changes, inevitable in light of unprecedented demographic pressures. The caveat is that 'decently-served' refers to an entire 'system of tertiary education' and not to the fortunes of every single kind of institution. In short, in today's world of vast student numbers and infinite demands upon universities to assure the overall welfare of society, natural protectors do not exist. The world is Darwin's and mutations are necessary.

The other three authors, with flashbacks, especially on the part of Crow and Dabars, who have read widely, establish ideal-type universities which Massy calls 'the traditional university' and the others the 'generic public university'. Their main thrust is similar to that of Tapper and Palfreyman. Political and economic and certainly demographic pressures emanating from all sectors of contemporary American society require serious alterations in many of the habits to which universities have become accustomed. However, in an American contest, the onus for major change falls more squarely upon the academic professoriate and individual institutions. American colleges and universities have always functioned within a competitive market environment, but with a few exceptions—states that have adopted master plans—the market has been unregulated. But the authors still believe that the academic barons have ignored many of the market signals—or they have misread them. The result is that in elevating 'abstract knowledge' beyond problem-solving, and in placing individual and institutional reputation above public service, universities are neglecting their primary responsibilities. The accusation is not new. At times a moral tone enters, although this is far truer of Crow and Dabars than of Massy. He finds 'warts and flaws' in the contemporary research university, which means that piecemeal adjustments are possible, although he himself has suggestions for improvement. His main target is teaching—that is to say, student learning, and he finds the current penchant for metric measurements of 'outputs' to be misleading. He is very likely correct.

For Michael M. Crow and William B. Dabars, teaching is also a leading issue. The difference is that Massy speaks about incremental reforms actually in vogue, if not systematically. The other two place the matter of pedagogy into the context of what they title 'the New American University', using their own institution, Arizona State University, as an example of what can be achieved under less than optimal resource circumstances. When scholars and journalists today mention teaching in higher education, they usually suggest a conflict between teaching and research at undergraduate levels, but how that conflict is discussed widely differs. Massy recognizes the historical advantages of the research university and wants to use them more effectively in undergraduate instruction. By contrast, Crow and Dabars take a more negative approach: specialization is their *bête noir*. Their criticism is hardly new, but what is very different is that they are institution builders, arguing their case from scratch, or more accurately, building upon a recovery of the American tradition of the democratic public service university embodied in the vision of the Morrill Land Grant University Act of 1862 and successor legislation.[1] Obviously they believe that institutional reputation-mongering and academic career enhancement interfere with a larger and more selfless understanding of how universities can best contribute to society.

'Society' is a convenient metaphor for discussing the bewildering and rival interests of our contemporary world. It is useful but not always helpful to academic leaders who face real and definable communities in the performance of their academic business. But for the sake of discussion let us admit that a broad correspondence however imperfect between what universities do and what people, interest groups, or governments want has been the rule in university history. (I leave aside the alarming issues of the purge of universities and their destruction by totalitarian and authoritarian governments). The correspondence changes or adjusts when salient historical changes occur. Alterations in class structure, occupational requirements, urban growth, or schooling have an impact but never predictably and not outright. Some changes—those associated with the beginnings of industrialism, for example—did not require university attention. But universities are not passive institutions as some criticisms hold. The role of universities in creating and advancing the digital revolutions that have come rapidly upon us is a case in point. Medical discoveries are another. Science and scholarship entail a strong personal commitment—why do them if not? But to see such commitment as only self-interest is to misstate the many sides of human ambition.

The context for understanding the arguments advanced in all of the books being reviewed is one that is daily reported in the press and endlessly discussed in university halls. The withdrawal of government support from public institutions, at least at levels regarded by academic leaders as essential for the functioning of institutions with a research mission, is one issue. Within regulated and unregulated markets, this has stimulated an unending search for revenue, and some of the solutions, notably installing tuition charges where none existed, have engendered even more difficulties. Tuition fees are allowed in England, and then capped by government, which subsequently relents and grants exceptions. They continue to rise in public and private universities in the United States. Price discrimination is used. Public universities try to attract more high-flying students from out-of-state (wealthy overseas students have been targets in both countries). State governments as in California negotiate with universities to limit the practice of luring undergraduates from other American states. Both public

---

[1] For the record, the vision of public service carried in land grant legislation was however expressed in many different ways, depending upon the type of institution created or supported by the acts. The inquirer is astonished by the variations.

and private universities search for donors or revenue streams to defray tuition costs for students of lower income levels. The American press, barely aware of attempts by institutions to make education more affordable, are more interested in alarming headlines. Politicians explore and install loan and payback schemes. They make promises. Can they be kept? Australian schemes usually come in for praise.

The size of the higher education population today—astronomical when compared to the handful that for centuries attended universities—alerts politicians to educational crises whose resolution does not make academic communities particularly comfortable. Ideological differences within the governing classes regarding public taxation affect budgets. Theories about optimal learning environments, dismay (within and without universities) over the tendency for growth of administrative staff to outpace that of academic staff, charges that large public institutions ignore or downplay undergraduate instruction in order to further careers based on research results have produced an 'accountability' environment new in history and in scale. All advanced democracies are affected. Cost containment is always a challenge because universities must continually upgrade plant and technology or compete for talent, but at least those kinds of issues are clear. Deferred maintenance deals with the first. The second requires a package of inducements often hard to compile. The improvement or reform of undergraduate instruction is far more mysterious because the variables are elusive. Cognitive theories of learning are technical and abstruse and generate disagreements. Criticisms about time-tabling are assuredly legitimate, as are questions about the manner in which credit units are assigned to subjects. Students do not learn at the same rate or in the same way. Late bloomers have to be accounted for, and peer relationships as well as parental upbringing are important but do not readily translate into measurable improvements in learning.

Numbers are always a problem, but theoretically universities can instruct huge numbers. If the lecture halls are full, as they are in many countries, put the undergraduates outside and use loudspeakers, or now, simulcasts and video streaming. But then another issue arises, one that also figures prominently in all discussions about structural and budgetary changes in higher education. Do reforms strengthen or harm quality, the quality of instruction and the quality of student performance? We do not have much in the way of historical analysis of reforms in curricula or teaching formats to guide us. No past baseline exists against which to quantify the many disciplinary innovations that have occurred over time. We are most frequently left with guesses and impressions: the jottings of students remarking upon the nature of instruction, eager younger faculty intent on departing from what the Victorian Walter Bagehot called 'the cake of custom', claims that the re-organization of disciplines will make a difference, or that standardized testing offers a solution. An argument for tutorial instruction as the best means of transmitting ideas and information is to my mind always compelling, but this most expensive of pedagogical structures is not an option in the age of mass-access higher education except in a few select universities.[2]

A recurrent staple of discussions over change within the academy is whether perceived standards of quality are at risk whenever the budgetary constraints and the need to upgrade facilities and compete for talent appear compromised. The 'quality' of instruction both as process and as outcome is itself a relatively recent issue given the long history of the university, traceable to the research revolution of nearly two centuries ago. Despite the difficulty of measuring student performance, it can be said with reasonable certainty that research (begging the question of its character and quantity) raised the standards of inquiry and the evaluation of evidence. This led to institutionalized peer review and the reign of the expert. The incorporation of research findings into undergraduate instruction elevated the demands of the classroom, putting an emphasis on critical thinking rather than on the regurgitation of received knowledge. Pushing these developments forward was the growth of compulsory secondary education. Better-prepared students were now available. The very idea of 'merit' as a factor in higher education, long in coming, was itself an element in assessing standards, a qualitative difference from 'worth'.[3] It is almost the case that quality was secondary in elite education in centuries past—the expensive education of the few—when the mission of universities was more or less limited to the transmission of what was known. 'Sponsored' not 'contest' mobility was the rule, benefitting those students who had birth or connections or who could qualify for 'gentle' status. Where social class position is primary, measurement is irrelevant.

When a research ethic fostering independence of mind entered into undergraduate instruction, transforming ancient ideas about liberal education, some public and, in the U.S., private universities were able to prosper more than others. They attracted the abler students, reducing the need for remediation, while elsewhere the quality issue forcefully emerged as school systems and teacher recruitment and training failed to keep pace with what universities expected. Not all the failings should be attributed to teachers. Possibly more than ever, they now have had to struggle with

---

[2] For the virtues of the tutorial, see David Palfreyman (ed.), *The Oxford Tutorial: 'Thanks, you taught me how to think'* (Oxford, 2008).
[3] Sheldon Rothblatt, *Education's Abiding Moral Dilemma, Merit and Worth in the Cross-Atlantic Democracies, 1800–2006* (Oxford, 2007).

pupil populations diverse in ethnic and class origins. Their discipline and learning abilities are greatly affected by family upbringing and social circumstances. But the quality issue is now universal, or at least it is being discussed as critical. Mass higher education has drawn attention to huge disparities in student achievement and wide variations in schooling. Universities able to attract students with the best measurable records are nevertheless under severe pressure to admit those from social categories regarded as disadvantaged. Assuring that they graduate requires considerable institutional attention, not generally forthcoming in universities with weak staffing ratios. And a further note on why quality has become uppermost in any discussion of reform or higher education policy is that market competition for graduates seeking employment in the digital age continually raises the stakes. Are there curricula or teaching reforms better shaped to current labour markets? But whenever such questions arise—it is not far-fetched to trace them back to the 'useful knowledge' movements of the Enlightenment—the debate between liberal and vocational education flames anew.

In their many works, required reading one should add, Palfreyman and Tapper have been discussing questions of quality, changing academic missions, markets, and 'donnish dominion'—academic self-government—with respect to English universities.[4] Their latest collaboration is enlivened by wit and an ironic detachment pleasing to any follower of Erasmus or Edward Gibbon. They advance a perspective derived from an overview of transformations occurring within the national organization of higher education in Britain (mainly England) in the second half of the twentieth century extending to the present. Since a great part of the story they tell recounts the polemical exchanges occurring between would-be academic policy wonks and policy wonks who would be academics, the opportunities for delightful eavesdropping are manifold. They take some pleasure in identifying paradoxes, contradictions, and absences of mind. Some genuinely funny pasquinades are an added bonus. The tone is refreshing.

Palfreyman and Tapper take the large view. They suggest that a tendency on the part of academic communities to regard all change instituted from the outside as a crisis is a handicap, for what is required is an understanding of the forces that invite intervention and the arena for action that such understanding actually permits. To decry all change from Whitehall, or even more, to regard large bites in the cake of custom as the outcome of a series of elaborate governmental conspiracies, is self-defeating. The demand for higher education requires a satisfactory supply response. So a first step

---

[4] The phrase comes from A.H. Halsey's wide-ranging historical discussion. See the *Decline of Donnish Dominion, the British Academic Profession in the Twentieth Century* (Oxford, 1992).

is to explain how and why government policies respecting higher education shifted from either benign neglect or friendly assistance to one in which the hand of government is omnipresent, although often with a 'lighter touch' (or such is the hope). A second step is to evaluate the outcome with respect to possible academic missions. The authors do not conclude that the situation is as dire as critics fear. Given the constraints on public spending owing to competing social goals, universities have not done as badly as its members believe. But it is the case, as the late sociologists Martin Trow and Burton Clark used to argue, that a greatly differentiated higher education system (Palfreyman and Tapper prefer 'tertiary') will distribute its rewards unevenly, or according to mission, research universities pulling in the lion's share of resources.[5] Furthermore, the Matthew Principle prevails. Those universities that were favoured before change occurred continue to be favoured. Newer institutions that try to emulate the historic leaders without developing a commitment to alternatives—perhaps an 'entrepreneurial style'—face disappointments. Palfreyman and Tapper, for example, do not think that most newer universities have been as innovative as circumstances might allow. The other books under review make one similar point. To die in the last ditch is not the smartest response to market pressures that have long been generating and have long been felt.

The increase in a demand for places in higher education commencing after the Second World War, stimulated by an earlier demand for more free places in secondary education, put added pressure on the British government as the principal funding source. Thus commenced a process of institutional growth that would very quickly challenge Treasury revenues. And not only was cost becoming more of an issue than before. The response of public opinion to taxing must always be a prime element of government policy irrespective of the party in office. Ideological perspectives can enter, but Palfreyman and Tapper downplay such distinctions. Even the great Conservative Margaret Thatcher, they say, was more interested in problem-solving than ideology. Soon the existing funding structures, notably the University Grants Committee, a sub-committee of the Treasury, proved incapable of addressing expansion. Even its shift to another government agency proved inadequate. There followed repeated attempts to construct a panoply of different ways to allocate expenditures: funding agencies, research and teaching assessment exercises, audit and accountability units, quality assurance bodies—all of them burdensome, time-consuming,

---

[5] Cambridge, London, Oxford, and Imperial College are the top four in a listing of European Union funding since 2014. The fear is that Britain's withdrawal from the Union will end the awards. See 'British Scientists Brace for a Brexit Loss: Grant Money', in *The Wall Street Journal* (August 16, 2016).

controversial. The outcomes of such inquiries and deliberations were often dubious, annoying to be sure when contrasted to the days when university decision-making was 'bottom-up', the dominion of the dons.

An enormous and greatly differentiated network of higher education institutions – universities, polytechnics, further education institutions (sometimes included in tertiary, sometimes not) replaced something of a smaller community of similar universities ('select' or 'elite') sharing hallowed features. Theirs was a simpler world of universities, noted for high quality and excellent undergraduates and greatly admired by visiting Americans, whose own differentiated higher education system seemed to allow for functions and activities decidedly *infra dig*. But that was 1960. Decades later, even within the older universities themselves, lay governing councils (akin to but not quite American boards of regents and trustees) began to play a larger role, challenging collegiate decision-making and in some instances, notably Oxford, beaten back by the academic *baroni*.[6]

At one time it might be possible to regard the changes in England (or Britain generally) as an unwanted Americanization of higher education. There were in fact British admirers of America's second-chance culture, the efforts made to improve access through differentiation and student transfer, even an emphasis on the commuter student in order to break the price stranglehold of the residential model. Yet, again as Trow and Clark had argued, the phenomenon of mass and then universal access to higher education was a feature of modern society, an egalitarian if not always clearly operative element, and sooner or later the demographic impact would need to be faced.

Palfreyman and Tapper relate the evolutionary (one could also say mercurial) character of government policies, full of false starts, changes of direction, uncertain readings of demand, and struggles to finance an unfamiliar congress of institutions.[7] An unsettled state of decision-making and constant experiments were understandably confusing. Education depends upon planning and predictability. Sudden changes are always damaging in some way. But 'cumbrous' and 'slow' are the words that the authors employ in reviewing the transformations. After all, we are talking about free societies and respect, even if at times begrudging, for established institutions. Many civil servants and cabinet ministers were graduates

---

[6] Despite the informed pleas of father and son, Anthony and Robert Kenny: *Can Oxford Be Improved? A View from the Dreaming Spires and the Satanic Mills* (Exeter, 2007).

[7] Michael Shattock adopts a similar perspective, suggesting that there are in fact advantages to incremental changes, notably because society itself is always uncongealed. See 'Parallel Worlds: the California Master Plan and the Development of British Higher Education', in Sheldon Rothblatt (ed.), *Clark Kerr's World of Higher Education Reaches the 21ˢᵗ Century, Chapters in a Special History*, (New York/London, 2012), 107–28.

of the select universities and revered them, even if others, of newer provenance, harbored no such loyalty.[8]

What is possibly more interesting to the authors than the general fact of inevitable change are the kinds of structures and models dreamed up to manage outcomes that were always elusive. Sometimes they originate in cultural values all along present, at other times in economic developments largely unforeseen. Often enough, the innovations are puzzling. For example, why should a Quality Assurance Agency be necessary when the high quality of British universities was generally acknowledged? Why not rely on the time-honoured quality control of academic selection, peer review, and external examining (none of which have actually disappeared)? Or perhaps quality is not really the issue, the object in view being a mechanism for distributing resources more 'objectively', indicating some distrust of the decision-making prowess of dons.

The larger answer lay in the expansion phenomenon itself. Would the traditional forms of student assessment prevail when the numbers were now so great, schooling uneven, ethnic and class diversity so varied? Expansion could not be avoided, but expansion meant recruiting undergraduates from family backgrounds without experience of higher education, or from secondary schools without reliable histories of excellence. A differentiated system was perhaps not capable of maintaining uniformly high standards of teaching or research. The American response was almost to avoid the issue entirely, at least publicly, and to forego any attempt to establish uniform standards of achievement. A federal constitution nobbled efforts to create national benchmarks; and where such efforts have been attempted, as in schooling, one result has been continual strife between the individual states and the Capitol. It could be said that American beliefs in the common man or 'worth' made the task of assessing student achievement easier. 'Merit' had always been problematical in any case.[9]

The quality issue dogged the expansion in the numbers of tertiary institutions from the outset. When Lord Robbins and his colleagues in their celebrated report of the 1960s advocated an increase in the numbers of universities, the issues of greater cost and a cheaper product came to the fore. The inherited model was the expensive select research university with favourable staffing rations. Could or should every academic be a researcher, in name if not in fact? Why not place constraints on the system of research? Research assessment exercises could be used to supplement peer review or

---

[8] But this historical association between civil servants and politicians and Oxbridge started to shift as the century advanced. A comparable situation occurred in California when University of California graduates no longer dominated the state legislature.

[9] Joseph F. Kett, *Merit: The History of a Founding Ideal from the American Revolution to the Twenty-first Century* (Ithaca, 2013).

even identify centres of research excellence. Palfreyman and Tapper point out that exceptional departments or units within all universities could have been designated as such centres, but the lobbying efforts of the more select universities, now in the process of creating leagues to promote common missions, kept the focus on them. Thus arose the Russell Group and thus the branding phenomenon, building on prestige and therefore, almost without appreciating the irony of the situation, giving reign to the hated market as a player in the emerging tertiary educational environment.

All societies undergoing similar secular transformations draw on combinations of legacy cultures, ad hoc solutions, and bureaucratic policies meant to solve problems. They often end in creating them.

After the better part of a century, the main result of tinkering, backtracking, and second thoughts was what the authors call the 'rise of the regulated market'. Markets always exist, and they are multiple, but the prevailing sentiment in the dominion of the dons was that universities must control supply through its degree-granting and certifying authority. In turn, supply leads demand in teaching and research, which frees institutions to decide which disciplines and fields of study are on offer irrespective of enrolment. Supply also decides pricing. The logical chain continues: pricing determines student selection and also—it is a common enough assumption by our authors—quality.

In a 'regulated market', government policies affect the supply function of a university, determining which disciplines will receive favoured fiscal treatment, the kinds of research that will be supported, student numbers, and missions. Government establishes the parameters within which negotiations regarding all of these occur. This does not prevent particular institutional flexibilities but limits are established and a certain amount of external steering is in place. A notable example has been the simultaneous imposition and capping of tuition by Westminster. Exceptions are permitted, as in the case of the Oxbridge colleges. But allowing for tuition charges in a system of higher education once almost solely dependent upon the Treasury and local authority student grants (excepting for Oxbridge college endowments) has also led to increases in the student debt load. This in turn has prompted policies and discussions aimed at mitigating what can be an enormous handicap for graduates without means.

In theory, an unregulated market would allow either supply or demand to dominate, alternating in influence according to circumstances, pricing adjustments being an on-going feature of continual bargaining relationships between higher education institutions and student markets, the state standing aside. This is a contentious issue in America as well. The one conclusion that all of the authors under review agree upon is that students are not consumers in the classic market sense. Unlike products purchased under customary market arrangements, students do not have any experience of the education on offer. They lack the knowledge that enables them to distinguish among competing academic programmes and to find, within a complex and confusing differentiated collection of institutions, the one best suited to their needs, ambitions, or careers. In the end, student decisions are made either in response to hearsay, to family traditions, campus marketing efforts, cost, or convenience. Those whose resources allow attendance at prestigious universities are apt to consider higher pricing as the best indication of superior quality. Palfreyman and Tapper do not accept this equation.

Whatever the official position, educational pecking orders exist in every nation, implicit if not explicit. In England, the distinction of institutional superiority has been explicit ever since the founding of the University of London in the 1820s challenged the privileges of Oxford and Cambridge. The solution, based on precedents newly invoked, was to restrict degree-granting authority to institutions legally identified as 'universities' and to bundle the new and increasing numbers of Victorian regional or civic colleges under the aegis of a central examining 'university', London being the model. The twentieth century saw the enlargement of degree-granting opportunities or their near equivalents in a strengthened polytechnic centre, until, in 1992, the distinctions between universities and polytechnics were abolished by parliament. But as the polys had received local authority funding and were expected to be innovative and, *inter alia*, serve as places for part-time attendees, their formal elevation in rank left them clamouring for greater recognition, which meant money. Whitehall had once again introduced changes upon changes that created new problems requiring new solutions. Every such policy shift, obedient to new confusions and uncertainties regarding standard issues like excellence or the cutting and re-allocation of funding because of inflation exacted a heavy price. This led to reconsiderations. It produced attempts to enhance student access (a 'widening participation agenda') with quality control measures, to decide which disciplines contributed most to national strengths: the STEM subjects receiving specific support, the humanistic disciplines dependent upon tuition charges.

Angry debates followed as to whether higher education was a private good to be financed by those seeking it or a public good, subsidized by the state. If a public good, was it then preparation for citizenship, the ancient ideal of what has been called the 'Republican or Atlantic' tradition, or something else more understandably utilitarian, perhaps job preparation which, in one blending of alternatives, could actually be associated with citizenship? After all, a satisfied, employed graduate was likely to be responsible and loyal.

Ever since John Henry Newman's captivating if also confusing sets of lectures on the true and essential meaning of a university, delivered in the middle of the nineteenth century, the Anglophone world has tried to pin down exactly what the 'idea' of a university was, had been, and ought to be. This has produced its own shelf of books purporting to locate the essence of a university education in graduates regarded as *gebildete*. These were distinguished by the quality and sensitivity of their minds. The great strength of Palfreyman and Tapper is to show, through analyses of the voluminous proposals, legislation, white papers, bureaucratic mediations, and accidents of history, how little is left of the 'idea' of a university. A different way to state the outcome is to conclude that the search for an authentic idea of a university is fruitless because the social requirements for supporting the search no longer exist. When universities were few, degree-holders also few, curricula less varied, and the knowledge base still manageable, a search for the beating heart of the university was plausible. But the conceptual issue, say the two authors, is now the 'idea of a university system'. A system is a sociological or policy construct that describes a set of interconnected linkages, one part affected by the other. Over decades, a centralized state has moulded a system. A system was required because multiple demands had to be distributed and syncopated in some operative way. A wholly open market system was too unsteady, lacking clear direction. Hence the system was regulated. After all, the state in Britain had become an active participant.

True, the linkages binding the system together were continually threatening to break. But undergraduates and postgraduates, business, global enterprises, service sectors dependent upon educated graduates, and the European Union (before the Brexit vote of 2016) interfered with what remained of donnish dominion. But suppose there was true market competition, 'unfettered', and no system of linkages existed. What would the central decision-makers expect? They would expect far more disparities between winners and losers, between haves and have-nots, than egalitarian beliefs could endure. In short, the outcome might well be like America, with a few exceptions. The solution, more stumbled upon than at first imagined say the authors, was to push institutions closer to market forces while mitigating the more disastrous consequences of unmanaged market rivalries. Interestingly, because Palfreyman and Tapper have provided a highly useful idea, the State of California Master Plan for Higher Education of 1960 can also be said to rest upon the conception of a regulated market. While central state government interference was restrained—the Master Plan allowed California's colleges and universities to sort out working patterns of cooperation—the full effects of open market competition were nonetheless mitigated. Three public systems were defined by separate if occasionally overlapping missions, and budgets assigned on that basis. Since missions were constrained, markets were segmented by price. The principal link was student transfer, which had to be guaranteed. The Plan was supported by statutory (rather than constitutional) law so that it could be more easily amended.

In the more comprehensive national regulated market system emerging in England, mission differentiation (or segmentation) is decided by the participating institutions employing whatever market clout they can muster. The present situation places much more responsibility for pursuing successful marketing strategies on campus leadership hierarchies or 'senior management teams', or entrepreneurially-minded academics. Warwick is a prime example.[10] One objection by dons to the emergence of strong leaders is that collective decision-making—'dominion'—appears weakened. But academic collegiality, government by committee or by senates, lacks the immediacy and the capacity to plan that economic uncertainties require. This at least is a prevailing argument.

The regulated market, say Palfreyman and Tapper, is in fact a compromise, an attempt to soften the punishments that markets can inflict or, conversely, to enhance innovation and experiment. Has that happened? Yes, in some instances, but the authors think that opportunities have been lost, especially with regard to the reform of undergraduate teaching or the provision of lower-cost vocational instruction. A regulated market is certainly a form of top-down control over the main elements of a higher education system, but it is hardly crippling. For it to work properly, all sectors of the academic community must co-operate. The authors even speculate that younger generations of academics might approve of operating within a regulated market, preferring it to 'an underfunded Cinderella public sector fate (as could await Scotland's universities, and probably also those in Wales)' (115). Clark Kerr, the principal architect of the California Master Plan, spoke of the Plan as a 'framework' and not a finished outcome. A regulated market is precisely a framework within which actors have considerable latitude, even a chance at some 'gaming' of the system. But as market failures are still possible, what will become of the 'Coketown University MBA'? Will the state then step in, the authors wonder?

The story being told here is carried along by a close review of the history of policy shifts and changes. It is accompanied by a healthy scepticism about the wisdom of policymakers and their ability to steer contemporary higher education systems. Research and teaching outcomes can never be wholly predicted whatever agencies are established to monitor the process.

---

[10] As explained by Burton R. Clark, *Creating Entrepreneurial Universities, Organizational Pathways of Transformation* (Kidlington, Oxford, 1998).

The tradeoffs between mass access and quality will continue to be elusive. Possibly all parties will gain a better understanding of how markets actually work, avoiding simple-minded conclusions and platitudes about efficiency gains. The central planners might also finally understand that in the process of encouraging universities to be more market-oriented, central control is accordingly weakened. But the dons are also not spared, those in particular who forget that we are in the twenty-first century. Finally, the dons will not have dominion of a former type, although lesser fiefdoms will survive.

An educated person is neither a product nor a consumer. How simple the task of education would be if that were accurate. And yet the authors close their comprehensive analysis by wondering whether in fact students of the future will become informed actors in any kind of market economy with respect to their educational choices. Will they force universities to seriously reconsider their pricing mechanisms and teaching formats?

Other conclusions? The regulatory market model receives the approval of the authors because it has proven reasonably successful in broadening and accommodating the plural demands of contemporary society. It is a fact achieved after much bumbling, and there is something to be said in history for bumbling. The very nature of the Britannic state, its mixture of centre and periphery in decision-making, made continual policy revisions virtually inevitable. Politicians go in and out of office, and incoming ministers have different ideas as to how to address the issue of student demand for higher education, the ultimate origin of both funding and quality issues.

Bumbling, its trial and error mode of proceeding, made possible recognition of an emerging complex of interactions between the state, quasi-state agencies, markets, universities, and innumerable stakeholders that could in a sense be formalized with a series of apt policies. An actual 'tertiary system' emerged with all the strengths and the weaknesses of linkages.[11]

A regulated market permitted creative responses, even while loyalty to older arrangements remained. But eventually the dons could no longer threaten to die in the last ditch in defence of the privileges of an ancient estate. Within a regulated market, they were cajoled with fee-granting powers, encouraged to seek new sponsors and join the search for investments to an extent unforeseen. Science parks and other developments were

---

[11] For over thirty years, Henry Eztkowitz, who has taught in the United States and in Britain, has been calling attention to what he calls the 'triple helix' relationships between universities, governments, and industry. An open access, peer-reviewed journal is now offered by Springer under that name. Eztkowitz's work is mentioned often and relied upon in the Crow and Dabars book discussed in this review.

undertaken, and even mergers occurred.[12] The dons and their universities were allowed to establish new kinds of lobby groups, associations to represent the segments of an openly partitioned higher education community.

In 1960 almost none of this could have been imagined even though at the time of Robbins it was thought a revolution was occurring. How little anyone knew. Glossy brochures have since poured forth extolling the virtues of particular institutions, listing achievements, reporting national and global rankings, stirring up alumni support, touting contributions to public and private good. How American it seems, with all the ambivalence that such a reference conjures up in particular quarters. The universities were certainly often bludgeoned into looking beyond college walls to grasp the greater national picture.

Market competition can be deplored—in truth, there is much to be deplored about the shouting and huckstering that have come forth in a winner-take-all environment. But there are certainly established gains. In place of a once settled position in the firmament of government approval, enjoying the admiration of the Great and the Good, the dons are no longer passive. Their educational world is in flux. Henceforth it will always be in flux. (An historian makes such predictions with fear and trembling.) Therefore the dons have had to reposition themselves, not once but many times, reconstructing the legitimacy and status once assumed as natural. As an added element, the authors maintain that the regulatory framework can and probably will include the private purveyors of higher education. As such, restrained from the outset, for-profit on-line education promoters can be warned against the shenanigans and misuse of taxpayer student loan money notoriously besetting the American providers of unfulfilled market promises.[13]

Palfreyman and Tapper use the word 'reshaping' to describe the evolutionary half century leading to the regulated market. William F. Massy

---

[12] The University of Cambridge Alumni Magazine, *Cam*, Issue 78 (Easter 2016) describes an astonishing array of research start-ups and spin-offs, huge amounts of construction, vast new areas of economic development, and the selection of the city by global firms such as AstraZeneca eager to locate themselves near cutting-edge intellectual activity. This is a Cambridge virtually unknown a half century ago.

[13] Another particular sin of the for-profits is contributing to the manufacture of an academic proletariat. According to a very recent discussion, adjuncts comprise just over 50% of academics in America, a huge increase from the 25% or so in 1970. Insofar as the total numbers of academic positions has increased twofold in the same period, the actual numbers of adjuncts are staggering. PhD over-production in particular fields provides a supply of academics in need of work. English literature and history are particularly affected. See Phillip W. Magness, 'For-Profit Universities and the Roots of Adjunctification in US Higher Education', in *Liberal Education* (Association of American Colleges and Universities), 102 (Spring 2016), 50–9.

from Stanford University, an engineer by training who also describes himself as a micro-economist and management scientist, adopts the word 'reengineering'. The first word (in context) points to an outcome occurring slowly over time, one that often outwitted those in high places eager to steer it. The second is a more instrumental word and is aligned to advocacy. It is not the actual process of change that concerns Massy, not the granular details of policy-mongering and second-guessing that befuddled the movement of higher to tertiary education in England. Instead, backed by tables, graphs, and lengthy discussions of actual innovations and educational experiments, he lays out a set of necessary changes that ought to be incorporated into the current higher education world of the United States. He talks about 'warts and flaws'. His account assumes a history, the history that led to the dominant higher education institution of modern society that he calls the 'traditional university'. However, his object is not to utterly transform that institution but to challenge particular core assumptions. He wants to identify its strengths and preserve it against the dangers of an aroused public opinion and, egged on by that, politicians inclined to meddle. We are consequently in the same contemporary world as Britain, a world of demographic pressure, egalitarian thrusts, rising tuition charges, competing interests, inputs and outputs, value-added education, and the tensions between liberal and practical curricula that characterize so much of the recent history of higher education.

And yet the profound difference between the political settlement of Britain and the United States rules out a national conception of a regulated market, although, as earlier indicated, individual states like California have approached that outcome. The greatest political difference between the two nations (besides the doctrine of the separation of powers) is America's federal system, a constitutional arrangement for distributing governmental responsibilities that has remained a source of anger and conflict from the very moment of its conception. While the provision for education is the responsibility of the states, Washington has contributed greatly to the making of the 'traditional university' by supplying the bulk of the research funding without which that institution as Massy views it would not really exist. Research funds and other centrally disseminated funds are awarded through research councils as in Britain. Other support derives from government departments and is competitively awarded to individual researchers. Rules and guidelines regarding the hiring of research personnel, opportunity funds, and human subjects research indicate that government's hand is always present. As in England, a small number of research universities dominate the competition.

Massy does not think that such government regulations as exist or even the forces of market competition of which Americans have long boasted have succeeded or will succeed in meeting the challenges of a 'new disruptive technology' and 'new postsecondary education models'. Or to refer back to Palfreyman and Tapper, no national regulated market exists in the United States to push universities, however gently, towards possible innovations. Massy does not advocate such an outcome, impossible in any case. Like everyone else, he mentions markets, and he means what most observers mean: pricing, quality, and campus efficiency (productivity). He too objects to those who use market analogies to typify education as a commodity and students as consumers. 'Business models' and 'industrial production' viewpoints ignore the importance of scholarship as a factor in education. The traditional university is humanistic in being personal, at least in its inheritance if not with respect to every student. Commuting students do not get the fullest exposure to a university's environment, but they do get some, he says. As commuters form the vast bulk of tertiary students in the United States, the benefits of residence are restricted to a minority. Massy does not say this.

Massy makes a strong distinction between the for-profit sector and the traditional university. The first aims at creating a brand. Universities have a mission. For-profits divert their subsidies to shareholders. The traditional university must retain its subsidies and reinvest them. Furthermore, says Massy, despite outside criticisms of the value-added performance of universities, market discipline in itself insufficiently measures educational quality because profit is the goal. And, as anyone who lives and breathes in a university environment understands, many academic disciplines do not attract the numbers that a strict accounting regards as a break-even point. But these disciplines have importance for the transmission of culture. So the issue for the traditional university is how to strengthen missions, maintain quality, and keep what the Germans of the nineteenth century called the unity of teaching and research, while bearing in mind that most of the traditional universities (those without a substantial endowment base, for example) are under revenue burdens bound to get worse.

Utilizing new kinds of mathematical measurements and the reported results of cognitive learning theories, Massy concentrates on the individual campus, repeating en route that no single template for disposing of warts and flaws exists. He lists five of the dominant ones: academic individualism based on the specialty (but a way forward lies in the science model of teams and, as at MIT, modular courses); too little oversight of individual teaching by deans and provosts, creating problems in the apportionment of time between teaching and research;[14] inexperience in matching quality to cost in teaching (apart for those in the business of obtaining external grants); inadequate understanding of how to measure student engagement as opposed to learning outcomes—Massy has an interesting set of pages on this topic; and, surprisingly, a tendency to cater to student markets in some respects (e.g., using metrics such as time to degree or graduation rates or selectivity—'surrogates' for quality measurement). Such data, he maintains, are not helpful—this ought to be openly acknowledged—and do not, in any case, truly grasp the actual nature of the learning experience. Reliance on national and global rankings to indicate quality is also a flaw. As such rankings are generally based on research recognition, they mean little with respect to undergraduate instruction, if more so regarding postgraduate degrees. And Massy, as others, also notes how universities send the wrong market signals to would-be students, luring them by the promise of 'gourmet food and climbing walls'. One might add to the list the enormous expense of maintaining huge athletic facilities, which do not in any way benefit all students equally. Once again we encounter the view that if price assumes quality, institutions have an excuse for raising fees. (Where discontents may arise, a colleague of mine once said, 'we don't give refunds'.)

Reforms need to be undertaken, Massy continues, because public trust has eroded. Parents and students wonder whether universities have provided value. Refreshingly, with regard to the tiresome argument that a research mission leads to the neglect of undergraduates, Massy is on the side of the professoriate. They are conscientious about teaching, he says—pointing to what he enumerates as many workable learning strategies—but they are far too cautious in meeting the outside educational challenges.

This is a thoughtful book by an author who has a formidable range of experience with different formats for teaching. He is acquainted with experiments in cognitive learning and pilot programmes around the nation. He understands that the best reforms are those that avoid a thunderous

---

[14] The unit-credit system of measuring 'work loads' in courses is certainly haphazard. Massy does mention other kinds of constraints on teaching, such as calendars, class schedules, and 'busy professors'. Does this latter reference to impediments to achieving better synergies between teaching and research include the amount of faculty time in research universities devoted to committee work in departments, colleges, senates, consulting, service in professional associations, the planning for academic meetings, the award of scholarships and fellowships, supervision of special programmes, or the administration of organized research units? These tasks are multiplied in the case of multi-campus systems that have an overarching Senate. Any practical approach to addressing the flaws comes up against a barrier of commitments that go well beyond any discussion about how to adjust teaching and research.

attempt to re-do centuries of development but must proceed step-by-step, institution by institution, allowing best practice to emerge. He speaks about 'coalitions of the willing' and, like others who advocate reforms, about the necessity for top-down guidance within institutions. Leadership is the ability to provide a vision. This is often an alternative vision based on the shifting grounds of historical circumstances. Academic leaders can then persuade able colleagues to join in the endeavour, and they reject— let us give special credit to Massy on this point—the clichés about markets and higher education that inform so much journalistic writing about universities. His arguments are tough, intricate, and demanding.

Not all of us will agree that the flaws and warts are as detrimental as he says. Furthermore, his focus on the 'traditional university' or at another place called 'four-year, non-profit institutions', overlooks the importance of other kinds of higher education colleges in a greatly differentiated national system where pricing mechanisms work differently. One of their functions, as sociologists of higher education once explained, was to deflect attention away from envy of the more select sector by contributing mightily to an educational goal of opportunity. Has that worthy objective failed? Massy's analysis does not provide an historical context for the flaws and warts that he identifies. Why were they once neither flaws nor warts? Or were they functional at some other level or possessed of meaning that the present fails to recognize? That is the problem that Samuel Taylor Coleridge set out to discover when he challenged the utilitarian philosophers of his day. But such is not Massy's intention, and he is to be congratulated for thinking so empirically and broadly about how to preserve the deepest benefits of a special type of institution. The technical parts of his discussion are available in extensive appendices.

Reshaping, reengineering, and now, as the final book in this review appears, the instrumental word shifts to 'designing'. *Designing the New American University* has been widely praised, even as a follow up to Clark Kerr's famous Godkin Lectures that made 'multiversity' a synonym of the present-day university. Michael Crow is president of Arizona State University, which reached full-blown research recognition in 1994. William Dabars is a research professor at the same university. They take on the usual suspects, and we find the same targets as in Massy or that Whitehall denizens found in Britain, although their case is stated with passion. They advocate a more revolutionary overhaul of the university, while recognizing that no single template exists. Nevertheless, they put forward a strenuous defence of their own, which engenders a less favourable view of other institutions.

Once again the charge is made that universities, public ones in particular, are more interested in abstract (a 'comfort zone') than in useful knowledge and problem-solving. Just understanding nature is not enough. The emphasis should be on 'an epistemology of knowing' rather than on an 'epistemology of possession'. The service function that formed a core of the Morrill Land Grant Act and was given special form by the California Master Plan needs to be re-awakened and strengthened. A 'true public university' requires a 'broader social embeddedness'. The writers excoriate the 'Generic Public University', with its 'Harvardization' or Berkeley envy, and repeatedly attack 'entrenchment in obsolete institutional design, lack of scalability, and residual elitism'. Chinese universities are building from scratch, they warn, and will leave American ones behind. 'We are losing our adaptive capacities' (19, 25, 26, 223). And like all current critics who have lived through the many debates and legal challenges regarding affirmative action, *de facto* quota admissions, and selectivity, they argue that generic universities have zealously pursued prestige. Consequently they have failed to broaden their demographic intake. They have refused to recognize that talent is more widely available and takes unconventional forms. Many more are qualified for a superior education than current selection practices suggest. Admissions officers rely overmuch on standard admissions testing (which, indeed, appears to be losing loyalty.)

The authors deplore course specialism and point to the other existing models as remedies—more inter-, multi-, pluri-, cross-disciplinary activity, harder to assess under peer review models it is true than the results of individual scholarship. But teamwork is a necessity: the focus should be on community and the welfare of the whole more than on the search for fame and fortune. Picking up on a biological theme, the authors assert that 'rational self-interest' achieved through competition is an evolutionary trait, a necessary requirement for self-preservation. However, social systems have grown more complex, global problems have magnified, and the limitations of individual actions are ever more obvious. This critique of liberal individualism is commonplace, but in all fairness rational choice theories are certainly widely expressed and have political followings.

But to continue: 'Our only option is to accept the inevitability and the limitations of individual rationality and to take it into account in formulating public policy and collective action' (230). Departing from this sober appraisal, the language of the authors becomes even loftier and more judgmental, broadening into an indictment of the history of western thought itself, at least in certain particulars. They draw into that indictment a collection of moral accusations whose sources readers of cultural and political history can instantly identify. 'Our science remains culturally biased and isolated. Western science is derivative of a philosophical model of domination and the manipulation of nature, as opposed to the acceptance of natural systems and dynamics'. There are more harsh words for market economics from the perspective of competitive individualism in the pursuit of wealth: 'An ironic effect of technology-created wealth is the growth of an affluent class that prizes individualism over civic engagement and that feels insulated from the need to understand and confront the complex-technology related issues' (232). Fortunately for the sake of a more rounded view, policymakers and politicians come in for a measure of censure for being scientifically illiterate. Given that opening, more could certainly be said about political partisanship where solving problems has become a matter of ideological principle rather than of analysis or action. Something could also be said about how ideology itself has invaded the university, not only with respect to academic missions but providing openings to all kinds of unpleasant advocacy and misuse of freedom of speech and inquiry. How about these as warts and flaws?

The list of deficiencies offered by Crow and Dabar is not new, if provided with greater heat than Massy's more measured catalogue of contemporary errors. Chapter Six of *Designing the New American University* is particularly stinging in its critique of the research university's attachment to economic individualism. The account is a far cry from the observer-participant, wry but forgiving voice of Palfreyman and Tapper. In place of respect for the anfractuosities of history, we have blame. Kerr had his reservations about the multiversity, but he understood it as a necessary outcome or 'artifact' of history, to be understood rather than deplored. A well-known philosophical conundrum in historical thinking, or meta-historical work, probably less debated today, is whether to attribute flaws, warts, and uncomfortable outcomes to deliberate human agency or simply to acknowledge the existence of impersonal forces moving through time. The tone of a discussion always reflects the dilemma, more charged when personal involvement enters, more dispassionate as the historian moves away from accusation towards understanding.[15]

The contemporary university is under attack from all sides, from those who castigate donnish reluctance to accept the marketplace except on the supply side, obedient to guild traditions of restricting demand to gain pricing advantages ('rent' in economic terms), to those who find it too committed. Or perhaps it is more accurate to say that the criticism refers to a professorial acceptance of the use of the market as an arena for negotiating career gains or employing exit strategies to secure personal recognition regarded as superior to collegial or common institutional values.

A revolutionary call for action, especially one that stresses the importance of problems that ought to be addressed by systematic and collective academic behaviour, might be interesting reading but not much more

---

[15] With the caveat that some historical events are so horrific that an 'objective' reckoning is not only pointless but immoral.

without specific corrective examples. And here Crow and Dabars can point to a great achievement. It is the redesign or as they say 'design' of a state university once of lower standing as conventionally appraised but now the recipient of national attention, praise, and a collection of awards and honours that are the staple of the kind of branding agenda that would seem out of sorts with the grander educational goals forming the substance of the book. The collection includes a listing of 'productivity' figures' and a dizzying array of supporting statistics. Unflatteringly, this can be regarded as a way of seeking legitimacy. However, an appeal is also being made to the view that a sense of the importance of the public good now lost or attenuated is not incompatible with the claims to excellence routinely identified with elite segments of higher education.

Establishing a 'New American University', the leadership of Arizona State rejected an incremental approach. Instead, they followed what they attributed to Chinese universities by building from scratch. Traditional aims of the public research university or Morrill Act model were however retained. Discovery, the advancement and dissemination of knowledge, and social engagement remained catchwords. Especially important—and it was a basic cornerstone of the California Master Plan—was inclusion. Every public university today has this in mind, and it is part and parcel of the British 'widening participation agenda'. Nevertheless, Arizona State made attracting students from all segments of society an outstanding priority, a particularly challenging task in a state with a large, low-income Latino population. The California Master Plan incorporated this goal. But Arizona State relies less on student transfer between differentiated segments. The University brings students of varied abilities into a framework that, according to the authors, is 'student-centric'. The employment of on-line instruction is one means of increasing numbers. Close to 10,000 undergraduates are enrolled in fully on-line instruction, along with an additional 3500 postgraduate students. The same faculty are used in both on-line and classroom instruction, which can be interpreted as a worthy effort to avoid contributing to the further creation of an academic proletariat composed of untenured part-time lecturers. Digital technology is also used for personalized or customized learning and advising. Many of the programmes are interactive, or interdisciplinary, although conventional disciplinary departments exist. The university is divided into four differentiated campuses led by deans and directors, according second-level administrators a prominent role in all educational undertakings. These efforts, strategies, and structures are undertaken to provide lower-cost instruction in an era of lessened political support, while, so the authors maintain, providing the personal and tailored student experiences ordinarily missing from large state-assisted universities.

The final chapter races to a conclusion with a bewildering account of educational opportunities available at Arizona State University, including collaboration with overseas institutions. Unfortunately, intemperate and gratuitous remarks about the inherited research culture of the 'generic public university' continually intrude with phrases such as the 'barbarism of specialization' or 'rigid social constructs' (244, 307). Any sensible historical overview of how knowledge grows, accumulates, divides, and then sub-divides and why inquiry inevitably focuses on small points awaiting synthesis suggests a wholly different understanding of knowledge extension. Burton Clark has re-explained how disciplinary specialisms eventually move laterally into adjacent fields of inquiry, or, even help create adjacent fields of inquiry.[16] Some learned men and women do it better than others, but that is true of any professional or intellectual activity. It is sounder to simply recognize this historical process and to admit that detailed investigation is a basic part of knowledge acquisition. Problem-solving simply cannot take place in the absence of methods and ideas that promote new ways of understanding social or natural phenomena. How that desirable outcome is to be reconciled with pedagogical views of the importance of self-discovery, personal growth, general culture, or citizenship has been an on-going feature of the history of what is to be learned at university. In this respect, shorn of their strident elements, the thoughts of Crow and Dabars are very welcome.

But because the transfer of learning and thinking skills from one person to another is so personal and individuated, it remains an open question whether one format or one teaching structure or one kind of technology is superior to others. The New American University, to be fair, may be addressing these matters more broadly by involving the whole of the faculty, but it is also the case that any other kind of university contains a multitude of pedagogical approaches. Massy provides many examples of experimentation across the United States. Research and specialism are hardly the enemy of good teaching.

In response to criticism that disinterested research has been downplayed at Arizona State University, the authors answer that any such loss is outweighed by the institution's devotion to the resolution of social problems (268). Perhaps, but the issue need not be so polarized. It can and should

---

[16] 'The Problem of Complexity in Modern Higher Education', in Sheldon Rothblatt & Björn Wittrock (eds), *The European and American University since 1800, Historical and Sociological Essays* (Cambridge, 1993). See especially the remarks commencing on page 275: 'modern disciplines are inherently imperialistic. Anthropologists who used to hanker after lost tribes now turn back on their advanced societies to pursue domains as they please—the ethnography of the classroom, or the hospital, or the business firm…You cannot keep economists out of anything'.

be argued that the lines between pure or basic and applied research have always been fuzzy, or to use the word of some of the authors, 'abstract' knowledge cannot always be separated from its applied correlates.

An outsider can certainly admire how the leaders of the New American University took bold steps to meet the manifold challenges of demography, public service, an under-prepared student population, and weak political support. Racing against time, Arizona State University rose to prominence and recognition in many of the indicators used in national and global rankings. But without direct personal experience of the comprehensive reforms undertaken in Arizona, it is difficult to provide an overall assessment of the pedagogical benefits of digital technologies so strongly argued. Yet as all of the books being reviewed establish beyond doubt, we have reached an historical moment when every university in a genuinely democratic nation is undergoing rapid or slow alterations in how numbers can be accommodated and educated for successful lives. The impetus for change is internal as well as external. It does appear correct to imagine that if the academic community does not itself give continual thought to how the twin challenges of access and quality are to be balanced, others will do it for them, either within the matrix of a regulated market, or by the uninformed actions of a political class pushed to extremes by public anxiety, while a predatory for-profit sector waits in the wings.

The New American University may have been designed from scratch, but as is clear from the accounting, imports from all areas of the history of the university as a special kind of institution were used, sifted, and recombined. Hence Arizona State University is, for all of its substantial innovations, also a latter-day version of the American multiversity. In truth, the authors indicate as much. The institutes, spin-offs, incubator projects, and other non-departmental aspects of the New American University are part and parcel of the multiversity. The multiversity's commitment to problem-solving at all levels is well established. Before he died, Kerr even began to think that the multiversity was too 'multi'. Possibly the New American University has stressed these features to a greater extent, or because its designers deliberately set forth in a race against time, the outcome was achieved with a particular kind of remarkable intensity.

Crow and Dabars often allude to the importance of Oxbridge and Berlin in the making of the American university. Scotland, which gave so much to the making of the American university, is oddly entirely omitted, a common enough error.[17] The authors close their book with inspirational

---

[17] R.D. Anderson's writing on Oxford and Cambridge is listed, but not his highly informative book on the history of Scottish education: *Educational Opportunity in Victorian Scotland, Schools and Universities* (Oxford, 1983).

educational passages from Thomas Jefferson's Rockfish Gap Report of 1818, probably the most brilliant reciting of the importance of education in a free society that Americans have ever known. But we ought also to remember that the teacher who influenced him most at the College of William & Mary was a natural philosopher and mathematician from Scotland named William Small. Educated at Aberdeen University, he carried the astonishing culture of the Scottish Enlightenment to the distant plantations of Virginia. Economic individualism was part of it—Adam Smith and Co.—and so was that 'philosophical model of domination and the manipulation of nature'.

University of California, Berkeley

Andrew Reeves, *Religious Education in Thirteenth-Century England: The Creed and Articles of Faith* (Leiden: Brill, 2015), 218pp. ISBN: 9789004294431

Virginia Davis

This monograph examines how English laypeople and the many parish clergy who had had only rudimentary education learned the basic doctrines of the Christian religions as expressed in the Apostles Creed and the Articles of Faith in the thirteenth century. In a well-informed and detailed work Reeves explores the nature and extent of the transmission of the theological learning developed in the Schools, particularly of Paris, to local parish priests and to their parishioners in the thirteenth century. The focus is on the period between the Fourth Lateran Council of 1215, whose programme designed to strengthen the faith of the laity was a landmark in the development of pastoral care, and 1281, when Archbishop Pecham's constitution, *Ignorantia sacerdotum*, bemoaned priestly ignorance and addressed the issue of the education of the faithful by the clergy in a manner which was to underpin most English catechetical programmes for the remainder of the middle ages. A key focus of the book is on the importance of making sure that Christian laypeople knew doctrine, although the author also recognizes that thirteenth-century pastoral care placed great emphasis on sin and its remedies.

Chapter 1 discuss the theological and historical background in the period leading up to 1215, in particular exploring the systematization of theology and canon law in the Schools of Paris. This systematization was seen as important to aid the salvation of laypeople. Theologians were conscious of the necessity of the cognitive aspect of faith; men and women needed to understand what they had learnt, and they sought to ensure that this was the case. Theologians and canonists formulated the notion that the Christian faith could be reduced to a set of fundamental principles in which the whole of the faith was contained, which came to be referred to by contemporaries as the Articles of Faith. A translation of the Apostles' Creed and translations of the Articles of Faith as articulated by three churchmen and theologians, Richard of Wetheringsett, and Robert Grosseteste in *Templum Dei*, and John Pecham in *Ignorantia sacerdotum* is provided in the appendix.

This in-depth discussion of the theological background is followed by a wide-ranging discussion of how the English episcopate sought to implement the pastoral programme handed down from the Fourth Lateran Council, both to a body of parish clergy, who had little education apart from an apprenticeship in carrying out the sacraments, and no knowledge of the sophisticated theological discussions which underpinned their faith, and to the wider body of laity across England. Close reading of synodal statutes, episcopal injunctions, and clerical treatises has enabled the author to identify in detail the procedures designed for the religious education of clergy and laity with an emphasis on the importance of archdeacons and rural deans in this process of dissemination and priestly education. He identifies a four-tiered system of educating the laity. The first step was for children to be educated in the Creed and Articles of Faith by their parents; the second was for priests themselves to teach the children of their parish; the third would have been instruction from the pulpit while the fourth was remedial instruction, usually in confession.

Chapters 3 and 4 focus on the importance of preaching, firstly by parish priests and canons regular, focusing in particular on Richard of Wetheringsett's *Que bene praesunt*, intended to be an accessible text for priests outlining the fundamental principles of the Christian faith to their flocks. Pastoral care in the thirteenth century was also fundamentally changed by the arrival of the mendicant orders who performed an important role as teachers and preachers of Christian doctrine. Reeves examines the interaction between the Franciscan John of La Rochelle's treatise on the Articles of Faith and his model sermons, and does likewise for the Dominican William Peraldus' discussion of faith in his *summa* on the Virtues and Vices to his model sermons. The works of both of these continental authors enjoyed a wide-ranging circulation in thirteenth-century England.

The final two chapters cover areas on which there has been much recent scholarly attention on which Reeves draws to explore his key themes. Chapter 5 covers vernacular religious literature, arguing that Anglo-Norman religious works allowed the less learned clergy to learn the fundamentals of the Christian religion to educate their lay flocks, while amongst the ranks of pious lay aristocrats there was a strong demand for religious instruction evidenced in book ownership and the commissioning of religious miscellanies. The final, shorter chapter provides an overview of how laypeople would have had the doctrines they had learnt verbally reinforced by their experiences of the liturgical ceremonies and the art to be seen in parish churches and mendicant convents.

The strength of this monograph lies in the fact that the author, who is very well grounded in the theological literature of the twelfth and thirteenth century, uses his extensive knowledge to tackle a clearly defined practical question, namely how did the church ensure that laymen and women in the thirteenth century acquired at least a basic understanding of the doctrines of the Christian religion as exemplified in the Creed and Articles of Faith? This is a question which lies at the heart of our understanding of the role of religion in everyday life. Its conclusions, that the English layperson would have had a good access to the doctrines proclaimed by the church, are well grounded in the wide range of evidence presented in this book. Reeves builds effectively upon the work in particular of C.R. Cheney and of Joseph Goering to make an original and valuable contribution to our understanding of the English church in the thirteenth century. His detailed discussion of the means whereby the sophisticated theological debates to be found in the twelfth- and early thirteenth-century Schools was transmitted to the laity is one which is certainly of interest to historians of universities. Overall the monograph is a genuinely valuable contribution to our understanding of how the tenets which lay at the heart of Christian doctrine in the thirteenth century were transmitted to the laity and the importance which ecclesiastical leaders accorded to this process.

Virginia Davis
Queen Mary University of London

F. Donald Logan, *University Education of the Parochial Clergy in Medieval England: The Lincoln Diocese, c.1300–c.1350* (Toronto: Pontifical Institute of Medieval Studies, 2014), xiv + 197 pp., 6 tables. ISBN: 9780888441881

Virginia Davis

The 1298 publication of Pope Boniface VIII's constitution *cum ex eo* marked a landmark in the provisions of university education for the parish clergy, opening the way for parish rectors who had not yet been ordained as priests to absent themselves from their parishes for up to seven years to attend university. This constitution was the culmination of a long period during which popes, councils, and bishops had sought to tackle the problem of uneducated parish priests. Yet while its promulgation has been praised as a significant step forward for the provision of an educated parochial clergy, relatively little attention has been paid to how this constitution was implemented across Europe. This new study by Donald Logan tackles this question with a focus on the diocese of Lincoln, the largest in England with nearly two thousand parishes. The survival of an extensive run of episcopal registers for the diocese has allowed an in-depth examination of *cum ex eo* in action. Logan's research explores not a single process but a dual one; in addition to the *cum ex eo* procedure there was a parallel procedure which allowed a considerable number of parochial rectors who were already priests to attend university. Logan's work emphasizes the distinction—not hitherto spelt out in such detail—between *cum ex eo* dispensations and *licencia studendi*. The licences were based on the papal decretal *Relatum est nobis* (c.1180) which allowed bishops to exempt parish priests from residence in their parishes for the purpose of study or some other reason.

Together the dispensations and licences contributed significantly to the enhancement of clerical education in fourteenth century England and, as Logan suggests, may have contributed to a substantial increase in the numbers of students at university in the first half of the fourteenth century.

Logan begins by discussing canon law and its requirements for clerical learning, exploring the general educational requirements required for ordination and what the records of the diocese of Lincoln reveal relating to the examination of candidates for ordination and institution to benefices. The thirteenth-century evidence reveals that bishops tested candidates and had some expectations as to the required basic level of learning. The central chapters of Logan's study focus on a detailed examination of the practice of issuing both types of permission to be absent from a parish within the diocese of Lincoln, showing that the procedure of dispensation *cum ex eo* became firmly established in the twenty years after its promulgation, especially during the episcopate of John Dalderby (1300–20). The following twenty years—the episcopate of bishop Burghersh (1320–40) saw a step change in the granting of permission to study at university to parish rectors. Burghersh continued to issue *cum ex eo* dispensations to non-priest rectors but he vastly expanded the number of licences to study being issued to rectors already in priestly orders. His successors in the 1340s continued these practices.

Logan's study is based on a meticulous examination of the evidence of the episcopal registers which has allowed him to chart the trends towards more extensive opportunities for parochial incumbents to attend university. His work goes far beyond this however, exploring issues such as how the financial arrangements for the rectors worked, where the absentees studied, and their preferred subjects. This volume sheds light on the history of the University of Oxford, where over ninety per cent of the clergy from the diocese attended whether via licence or dispensation. Logan's sampling of registers of other dioceses and of recent calendars suggests that the pattern he has identified for the diocese of Lincoln is likely to be a wider English phenomenon.

The very extensive appendix (89–172), consisting of a register of the rectors of Lincoln diocese 1300–c.1350, is an important prosopographical tool in its own right. The appendix is arranged alphabetically by candidate's name with the details of where he was to study and the degree (if mentioned), length of time, and dates. Of the over 1200 names, only about five per cent are also recorded in A. B. Emden's magisterial registers suggesting—as Logan does (80) that there may have been a substantial increase in the number of students at the university in the first half of the fourteenth century.

This volume makes a significant contribution to our understanding both of clerical education and of the importance of the experience of university for the education of the fourteenth-century clergy. It is clear that many of the men who attended university in this period with either sort of licence already had practical experience of parochial ministry within the parish and would have brought this life experience to the world of the English university.

Queen Mary University of London

Olga Weijers, *A Scholar's Paradise. Teaching and Debating in Medieval Paris* (Turnhout: Brepols, 2015), 257 pp. ISBN: 9782503554631

William J. Courtenay

This book grew out of a series of lectures that Olga Weijers gave at the École Pratique des Hautes Études in Paris in 1993–1994, and which, in an earlier version, were published by Brepols in 1995 as *Le maniement du savoir: Pratiques intellectuelles à l'époque des premières universités*. Since then Dr. Weijers, a leading scholar on the faculty of arts at the medieval University of Paris, has reorganized and expanded that work on the basis of subsequent study on the methods of teaching and disputation. The result is impressive and should attract a wide audience from university undergraduates to specialists in medieval intellectual history and history of universities. The book is written to be accessible to an audience of non-specialists. Instead of notes there are a few parenthetical references linked to bibliographies at the end of each chapter or to a short general bibliography at the end of the book. The work presents a detailed picture of the origins, structure, and development of the academic community at Paris in the thirteenth and early fourteenth centuries, concentrating on the faculty of arts. It is divided into fifteen relatively brief chapters. Chapter 1 places the university community in the topographical context of the medieval city, with its division between the commercial community on the right bank (the *ville*), the royal and episcopal quarters on opposite ends of the Île-de-la-Cité, and the scholarly quarter on the left bank, with its lecture halls and rented property for students and masters in arts, theology, law, and medicine, as well as most of the teaching convents of the religious orders. Chapter 2 covers the administrative structure and curriculum of the various faculties, while Chapter 3 describes the classification of knowledge, the branches of learning, and the content of teaching in the various disciplines. Chapter 4 shifts attention to the respect for and means of handling authoritative texts, particularly the works of Aristotle and the introduction of textbooks.

The next series of chapters focuses on methods of teaching and the skills of analysis and argumentation. These chapters benefit from the years of study Weijers has given to the technical meaning of terms in the medieval academic vocabulary. Chapter 5 concerns the *lectio*, commenting on texts, ordinary and cursory lectures, and related matters. Chapter 6 is on the development of the *questio* and its use in commenting and lecturing, while Chapters 7 and 8 are on the *disputatio*, its evolution, the methods of argumentation and finding fallacies, and the different types of disputation. From there the book shifts to academic ceremonies and events (Chapter 9), scholastic Latin, the analysis of language, and the place of oral and written expression, and *reportationes* or extensive notes, sometimes verbatim, taken on oral lectures or disputations (Chapters 10 and 11), the layout of manuscripts and the use of diagrams and images, with eight examples (Chapter 12), aids to study such as dictionaries, tables of titles and questions, and subject indices (Chapter 13), condemnations of suspect opinions (Chapter 14), and a biography of a scholarly career in the thirteenth century, using that of Robert Kilwardby (Chapter 15).

The book is well written, with few typographical errors, e.g. *parienses* instead of *parisienses* on p. 225. It presents dimensions of instruction and writing at the University of Paris, or any medieval university for that matter, rarely mentioned in books aimed at the general reader, and does so successfully for the most part. Although the book concentrates almost exclusively on the thirteenth century and on the faculty of arts and says far less about texts and teaching in the higher faculties of theology, canon law, and medicine, that imbalance can be justified on various grounds. Since all secular students in theology and medicine had studied in a faculty of arts, and law students were expected to have familiarity with the content and methods used in the faculty of arts, as was also true of students in the religious orders, an understanding of the faculty of arts is fundamental for understanding the medieval University of Paris. Second, most of the techniques of analysis, teaching, and debating as well as the format of examinations in the higher faculties were similar to or paralleled those in the faculty of arts. Third, the works of Aristotle were extensively used by masters and students in the faculties of theology and medicine. And finally, this emphasis allows the reader to profit from the detailed knowledge and insights of the author, a leading authority in this area. Chapters in which the author depends on the research of others, such as the chapters on the use of images and diagrams or on the condemnations of the opinions and works of Parisian scholars, are not as informed or balanced as they might have been.

Those interested in the subject of this book should still consult Weijers's *Le maniement du savoir,* which contains additional material and many more full-page illustrations of Parisian academic manuscripts. These are, in many ways, two very different books. *A Scholar's Paradise* is for a more general audience and could well become the best and most accessible book in English on the origin, structure, contributions, and importance of the University of Paris and, by extension, the importance of the university as an institution in medieval western society.

University of Wisconsin
Madison, Wisconsin

Bjørn Okholm Skaarup, *Anatomy and Anatomists in Early Modern Spain* (Farnham/Burlington VT: Ashgate, 2015), xii + 285pp. ISBN: 9781471448162

Vivian Nutton

This book 'fills in a much-needed gap' in English-language medical history. It covers in detail the development of anatomy in Spain and Mexico from 1500 to the end of the seventeenth century, pointing out particular instances where the Spanish experience can contribute substantially to wider debates, most notably Juan Tomas Porcell's autopsies of plague victims in a hospital at Zaragoza in 1568 and the detailed plan of 1586 for a 'house of anatomy' there. Dissections in Spain usually took place within a hospital, and only Salamanca in 1554 built a specific free-standing anatomy theatre. There are also some good examples of the co-operation between artists and anatomists, and even some surviving early manikin models. Skaarup successfully refutes O'Malley's exaggerated description, based on Vesalius' comments on his time in Spain between 1559 and 1561, of benighted doctors and surgeons lacking all interest in anatomy, although the situation at court may have been less favourable to investigating bones than outside. Recent research has also demolished the old canard that Vesalius made his pilgrimage to the Holy Land in 1564 either as an attempt to escape Spanish hostility or as penance for an unintended vivisection: he went as a royal representative to deliver the annual subsidy for the Christian churches.

The overall picture painted by Skaarup agrees with that of Granjel a generation ago, who argued for a major change around 1550. Before then an interest in anatomy can be shown only for the university of Valencia, a new foundation intended to promote the new Italian humanist values over the older medieval 'arabized' learning. A building for dissection was already in existence within a hospital there by 1524, and professors like Pedro Jimeno, who may have heard Vesalius in Padua, and Luis Collado were early adherents of Vesalius. Indeed, the swift adoption of Vesalian anatomy elsewhere, often aided by former Valencians, is one of the striking features of this story. The introduction of regular dissections at Salamanca, Valladolid, Zaragoza, Alcalà, and Barcelona in the 1550s and 1560s shows the impact of this new anatomical medicine and the impetus given by Vesalius, at least indirectly through his writings. A copy of the *Fabrica* was among the books brought in 1561 to Mexico City by its first professor of medicine, Juan de la Fuente, a graduate of Alcalà. In 1563 a new teacher at Salamanca, Augustin Vazquez, was reprimanded for using Valverde's anatomy book rather than the *Fabrica* itself, although, as Skaarup makes clear, Valverde's shorter text, available also in the vernacular, was arguably a more effective tool for teaching. The number of statutory dissections was remarkably high at that time in some universities compared with elsewhere. Cosmè de Medina, the first holder of the chair of anatomy at Salamanca in 1552, undertook to carry out at least thirty annual dissections, backed by a royal decree that authorized the acquisition of bodies of executed criminals and others from the hospital.

But this sudden interest in Vesalian anatomy, comparable in speed and extent only to that at German Lutheran universities, did not last, and one of the merits of this book is to emphasize the obstacles faced by those who wished to dissect human corpses. On top of a considerable popular reluctance outside the university to having humans dissected, even if all the authorities were in favour (something also documented for Germany and Italy), medicine, and anatomy in particular, cost money. Medina's plans had to be scaled back, and the chair at Alcalà was filled only intermittently, while Valladolid had a specific anatomy chair for only a matter of months. At Salamanca the anatomy theatre fell into disrepair, and, when finally it was demolished, there was official rejoicing that a place of death was now replaced by a place of recovery as a hospital building. At Valencia, where anatomical teaching survived and numbers of dissections increased in the eighteenth century, the medical faculty accounted for almost half the budget of the university, with constant pressure on what could be done.

Skaarup also draws attention to a lack of publications in anatomy from university teachers of anatomy, lamenting that only a handful of relevant books were written even at Valencia, with only five between 1600 and 1650. Other universities were even less productive. How far this is an anachronistic complaint is unclear, since many anatomists long considered that it was their teaching of their own students that mattered, not writing, let alone a research publication. Those who taught anatomy to surgeons at the monastery at Guadalupe, from the 1550s onwards, and who gained a high reputation in Spain and in Spanish America for their dissections and teaching, have left little record of their achievements, and their names are largely lost. Skaarup lists only five books by doctors who had taught or studied there, of which the most interesting, the *Historia natural* (1565–9) of Francisco Hernández, remained unpublished until the last century.

But there were other reasons for the swift decline of anatomy. Increasing suspicion of Moriscos and other crypto-Christians bore hard on the University of Valencia, which had been founded to bring together the best of Islamic and non-Islamic learning. Lluis Alcanyis, who held the second chair of medicine, which later became the anatomy chair, was burnt at the stake in 1506 for being a *judaizante*. Increasing government regulation after 1550 also hampered contact with the world outside the Spanish dominions. The number of Spanish students at Montpellier, for instance, dropped by over 90 per cent, and the growing inwardness led to what some authors have termed 'tibetization'. But it is also worth noting that a century later Spanish medical writers were among the first to accept Harvey's theory of the circulation of the blood and continued to defend it against all objections, in part the result of an influx of Italian physicians to universities such as Zaragoza and Barcelona in the 1650s.

Skaarup wisely notes that there will have been many other local considerations, financial, intellectual, and personal, that are not revealed in the archives. He himself stresses the co-existence in Spain alongside Vesalian anatomy of both the older 'arabized' medicine and the more modern humanist medicine, neither of which set great store on anatomy. Dissection was something that could be left to surgeons, and many of the treatises discussed in this volume are works on surgery and aimed primarily at surgeons. Paradoxically, the university with the only continuous record of activities in anatomy, Barcelona, was also the most conservative, favouring the ideas of Vesalius' Paris opponent, Jacobus Sylvius, in its regulations almost until the end of the sixteenth century, when in a syllabus consisting almost entirely of Galenic texts the professor of anatomy could simply choose 'a book'. Elsewhere anatomists reverted to material their predecessors had rejected. At Valencia Juan Calvo returned to the Galenic views on the heart and liver that Collado had rejected thirty years previously. For all his interest in autopsy, Porcell at Zaragoza was a firm believer in the humoral medicine of Galen and Avicenna. At Alcalá none of the leading physicians showed the same interest in Vesalius as had its leading figure in the 1560s, Francisco Valles, while at Salamanca, where the enthusiastic audiences that had greeted the new Vesalian anatomy were long in the past, the statutes of 1594 demanded that the professor of anatomy lecture over two years on the whole of Galen's *De usu partium* and nothing else since 'these books contain all that is worth knowing'.

The centralized institutional structure of Spanish medicine also contributed to this ossification, for it gave considerable power to the Protomedico. From 1592 to 1611 this post was held by the Valladolid professor, Luis Mercado, a prolific writer and a firm Galenist, who, whatever his merits as a medical observer and therapist, saw little value in anatomy. Good medicine, he averred, had been practised in Spain for more than two hundred years without this discipline. His own treatise on surgery was a compilation from books, by contrast with the more empirically oriented manual by Dionisio Daza Chacón. Mercado could use his position to ensure that in 1594 by royal decree his textbooks, his *Institutiones,* became part of the core curriculum throughout Spain and were the only ones permitted in the examination of medical students. Others might object, blaming the ruin of medicine on their use in examinations, but they could do little against the royal fiat. Not only did this impose a rigidly Galenist approach to all areas of medicine, but it also gave little encouragement to those who wished to revive the study of anatomy. The achievements of the pioneers of Vesalian anatomy were forgotten, and Spanish anatomy passed into an oblivion from which this book rescues it in part.

Although it is clearly organized, Skaarup's study still shows signs of its origin in a 2009 thesis. It is repetitive at times, and although aware of debates within historians of Spain about the changing environment of the late sixteenth century, the author is less sure about the wider picture of the history of medicine. *Pace* p. 21, Bologna was arguably at least as significant as Padua in the sixteenth century, although Papal control disrupted a flow of non-Italian students from the 1540s onwards. Leonardo da Vinci's collaboration with the young Pavian Galenist Marcantonio della Torre is extremely likely, but none of his anatomical drawings would fit the sort of book that, according to Vasari, the two were planning, let alone a textbook of anatomy.

Skaarup has provided his readers with much food for thought. How often was the Spanish example of setting up dissection rooms or buildings within a hospital followed elsewhere? How far does the pattern of ownership of books by Vesalius compare with what is known, for instance, for England? Most important of all, the focus of this book lies away from the famous trio of Padua, Bologna, and Paris and, for English students, Oxford and Cambridge. Spain's universities were not large, and medicine did not play a great part within them. Yet, for that reason, they may be typical of most medical schools across Europe in their structures and in many of their problems, especially those of finance. This book shows very well the difficulties faced by those who wished to introduce dissection as an essential part of the education of a doctor, as well as the objections that might be made. How many of them were owed to peculiarly Spanish circumstances, such as the influence of Mercado, and how many can be found across Europe are important questions that still await investigation. But with this book as a guide, one can now safely introduce Spanish comparisons into the history of renaissance anatomy.

Department of the History of Medicine,
I.M.Sechenov First Moscow State Medical University

Víctor Navarro Brotóns, *Disciplinas, Saberes y Prácticas. Filosofía natural, matemáticas y astronomía en la sociedad española de la época moderna* (Valencia: Universitat de València, 2014), 496 pp. ISBN: 9788437094465

Luís Miguel Carolino

In the revised version of his widely influential *Ciencia y técnica en la sociedad española de los siglos XVI y XVII*, the late José María López Piñero decided to exclude the physical-mathematical sciences on the grounds that those topics would be thoroughly covered in a book to be published by Víctor Navarro Brotóns, a leading scholar in the field of history of science in Spain and its empire in the early modern period. Navarro Brotóns's book has just come out under the title *Disciplinas, Saberes y Prácticas. Filosofía natural, matemáticas y astronomía en la sociedad española de la época moderna.* This book offers a fresh and comprehensive view on the practice of science and natural philosophy in early modern Spain. The author takes great pains to understand Spain in its wider, early modern context, which means to go beyond the Iberian Peninsula and include Spanish America, the Philippines, and European regions under Spanish Habsburg rule.

Disciplinas, Saberes y Prácticas consists of a collection of articles published over the last twenty years. Despite stemming from different papers, this book is remarkably homogeneous and very well balanced in its approach to 'physical and mathematical knowledge' in early modern Spain. Navarro Brotóns begins with an extensive discussion on the sensitive problems related to the history and the historiography of science in Spain, followed by eighteen chapters meaningfully organized in three parts: 'The sixteenth century and early seventeenth century: the scientific Renaissance'; 'The seventeenth century and early eighteenth century: scientific activity during the Scientific Revolution'; and finally 'The eighteenth century (up to 1767)'. Underlying this organization is the fundamental view according to which science and scientific activities flourished in Spain particularly during the sixteenth century, entered a period of relative 'decline' (*decadencia*: a concept that Navarro Brotóns uses not without qualification) as the seventeenth century progressed, and revived in the eighteenth century.

During the sixteenth century, the teaching of natural philosophy and science in Spanish universities experienced an auspicious 'Renaissance'. Universities such as Valencia, Alcalá, and Salamanca welcomed nominalist philosophers educated in the Oxford and Paris Calculator tradition as well as advocates of corpuscularian theories of matter. University authorities also favoured the introduction of new areas of knowledge such as cosmography, geography, and nautical science in the university curricula. In addition to the universities, there emerged new institutions closely related to the needs of an Empire in the making, such as the *Casa de Contratación* or the Imperial College of Madrid established by Philip II in 1609. These institutions were crucial in the development of the practical mathematical tradition in the Spanish empire. This 'scientific Renaissance' is embodied in characters such as the theologian Diego de Zúñiga, who argued that Copernican theory provided a better explanation for celestial motions than the previous planetary systems, or Jerónimo Muñoz, a professor of mathematics, astronomy, and Hebrew, whose *Libro del Nuevo Cometa* (Valencia, 1573), which argued against the Aristotelian tenet that comets were celestial phenomena, became widely known in Europe thanks to Cornelius Gemma and other authors like Tycho Brahe, who discussed Muñoz's observations and calculations in detail. As in other European countries, in Spain the observation of the comets and new stars between 1572 and 1618 also proved instrumental in fostering the crisis of the traditional scholastic worldview.

Nevertheless, the Spanish 'scientific Renaissance' lost much of its momentum in the early decades of the seventeenth century. At the turn of the century, Spain was apparently in a good position to succeed in the so-called Scientific Revolution. Yet the following decades proved that this was not the case. The mathematization of the world has been recognized as a central feature of the Scientific Revolution. The idea that not only the heavens but also sublunary phenomena were mathematically comprehensible represented a crucial change that eventually led to Galileo's and Newton's assumptions that motion is a neutral state of bodies in a homogeneous, infinite, and geometrized space. In this process, practical mathematics played a crucial role. In Spain, the integration of practical mathematical disciplines into university curricula and at state-sponsored institutions during the sixteenth century could have paved the way for a further incorporation of mechanics into natural philosophy, along the lines of Galileo's approach. Nevertheless, this did not happen. In fact, cultural contacts with Europe were increasingly hindered by the prevalence of Scholastic thought in Spanish universities and, above all, by the strengthening of the Counter-Reformation movement in Spain.

If this country failed to experience some of the main scientific changes that occurred in other European countries, this does not mean that scientific activities did not thrive in Spain and its empire. As Navarro Brotóns suggests, a special role was played by the Jesuit mathematicians during the seventeenth century and part of the eighteenth century. Since Jesuits co-ordinated an international network of scientific correspondents and were responsible for the main teaching positions in mathematical sciences, they contributed not only by shaping science in Spain but also by animating the exchange of astronomical information between Spain, Italy, Flanders, and Mexico. The *novatores* were another important group of figures who played a crucial role in the revival of Spanish science in the late seventeenth century and eighteenth century. These European-inspired authors strove to introduce to Spain the *nova scientia* of Galileo and his disciples and, to a lesser extent, Descartes's philosophy. Throughout the book, a detailed survey of institutional histories is very well combined with a conceptual analysis of key printed material and manuscript texts.

By organizing the volume in this way, Navarro Brotóns has given its readers an innovative, and certainly the most up-to-date, account of scientific activity in Spain and its empire during the Scientific Revolution. The result of decades of committed research, this magisterial work is highly recommended for historians of early modern science and for all those broadly interested in the Iberian cultural history.

Instituto Universitário de Lisboa (ISCTE-IUL),
CIES

Heather Ellis, *Generational Conflict and University Reform. Oxford in an Age of Revolution* (Leiden/Boston: Brill, 2012), viii + 257. ISBN: 9789004225527; E-ISBN: 9789004233164

Mark Curthoys

This book seeks to re-interpret the changes in the curriculum, examination system, and institutional structures at Oxford University, over nearly a century and a half (1714–1854), in the light of what it contends was a growing tension between undergraduates and their tutors. It argues that generational conflict between seniors and juniors was a key factor in the process traditionally labelled 'reform' at Oxford. Cambridge underwent a similar process of institutional renovation, like Oxford ultimately by government intervention, but the book insists on Oxford's distinctiveness from Cambridge, where curricular reform took place earlier and where also, it is contended, there was less acute generational conflict. At the same time, the work seeks to assert continuities between developments in Oxford and those on the continent of Europe, and detects revolutionary tendencies among Oxford students, hitherto regarded as overwhelmingly conservative and supportive of the established order, while also calling into question the assumed cohesion of the British elite.

Like previous studies (notably by W.R. Ward and Sheldon Rothblatt) Ellis treats the new examination statue of 1800 as a pivotal moment. Here the statute is presented as a response to over half a century of what are described as troubled relations between senior and junior members. The book traces how, in the wake of riots by Jacobite students in the first half of the century, college authorities tightened their control over student reading. There was a more systematic enforcement of the traditional syllabus and a narrowing of the classical curriculum to prevent, in the context of the

American and French revolutions, the use of texts which might encourage the spread of radical ideas. The result was an increasing emphasis on educational tasks more associated with schools, using texts which were also commonly studied by schoolboys, in a process culminating in the 1800 statute. The conservative characteristics of the statute are re-emphasized and seen as part of a larger process whereby seniors reasserted their authority over junior members in the early decades of the nineteenth century. Positing the emergence of a more united student body, Ellis suggests that as a result of these developments there was a widening breach between seniors and juniors in the early decades of the nineteenth century, demonstrated by criticisms of the narrowness of the curriculum and the arbitrary discipline imposed on undergraduates. The juniors, in this argument, far from accepting the new system, challenged it and were among its strongest critics, prompting attempts by the seniors in the late 1820s to reassert control. The subsequent Tractarian movement, in which young men came to be especially prominent, gained approval in its early stages from senior members of the University because the doctrines of childlike obedience which it emphasized to its student adherents offered a reinforcement of established authority. Only later did the Tractarians—presented here as evolving into a radical youth movement—come to undermine the very establishment which they had originally defended. Relations between junior and senior members, again said to be deteriorating, are put forward as a factor in the appointment of a royal commission in 1850, and the Act of Parliament (1854) which is the terminal point of the book.

All this makes for an intriguing argument, sustained over a long historical period; and even more so through its attempt to apply the currently topical concept of generational conflict—compelling in the early twenty-first century as a description of the disparities in wealth and opportunities between the generations—to an *ancien regime* institution. It does this by examining 'the published discourse of reform' through the abundance of pamphlets, periodicals, and other published contemporary commentary which freely invoked the terms 'senior' and 'junior' though, as the introduction acknowledges, 'junior' in particular was an unstable term which could, in different contexts, refer variously to undergraduates, BAs, younger MAs, and also college fellows and tutors. The conflicts described in the book were not, as a result, entirely between generations, but were also between status groups: tutor/pupil conflicts might arise between teachers and students not many years apart in age; while constitutionally the tutors (as juniors) might come into conflict with seniors (heads of colleges), especially in the years leading up to the reform of the university's constitution.

These distinctions are especially important to bear in mind given the weight that the argument attaches to the authorities' fear of 'junior rebellion', a concern tangible enough in the case of the Jacobite riots, though less obviously so on other occasions when the term is applied. The views of juniors who went into print to criticize the curriculum and examinations in the early nineteenth century are presented as a junior programme for reform, which brings out otherwise submerged dissenting voices—but placed in the context of the over 1000 undergraduates who (voluntarily) came forward to seek honours in the new examinations over the same period, it may that be junior rebellion was a limited concern for the Oxford authorities. The point, though, is very much taken that the behaviour of juniors (whether Jacobite sympathisers, proselytizing crypto-Catholic tutors, or dissipated high-born rakes) could subvert the collegiate university's claims to exercise moral supervision and to uphold religious and political orthodoxy among those young men entrusted to it. The book is indeed well framed at either end of its chronological range by threats, fulfilled in 1850, of government intervention in the face of such concerns. But the Oxford authorities' overwhelming perception was of a threat to the establishment (including the university) externally, by religious and political radicals, and their anxiety about undergraduate education was to ensure that the establishment had intellectually armed defenders, and particularly an educated clergy, whom it was Oxford's especial role to supply. It was arguably this priority, rather than curbing generational revolt within Oxford itself, that lay behind many of the developments over this period.

At the same time, the University educated men of high social rank and independent fortune, exemplified by the Jacobite student who, in the late 1740s, is quoted as proclaiming 'I am a man of an Independent Fortune and therefore afraid of... no one'. Keeping such students at their studies, and out of trouble, was a recurring disciplinary problem for the Oxford authorities, and one which did lead to outbreaks of riot (notably at Christ Church in the 1820s). But this had at its root issues of social standing rather than generation. More account might be taken of such distinctions within the student body, which was perhaps more fractured in this period than the all-embracing description of 'juniors' might suggest. By introducing the concept of generational conflict into discussion of university reform, this ambitious study succeeds in directing attention to the 'junior' voice in key developments within the University, and in its discussion of academic discipline suggests wider questions about the status of young men in late eighteenth- and early nineteenth-century Britain.

University of Oxford

Klaas van Berkel and Bart Ramakers (Eds), *Petrus Camper in Context. Science, the Arts, and Society in the Eighteenth-Century Dutch Republic* (Hilversum: Verloren, 2015), 316pp., ill. ISBN: 9789087044671

Rienk Vermij

During his lifetime, the Dutch professor of medicine Petrus Camper (1722-89) enjoyed an enormous, European-wide scholarly reputation. He was a versatile scholar, active in comparative anatomy, obstetrics, zoonosis, and other fields. But though a towering figure in his own time, from two hundred years later his contribution is somewhat hard to identify. He wrote a major work on pathological anatomy, but most of his ideas were published in academic and other orations or small essays, often written for special occasions.

The present volume therefore does not focus on Camper's contribution to medicine. As he has been the subject of a recent (2008) Dutch biography and several other studies, there seems little to add in this field.[1] There is nonetheless a paper on Camper's best-known contribution, his introduction of the 'facial angle', by Miriam Claude Meijer, who has written on this topic before.[2] The facial angle, a way to compare skulls in a quantitative way, has gained a rather bad reputation, as in the nineteenth century it was often used to classify humans on a racial scale. This, however, was against Camper's original intention: he was outspoken in his rejection of racism, a point which certainly bears repeated emphasis.

[1] J.K. van der Korst, *Het rusteloze bestaan van dokter Petrus Camper (1722–1789)* (Houten, 2008).

[2] Miriam Claude Meyer, 'Petrus Camper et les variétés crâniennes', in Nicolas Bancel, Thomas David et Dominic Thomas (eds), *L'invention de la race. Des représentations scientifiques aux exhibitions populaires* (Paris, 2014), 43–57.

The main focus of the volume, however, is not on Camper's medical or scientific work, but on his position in society. It thereby approaches Camper from a new angle and presents an interesting case of the role of science and medicine in the period of the Enlightenment. So, instead of Camper's medical work, his political role and his artistic ideas and accomplishments get pride of place. There are papers on Camper as a landowner and Frisian politician (Jensma), on his connections to other intellectuals of his time (Van Sluis, Hildebrand), on his impact on the university of Groningen, where he taught for several years (Caljé), on the literary form of his writings (Ramakers), on his illustrations for William Smellie's anatomical atlas (Cunningham), and on his efforts toward a new town hall for the city of Groningen (Schmidt). Camper's social standing, it becomes clear, was not simply that of an intellectual or professor. His identity was much more defined by his wealth and his status as a member of the regent class, with the accompanying activities and political connections. Goffe Jensma, in his article on Camper as a regent, goes so far as to say that 'Camper was much more a seasoned Frisian regent who dabbled in science than a pure-blooded scientist who happened to have married a woman of more than average means'. (43) Just like his many other activities, his scholarly work should be seen in the larger framework of his social responsibilities and the new ideal of citizenship as it emerged in the period of the Enlightenment. The editors emphasize the necessity of a political biography of Camper. Van Berkel in his own contribution makes a start by describing one particular episode from Camper's career as a regent.

The volume therefore offers a valuable contribution, but there are also some weak points. The papers were originally given at a conference on Camper at Groningen in 2010, and the volume shows all the weaknesses which affect such a work when it is not guided by a strong editorial hand. For people outside the field, the editors' introduction on Camper and the present state of Camper studies is a bit short. In the papers themselves there is some repetition, in particular in the three papers on Camper's aesthetics (by Krul, Van de Akker, and Schmidt), where all authors have to draw on the same text, a lecture by Camper on beauty. Moreover, these three authors' interpretations appear slightly different on points of detail, but none of them mentions the other papers. Apparently, they did not go to the 2010 conference to listen to each other. Finally, one would have hoped for something of a general conclusion: how does the new approach change our view of Camper? In particular, one would like to know to what extent Camper's reputation in the medical world of the eighteenth century was due to his social standing rather than to his actual work. Cunningham emphasizes the importance of Camper's sociability in his relations to English physicians. Hildebrand points out that in his relations with

German scientists, Camper acted very much as a mentor and godfather, but drew little benefit himself. Raised in the empiricism of 'Newtonianism', he stuck with anatomy as the central discipline in medicine and cared little about the up-and-coming field of experimental physiology. So, are we right in concluding that it was his social rather than his intellectual standing that defined Camper's position?

The main question left is how these results fit in with our general understanding of the Enlightenment. Was Camper typical of his age? What does his case say on how we should study eighteenth-century science and medicine? Unfortunately, neither authors nor editors do raise these questions. Therefore, for people outside the small circle of Camper specialists, the book is not as useful as it could have been. Still, it presents an interesting case that certainly deserves to be considered by students of Enlightenment science in general.

Department of the History of Science
University of Oklahoma,
Norman, Oklahoma 73019-3106

Dan Inman, *The Making of English Theology: God and the Academy at Oxford* (Minneapolis: Fortress Press, 2014). ISBN: 9781451469264

Johannes Zachhuber

Recently, the introduction of a new undergraduate syllabus in Theology and Religion at the University of Oxford caused a minor stir in the national and even international media. Outlets such as the *Daily Telegraph* and the *Daily Mail* saw it as a further sign of the de-Christianization of the United Kingdom and a break with an 800-year tradition at the nation's oldest university. For those intrigued by the vehemence of this response, Dan Inman's well-written and reliably researched monograph, depicting the history of Oxford's Faculty of Theology from the early nineteenth century to the middle of the twentieth, provides at least two essential clues: firstly, practically all of the several attempts to tinker with theology at Oxford during this period have called forth reactions of this kind. Secondly, the status quo those critics were defending has in no case been a centuries-old tradition but usually the compromise reached a few decades previously.

An honour school in Theology did not exist at Oxford until 1869 when it was introduced against the fierce resistance of conservatives who at the time feared that such a degree course would turn the 'queen of the sciences' into a discipline like any other. The struggle, which is at the centre of Inman's first two chapters, lasted for a whole generation and is highly instructive. Until the mid-nineteenth century, Oxford—as well as Cambridge—was in effect still an institution of the Church of England. On matriculation, students had to subscribe to the Thirty-Nine Articles; their tutors were ordained clergy (until at least 1877), and ordination was also the chosen destination for the majority of students. Until 1932, all students had to present themselves for mandatory examinations in Divinity.

Professional training, on the other hand, was alien to the ethos of Oxford at whose core remained the humanistic ideal of a classical education aimed at the formation of gentlemen. A further factor was the perseverance of the medieval system of independent—and often well-endowed—colleges, whose fellows were far more numerous and, throughout the period described in Inman's book, generally more influential than the relatively few faculty-based professors.

If one wanted to be more provocative than Inman, who is mostly kind and generous to the individuals and the institution he studies, one could say that Oxford in the early nineteenth century was exactly the kind of university progressive educationalists across Europe were keen to see abolished or at least utterly reformed. Its social utility at a time of unprecedented economic and cultural challenges was as limited as its potential for intellectual innovation was modest. More radical solutions were, of course, introduced in much of continental Europe at the turn of the century, and the perseverance of England's medieval universities can easily appear as a less interesting case of institutional conservatism.

It is against this backdrop that Inman introduces his most interesting argument by suggesting that Oxford's idiosyncratic development deserves to be taken more seriously than it often has been, at least by historians of theology. While there are no figures rivalling the leading lights of German theology during this period—interestingly the two most prominent theological authors associated with Oxford of the time, John Henry Newman and C.S. Lewis, never became professors of theology, albeit for different reasons—the specific situation at Oxford led to the emergence of a specific form of intellectually engaged, ecumenically open theology by the middle of the twentieth century. In other words, English theology has found its own path into the modern world, and if this path was neither that sought by progressives nor that defended by conservatives, its outcome was all the more original and attractive. In fact, as Inman makes clear in his opening chapter, he believes that the Oxford model could help settle current controversies about the discipline's place in the university.

Inman's plausibly structured narrative ultimately aims to substantiate this claim. The first two chapters present Oxford's development from 1833 until 1882, and thus mainly conflicts about the role of theology in the University, during a period of loosening ties with the Church of England. A third chapter takes the history to the outbreak of World War I and, more to the point, the ultimately failed attempt by Henry Scot Holland, Regius Professor of Divinity, to transform Theology into a Religious Studies degree. The final chapter sketches developments until 1945. While earlier chapters ended with frustrated or stunted efforts to reform the subject, here at last, in Inman's narrative, Oxford discovers its own mode of practising theology in the modern university informed by lasting links with the Church of England but without a strictly confessional identity. Theology at Oxford thus marks, so Inman convincingly, a *via media* between the 'undenominational' faculties that have become the norm in most British and American universities since the nineteenth century and the strictly confessional faculties in much of continental Europe.

It is perhaps more questionable whether Oxford also offers anything to those who bemoan theology's subjection to rigorous 'scientific' standards. Inman seem to think it does, but his case is weaker in that regard. As the book shows, Oxford's conservatives in the nineteenth century, while affirming the fundamental significance of theology for the university, struggled to define its intellectual content. 'Historical' and 'speculative' approaches were roundly rejected, and the outcome, as Inman illustrates on the basis of examination papers from the period, was theology reduced to little more than Scripture knowledge and apologetics. Any form of intellectual engagement with the subject's big questions was apparently suspected of pandering towards liberalism and therefore excluded from the syllabus, inevitably with rather dire results for theology's academic prestige. When this gradually changed, Oxford's theological reputation was increasingly built on biblical and historical scholarship operating on a methodological basis shared with other, related disciplines rather than developing a mode of discourse specific to theology as demanded by the theological critics of university theology.

Inman's study is largely restricted to Oxford's own history with the occasional glance at other English universities. There is in principle nothing wrong with this approach; for Inman, however, it creates a specific problem insofar as the developments he relates are to a large extent played out with reference to contemporary trends in Germany. As much as liberal attempts to reform Oxford were motivated by a desire to emulate the success of the German research university, the German provenance of that model was a major reason for others to reject it. Concerns ranged from a general fear of continental radicalism following the French revolution to more specific worries about the critical approach adopted by leading German theologians of the time. Quite how the latter development was supposed to be linked to institutional reforms, emblematically exemplified by the foundation of the University of Berlin in 1810, was never entirely clear. Inman himself is content with rather vague references to 'Berlin' or 'Germanization' throughout the book, and this probably describes with accuracy the prevailing mindset of the conservatives he is dealing with. Yet it might have been helpful had Inman himself probed a little deeper at this point, especially since he ultimately wants to establish the significance of Oxford's own path towards theological modernity. What precisely was at issue between the (Protestant) German model and the one that emerged at Oxford? Was it the adoption of historical criticism? Was it the embrace of the organizational forms of modern *Wissenschaft*? Or was it not perhaps primarily the absence from Oxford of the rigorous discipline required of institutions whose purpose was the training of ministers for a confessional church? Along the lines of Inman's own argument, it would not appear far-fetched to suggest that the last aspect was of fundamental importance as it facilitated the emergence of a modern theology germane to Oxford. By contrast, resistance against the former two developments was more of a rearguard action which could safely be suspended once modern theology at Oxford had come into its own.

In a well-written book, Dan Inman provides an account of a fascinating and little known chapter in the history of the University of Oxford. The book raises important questions about the character of modern theology and its place in the academy. Inman writes accessibly although a glossary of the many Oxford-specific terms would have been desirable.

Oxford

Paul Shrimpton, The 'Making of Men'. The Idea and reality of Newman's university in Oxford and Dublin (Leominster, Herts: Gracewing Publishing, 2014), 587pp. ISBN: 9780852448243

Sheldon Rothblatt

John Henry, Cardinal Newman died on August 11, 1890 at Edgbaston, Birmingham, the site of the beloved Oratory that he founded and cherished. His was a long and full life. Educated at Trinity College, Oxford University, he translated to Oriel College as a fellow despite an unexpectedly poor performance in the honours examinations. A man of God who sought holiness, he was also an educational reformer by instinct and by religion in the decades when so many Oxford undergraduates were, to put it mildly, a hearty bunch keen on entertainment and lax in academic focus. While an undergraduate, annoyed by a certain Augustan indifference awaiting transformation into Victorian piety and high-mindedness, Newman co-founded a short-lived journal or student newspaper, already expressing sentiments and ideals that new generations of undergraduates and youthful Oxbridge tutors, fresh from reformed secondary boarding schools recent and ancient, would later bring to the senior foundations. He is credited, or can be credited, with being the first or certainly amongst the first of Oxbridge tutors to instill discipline and meaning into a moribund system of college instruction, what has been called and Paul Shrimpton, in his absorbing book, also calls a 'pastoral' mission. This led to a famous punch-up with the Provost of Oriel, Edward Hawkins, who looked upon Newman's zeal as a departure from common practice. Anyone familiar with the fights between Hawkins and Newman understands that Newman's conception of the tutor's role was at the heart of the disagreement. This has been noted before the arrival of Shrimpton's book but never with the depth and perception that his analysis brings to it.

The irony of the situation is that amongst the Oxbridge colleges, Oriel was known as the most intellectual, its fellows committed to what in the 1830s was a relatively uncommon institutional salute to the life of the mind. They were referred to as 'Noetics' to make the point. But Newman, an intellectual *par excellence,* a deeply learned thinker and compelling writer, was nevertheless dissatisfied. He wanted more. He wanted intellect to be in the service of teaching, and teaching devoted to 'the making of men'. But intellect itself, while necessary, was insufficient without the direction of religious faith and the guidance of religious virtue. If, in his view or those of friends, the Church of England after a century of lapses and indifference could not provide the necessary inspiration, some of the ancients, suitably corrected, would serve – Aristotle's *Nichomachean Ethics*, for example.

In the earliest decades of the nineteenth century the Anglican Church experienced a number of different jolts and challenges, to put the situation mildly. These would continue for much of the century as religious truth and religious organizations are always affected by contemporary influences. There were many as Britain underwent multiple social and economic transformations. For Newman, the Oriel fellows were taking the wrong route, more towards Broad Church and a 'liberal' approach to religious obedience. Roman Catholicism provided a more secure base and a steadier arc for him and a famous set of converts in what is usually referred to as the 'Oxford Movement'.

'Liberal' is a word always subject to interpretation and history. Newman, as Shrimpton points out (and others as well), was in the context of the Roman Catholicism of his day rather more broad-minded than members of the ecclesia. He was not a reactionary. He was not a 'conservative' except in the widest meaning of that confused and abused word: history, continuity, perspective, and proportion. What he feared, and they could unsettle any pastoral teaching aims, were utilitarianism, relativism, skepticism, agnosticism, secularism and any of the other 'isms' commonly associated with modernity. The teacher who lacked core convictions, saw every moral issue as problematical, and could not balance a tolerance of human imperfection with the need to keep students from going off the rails would never succeed in making them decent and civic-minded adults once they entered the world at large.

The 'making of men' is a latter-day version of 'character formation', one of the oldest goals of liberal education, although each age and society must debate the kind of character to be formed, the means for doing so, and the formal support structures that allow the task to be achieved. For

Shrimpton, Newman is the best guide for understanding how institutions enable or ignore what he – clearly a dedicated teacher himself at Magdalen College School in Oxford – regards as central to any university education.

For many, past and present, Newman is irresistible, his prose eminently quotable and his passion compelling. A century and a half after his death, his writings remain a staple of historical and educational scholarship. His memory and name are preserved at innumerable American colleges, public or private, that possess a Newman Hall gathering and worshipping place for Roman Catholic students. Nevertheless, while often discussed, and at one time even a 'Great Books' author taught in American literature courses, his outright influence with respect to liberal education today is debatable. Or perhaps it is more accurate to say that his fate is tied up with that of liberal education generally in an age of high technology, finance, large-scale educational structures, and student populations stratified by social class, ethnicity, identity politics, and income.

The literature on Newman and certain of his important contemporaries is vast, but, as Shrimpton notes, most of the scholarly attention has been devoted to analyses of the famous lectures or 'Discourses' that he delivered when summoned to Ireland in the middle of the nineteenth century to become the founder and rector of a Catholic University. That enterprise, as conceived by Newman, was short-lived, disintegrating after his departure (he was rector for four years, the last infrequently in residence). It was revived for some decades but as a Jesuit seminary on a wholly different basis. It was afterwards briefly a university college affiliated to a Royal University of Ireland (on the model of what was once called the Royal University of London, and then just London University) and finally, in the beginning of the twentieth century, absorbed into the National University of Ireland.

As a work of thought and style, the celebrated 'Discourses' on the 'idea' of a university is almost the starting point for any discussion of the function, missions, and role of a university, at least in the English-speaking world. Books and articles that attempt a definition of higher education obedient to a core or 'idea' appear regularly, but never with Newman's certainty or apparent certainty (some of what he wrote was deliberately overstated to make a particular point). Even when his *Idea* is regarded as superceded, or impractical, his name is summoned up as if to grant legitimacy to any other intellectual position. Shrimpton is no fan of the multiversity; but even Clark Kerr, who virtually created the neologism and gave it form in a series of famous lectures at Harvard, paid wistful obeisance to Newman. The multiversity, like the cultures and societies that give it life, is a messy construct, an artifact, said Kerr (almost desperately?), of history itself. A graduate of the famous Quaker college of Swarthmore in Pennsylvania, Kerr tried his own blend of a Cambridge collegiate university with an American multi-campus state university by establishing the Santa Cruz branch of the University of California when he was president. In his own mind, the blend failed, and in that sense his hopes like Newman's were thwarted. However, unlike Newman's foundation in Dublin, Santa Cruz is a flourishing component of a huge state university, if more like the other campuses than Kerr's sometime conception.[1]

The 'Making of Men' can be divided into three parts. The first comprises the early years of Newman's life and provides background for the intellectual and theological bases of Newman's mature thinking. Much of this work is familiar from other authors but is necessary to Shrimpton's overall plan to show how Newman's prior experience and thinking fed into the enterprise of institution-building. The second part is a long and heavily-detailed account of Newman's work, including his everyday work, of building and administering a university in Ireland. Shrimpton, as is his intention, has succeeded in going beyond the usual accounts of Newman and his well-known *Idea*. He has recovered and mastered an immense quantity of forgotten or overlooked correspondence, reports, working papers, memoranda, account books, archival miscellanea, and Newman's unpublished essays or second thoughts. This is fine scholarship, demonstrating a long and arduous commitment to an understanding of Newman's achievements. Shrimpton also makes use of Newman's published writings that fill in, as it were, the gaps in the famous lectures to provide a fuller discussion of his thinking.

The third part of the book is brief but intense. Shrimpton now joins the company of today's critics of universities and higher education in general in deploring many of the educational developments that have pushed contemporary universities away from a commitment to liberal education as character formation. This section is filled with personal feeling. It interweaves Newman's thinking with our present-day world (mainly England and the U.S.) and provides a counterpoint, but it is more the author lending his voice in support of arguments about what is at fault in the present-day university than an altogether new critique. However, as in all parts of this book, we can be grateful for careful and unflaggingly attractive prose.

As a young tutor and fellow of Oriel, Newman attempted to reform the inherited system of college lecturing through pastoral teaching. He took into account the student's individuality, paid attention to his moral and spiritual state and stage, and in general provided the combination of

---

[1] See the essays edited by Sheldon Rothblatt, *Clark Kerr's World of Higher Education Reaches the 21ˢᵗ Century, Chapters in a Special History* (Dordrecht: Springer, 2012).

personal concern and pedagogical attention that have come to be valued as the great achievements of the Oxford and Cambridge system of collegiate instruction. Criticisms notwithstanding, the Oxbridge inheritance remains a model at least of what an ideal undergraduate teaching structure might be, even if, owing to other influences, the shaping of the critical intelligence takes precedence over a directed shaping of character in the round.[2]

When summoned to the task of founding a Roman Catholic University in Ireland, Newman systematically elaborated on the pastoral conception in ways that, thanks to Shrimpton, we can find astonishing. Oxford was present throughout – we have known that - and it was the Romantic Oxford that Newman could never really forget. It was in fact the Romantic generation of Oxonians that bequeathed to history the sentimental melodies of dreaming spires and lost causes. (At one point, other evidence to the contrary, Shrimpton underplays Newman's emotional attachment to Oxford, the *genius loci* that for him made an educational institution stand out.) The heart of the pastoral conception was the college, small, intimate, residential, where tutors and students commingled. Newman established colleges or licensed boarding houses, including one for medical students, and these underwent the vagaries associated with trying to house a mixture of immature or obstreperous students of different ages. The mix challenged all his attempts at discipline and virtually strangled his conception of *in loco parentis*. He was often criticized by the Irish episcopate for sparing the rod, if not literally, and for allowing students too much freedom in apportioning their time. Newman was not at heart a true disciplinarian, that is to say, he was an English/Oxford convert to Roman Catholicism and not an Irish cleric who conflated school and university. In the making of men, especially those destined to enter a world where some habit of self-reliance was necessary, youthful hi-jinks were to be reasonably tolerated as part of the process of coming of age. Not a sports buff himself, Newman saw value in team sports – very Victorian as Shrimpton notes - and to countermand the deleterious influence of local gaming venues, he even made space available for a billiards table.

Shrimpton is at pains to demonstrate Newman's attention to detail in carrying out the definition of a university, distinguishing it from a college and especially from a seminary, the type of institution best known to the Catholic hierarchy. In fact, the challenge of the seminary view of education constantly hindered Newman's realization of his vision of an institution that is faith-based but open to freedom of thought and the ability to

---

[2] This distinction is only convenient. Even attention to the critical shaping of mind redounds to the shaping of character.

reason. A university was a collection of disciplines – religion was one of the disciplines – and contrary to the impression gained from a reading of the first page of the published *Discourses on the Idea of a University* - Newman was not opposed to research or to professional education. He apparently overstated his opposition to make a point, thereby unfortunately misleading those who applauded his soaring tribute to liberal education. A medical school was in fact the best-known part of his achievement in Ireland. He wanted scholars, and he often could not find them, relying heavily on English converts and his circles from Oxford days. But the pastoral function was the essence, a liberal education was the goal, and residential instruction gained in a college-type of organization complemented the organization of professorial instruction. This was the formula that would prevail at Oxford and Cambridge after the massive inner reforms of the second half of the nineteenth century. The Catholic University in Ireland was a combination of the Oxbridge college of the future committed to a pastoral educational mission and the university as a collection of disciplines, understood by Newman in its historical evolution and by the Irish bishops as the Louvain professorial model recently established in Belgium. But while the bishops inclined towards clerical leadership, Newman pushed the necessity of a lay element, fearing that the clergy as he knew them were often narrow-minded men.

Shrimpton provides the particulars of Newman's residential schemes, his struggles to recruit undergraduates, his attempts to meet expenses, always a disheartening challenge, his efforts to attract and pay suitable tutors, professors, vice-rectors, and staff and even his success in conceiving and building a splendid university church in a byzantine basilica and not gothic style, with rather more interior bling and better sight lines. He was often away at the Oratory in Birmingham and conducted his business from afar, relying on those in residence to carry out his dreams, which only a few could ever do. His relations with many of the bishops were not smooth, and those with Archbishop Cullen were particularly challenging. Although Newman was Cullen's choice to establish a Catholic university, he came to regret the decision. Colin Barr has written on this in ways unflattering to Newman. Cullen was not a well man, suffering from stress and insomnia, and Barr suggests, or has Cullen suggest, that Newman pushed him over the edge into a nervous breakdown.[3] Shrimpton, as expected, takes Newman's side, quotes from his letters, and supports the portrait of a two-faced ecclesiastical grandee.

---

[3] Colin Barr, *Paul Cullen, John Henry Newman and the Catholic University of Ireland, 1845–1865* (Notre Dame, IN: University of Notre Dame Press, 2003), 133, 172.

The scheme to establish a Roman Catholic University in Ireland collapsed, certainly as Newman designed it, but the surprising fact is that he was able to do anything at all. (By contrast, the Catholic Oratory School that he established in England worked). The odds were against a university, flushed out with colleges and heavily staffed with lay teachers and professors, from gaining any ground whatsoever. First, as indicated, the Irish episcopate did not fully grasp Newman's intentions and knew of a different model for higher education more closely aligned in spirit to secondary schools. But no mention is made in the book of the increasing rightward movement of the papacy in the nineteenth century, although there is a passing reference to the German theologian, Ignaz von Döllinger, the mentor of the Cambridge historian Lord Acton, who was excommunicated for his liberal sentiments. Second, the absence of an adequate system of feeder schools nobbled the intake of qualified undergraduates. Newman had to recruit from England or from abroad, and those results were hardly uniform. Third, financing the enterprise, made more difficult by Newman's insistence on residential education even though only a few could manage the cost, was a major headache. Where the market was soft – Ireland was wretchedly poor - subsidies from diocesan funds were essential, but they made Newman reliant upon monetary sources that weakened his authority. Fourth, Ireland was an educational laboratory for England. A number of free-standing secular colleges that competed for students and would one day report to a central examining body modeled on the University of London limited the available pool of candidates. A fifth reason was that the Catholic University did not have legal authority to grant degrees. While the degree had not yet assumed the credentialing importance of today, it remained a factor in attracting students, especially if they were upwardly mobile or ambitious. A sixth reason was that the Irish gentry and professional classes, whose children Newman hoped to attract, were lukewarm about the new university. It was as yet unbranded. It did not possess the status deemed appropriate for persons of rank. And lastly, Ireland was becoming politicized following the terrifying famine of the 1840s. A growing Irish nationalism was at odds with a university conception so closely associated with English domination, English ideas, and English institutions, at bottom Protestant in the estimation of the Irish Roman Catholic hierarchy.

No student of human affairs can ever be shocked by learning that heroes have feet of clay, and yet Newman's compelling literary style leads readers to imagine that he of all intellectuals is an exception. Here again Shrimpton and Barr are at odds. As a devoted admirer of Newman the thinker and the builder, Shrimpton also portrays him as a man of generous outlook, fine manners, surrounded by friends, clubbable even. He had a humorous side (certainly apparent in a reading of his novel about Oxford, *Loss and Gain*), and no one could ever doubt his energy. He did the work of two, and really, as Newman described in a letter, to the point of exhaustion. For Shrimpton, Newman is a 'great Christian humanist',[4] and those who came to the new university did so, he maintains, from a 'fascination and love for Newman'. Yet Shrimpton grants that there were those for whom Newman appeared cold and daunting, even severe of aspect. Barr picks up on this side of him. Archbishop Cullen called Newman 'angular', and Barr goes beyond this to quote Newman as calling the Irish 'such beasts' and referring to them as 'Paddies'. Barr states flatly that by present-day standards Newman 'harboured racist views' toward the Irish, was never truly comfortable with them or with foreigners in general. But if this is the case by today's standards, Barr concludes that Newman was probably less anti-Irish than the English of his day, although Cullen himself, always under pressure from nationalists, was not particularly enamored of Englishmen. Barr also grants that Cullen was not always courteous towards his chosen rector.[5] Clearly the two were not destined to get along.

Accounts of institution building are always arresting. There is the excitement of erecting from scratch, the Gordian knots, the visions of the pioneers, the combination of borrowings and variations, the interplay of personalities and rivalries. Idealism is foremost, the perennial search for styles of pedagogy that will, if given a chance, allow human potential at its finest to emerge. Much is at stake, to include an investment of ego and the constant scraping of the bottom of the barrel to obtain the wherewithal to transfer an idea into a reality. Often if not mostly, the vision does not survive, because as in the case of the Catholic University the circumstances were not propitious, or because of flawed leadership (Black Mountain College in North Carolina?) or because the institutionalization of an 'idea' falls athwart of inheritances at war with a pioneering intent (Santa Cruz). Above all, how is the *genius loci* to be grasped, the intangible element that silently informs space, that struggles to be captured, and is contrary to the dross of this world?

Having invested so much thought and time into Newman's work as a builder of institutions, and having succeeded so well in providing an illuminating account of his comprehensive outlook and his union of history, religious commitment, and existing educational models, Shrimpton concludes with reflections and commentaries of his own (although these are not absent from the main text itself). He deplores the bureaucratization of higher education, the enemy he says of *caritas*. He rounds up the usual suspects. Impersonal distant learning, electronic wizardy, the substitution

---

[4] And as a Christian, Newman's attitude toward Jews would be interesting, to say the least. But this is not a topic that attracts the main body of Newman scholars.
[5] Barr, 103, 109, 137.

of career for human development, the 'self-destructive temptations of popular culture' – these aspects of today's higher education world are often excoriated. And to be sure, Newman is frequently cited as an authority for deploring the sins and failings of post-industrial democracy. As for liberal industrialism, Newman saw it becoming a 'bazaar', a marketplace of shrill competing ideas with the best ones lost in the shouting. (Kerr did not know that Newman actually foresaw a kind of multiversity or a multiversity which he identified in the making of the University of London.)

As noted, the institutional soul of Newman's conception of what a university means was pastoral teaching as revived by him at Oxford, at the time closely aligned with but never subordinate to the Church of England. Pastoral teaching as idealized by Newman was Christian. Shrimpton understands it as such, but believes the practice is applicable to a plural religious environment. How wonderful if the humanity of the undergraduate could be drawn out to its fullest ethical dimensions by the humanity of the teacher. Newman had the college in mind, and the college of his time was tiny. Elite systems of higher education, whether selection occurs by merit or by social class (by default Newman had to choose from the latter), can always provide careful attention to student learning. But the admixture of demography and democracy, high technology, and the need for a society to generate wealth if social goals are to be met makes mass higher education a reality that defeats Newman's beautiful plan for personal regeneration and development. No society can base mass higher education exclusively or even partly on an elite model.

Shrimpton adds to the voices that maintain today's higher education systems are in 'crisis'. A Roundtable of scholars has no trouble identifying all kinds of annoyances, structural impediments, and departures from serious moral and intellectual inheritances (I have favorites), but by and large national higher education systems in the developed countries are functional, many containing great segments of creativity. Doubtless they are overstretched, taking on more responsibilities than any nineteenth-century European or American university could imagine. But I would think that the real crisis lies further down in the educational food chain where basic skills and proficiencies must be acquired, but that too is a platitude.[6]

---

[6] No one along the political spectrum in the United States is satisfied with pupil performance in state sector schooling, especially in the achievements of disadvantaged children. A succession of would-be national reformers seem stymied in their efforts to improve the results indicated in standardized testing. The latest Programme for International Student Assessment (PISA) run by the OECD reveals that pupils in Singapore are about three years ahead in mathematics. Estonia has a good record in raising the scores of the poorest children. *The Economist* (Leader on Global education, December 10, 2016.) The examples are endless. Newman, says Shrimpton, believed that examinations had their uses subordinate to his larger purposes.

"Character formation' is a valued ideal for liberal education, but why suppose that it does not quietly exist in the thousands upon thousands of courses given in universities each day, hidden from view perhaps and undertaken on personal initiative? The tutorial may be the optimal structure for encouraging pastoral attention, but it is easy to overstate the impersonal or bureaucratic element in today's provisions for tertiary education. Somewhere in the labyrinth of corridors of the large contemporary university, niches exist for those whose view of education is sympathetic to Newman's. Helter-skelter perhaps, but we may have to settle for less. American colleges and universities are constantly experimenting with different teaching structures and strategies such as honours colleges within research universities, undergraduate thesis writing, special small seminars for new undergraduates, schemes for having faculty dine with undergraduates in residence units. And although Newman's university was not yet filled with postgraduate students, a development some ways off, discipleship itself is a form of pastoral teaching. *In loco parentis* was designed for the very young, but the graduate research experience provides some justification for believing that the personal influence of the mentor extends beyond the period once termed 'the dangerous years', the years during which young persons could easily be led astray.

Yet a characteristic of the higher education universe of today is that it is composed of students of all ages and backgrounds who are receiving instruction in many kinds of venues, some of them inexpensive as befits their means, some exploitative in a huge for-profit sector. Newman's difficulty with his handful of students is paltry compared to the bewildering variety of student types today. A number of them return to higher education belatedly, some after years of work. Single mothers struggle to snatch a few hours of study time from the impossible demands of keeping aloft economically. Another body attends classes part-time from necessity, but the overwhelming majority in the United States (or Latin America) live away from the university and commute. While we might suppose that all would benefit from any available personal attention, their characters are largely formed, formed by upbringing, by communal associations, by churches, by the work experience. From their perspective, the fortunate ones in receipt of the fullest form of a university experience are both lucky and pampered. The formula of tutorial instruction, pastoral teaching, and a collegiate residential setting was for the few, the happy few, those with means, those who had access to means.

And so it was in the Scotland of Newman's day where students were, like the Irish, possessed of lesser means, living at home or in cheap lodgings. Did Newman have views about Scottish education apart from those stirred up in the well-publicized educational controversy between Oxford and the Edinburgh Reviewers of the early part of the nineteenth century? Scotland's system of professorial lecturing, Scottish schools of moral philosophy, Scotland's idea of liberal education as disciplinary breadth took the relative family poverty of undergraduates into account, and Scotland's Enlightenment crossed the Atlantic to find a major place in the evolution of the American higher education system.

Newman's scheme for Ireland was encompassed within what Shrimpton and others would call faith-based institutions. Referring to such institutions, to include several Jewish ones in the United States, Shrimpton regards them as probably the best solution to the crisis in higher education. But several of the authors cited in his notes, authors deeply committed to Catholic and Protestant values and institutions, are in fact disappointed with the evolution of faith-based institutions, so strong have been the influences of secular learning and the overwhelming dominance of graduate research education in the formation of teachers.[7] There can be no disagreement with Shrimpton's contention that the university ought not neglect the obligation to encourage the formation of an educated citizenry. The problem is that our students, subject to the multiple influences of an age with more openings for personal choice in consumer-directed cultures, do not always turn out as teachers might wish, no matter the degree of pastoral teaching. We may deplore this; but just as circumstances defeated Newman, so are they present in even more perplexing and complicated forms today.

Newman was more flexible in his thinking than we suppose – Shrimpton has made that point. He was certainly more open-minded with regard to human error and thought than a more conservative ecclesiastical hierarchy desired, sometimes even searching for ways to get round the list of the Catholic index of prohibited books, straddling the line for the maintenance of dogmatic certainty. But we may suppose that no degree of flexibility of mind could have prepared him for the cacophony of differences so marked at present.

University of California, Berkeley

---

[7] See George M. Marsden, *The Outrageous Idea of Christian Scholarship* (New York and Oxford: Oxford University Press, 1997); Marsden, *The Soul of the American University, From Protestant Establishment to Established Nonbelief* (New York and Oxford: Oxford University Press, 1994); J.T. Burtchaell, *The Dying of the Light, The Disengagement of Colleges and Universities from their Christian Churches* (Grand Rapids, MI: W.B. Eerdsman Pub. Co., 1998).

Jean Grier and Mary Bownes, *Private Giving, Public Good: The Impact of Philanthropy at the University of Edinburgh* (Edinburgh: Edinburgh University Press, 2014), vi+218pp. ISBN: 9780748699575

Robert Anderson

Between the 1940s and the 1970s, the expansion of British universities was funded on a large scale by the state. Since then, increasing pressure on state resources, reinforced by the growth of market ideology, has forced universities to take a much more active role in seeking alternative sources of finance. These include tapping the goodwill of alumni and appealing to the philanthropic impulses of wealthy individuals, and many universities have set up sophisticated fundraising programmes to develop the process. This account of 'private giving' is the product of initiatives of this kind at Edinburgh University. It is partly historical, but focuses particularly on recent gifts, no doubt in the hope that readers will be tempted to follow suit. The book is lavishly illustrated and attractively produced. For university historians, however, the book has some deficiencies. The authors have used the standard secondary works to provide a concise historical account of the university, but do not claim to have carried out original research, apart from some dips into Senate minutes, and there are occasional errors and confusions. It is not true, for example, that in the nineteenth century all Edinburgh professors were born in Scotland (32); and the newspaper *The Student*, founded in 1887, was not the first British student newspaper (179): Aberdeen got there first with *Alma Mater* in 1883.

Scottish universities lacked the inherited wealth of Oxford and Cambridge. In the nineteenth century they received significant support from the state, but from the 1860s also made serious efforts to appeal to private donors and build up endowments. Alumni were directly targeted, and typically made small gifts or bequests in grateful acknowledgement of their own education. Larger sums came from wealthy individuals, often local businessmen who had not themselves attended the university, to pay for new chairs or buildings. By 1914 Edinburgh University received about 19 percent of its income from endowments, compared with 46 percent from student fees and 34 percent from the state.[1]

This pattern continued in the inter-war years, when state grants were administered through the University Grants Committee, but were limited to current rather than capital expenditure. New buildings especially depended on private donors. Here, however, this book has a surprising omission. With its emphasis on private giving, it virtually ignores the role of the charitable foundations which appeared in the twentieth century. The first and one of the wealthiest was the Carnegie Trust for the Universities of Scotland, founded by the Scoto-American tycoon Andrew Carnegie, which began operations in 1901, supporting both teaching and research. Between the wars, the largest single donor to the university comprised the two American-based Rockefeller organizations – the International Education Board and the Rockefeller Foundation, which between them gave about £200,000, for zoology and surgery respectively. Neither Carnegie nor Rockefeller get more than casual mention here. Nor do individual donors from this period, several of whom gave over £100,000. One of them is the victim of a confusion between names. A passage quoting Sir Alexander Grant, Principal of the University in 1868–84, is accompanied by a portrait with his name attached, but which is in fact of another Sir Alexander Grant, an Edinburgh biscuit manufacturer who was a generous donor in the 1920s both to the university (mainly for geology) and to the National Library of Scotland. But he gets no credit here.

The emphasis, reasonably enough, is on recent years, but the treatment is not very systematic. No statistics are provided to show how private income has varied over the years, how large the university's endowments are (they are certainly large by British standards), or what proportion of the university's income derives from them. One suspects that the authors worked by asking each university department to provide its own examples of philanthropy, and the results are inevitably rather uneven and anecdotal, though also informative. There are useful sections on the university's outstanding collection of musical instruments, and on its art collections, which deserve to be better known. There is also much information on sporting facilities and achievements, and on student social life and halls

---

[1] Robert Anderson, 'The state and university finance in modern Scotland', *Scottish Affairs*, no. 85 (Autumn 2013), 29–52; Robert Anderson, 'Il finanziamento delle università britanniche in una prospettiva storica', *Memoria e Ricerca*, 48 (2015), 11–33.

of residence. These are all areas which have benefited from private giving, even if they are not essential to the university's core functions of research and teaching.

One chapter is devoted to 'research and scholarship'. This is again informative, but it illustrates, rather than confronting, some of the problems of relying on private philanthropy. Donors like to fund a specific project to which their name can be attached, rather than adding to the university's general endowment. Some fields are popular, above all medical treatment and research, to which the *Harry Potter* author J. K. Rowling has recently made a very large gift. Others, like research in the humanities and social sciences, attract only marginal interest. Corporate capitalism has largely eliminated the locally-based fortunes which were so significant to university philanthropy in the nineteenth and early twentieth centuries. Nor, in our own period, does the book mention the questions of academic freedom which arise when chairs or institutes are funded by authoritarian governments in Asia or the Middle East. In supporting research, can individual philanthropy do more than supplement the basic funding coming from the state-financed research councils, charitable foundations, and industry?

Another key chapter is on 'bursaries, scholarships, and prizes'. This used to be a favourite field for individual legacies and donations, and for the Carnegie Trust, which carried out its founder's offer to pay the university fees, in whole or part, of all Scottish students. These arrangements were eventually superseded by the growth of public financial support, from the central state and local authorities, and after 1962 Scottish students, like those elsewhere in Britain, had their fees paid by the state and received generous living allowances. Since the 1990s, the state's support for students has been progressively reduced, or converted into loan form, and poorer students have again become a subject for philanthropy. We learn of one donor who was so grateful for his own free education that he personally finances thirteen students 'from disadvantaged backgrounds' (117). This is admirable, no doubt, but thirteen bursaries do not go far in a university with 35,000 students.

Here politics enter into the picture. According to Grier and Bownes, 'With the exception of a brief period in the twentieth century … gaining a university education has always represented a financial sacrifice for all but the very wealthy' (118), which may be true in a long-term perspective, but seems a dismissive treatment of one of the most important achievements of postwar social policy. 'As the global marketplace for higher education becomes more competitive', they write, 'the University will continue to develop its use of bursaries and scholarships to ensure that it can attract the very brightest and best students regardless of their personal circumstances'

(119–20). But for forty years all universities in Britain were able to practice 'needs-blind admission', and there were no financial barriers to students from 'disadvantaged backgrounds', though there were certainly social and cultural ones (and still are). Moreover, while in England payment of fees by the state has been replaced by student loans to be repaid on an income-contingent basis, in Scotland (which has had its own parliament since 1999) higher education remains free. This is only indirectly acknowledged by Grier and Bownes (39). The issue of student fees remains prominent in British electoral politics. The current Scottish National Party government regards the refusal to charge them as a flagship policy, and has invested much political capital in it. It might well feel from what is said, or not said, here that Edinburgh University is spurning this generosity and turning its back on its natural market in pursuit of a global one.

This book clearly reveals the vision of the future held by the administrative elite of leading British universities, and does not avoid the clichés of competitive managerialism. Edinburgh University is a 'world-class institution' (39) whose 'iconic buildings' (62) house 'cutting-edge research' (202: if there is any blunt-edged research going on in British universities, we never hear of it). The Scottish universities see themselves, to quote a recent statement by their representative organization, as 'large and increasingly complex businesses operating on a global stage'.[2] They are obsessed with their position in international league tables, and dream of being up there with Harvard and Princeton, floating free of their local communities and the national educational system. But out of nineteen Scottish universities, only five or six have the intellectual prestige, international links, and wealthy alumni needed to build up significant endowments. It is very desirable, for the sake of their independence, that universities should have as many different sources of income as possible. But for the foreseeable future, the basic funding of British universities is likely to come, directly or indirectly, from public resources, and the contribution that can be made by private philanthropy needs a more rigorous assessment than it gets here.

School of History, Classics and Archaeology
University of Edinburgh
Edinburgh EH8 9AG
United Kingdom

---

[2] Anderson, 'The state and university finance', 51.

John W. Boyer, *The University of Chicago: A History* (Chicago: University of Chicago Press, 2015), 676pp. ISBN: 9780226242514

Roger L. Geiger

The University of Chicago is one of the world's great universities by any reckoning. In the United States, it is noted for the intellectualism of its undergraduates and for epitomizing academic freedom, merit, and unfettered inquiry. Its founding in 1892 is generally known, as are its two iconic presidents, William Rainey Harper and Robert Maynard Hutchins; but the university's past is also encrusted with myths, especially locally; and they have been an active factor in its development. Further, while University of Chicago faculty have provided academic leadership in many fields, the institution itself has in significant ways been out of sync with the trends that have shaped other American universities. These issues and much else are examined by John Boyer in the first modern history of the university. The author, a prolific historian of modern Austria and since 1992 Dean of Chicago's unique undergraduate college, has been researching aspects of the university's history over the last twenty years. This volume is a frank and penetrating study that not only rectifies myth, but also places the university in the broader history of American universities.

Boyer provides a welcome account of the little-known first University of Chicago (1856–86), a not atypical denominational college which succumbed to bankruptcy after failing to find support among local Baptists or the burgeoning metropolitan community. The new university was shaped almost single-handedly by William Rainey Harper, the manic genius who cajoled multi-million-dollar gifts from John D. Rockefeller. Harper was animated by so many ideas and projects that both contemporaries and historians have concluded that 'no one could know the complete Harper' (144). But uppermost among his goals for the university was a dedication to the cultivation and advancement of academic knowledge. He recruited the best scientists and scholars available and, amazingly, created a research university that rivalled Harvard in less than a decade. But the University of Chicago was more than that: It was the original multiversity—to borrow Clark Kerr's later term—dedicated to spreading knowledge through research and scholarship, undergraduate and graduate education, and encompassing academic, professional, and vocational fields, extension education, and a university press. Harper's diverse initiatives were sometimes altered in light of experience, as was the rhetoric that promoted them. This was largely the case with undergraduate education.

If the structure of undergraduate education was unsettled at the founding, this reflected controversy raging in the early 1890s over how preparatory, collegiate, advanced, and professional education should fit together. However, at Chicago the nature and role of the college remained problematic for the ensuing century. Harper originally favoured subordinating the undergraduate college to 'University work' (81), i.e. graduate education and research. He divided undergraduate study into the Junior and Senior Colleges (another innovation), and suggested that the former might be accomplished at other places. But as the size and salience of the college grew, Harper fully embraced this role. Yet undergraduate education at Chicago was distinctive in several respects. For its first four decades, up to 70 per cent of students were from Chicago, and most lived at home or in rented rooms (the university had few residence halls). More than half of its graduates had transferred from other institutions, perhaps in order to avoid the stiff entrance examination. The quarter system devised by Harper—a brilliant innovation—obviated the class cohesion that shaped collegiate life elsewhere. In fact, the anti-intellectual collegiate culture that was the bane of American higher education in this era was largely absent from Harper's university.[1] Its students were commuters, often older and working part time. They attended the university to learn, not to socialize, and by and large formed a body of serious students. Mostly from middle or upper-middle class homes, they largely prepared for careers in education, business, or the professions. But their student experiences were not of the kind to create enduring loyalties to the university or classmates.

Boyer's portrayal suggests that the early University of Chicago, in its combination of openness and quality, may have been the most democratic institution in American higher education. It was beholden to no wealthy

---

[1] Harper embraced big-time football by hiring the first true coach, Amos Alonzo Stagg; and fraternities housed 14 per cent of students, which was less than at contemporary institutions. Hutchins actively discouraged fraternities and abolished football in 1939. Later, after 1945, the college was known for asceticism and the absence of social life.

elite or exclusive constituency, since its benefactor—Rockefeller—made no claims on the institution. Students came predominantly from the Chicago public schools and were taught alongside graduate students by senior professors. Graduate students comprised one-half of enrolments and included future academics as well as mid-life professionals seeking masters or doctoral degrees. In few other institutions did such a cross-section of the middle class receive instruction from eminent scholars and scientists.

After Harper's untimely death in 1906, leadership of the university gravitated to the senior professors, who had little regard for a multiversity and an overriding commitment to 'University work'. Rockefeller's final gifts (1910) provided an ample endowment to support such aspirations; and the cautious stewardship of President Harry Judson (1906–22) avoided any new initiatives. Harper's university endured until World War I, but fissures appeared soon afterward. Enrolments ballooned while inflation crimped resources, and the resulting pressures provoked an internal conflict between graduate and collegiate instruction. The teaching of undergraduates clearly deteriorated and their meagre facilities became increasingly inadequate. At the same time, senior professors, including president Judson, advocated privileging graduate education and possibly jettisoning the junior college altogether.

Boyer considers Judson's successor to have been a potential saviour. President Ernest Burton (1923–5) clearly perceived the university's predicament: in order to preserve a great research university, both the college and relations with Chicago donors needed to be strengthened. His sudden death in 1925 doomed both of these efforts. He had strongly advocated building residential colleges to provide a more complete undergraduate experience, but senior faculty insisted that resources be devoted to graduate education and research. Just one residence hall was built. He launched a professional fund-raising campaign to build community support and supersede dependence on the Rockefellers, but his successor cancelled the campaign. Academic instruction flourished nonetheless, with copious funds coming now from the various Rockefeller trusts for both buildings and faculty research. All told, during its first half-century, 60 per cent of Chicago's gifts came from Rockefeller sources (185), but when that era ended, *c.*1940, the university had failed to develop alternative donors from the Chicago community or its alumni. That failure would weigh heavily on the future development of the university; however, it was intertwined with the conflict over the status of the college—and soon dominated by the overweening presence of Robert Maynard Hutchins (1929–51).

Hutchins's presidency began with an innovative resolution of the college wars. Dubbed the New Plan, it restructured the university into four upper division colleges (Humanities, and Social, Biological, and Physical Sciences) responsible for junior-senior and graduate coursework and the awarding of degrees. A fifth college was devoted to the general education of freshmen and sophomores. Its courses were taught in year-long survey courses capped with comprehensive, multiple-choice examinations drawn up by a separate examining board. These arrangements gave professors control over all advanced teaching and learning, while establishing the most ambitious general education curriculum of any major university. Although it was negotiated prior to his presidency, Hutchins endorsed and took credit for the New Plan. Then, almost immediately, he reversed course and began manoeuvring to undermine it.

The central chapter of Boyer's study, and indeed of the history of the University of Chicago, treats the quixotic quest of Hutchins to reshape the university—and American education. Hutchins possessed enormous eloquence and charisma,[2] but he also sought intellectual distinction that was beyond his ken. He had fallen under the influence of Mortimer Adler, an abrasive and arrogant autodidact whom he brought to Chicago: 'Both men aspired to traditional philosophical learning of great seriousness and scope, and both, for better or worse, aspired to remake the University in pursuit of that ideal' (242). Hutchins soon began attacking what he called 'the information disease', and belittling the New Plan survey courses— 'a hasty look at all the facts in a given field does not seem very useful from any but a conversational point of view' (244). Rather, he and Adler sought a university dedicated to *ideas*, taught through immersion in Great Books. Hutchins thus was openly dismissive toward specialized research and scholarship, and hence the accomplishments and expertise of most of the university faculty. 'Facts are the core of an anti-intellectual curriculum', he wrote, the 'gaze of the University should be turned toward ideas' (245). For the remainder of his presidency, Hutchins was virtually at war with the divisional faculty. But his principal interest was in the college, and there he prevailed.

Hutchins concluded that general education required four years rather than two, and that it should be given in grades 11 through 14. During the turmoil of World War II he managed to obtain trustee approval for such an experiment, creating in 1942 what is known as the Hutchins College. The baccalaureate course consisted of fourteen standardized year-long courses, taught in discussion sections by a separate college faculty. At its height, after 1946, students enjoyed lively classes taught by remarkably

---

[2] Hutchins is the most quoted figure in Robert Birnbaum's collection of higher education quotations, with 50 percent more entries than second-placed Charles W. Eliot: *Speaking of Higher Education: the Academic's Book of quotations* (Westport, CT, 2004).

talented instructors (judging from subsequent academic achievements; none stayed with the college). Ironically, this learning was ruled by standardized tests: Students were 'admitted, classified, counseled ... given scholarships and awarded baccalaureate degrees upon the basis of standard tests' (258). However, as was the case with other experimental colleges, the intensive pedagogy appealed to minority tastes. College enrolments, which had been above 3,000 before the war, plummeted to half that number. The attempt to enrol students at the 11th grade level was a disaster. High school principals resisted losing their best pupils. The stereotype of the Hutchins College student was that of a 'quiz kid'—a nerdy would-be intellectual. And the college's degrees, certifying no specialized preparation, were not recognized for advanced studies.

The collapse of college enrolments exacerbated the deterioration of university finances. Hutchins had operated with budget deficits since 1938, reaching ten per cent of expenditures in 1950–1, and he had drawn down endowment assets to cover them. With a large graduate enrolment and eminent research university faculty and facilities, the University of Chicago was an expensive operation, needing tuition revenue but ultimately dependent on revenues from the endowment. Its finances hit rock bottom in the early 1950s. Just when other universities were beginning their postwar take off, Chicago endured what Boyer calls the 'age of survival, 1951–1977'. The issue was 'whether the University could survive as a first-rate institution' (338). Indeed, budgets and enrolments, confounded by the mythic traditions of the Hutchins College, would plague Chicago for the next four decades.

When the Ford Foundation provided Hutchins with a graceful exit, Lawrence Kimpton was appointed to save the sinking ship. An able administrator, Kimpton needed several years to dismantle the most damaging features of the Hutchins College—early admissions and the fixed four-year general education course. By this time the college had acquired its own separate faculty, who passionately defended its ethos and structure. Only in 1957 was it possible to reestablish a normal entry level and a college course consisting of two years of general education followed by two years of divisional courses. Kimpton believed that a huge increase in undergraduate enrolments was needed to stabilize the university, but only a small increase to 2000+ was achieved. It took almost as long to balance the budget through draconian cuts and the first fund-raising campaign since Hutchins's half-hearted effort at the end of the 1930s. It was a modest success, but at the end of the 1950s Chicago faced the same chronic problems—under-capitalized and under-enrolled.

The next significant leader was Edward Levi, first as provost (1962–8) and then as president (1968–75). Boyer gives Levi credit for rehabilitating the distinctive intellectual spirit of the university. His first priority was to rebuild the senior faculty after the losses of the 1950s. He bolstered salaries and created special chairs, with vital assistance from the Ford Foundation, thereby helping the university to remain in the front ranks of American research universities. But Levi was also a friend and admirer of Hutchins. He reorganized the college (again) with the intention of integrating general education with divisional specialization while preserving, even emphasizing, its intellectual rigour and liberal nature. Under Levi, Chicago weathered the student rebellion of the late 1960s and the dismal financial climate of the 1970s. Morale rose, the 2,000+ students received a rigorous education with few social amenities, and the university maintained a large and distinguished faculty that it could scarcely afford.

The state of the university brightened during the long and peaceful presidency of Hannah Gray (1978–93). A resourceful administrator, Gray also perfectly articulated the university's cherished ideals of intellectual excellence and academic freedom. She endured the usual financial roller coaster, achieving stability in the 1980s only to be swamped by cost escalation and recession at the close of her tenure. Enrolments finally started to rise under Gray as she brought much needed improvements in student life. But the college was still subject to what Boyer calls the 'heritage effect'; the university's 'commitment to general education as a defining principle of liberal education' (402). In 1985 the general education core was revised once again, this time to create a required two-year curriculum for all students, thus restoring a mandate similar to the New Plan and the Hutchins College.

When Hugo Sonnenschein became the new president of the University of Chicago in 1993, he directly addressed the university's chronic weaknesses: the narrow appeal of the college—Chicago received less than half the number of applicants of peer institutions; and under-capitalization—it had roughly one-half the endowment support per faculty of its peers (423, 409). To maintain its standing the university needed to increase its capitalization—the endowment; and it needed to increase the number of tuition-paying undergraduate students. He immediately intensified the fund-raising effort, with some success, and began the more laborious process of attracting more students to the college. This meant changing the 1985 general education core, which was constricting for students, difficult to staff, and reflected a superannuated heritage. By 1998 the faculty, with great trepidation, instituted a reduction and modernization of the general education core. A vitriolic reaction then ensued from traditionalists among faculty, students, and alumni. The university was accused of lowering intellectual standards to attract more students and—most reprehensible—to increase income. The vituperation heaped upon Sonnenschein may well have hastened his exit in 2000. But he was soon vindicated.

The reforms of these years overcame the chronic weaknesses that had plagued the university. Moreover, Chicago found itself on the right side of history for a change, namely, participating in the burgeoning demand for admissions to highly selective institutions, and the philanthropic munificence enjoyed by top private universities. Applications rose from *c.*5,000 in 1993 to over 30,000 in 2013; undergraduate enrolments grew from 3,500 to over 5,000, the same as Yale and Princeton; and the quality of Chicago undergraduates rose to equal that of peer institutions. In addition, thriving professional schools of law and business added to the prosperity of the university.

In this volume Boyer has provided essentially an administrative history of the University of Chicago. He is particularly adept at portraying the personalities and policies of the presidents, and the roles of other important figures are also factored into the analyses. A particular strength of this study is documenting the influence of trustees, who played a far more constructive and altruistic role than that insinuated by Thorstein Veblen in *The Higher Learning in America.*[3] The book provides sufficient characterization of the university undergraduates, who comprise a principal variable in this history. It contains no subjective accounts of inspired pedagogy purveyed in great books or general education survey courses, for which this reader is appreciative. Also absent is any attempt to describe the monumental contributions of Chicago scholars and scientists, who shaped at different times the traditions of sociology, physics, economics, and law, among other fields: subjects covered in a different literature. In recent years the history of American higher education has been enriched by institutional histories of extraordinary quality.[4] John Boyer's history of the University of Chicago deserves a place among them.

Pennsylvania State University

---

[3] See 107, 112. Veblen was a faculty member at Chicago, 1892–1906, when the book was drafted: Thorstein Veblen, *The Higher Learning in America. A Memorandum on the Conduct of Universities by Business Men,* ed. Richard F. Teichgraeber (Baltimore, 2015; first published 1918).

[4] Among the best: Robert A. McCaughey, *Stand Columbia: A History of Columbia University in the City of New York, 1754–2004* (New York, 2004); James Axtell, *The Making of Princeton University: From Woodrow Wilson to the Present* (Princeton, 2006); David B. Potts, *Wesleyan University, 1910–1970: Academic Ambition and Middle-Class America* (Middletown, CT, 2015).

Tomás Irish, *The university at war, 1914–25. Britain, France, and the United States* (Basingstoke: Palgrave Macmillan, 2015), x + 254 pp. ISBN: 9781137409447

Tomás Irish, *Trinity in war and revolution, 1912–1923* (Dublin: Royal Irish Academy, 2015), xix + 300 pp. ISBN: 9781908996787

Robert Anderson

Few institutions were affected as drastically as universities by the First World War. They were emptied of students as young men departed for military service, and in many parts of Europe they suffered physical destruction; boundary changes during and after the war meant that many universities in central and eastern Europe found themselves in new countries. At a deeper level, the outbreak of war in 1914 marks the end of a phase of history when an international university community seemed to be emerging, united by the ideals of progress, science, and freedom of thought. This was marked by the numerous university anniversary ceremonies – including that at Dublin in 1892 described in Tomás Irish's *Trinity in war and revolution* – which assembled a company of scholars and scientists from all over the world to exchange celebratory addresses and honorary degrees. But nationalist tensions were never far below the surface, and in 1914 the optimistic ideal was shattered. One well-known aspect of this was the way in which the reputation of the German universities, still at the head of the international league table in 1914, was compromised by the unconditional support of German professors for their country's cause. French and British war propaganda made much of this, leading after the war to a boycott of German universities at scholarly gatherings. But allied academics, notably historians like Ernest Lavisse in France, were hardly less chauvinist.

This is the starting-point for Irish's *The university at war, 1914–25*. His book is not a comprehensive history of universities in the First World War, but puts forward an interesting, solidly documented, and well-argued thesis. The British historian and politician H. A. L. Fisher described the war as a 'battle of brains'. Irish argues that the three western allies had a concerted campaign to mobilize academic ideals as a weapon against Germany, and as a way of strengthening cooperation among themselves. He shows that American universities were engaged in this project from the start, helping to pave the way for America's entry into the war in 1917, and leading to a permanent reorientation of international academic links. One trigger for American involvement was the destruction of the university library at Louvain in 1914. Though seized on by the French and British as a symbol of German barbarism, it was in America that Louvain gave rise to a sustained propaganda campaign, and that generous funds were raised for postwar reconstruction.

One of Irish's themes is the linkage in all three countries between the academic and political worlds. This was closest in France, where the values of the Third Republic and those of the French universities were symbiotic. Irish's French material will be unfamiliar to many readers, and he shows how the centralized nature of the French system, and the networks based on elite institutions like the Ecole Normale Supérieure, fed into politics and supported a narrative of the war as a defence of democracy and human rights. This was a country where professors became successful politicians, like the mathematician Paul Painlevé, who became successively minister of war and prime minister. The American and British political classes were less permeable to outsiders, but Fisher was brought from Oxford to be minister of education, and Woodrow Wilson had of course been president of Princeton. Even Russia (not discussed by Irish) seemed to be following suit when the historian Pavel Milyukov became foreign minister after the February revolution.

In the course of his discussion, Irish gives accounts of a number of significant issues, including the anti-war movements in Britain and America (though in France, where the enemy was present on the nation's soil, this was hardly a factor), the fate of German scholars in British universities, and debates on academic freedom in America. He also discusses at some length important post-war developments, including the role of academics in the Paris peace conference, the crucial role of the war in making science a priority for state support, the promotion of student exchanges in a spirit of internationalism, and the commemoration of the fallen. The war left a legacy of French cultural prestige in Britain and America, and brought American universities, little known in Europe before 1914, permanently to the centre of the international stage. Charitable foundations like the Carnegie Endowment and the Rockefeller Foundation were to have extensive European operations in the interwar years.

The broad perspectives of Irish's general study are complemented by his history of Trinity College Dublin (TCD, also known as the University of Dublin) in the crucial years for Ireland which, under the shadow of the European war, included the Easter Rising of 1916, the war of independence, the establishment of the Irish Free State, and the Irish civil war. These were difficult years for an institution which had been seen as a bastion of pro-British unionism. Unusually for the time, Dublin was a city with two universities representing rival traditions, as University College Dublin, with its roots in J. H. Newman's Catholic University of 1854, had become the home of Catholic nationalism and a seedbed for political activists. Trinity College, originally an Anglican foundation, had ceased to be formally Protestant, but in 1912 only 13 percent of new students were Roman Catholics, and it drew its students disproportionately from the Anglo-Irish elite and the Dublin professional classes.

But many also came from the middle classes of Protestant Ulster, and problems for TCD did not have to await the outbreak of war. The passing of the Irish Home Rule Act in 1912 created a crisis because of the political dispute over whether this should extend to Ulster. If Ulster was excluded from Home Rule, TCD would be left in an exposed position as the university of a beleaguered southern minority. Yet the university's representative in Parliament (British university graduates at this time had a separate parliamentary vote) was the leader of Ulster Unionism, Edward Carson. The Ulster question was unresolved in 1914, and the outbreak of war caused further tensions. Many TCD students came from families with traditions of military and imperial service to the British state. They embraced the war effort, while Irish nationalists were increasingly hostile to it. In the 1920s and later, memory of the war and monuments to the war dead were to be contentious issues.

TCD, occupying a large walled campus in the centre of Dublin, was often described as a unionist 'garrison'. Irish shows that this was misleading, as there were different strands of opinion within the university, including a growing sympathy for nationalism. But it became literally true during the Easter Rising, when the college was used as a base by the British army. The university largely escaped direct involvement in the military events which surrounded the establishment of Irish independence, but its position was permanently weakened. An institution which had been confident of its position in Irish society and culture, with its own brand of Irish identity, Tomás Irish argues, now had to work in a hostile environment. This was partly a matter of finance. Like Oxford and Cambridge, TCD had endowments which allowed it to manage without state funding before 1914. It had stood aloof from the general development of Irish university education, which had led to its rival University College sharing in state grants. TCD's limited means inhibited the expansion of disciplines, especially in science, and now wartime inflation led to financial crisis. The new Free State, itself impecunious, refused to give more than a small temporary grant. It was only in 1947 that TCD began to receive permanent support from the state - Irish gives quite a full account of developments after the First World War, going beyond the date of 1923 in his subtitle. Since then TCD has regained its central position in Irish life and shed the lingering memory of minority status.

Irish's book covers (with some attractive visual material) many of the standard themes of institutional university history, including student life, the development of the curriculum, the social and geographical backgrounds of students, and the idiosyncrasies of TCD's senior members. One of his strengths is his subtle account of the problems of identity which the difficult position of TCD posed to its members and graduates. In both of these books Irish stresses how, through its graduates and its cultural influence, a university creates communities and networks which extend throughout a society, and help to make ideas a political force. One book is a model transnational study based on sources in three countries, the other a penetrating account of a single university's response to a unique national crisis. To produce two such differently focused books simultaneously is an impressive achievement, and they make an important contribution to university history.

School of History, Classics and Archaeology
University of Edinburgh
Edinburgh EH8 9AG
United Kingdom

Michael Segre, *Higher Education and the Growth of Knowledge. A Historical Outline of Aims and Tensions* (New York/London: Routledge, 2015), 197pp. ISBN: 9780415735667

Steven J. Livesey

In this short (197 page) monograph containing eleven chapters and two brief appendices, Michael Segre presents 'a historical outline attempting to show how many closed aspects of the university comprise a superfluous heritage' (2). As this description suggests, he does so using the prism of Karl Popper's *The Open Society and its Enemies* (1945) as his guide. But Popper is Segre's guide not merely for social theory, but for his philosophy of science writ large as the pursuit of truth inseparable from its social context, an activity that flourishes best in an open society and subject to criticism. Beginning with ancient Near Eastern literate societies, he traces the history of education and learning through the European medieval, Renaissance, and early modern universities, Enlightenment technological schools and Humboldtian reform movements, arriving finally at contemporary American and European institutions that have expanded their reach worldwide. It is a breathtaking, prodigious survey of 3000 years of intellectual history.

Along the way, Segre enumerates the closures that restricted the growth of knowledge in the Western tradition. His principal target is the monopoly of the religious hierarchy over higher learning and its consequent dogmatic and unscientific perspectives. In both Mesopotamia and Egypt, learning was tied to religion as a prerogative of the priest caste. Segre's discussion of pre-Socratic philosophy is dominated by Pythagoras, who was influenced by or associated with priestly castes. In ancient Judaic culture, first one tribe, the Levites, and subsequently the rabbinical caste assumed the guardianship of knowledge; in the early renaissance of Islam in the ninth century, *majālis* served as sites for discussing medicine, philosophy, and religious law, followed by the rise of the madrasa as the premier forum for Islamic as well as foreign sciences. Western monastic schools were *ipso facto* religious institutions, but beginning with the first statute of incorporation, medieval universities were dominated legally as well as educationally by the Church. Segre considers Galileo's *Letter to Christina* and Kepler's introduction to the *Astronomia nova* as the historical watershed between religion and science; with Bacon comes the creation of a new secular religion based on science, with its own rites, saints, and clerics, thereby replacing one form of 'religious' authority with another.

Particularly when he turns to the formation of the university, Segre focuses on guild structures. The society in which the medieval university was born was a closed society in Popperian terms, in which all innovation had to be legitimated by the pope or emperor. While aggregations or guilds can be beneficial, they can also become closed societies, whose interests revolve around the well-being of members, including preserving a monopoly on membership while discouraging excellence and progress.

Although modern universities are the product of technological schools of the eighteenth century, founded as replacements for guilds that were no longer suitable to train a large corps of technologically skilled engineers in the modern state, these new institutions retained many of the guiding principles of the old guild schools. Modern universities, like the medieval ones they replaced, are primarily vocational training centres; the earlier bodies preserved a priest caste, while their modern heirs confer diplomas in scientific disciplines that are (in the words of James Conant) 'certificate[s] of vocational competence' (185). To achieve this vocational training, universities employ systematic, unidirectional teaching methods with exams, grades and honours, all of which contribute to dogmatism, careerism, elitism, and stress.

According to Segre, this emphasis on agonistic education derives from Plato, whose formula for ideal education emphasized subjecting students to 'toils and pains and competitions' [*Republic* III, 413d] as a means of winnowing excellence. In fact, Plato's Academy, like modern 'centres of excellence', emphasized conformist learning, the cornerstone of a meritocracy, which is often confused with a search for excellence:

'Normal' experts, that is, meritocrats, might have been helpful in France during the Revolution and the Napoleonic empire. Creating a meritocracy, nevertheless, has its drawbacks. Meritocrats would not be very helpful or realistically appropriate, for example, in a modern Third World country that favors nuclear physicists over agronomists. The world financial and economic disaster that began in 2007 was caused above all by meritocrats, deemed 'prestigious experts'. Today, in addition, there are often no clear ideas as to what meritocracy should be, that is, what merits to value. For example, a democratic government, such as Italy's in the last decades, repeatedly declared that it encourages meritocracy (hoping to encourage excellence, but confounding 'merit' with 'excellence') without really knowing what it is and who should be favored. Much the same can be said of the 'evaluation' of the quality of a university on both a national and an international level; it is conducted on the basis of arbitrary quantitative parameters that have sometimes little to do with excellence of any kind at all. Meritocracy is not necessarily compatible with the development of free thought and science. As opposed to merit, excellence lies in originality, and originality implies autonomy, the psychological basis of the ability to think outside the box, than [sic] upon conformity to whatever fashion flavors in the box. In turn, this 'thinking outside the box' must be submitted to and regulated by criticism, which reduces possible harmful developments. These are the principles of controversy in an open society and should be the goal of universities (173).

Save for small glimmers of reform in the nineteenth century—Humboldt in Germany and Charles William Eliot at Harvard—the modern university retains the medieval closed nature that serves as an incubator of a managerial class, and through partnerships with extra-university institutions preserves social and economic stability. Those who do not fit this mould 'are barred from universities, and even from publishing by high-status publishers of "prestigious" scientific reviews or publications, for their non-conformism' (178).

Segre begins his monograph with a personal reflection: 'It is with mixed feeling that I undertake writing this book; it criticizes an institution, the university, to which I have belonged for more than four decades and toward which I owe a profound debt'. I suspect that most readers of the book who have spent time on both sides of the student-teacher divide will share this ambivalence, since each of us sees different warts on the body of the institution, along with the debts we owe to it. Beyond the issues already related, Segre occasionally illuminates particular contemporary curricular misgivings by drawing parallels with historical figures. Speaking of Galileo's time as a university professor in Padua, he adds his critique of modern university education:

As is also the case in almost every university today, to obtain their degree, Paduan students had to accumulate credits (called *ponti* or 'points'). Modern universities not only persist with this deplorable practice, but even increase it, disregarding that, as argued by Popper in *Objective Knowledge* as well as by other philosophers, knowledge cannot be quantified, much less measured. In Padua, these *ponti* were already a lure for corruption: they were increasingly awarded outside the lecture hall, presumably in exchange for money. . . . [W]e have a basic problem related with university studies yesterday and today. If a student studies in order to grow intellectually or professionally, lessons or workshops are almost always interesting and instructive. If learning is exploited for social purposes and students study only to pass exams or accumulate credits, marks, or degrees alone, then interest diminishes and study can degenerate into stress, alienating the student's interest in the subject being studied and indirectly hampering science.... Much can still be done to make study more genuine, honest, and pleasurable. However, the relationship between science and society remains basically problematical. Science cannot progress without the help of institutions such as the university, but the institutions can get corrupted; only judiciousness and intellectual honesty and foresight can avoid this problem for the moment (138–9).

In the end, Segre concludes as he began, not with a proposal for improvements, but with a call for discussion of possible reforms, since as he notes, every university is 'open' or 'closed' in varying degrees, and every country has a university system peculiar to its national culture. To that end, it is difficult to take issue with a proposal that seeks improvement as well as criticism of a central institution of modern society. Nevertheless, I would offer two suggestions as preliminaries to this discussion.

The first is that restricting a discussion of educational philosophy and university organization to Popper's treatment of open and closed societies may limit the kinds of reform needed. Utopian reforms of universities may be seriously flawed, but the unintended consequences of Popper's famous piecemeal social engineering applied to universities may give us pause as well. And while Segre refers in passing to opposing camps represented by Durkheim and Marx on the one hand and John Stuart Mill, Weber, Hayek, and Popper on the other (6–7), a robust discussion of pedagogical and institutional reform demands greater review before a coronation of one perspective. To give but one example: Segre's frequent reference to unidirectional pedagogy that privileges one side of the learning process and encourages rote memorization over critical analysis might benefit from approaches as diverse as Habermas's notion of reflexive learning and Paulo Freire's criticism of a 'banking education model' that views learning as a process of accumulating bits of knowledge from the hands of the teacher and by contrast his support for an active, dialogic pedagogy.[1]

Second, because the university as an institution is a product of its embedding society, Segre's book is at once a history of Western civilization and philosophy as well as higher education and epistemology. Necessarily, some things are omitted, others abbreviated. Given the scope of the subject, Segre relies on secondary rather than primary sources. But the

[1] Jürgen Habermas, *Legitimation Crisis* (Boston, 1975), 15–16; Paulo Freire, *Pedagogy of the Oppressed* (New York, 1970).

choice of those sources is sometimes problematic: chapter 6, on the birth of the university, relies on Rashdall (1936), Haskins (1923), an *Encyclopedia Britannica* article (1960), Kibre and Siraisi (1978), and Le Goff (1957), surveys composed under a very different (and largely replaced) historical sensibility; though he refers in his bibliography to the more current history by Walter Rüegg and Hilde de Ridder-Symoens, it is not apparent that its material was used in the chapter. By the end of the middle ages, conservative universities could not appreciate the new technology of printing (94), while innovation was to be found in Renaissance academies, which 'were less prone to developing the tensions generated in universities' (100)—both highly contested claims in the literature.[2] In Chapter 10 ('Science Develops Outside "Academia"'), a similar array of sources leads to the expected conclusion of an ossified academic institution, and while Segre refers to some attempts to rehabilitate the university [notably an encyclopedia article by Gascoigne (2000) and Feingold's *Mathematician's Apprenticeship* (1984)], these are considered weak tea indeed; Feingold and Navarro Brotons's *Universities and Science in the Early Modern Period* (2006) is referred to in the bibliography, but there is no apparent use of it in the chapter.

In sum, this is a thought provoking book about an interesting and important matter, but a wider source net and a firmer philosophical foundation would make the ensuing discussion more productive.

Department of the History of Science
The University of Oklahoma
Norman, OK 73019

[2] On printing technology and the university, see Rudolf Hirsch, *Printing, Selling and Reading* (Wiesbaden, 1967), 51 and Curt Bühler, *The University and the press in 15th-century Bologna* (Notre Dame, 1958), 15–16. Segre is also apparently unaware of the kinds of intellectual confrontations that prevailed in the Renaissance: in George of Trebizond's notorious conflict with Poggio in 1452, Poggio charged Trebizond, accusing him of lying; Trebizond stopped him with a punch, after which Poggio attempted to poke out Trebizond's eyes. Later, Trebizond wrote that at that moment he thought of laying Poggio out by squeezing his testicles. John Monfasani, *George of Trebizond: A Biography and a Study of His Rhetoric and Logic* (Leiden, 1976), 109–10. Clearly, this wasn't a tension-free environment.